Cook ||||||||||| h
Katie Stewart

HAMLYN
LONDON · NEW YORK · SYDNEY · TORONTO

Photography by Anthony Blake · David Davies · John Donaldson

Photographs by courtesy of Syndication International

Line drawings by Joanna Troughton

Published by
The Hamlyn Publishing Group Limited
London · New York · Sydney · Toronto
Astronaut House, Feltham, Middlesex, England
© Copyright The Hamlyn Publishing Group Limited 1974
ISBN 0 600 35319 2

Printed in England by Cox & Wyman Limited, Fakenham

Contents

Useful facts and figures

In this book, quantities have been given in both metric and Imperial measures. Exact conversion from Imperial to metric measures does not usually give very convenient working quantities and so for greater convenience we have rounded off metric measures into units of 25 grammes. The table below shows recommended equivalents:

Ounces/fluid ounces	Approx. g. and ml. to nearest whole figure	Recommended conversion to nearest unit of 25
1	28	25
2	57	50
3	85	75
4	113	100
5 ($\frac{1}{4}$ pint)	142	150
6	170	175
7	198	200
8 ($\frac{1}{2}$ lb.)	226	225
9	255	250
10 ($\frac{1}{2}$ pint)	283	275
11	311	300
12	340	350
13	368	375
14	396	400
15 ($\frac{3}{4}$ pint)	428	425
16 (1 lb.)	456	450
17	484	475
18	512	500
19	541	550
20 (1 pint)	569	575

Note: When converting quantities over 20 oz., first add the appropriate figures in the centre column, *then* adjust to the nearest unit of 25. As a general guide, 1 kg. (1000 g.) equals 2·2 lb. or about 2 lb. 3 oz.; 1 litre (1000 ml.) equals 1·76 pints or almost exactly $1\frac{3}{4}$ pints.

This method of conversion gives good results in nearly all recipes. However, where the proportion between liquids and solids is more critical, for example in baking recipes, cut down on liquid measures slightly when using metric quantities or, as in Fresh strawberry cake (page 172), use standard eggs.
Liquid measures: The millilitre is a very small unit of measurement and we felt that to use decilitres (units of 100 ml.) would be easier. In most cases it is perfectly satisfactory to round off the exact conversion to the nearest decilitre, except for $\frac{1}{4}$ pint; thus $\frac{1}{4}$ pint (142 ml.) is $1\frac{1}{2}$ dl., $\frac{1}{2}$ pint (283 ml.) is 3 dl., $\frac{3}{4}$ pint (428 ml.) is 4 dl., and 1 pint (569 ml.) is 6 dl. For quantities over 1 pint we have used litres and fractions of a litre.
Tablespoons: You will note that often measurements are given in tablespoons; the spoon used is the British Standard measuring spoon of 17·7 millilitres.

OVEN TEMPERATURES

The chart below gives the Celsius (Centigrade) equivalents recommended by the Electricity Council.

Description	Fahrenheit	Celsius	Gas Mark
Very cool	225	110	$\frac{1}{4}$
	250	130	$\frac{1}{2}$
Cool	275	140	1
	300	150	2
Moderate	325	170	3
	350	180	4
Moderately hot	375	190	5
	400	200	6
Hot	425	220	7
	450	230	8
Very hot	475	240	9

A GUIDE FOR AMERICAN USERS

Imperial	American
1 lb. butter or other fat	2 cups
1 lb. flour	4 cups
1 lb. granulated or castor sugar	2 cups
1 lb. icing or confectioners' sugar	$3\frac{1}{2}$ cups
1 lb. brown (moist) sugar	2 cups (firmly packed)
12 oz. golden syrup or treacle	1 cup
14 oz. rice	2 cups
1 lb. dried fruit	3 cups
1 lb. chopped or minced meat	2 cups (firmly packed)
1 lb. lentils or split peas	2 cups
2 oz. soft breadcrumbs	1 cup
$\frac{1}{2}$ oz. flour	2 tablespoons
1 oz. flour	$\frac{1}{4}$ cup
1 oz. sugar	2 tablespoons
$\frac{1}{2}$ oz. butter	1 tablespoon
1 oz. golden syrup or treacle	1 tablespoon
1 oz. jam or jelly	1 tablespoon
4 oz. grated cheese	1 cup
4 oz. button mushrooms	1 cup
4 oz. chopped nuts (most kinds)	1 cup

LIQUID MEASURES

$\frac{1}{4}$ pint water, milk etc.	$\frac{2}{3}$ cup
$\frac{1}{2}$ pint water	$1\frac{1}{4}$ cups
1 pint water	$2\frac{1}{2}$ cups
2 pints water	5 cups

Note: The British pint is 20 fluid ounces as opposed to the American pint which is 16 fluid ounces.

The following list gives American equivalents or substitutes for some equipment, terms and ingredients used in the book:

Imperial	American
EQUIPMENT AND TERMS	
Baked/unbaked pastry case	Baked/unbaked pie shell
Baking tin	Baking pan
Cocktail stick	Toothpick
Deep cake tin	Spring form pan
Dough or mixture	Batter
Frying pan	Skillet
Greaseproof paper	Wax paper
Grill/grilled	Broil/broiled
Kitchen paper	Paper towels
Minced	Ground
Mixer/liquidiser	Mixer/blender
Muslin	Cheesecloth
Pastry cutters	Cookie cutters
Patty tins	Muffin pans/cups
Pipe, using a plain star tube in a piping bag	Pipe, using a fluted nozzle in a pastry bag
Prove dough	Allow dough to rise
Sandwich tin	Layer cake pan
Stoned	Pitted
Swiss roll tin	Jelly roll pan

INGREDIENTS	
Apple purée	Applesauce
Aubergine	Eggplant
Back bacon	Canadian bacon
Bacon rashers	Bacon slices
Beef/chicken stock cube	Bouillon cube
Belly pork	Fresh picnic shoulder
Black olives	Ripe olives
Boiling chicken	Stewing chicken
Broad beans	Fava or lima beans

Chicory	Belgian endive
Cocoa powder	Unsweetened cocoa
Coffee essence	Strong black coffee
Cooking apple	Baking apple
Cooking chocolate	Unsweetened cooking chocolate
Cornflour	Cornstarch
Courgettes	Small zucchini
Crystallised fruits	Candied fruits
Demerara sugar	Light brown sugar
Desiccated coconut	Shredded coconut
Digestive biscuits	Graham crackers
Double cream	Whipping cream
Essence	Extract
Gherkin	Sweet dill pickle
Glacé cherries	Candied cherries
Green grapes	White grapes
Hard-boiled eggs	Hard-cooked eggs
Haricot beans	Navy beans
Icing sugar	Confectioners' sugar
Marrow	Large zucchini or summer squash
Plain chocolate	Semi-sweet chocolate
Plain flour	All-purpose flour
Scampi	Jumbo shrimp
Self-raising flour	All-purpose flour sifted with baking powder
Single cream	Coffee cream
Sponge finger biscuits	Ladyfingers
Spring onion	Scallion
Sultanas	Seedless white raisins
Swiss roll tin	Jelly roll pan
Tomato purée	Tomato paste
Unsalted butter	Sweet butter
Vanilla pod	Vanilla bean

All spoon measures are level unless indicated otherwise.

Introduction

To cook well brings pleasure to your family and friends. Perhaps most important of all, it brings satisfaction and a sense of achievement to the cook.

Most of my friends are busy young wives who look after a family and cope with entertaining too. I am constantly impressed with the excellent meals they produce. Recipes don't have to be difficult to be good – and a good cook is not necessarily the person who slaves over the hot stove all day. Much more likely that she plans imaginative, simple menus and serves food that tastes good without being elaborate or fussy.

There are many important points to consider like buying the best quality, particularly when it comes to fresh foods. Knowing how to choose food, making the right choice for the recipe concerned. Becoming aware of the seasons and those foods which are at their best helps you vary your menus and that's also very important. Cooking is a craft that takes time and patience to learn, it's creative too and the individual touch counts for a great deal.

All kinds of recipes are required to meet different situations that arise in the home. Sometimes we need a quick recipe, a snack or a light lunch idea. Other times it may be some-thing less expensive for a family meal. On many occasions the search is for something sophisticated and delicious for a party. This book contains both family and party recipes, but the emphasis is on entertaining. Recipes and instructions are set out as clearly as possible to make their preparation easier and avoid frustrating failures. The more difficult recipes include step by step colour illustrations. The notes on advance planning are important. We cannot be in two places at once and it is vital to know if and how a recipe can be prepared ahead.

I've tried to anticipate the sort of information you might require like recipe suggestions for different types of parties and how to plan them. There is a chart showing food quantities required for large numbers and I have featured food storage in your refrigerator and freezer and how it can help you, plus lots of ideas for garnishes to make food attractive.

The hardest part about cooking is getting new ideas, and that's just what this book sets about providing you with.

Katie Stewart.

Making and using pastry

The art of making pastry lies in paying careful attention to detail and using the correct proportions. It is really a matter of knowing how and why and then sticking to the rules. There are various kinds of pastry, each producing a different texture and a variation in flavour. Some are more difficult to make than others and each one suits a particular type of recipe.

The nine basic pastries are given in this chapter, with at least one example of a recipe for using each pastry to its best advantage.

Know your ingredients

Flour: Use top quality plain flour for best results. Suet pastry is the exception where a self-raising flour is used. Self-raising flour may be used in shortcrust pastry. It's use gives shortcrust a rather soft cake like texture which is acceptable in dessert recipes. Plain flour is required for rich shortcrust pastry containing egg, and is essential for flaky and puff type pastries.

Fat: Butter, margarine, white cooking fat or lard can be used, or chopped suet in the case of suet pastry. The choice depends on the type of pastry. Butter gives flavour and a crisp texture. Margarine can be used in place of butter in the plainer types of pastry but take care to use a firm, hard margarine. Cooking fat or lard gives a shortness particularly to shortcrust pastry. Many cooks like to use a mixture of butter and white cooking fat in shortcrust pastry. In a rich pastry where flavour is important, butter should always be used.

Sugar: Sugar can be added to shortcrust type pastries to give a sweet flavour. It can be sieved into the dry ingredients in the form of icing sugar. If castor sugar is used it should be dissolved in the liquid ingredients first, to avoid a speckly appearance in the baked pastry.

Liquid: The liquid used to bind the pastry ingredients together can take the form of water, milk or egg or a combination of any of these three. If water is used, it should be freshly drawn cold water. Often a little lemon juice is added, as in the case of flaky or puff pastry, to help develop the gluten in the flour and make a good strong dough. Egg is used to bind the rich shortcrust pastries to get a good colour and a crisp, short texture.

Twelve point guide to good pastry

Illustrated in colour on pages 20 and 21

1. Pastry is always best if allowed to rest several hours before using. Place in a polythene bag and store in the refrigerator. Pastry stored unprotected forms a skin on the surface which cracks on rolling out. If left overnight and pastry seems stiff, let it stand at room temperature for 30 minutes before rolling out.

Use a small straight wooden rolling pin, rolling with the palms of the hand and fingers to guide the pin, so that pressure is even and light. Sprinkle flour from a dredger; too much over the rolling surface will be worked into the pastry, this alters the proportions and pastry will be tough. Sprinkle the pin with flour rather than the pastry and move the pastry all the time you are working, but never turn it over. The side next to the working surface is the smoothest and should finally be the side facing upwards.

To get maximum use and little waste, shape the dough to a small edition of the shape to which you wish to roll it; for a circle, turn pastry round and round all the time, for oblong or square shapes, roll first in one direction then another.

2. A tart tin with a loose base or a flan ring set on a baking tin can be used to bake a pastry case. It's useful to remember – when pastry is baked in a mould there is no need to grease the mould so long as the pastry contains 50 per cent fat or more.

Pastry should be handled as little as possible, so use the rolling pin to lift it. Place the pin at one edge of the pastry and roll back towards you, lifting the pastry round the pin, then unroll over the tart tin. Ease, never stretch the pastry into the tin, allowing excess to overlap edges. To get a pretty high rim that doesn't shrink back in baking, press $\frac{1}{4}$ inch ($\frac{1}{2}$ cm.) of the excess pastry back over rim to the inside. Roll the pin over the top to trim edges. Finally, using forefinger and thumb, pinch up the rim of pastry to stand above the tin.

3. When using a plain flan ring, press a $\frac{1}{2}$-inch (1-cm.) pastry rim inwards round the edge. Cut away pastry with the pin and then pinch the edge upwards. Make the edge pretty by using a pastry nipper. Pinch the high pastry rim holding nippers upright, facing inwards to flan centre.

Recipes often call for a pastry case to be baked without any filling, this is called 'baking blind'.

Make a paper lining to fit exactly by first folding a paper dart in greaseproof paper. Hold point to centre and then cut with scissors level with flan edge. Open out and use to line the flan ready for baking blind.

4. When baking blind, care must be taken to help the pastry maintain its shape during baking. First prick the base of the flan to allow air trapped underneath to escape – in the heat of the oven this would expand and push up the base. Prepare a paper circle as described in point 3. This paper lining serves as a container for dried beans, rice or macaroni, the weight of which helps keep the pastry down. Always return these 'baking beans' to a special jar and use only for this purpose. Crumbled kitchen foil can be used instead but care should be taken not to tear the pastry with the rough edges of the foil.

If liked, paint the rim of the pastry with lightly mixed egg yolk and water – best for a savoury recipe, to give a rich brown colour. Place the tray, with the above lined flan, in the centre of a hot oven (400°F., 200°C., Gas Mark 6) and bake for 12 minutes. The pastry will now hold its shape. Carefully lift away the centre paper with beans or the crumpled foil and lift away outer flan ring. Replace the baking tray with pastry case back into the oven for a further 5 minutes to crispen.

5. Barquette or boat shaped tins make elegant looking fresh fruit tartlets or cocktail canapés with savoury filling. Roll pastry out thinly and lift on to the rolling pin. Select about 6–8 large barquette moulds or 12 tiny ones and place close together on the working surface. Unroll pastry, allowing it to fall over the moulds – any mould showing should be tucked underneath pastry so all are covered. Trim a piece of excess pastry from the edge and shape into a ball. Use this to pat the pastry down into each mould. Then roll the pin over the tins, cutting off the excess pastry, the edges of the mould will show through. Separate the moulds and, using fingers, neaten pastry edges. Line each with a small piece of paper and a few baking beans. Place the moulds on a baking tray and place above centre in a hot oven (400°F., 200°C., Gas Mark 6) and bake for 10–12 minutes. Remove paper linings and return to the oven for a further few minutes to crispen.

6. For a professional appearance, use individual tartlet tins, they are easier to handle than trays of tart shapes. Roll pastry out thinly. Select a fluted round cutter, at least 1 inch ($2\frac{1}{2}$ cm.) larger in diameter than the tin, and stamp out circles of the dough. Carefully fit the pastry circles into the moulds, allowing the edge of the pastry to show above the rim of the mould. Prick the base of each and then, using forefinger and thumb, pinch the edges so that the rim stands fairly high above the rim of the mould. Run the forefinger around the outside of the mould, to slope the edge of the pastry slightly inwards. Line each with a small square of greaseproof paper and a few baking beans. Arrange the tins on a baking tray, place just above centre in a hot oven (400°F., 200°C., Gas Mark 6) and bake for 10 minutes. Remove paper and return to the oven for 2 minutes to crispen.

7. Pretty pastry shells can be made by moulding pastry over fluted or small shaped baking tins – queen cake moulds are the most effective. Roll the pastry out, select a large plain cutter about 1 inch (2½ cm.) larger in diameter than the tin and stamp out rounds of pastry. Mould the pastry over the outside of the tin, pressing to fit the shape well and bring the pastry up to the edge of the mould. Turn moulds downwards on a baking tray and prick the pastry on the base of each. Place just above centre in a hot oven (400°F., 200°C., Gas Mark 6) and bake for 12 minutes. When baked, tap each one sharply and lift the pastry away from the mould. Turn the right way up and each case will have a pretty fluted inside.

8. Fruit pies look especially pretty if topped with a woven pie crust. The crust can be woven loosely so that the fruit shows through or closely to make a closed top. Either way, first roll half the pastry to a circle, lift on to the pin and unroll over a shallow pie plate. Fit the pastry gently into the plate and trim away excess from around the rim. Roll out pastry trimmings and remaining pastry to a length and cut into thin strips using a pastry wheel. Fill the pie dish with the fruit, then for an open weave arrange about 5–6 strips across the pie in one direction. In the opposite direction, begin to weave the pastry top. Fold back alternate pastry strips and place one pastry strip across. Turn down the pastry strips and fold back opposite ones and lay across the next pastry strip. Continue until the top is covered.

9. An old fashioned plate tart depends on a pretty rim for a smart appearance.

Roll the pastry out thinly about ½ inch (1 cm.) larger than the pie plate all round. Lift the pastry up on the pin and unroll over the pie plate. Press the pastry gently into place and trim away excess at the edges with a knife. Prick the base with a fork to prevent the centre bubbling up and then finish the edges.

Edges may be marked with the floured prongs of a fork, looped end of a kitchen skewer or, better still, cut attractively. Cut into the pastry with the tip of a knife – 1 inch (2½ cm.) cuts about an inch apart all round the rim. Then lift each flap of pastry at one corner and fold over diagonally to make a point. Continue all round the pie edge. Fill the centre with jam or syrup.

10. A shallow pie plate is good for open pies, where a deeper filling is required. The rim around the edge offers scope for attractive decorations. Roll the pastry out thinly, at least 1 inch (2½ cm.) larger all round than the pie plate. Lift the pastry on the pin and unroll over the dish. Press the pastry gently into place and, with scissors, trim the excess to within ½ inch (1 cm.) of the edge. Now turn the edge under to give a thick rim. Using floured knuckles and forefingers, pinch the rim to make a scalloped edge, then pinch edges to get a sharp ridged effect. Prick the base of the pie and bake blind. Use for lemon meringues or chiffon fillings, alternatively fill with fresh fruit or custard mixtures and bake.

11. The more traditional shaped deep oval pie dishes are never lined underneath with pastry – the shape is too awkward and pastry would remain damp. For this reason the rim must be lined with strips of pastry and, when sealed with the top, make an edge that will hold in juices from filling during baking.

Roll the pastry out to an oval shape about 1 inch (2½ cm.) larger than the dish all round. Turn the empty pie dish over on to the pastry and, using a sharp knife, cut round the rim about ½ inch (1 cm.) away – this allows for a slightly rounded top covering the filling.

Grease the rim of the dish, lift the pastry trimmings and place cut side inwards around the edge of the dish. This way they will fit the edge of the dish without extra rolling or shaping – trim outer edges. Fill the pie with fruit or meat fillings and damp pastry rim. Lift the pastry top on pin and unroll over the pie. Press edges together with prongs of a fork, make a hole in centre and decorate with leaves cut from any trimmings. Brush meat pies with egg and milk and fruit pies with beaten egg white and sugar.

12. Sausage rolls are easier to make in batches. Roll pastry out thinly to a square. Trim edges neatly and then cut lengthways into two oblong strips. Divide sausagemeat in two and, with floured hands, roll to a length same as pastry strips. Place one down the centre of each strip of pastry. Lightly mix 1 egg with 2 tablespoons milk and brush down one side only of pastry strips. Fold undamped side of pastry over filling and seal with wetted edge – remember one wetted and one dry edge will seal but two wetted edges will not. Press edges together and seal with floured prongs of a fork. Snip tops with scissors and, using a sharp floured knife, cut each long roll into individual sausage rolls.

Shortcrust pastry

The fat is rubbed into the flour for shortcrust pastry. This distributes it in tiny particles throughout the mixture. The flour and small lumps of fat are passed through the finger-tips until the mixture resembles fine crumbs. For best results, use fat that is at room temperature. Hard fat, cold from the refrigerator, does not rub in easily and forms an unevenly blended mixture.

There are several types of pastry made using this method. For a plain shortcrust, use a mixture of margarine and white cooking fat. The margarine gives flavour and the white cooking fat adds a shortness to the pastry. In some cases sugar is added to make a sweet shortcrust. A richer shortcrust can be made using all butter and egg to mix. This makes a crisp short pastry and is used for dessert flans and tarts.

Flans made with all butter can be baked in advance and will keep well for 2–3 days in a closed tin.

Shortcrust pastry quantities

Pastry quantities given are for the amount of flour used. Other ingredients in the recipe should follow in the correct proportions.

SHORTCRUST PASTRY

Tartlets	8 oz. (225 g.) shortcrust pastry	18 2½-inch (6-cm.) tartlets
Flan or quiche tins	4 oz. (100 g.) lines	one 7-inch (18-cm.) tin
	4–6 oz. (100–175 g.) lines	one 8-inch (20-cm.) tin
	6 oz. (175 g.) lines	one 9-inch (23-cm.) tin
	8 oz. (225 g.) lines	one 12-inch (31-cm.) tin
Pie plates	4 oz. (100 g.) lines or covers	one 7-inch (18-cm.) plate
	6 oz. (175 g.) lines or covers	one 9-inch (23-cm.) plate
	8 oz. (225 g.) lines and covers	one 7-inch (18-cm.) plate
	12 oz. (350 g.) lines and covers	one 9-inch (23-cm.) plate
Oval pie dish	4 oz. (100 g.) covers	one 1-pint (¾-litre) dish
	6 oz. (175 g.) covers	one 1½-pint (1-litre) dish
	8 oz. (225 g.) covers	one 2-pint (1¼-litre) dish

Plain shortcrust pastry

Use plain shortcrust pastry for sweet or savoury pies, tarts, flans and tartlets. For an extra short pastry, use 2½ oz. (65 g.) fat and only 1 tablespoon water.

Makes 4 oz. (100 g.) pastry

4 oz./100 g. plain flour	2 tablespoons water
pinch salt	
2 oz./50 g. margarine and cooking fat, in equal parts	

Sift the flour and salt into a mixing basin. Blend the two fats together on a plate, using a palette knife. When evenly mixed, add to the flour.

Pick the mixture up in small handfuls and, using the fingertips, rub the fat into the flour allowing the ingredients to fall back into the bowl through the fingers. Do this until the fat is evenly blended throughout the flour and the mixture looks like fine breadcrumbs – there should be no loose flour in the bowl.

Sprinkle the water over the mixture and, using a fork or a round bladed table knife, stir and cut through the ingredients drawing the mixture together until it clings together leaving the sides of the basin clean. Turn out onto a lightly floured working surface and knead just once or twice to form a smooth dough.

Allow the dough to rest for 15–20 minutes before using. Either turn the empty mixing basin over the dough on the table or, if the dough is to be used later, place inside a small polythene bag and put in the refrigerator.

Use the pastry as directed. A hot oven (400°F., 200°C., Gas Mark 6) is correct for shortcrust pastry, unless otherwise directed. Bake on the shelf above centre.

Bacon and egg pie

This recipe is ideal for a picnic lunch, it is moist to eat and looks most attractive when cut in portions.

Serves 4

6 oz./175 g. shortcrust pastry	4 eggs
milk	salt and freshly milled pepper
for the filling:	
4 back bacon rashers	

Divide the shortcrust pastry in half and put one piece aside. Roll remaining half out to a circle slightly larger than a 7-inch (18-cm.) flan ring or shallow sponge cake tin. Line the tin with the pastry and damp the pastry rim.

Arrange the trimmed bacon rashers on their sides over the base of the pie, leaving four spaces for the eggs. Break an egg into each space between the rashers. Season each egg with salt and pepper. Arranging the bacon and egg in this fashion ensures that when the pie is cut each person will get both bacon and egg.

Roll out the remaining pastry and cover the top of the pie. Press the edges together to seal and trim off the extra pastry. Brush the finished pie with a little milk and place in the centre of a hot oven (400°F., 200°C., Gas Mark 6) and bake for 12 minutes. Lower the heat to moderate (350°F., 180°C., Gas Mark 4) and bake for a further 15–20 minutes.

When cold, cut in four portions and serve with salad.
Advance preparation: This pie can be baked the day before. Cool and keep in a cold larder.

Apple dumplings

Test the dumplings with a sharp knife blade to make sure the apples are cooked before removing them from the oven. Apples should feel quite tender.

Makes 4

8 oz./225 g. shortcrust pastry	milk and castor sugar for brushing
4 even sized cooking apples	
2 oz./50 g. castor sugar	

Prepare the shortcrust pastry and divide into four portions. Pat each piece to a round in shape and then roll out to a circle about the size of a bread plate. Allow to rest while preparing the apples.

Peel and core the apples, keeping them whole. Place one on each round of pastry and fill the centre with castor sugar. Bring the edges of the pastry together over the apples. Trim any uneven pieces and press the pastry gently to get a good shape. Turn over and place on a greased baking tray with the sealed pastry edges underneath. Make a hole in the centre of each to allow steam to escape and brush the dumplings with milk. Roll out pastry trimmings and cut in small diamond shaped pieces. Mark with a knife to make small leaves of pastry and use these to decorate the apples. Cut four pastry stalks.

Place the apples in the centre of a hot oven (400°F., 200°C., Gas Mark 6) and bake for 30 minutes. Remove from the heat, brush the apples with a little extra milk and sugar and return to the oven with the pastry stalks on the baking tray. Bake for a further 5–10 minutes until browned.

Place the pastry stalks in the hole on top of the apple dumplings. Sprinkle with extra sugar and serve.

Custard tart

An old fashioned recipe which never fails to be popular. A few seedless raisins add interest to the filling. Serve custard tart warm for dessert or carry cold on a picnic.

Serves 4–6

4 oz./100 g. shortcrust pastry	1 oz./25 g. castor sugar
1 oz./25 g. seedless raisins	few drops vanilla essence
for the custard filling:	½ pint/3 dl. milk
3 large eggs	little grated nutmeg

Roll out the pastry on a lightly floured working surface to a circle large enough to line an 8-inch (20-cm.) tart tin or a flan ring set on a baking tray. Line the tin with the pastry, trim the edges and set aside while preparing the filling.

Crack 2 whole eggs and an egg yolk into a mixing basin. Reserve the extra egg white. Add the sugar, vanilla essence and milk to the eggs and whisk thoroughly to mix. Strain the mixture into a jug.

Brush round the inside of the pastry case with the reserved egg white. This keeps the pastry base flat during cooking and helps prevent the pastry becoming soggy from the custard filling. Sprinkle the flan case with the raisins. Pour in the prepared custard and sprinkle with a little grated nutmeg.

Place the custard tart in the centre of a hot oven (400°F., 200°C., Gas Mark 6) and bake for 15 minutes. Lower the heat to moderate (350°F., 180°C., Gas Mark 4) and bake for a further 15–20 minutes or until the custard filling has set and is golden brown.

Serve warm with cream.

Sweet shortcrust pastry

This slightly sweet pastry is suitable for flans and small tarts with a sweet filling. It is also good for dessert pies.

Makes 4 oz. (100 g.) pastry

4 oz./100 g. plain flour	1 level tablespoon castor sugar
pinch salt	1½ tablespoons cold milk
2 oz./50 g. margarine and white fat, in equal parts	

Sift the flour and salt into a mixing basin. Blend the two fats together on a plate using a palette knife. When evenly mixed, add to the flour.

Pick the mixture up in small handfuls and, using the fingertips, gently rub the fat into the flour allowing the ingredients to fall back into the bowl through the fingers. Do this until the fat is evenly blended through the flour and the mixture looks like fine breadcrumbs.

Measure the sugar and milk into a small basin or teacup. Stir to blend and then pour over the dry ingredients. Using a fork or a round bladed table knife, stir and cut through the mixture until the ingredients cling together and the mixture leaves the sides of the basin clean. Turn out on to a lightly floured working surface and knead once or twice to form a smooth dough.

Allow the dough to rest for 15–20 minutes before using. Either turn the empty mixing basin over the dough on the working table or, if the dough is to be used later, place the dough in a small polythene bag and put in the refrigerator.

Use the pastry as directed. A hot oven (400°F., 200°C., Gas Mark 6) is correct for sweet shortcrust unless otherwise directed. Bake on the shelf above centre.

Apple amber

The combination of apple filling, slightly flavoured with lemon, and the crisp sweet meringue makes this a delicious pudding.

Serves 6

4 oz./100 g. sweet shortcrust pastry	2 egg yolks
	green food colouring (optional)
for the filling:	*for the meringue:*
1½ lb./¾ kg. cooking apples	2 egg whites
2 oz./50 g. butter	4 oz./100 g. castor sugar
3 oz./75 g. castor sugar	
2–3 pieces thinly pared lemon rind	

Roll out the pastry on a lightly floured working surface to a circle, large enough to line an 8–8½-inch (20-cm.) shallow round pie dish. Lightly grease the dish and line with the pastry. Trim the edges and set aside while preparing the filling.

Peel, core and cut up the apples. Melt the butter in a saucepan. Add the apples, sugar and lemon rind. Stir over a low heat until the sugar has dissolved, then cover the pan and continue to cook gently until the apples are tender. Using a wooden spoon, beat the apples to a purée, then rub through a sieve into a mixing basin. Add the egg yolks to the purée and, if liked, a few drops of green food colouring to give the mixture the palest green colour.

Pour the mixture into the lined pie dish. Bake in the centre of a moderately hot oven (375°F., 190°C., Gas Mark 5) and bake for 25–30 minutes or until the pastry is golden and the filling set. Beat the egg whites for the meringue until stiff and then gradually whisk in the sugar. Spoon over the apple filling. Replace in the centre of the oven at a lower temperature (300°F., 150°C., Gas Mark 2) and bake for 20–30 minutes or until the meringue is crisp and lightly brown.

Allow to cool before serving with cream.

Butterscotch tart

The sugar caramel gives the filling in this tart a very good flavour and dark colour.

Serves 4–6

4 oz./100 g. sweet shortcrust pastry	2 tablespoons golden syrup
for the filling:	2 level tablespoons cornflour
2 oz./50 g. granulated sugar	½ pint/3 dl. milk
4 tablespoons water	2 eggs
	few drops vanilla essence

On a lightly floured working surface, roll out the prepared pastry and use to line an 8-inch (20-cm.) tart tin, or flan ring set on a baking tray. Allow to rest for 10 minutes. Place above centre in a hot oven (400°F., 200°C., Gas Mark 6) and bake blind for 10 minutes. Remove any foil or paper and beans a few minutes before the end of the baking time. Set the pastry case to one side while preparing the filling. Lower the oven heat.

Put the sugar in a dry pan and heat, stirring all the time, until the sugar has melted and turned to a golden brown. Add the water – take care the mixture will boil furiously with the addition of a cold liquid. Add the syrup and stir over the heat until dissolved and the mixture is blended. Remove from the heat.

Blend the cornflour with the milk and stir into the caramel. Replace the pan over the heat and stir until the mixture is boiling and has thickened. Draw off the heat and cool for 2–3 minutes. Lightly mix the eggs and vanilla essence. Add to the caramel and mix thoroughly.

Pour this filling into the baked pastry case. Return to a very moderate oven (325°F., 170°C., Gas Mark 3) and bake for 30–35 minutes or until the filling has set.

Serve warm or cold with cream.

Rich shortcrust pastry

A richer shortcrust pastry keeps its shape well when baked. This type of pastry is ideal for open fruit flans, for tartlets – especially those baked blind and filled with fresh fruit – and for pastry which is used as the base for some cake recipes.

Makes 4 oz. (100 g.) pastry

4 oz./100 g. plain flour	1 oz./25 g. icing sugar, sifted
pinch salt	1 egg yolk
2 oz./50 g. butter	1 tablespoon water

Sift the flour and salt into a mixing basin. Add the butter, cut in pieces – take care that the butter is at room temperature and not cold from the refrigerator.

Pick up the mixture in small handfuls and, using the fingertips, rub the butter into the flour allowing the mixture to fall back into the bowl through the fingers. Do this until the butter is evenly blended through the flour. Add the sifted icing sugar and mix the ingredients.

Add the egg yolk and sprinkle over the water then, using a fork or round bladed table knife, stir until the mixture is evenly moist and crumbly. Using the fingers, draw the mixture together into a rough dough. Turn out on to a lightly floured working surface and knead to form a smooth dough.

Allow the dough to rest for about 30 minutes before using. Place the ball of dough inside a polythene bag and set in a cool place, preferably the refrigerator.

Use the pastry as directed. A moderately hot oven (375°F., 190°C., Gas Mark 5) is required for a rich shortcrust, unless otherwise directed. Bake on the shelf above centre.

Freezer note: It is not advisable to freeze this pastry uncooked. It is a good idea, however, to freeze baked flan cases or baked tartlet cases ready for filling. They thaw very quickly.

12

Cherry and almond tart

This tart has a moist, almondy flavour that comes from the topping of *crème d'amandes*. For a special occasion, blend the filling and mix the icing with rum for flavouring.

Serves 6

4 oz./100 g. rich shortcrust pastry	2 oz./50 g. castor sugar
	1 egg
1 lb./½ kg. dark red cherries	few drops almond essence
for the topping:	*for the glaze:*
2 oz./50 g. ground almonds	2 oz./50 g. icing sugar
1 level tablespoon flour	water to mix
2 oz./50 g. butter	

On a lightly floured surface, roll out the pastry to a circle large enough to line a greased 8-inch (20-cm.) flan ring or tart tin. Line with the pastry, trim the edges and prick the base with a fork. Stone the cherries, keeping them whole, and arrange over the base of the tart. Set aside while preparing the almond topping.

Mix together the ground almonds and flour. Cream the butter and sugar until light and then gradually beat in the lightly mixed egg and almond essence. Fold in the almonds and flour. Spoon the mixture over the cherries and, using a spatula, spread the topping to completely cover the cherries and fill the tart. Tap the tart sharply to encourage the filling to fall evenly. Place above centre in a hot oven (400°F., 200°C., Gas Mark 6) and bake for 35 minutes, or until the tart is brown and filling baked.

Sift the icing sugar and blend in just enough water to make a thick icing. While the tart is hot from the oven, spoon the icing on to the centre. This will soften with the warmth of the tart and should be spread thinly to cover the whole surface. Leave the tart to cool and the icing will set firm. Serve cut in wedges when cold.

Tarte aux pommes

Illustrated in colour on pages 52 and 53

Two types of apples are used to make Tarte aux pommes – sour cooking apples which reduce to a good purée for the filling and dessert apples which hold their shape well for the top. A clear shiny glaze of apple jelly makes this an attractive dessert. Very good for a buffet supper.

Serves 8

8 oz./225 g. rich shortcrust pastry	2–3 cloves
	for the topping:
for the filling:	3–4 dessert apples
2 lb./1 kg. cooking apples	icing sugar (see recipe)
6 oz./175 g. castor sugar	*for the glaze:*
1 oz./25 g. butter	½ pint/3 dl. apple juice (see recipe)
1 tablespoon water	
juice ½ lemon	8 oz./225 g. granulated sugar

Roll out the pastry on a lightly floured working surface to a circle large enough to line a 10-inch (26-cm.) tart tin or a flan ring set on a baking tray. Prick the base of the pastry and set aside while preparing the filling.

Peel, core and cut the apples into chunks. Reserve the apple peelings and pieces of apple core in a basin. At a later stage, place the peelings and cores in a saucepan with a generous 1 pint (6 dl.) water. Place the apple pieces in a separate saucepan, add the sugar, butter, water, lemon juice and cloves. Bring up to the boil, cover and simmer very gently for about 10-15 minutes or until the apple pieces are quite soft. Draw the pan off the heat, remove the cloves and whisk the mixture to a purée. Allow to cool and then spoon over the base of the pastry case.

Peel the dessert apples and slice thinly. Arrange the slices, overlapping, in circles to cover the surface of the tart. Add any peeling and cores to the pan of apple peelings.

Place the apple tart above centre in a hot oven (400°F., 200°C., Gas Mark 6) and bake for 30–35 minutes. When baked, the top will be brown and the apple slices cooked but still pale in colour. To get the apple slices edged with brown, so familiar in the traditional recipe, dredge the surface of the tart with icing sugar. Brush away any sugar that falls on the pastry rim and place the tart under a hot grill. The tart will be too large to go under completely, in which case simply turn the tart round so that the edges of the apple slices caramelise under the high heat. Allow the tart to cool while preparing the jelly glaze.

Bring the pan of apple peelings to the boil. Cover with a lid and simmer very gently for 1 hour. Strain and reserve ½ pint (3 dl.) of the apple juice. Add the sugar to the juice and stir over low heat until the sugar has dissolved. Bring up to the boil and cook rapidly for about 10 minutes for a set. Test in the same way as you would an apple jelly preserve. When setting point is reached, draw the pan off the heat. Allow to cool for 2–3 minutes or until the jelly is beginning to show signs of setting. Spoon quickly over the flan to completely glaze the surface.

Leave until cold when the jelly sets firm. Serve with cream.

Quiche pastry

This pastry is so called because it makes a particularly crisp, pleasant-to-eat crust for all savoury quiche recipes. Use it for any savoury flan.

Makes 4 oz. (100 g.) pastry

4 oz./100 g. plain flour	1 egg yolk
pinch salt	2 tablespoons water
2 oz./50 g. butter	

Sift the flour and salt into a bowl. Add the butter, cut in pieces – butter should be at room temperature and not cold from the refrigerator.

Pick up the mixture in small handfuls and, using the fingertips, rub the butter into the flour. Do this until the butter is evenly blended through the flour.

Lightly mix the egg yolk and water. Add to the ingredients and, using a fork, stir until the mixture is evenly moist and crumbly. Then with fingers draw the mixture together to form a rough dough. Turn out on to a lightly floured working surface and knead once or twice to form a smooth dough.

Place the ball of dough in a polythene bag and set in a cool place, preferably the refrigerator, for about 30 minutes before using.

Use the pastry as directed. A moderately hot oven (375°F., 190°C., Gas Mark 5) is required for quiche pastry. Bake on the shelf above centre.

Asparagus quiche

Buy the less expensive loose asparagus for making asp‡ quiche, only the tender green top parts of the stems are ‡ Serve the quiche for lunch, supper or take it on

Serves 4

4 oz./100 g. quiche pastry	1 tablespoon grated Parmesan
for the filling:	cheese
1 lb./½ kg. fresh asparagus	2 eggs
1 small onion	¼ pint/1½ dl. single cream
½ oz./15 g. butter	salt and freshly milled pepper

On a lightly floured working surface, roll the pastry out to a circle slightly larger all round than an 8-inch (20-cm.) quiche tin or use a shallow sponge cake tin. Line the tin with the pastry and set aside while preparing the filling. Place the lined tin on a baking sheet so that it is easier to handle once the filling is added.

Wash and scrape the asparagus stems, trim the ends evenly and place asparagus in a large bowl of salt water. Bring a pan of water to the boil, lay the asparagus spears in the pan of water and cook gently for 15 minutes or until just tender. Drain well and then trim the stalks down to the tender green tops and the heads.

Peel and finely chop the onion. Melt the butter in a frying pan, add the onion and fry gently for about 5 minutes until the onion is tender but not brown. Add the asparagus pieces and toss for a moment in the hot onion and butter. Spoon the mixture over the base of the pastry case. Sprinkle with the grated cheese. Lightly beat the eggs and cream together and season well with salt and pepper. Pour over the asparagus to fill the quiche. Place in the centre of a moderately hot oven (375°F., 190°C., Gas Mark 5) and bake for 40 minutes.

Cool then serve with a salad.

Cheese, egg and bacon tart

Serves 4

4 oz./100 g. quiche pastry	5 tablespoons milk
for the filling:	salt and freshly milled pepper
2–3 bacon rashers	2 oz./50 g. cheese, grated
2 eggs	pinch cayenne pepper

On a lightly floured working surface, roll the pastry out and use to line a 7-inch (18-cm.) plain round flan ring. Trim the edges and allow to rest for 10 minutes. Place above centre in a hot oven (400°F., 200°C., Gas Mark 6) and bake blind for 10 minutes. Remove any foil or baking beans and lift away the flan ring a few moments before the end of the cooking time.

Trim, chop and lightly fry the bacon rashers for the filling. Arrange in the base of the pastry case. Beat the eggs and milk, add a seasoning of salt and pepper, then stir in the grated cheese and cayenne pepper. Pour over the bacon and return the quiche to the centre of the oven. Bake for a further 20–30 minutes or until the filling is set and lightly browned.

Serve warm or cold with coleslaw salad.

Flaky and puff pastry

Both these pastry doughs bake and rise in layers or flakes. To achieve this, the flour is made into a dough and the fat incorporated at a later stage in a layer or pieces. The method of folding and rolling builds up layers of dough and layers of fat. To preserve these all important layers, it is vital that the pastry is never rolled too thinly, nor should the pastry be given more rolls and folds than recommended in the recipe. Over-rolling causes the layers to break down and blend together, thus spoiling the end result.

A mixture of margarine and white cooking fat can be used in flaky pastry but in puff pastry, where there is a high proportion of fat, butter should be used. Have the dough and fat of the same consistency. Fat should be at room temperature. If the fat is too hard, it will break through the layer of dough during rolling and folding and cause uneven rising.

Never hurry puff pastry when preparing it. Prepare it when doing other jobs as well. Roll and fold the pastry, then leave it to rest and go back. Don't tidy away each time, leave the rolling pin and flour out ready for the next working. Once prepared, the pastry will keep in the refrigerator for 2–3 days.

Flaky or puff pastry quantities

Pastry quantities given are for the amount of flour used. Other ingredients in the recipe should follow in the correct proportions.

Care should be taken if using bought puff pastry in any recipes. Bought puff pastry is sold by weight, therefore a greater quantity is required. A 7½ oz. (215 g.) packet frozen pastry would amount to the same as 4 oz. (100 g.) home made pastry and a 13 oz. (368 g.) packet would equal 8 oz. (225 g.) home made pastry.

Vol au vents	8 oz. (225 g.) pastry	12 3-inch (7-cm.) vol au vents
Cream horns	8 oz. (225 g.) pastry	12 horns
Sausage rolls	8 oz. (225 g.) pastry	18 2½-inch (6-cm.) rolls
Pie crusts	4 oz. (100 g.) covers	one 1-pint (¾-litre) dish
	6 oz. (175 g.) covers	one 1½-pint (1-litre) dish
	8 oz. (225 g.) covers	one 2-pint (1¼-litre) dish

Flaky pastry

Flaky pastry is excellent to use for pie crusts, sausage rolls, turnovers and mincemeat pies.

Makes 8 oz. (225 g.) pastry

8 oz./225 g. plain flour	scant ¼ pint/scant 1½ dl.
pinch salt	water
6 oz./170 g. butter and	
cooking fat, equal parts	

Sift together the flour and salt into a mixing basin. Blend the butter and fat together on a plate, using a palette knife. When evenly mixed, spread over the plate and mark into 4 equal portions. Add one portion to the sieved flour and rub in.

Sprinkle the water evenly over the mixture. Then, using a fork or a round bladed table knife, stir the ingredients, drawing the mixture together into a rough dough. Turn out on to a lightly floured working surface and knead fairly thoroughly to get a smooth dough. Place in a polythene bag and leave to rest in the refrigerator for 15 minutes before rolling out.

Roll out the dough to an oblong shape about three times as long as it is wide. Mark it into thirds. Over the top two thirds of the dough, place one third of the remaining fat in small pieces. Do this with the tip of a table knife, leaving the fat in small lumps and leaving a margin of $\frac{1}{2}$ inch (1 cm.) all round the edge. Distribute the fat evenly, allowing spaces between the pieces of fat so that plenty of air is trapped during folding. Fold the lower, uncovered third of the pastry up over the centre third, and the top third down over both. Take care to keep the corners square. Lightly press the open edges with the rolling pin to seal and give the pastry a half turn clockwise, so that the open edges face towards and away from you.

Roll the pastry out again. Dab on a third portion of the fat as previously described, then fold, seal and turn the pastry again. Place the pastry inside a polythene bag and leave to rest for 15–20 minutes in a cool place.

Roll the pastry out and add the last portion of fat as previously described. Fold, seal the edges and turn the dough. Roll out once more, this time without adding any fat. Fold, seal and turn the pastry and it is now ready for use. Allow the pastry to rest again, covered in a cool place for 30 minutes before using. Prepared flaky pastry dough will keep in the refrigerator for 2–3 days. It must be wrapped in foil or in a polythene bag to prevent the surface from drying out.

A hot oven (425°F., 220°C., Gas Mark 7) is required for flaky pastry. Bake on the shelf above centre.

Freezer note: Freeze in quantities of 8 oz. (225 g.) pastry – an amount which is suitable to use in recipes. Allow to thaw for 1 hour at room temperature or overnight in the refrigerator.

Sausage rolls

Larger sausage rolls are delicious for supper, smaller ones for a buffet supper, to serve with drinks or for a picnic. Add a little powdered sage or some finely chopped and sautéed onion to the sausagemeat for extra flavour.

Makes 8–12 sausage rolls

4 oz./100 g. flaky pastry	8 oz./225 g. beef or pork
good pinch powdered	sausagemeat
sage	beaten egg to glaze

Roll out the pastry very thinly to a rectangle about 8 inches (20 cm.) wide and 12–14 inches (31–36 cm.) long. Cover and rest the pastry while preparing the sausagemeat. Mix the sage into the sausagemeat and divide the mixture into two portions. With lightly floured hands, roll each portion out on a floured working surface to a 'rope' about 12–14 inches (31–36 cm.) long.

Divide the pastry into two strips lengthwise. Brush the right hand side of each pastry strip with a little beaten egg. Place the sausagemeat on the pastry, a little to the right of the centre. Fold the unglazed pastry over and seal it on to the side brushed with egg. With a sharp knife, cut each strip into 4–6 sausage rolls according to size required. Make two or three diagonal slashes on the top of each one.

Arrange the sausage rolls on a baking tray. Brush them with the egg and place in the centre of a hot oven (425°F., 220°C., Gas Mark 7) and bake for about 20 minutes.

Serve warm, or leave until cold and reheat before serving.

Freezer note: Sausage rolls can be frozen before or after baking. They should not be kept longer than a month. Freeze unbaked items uncovered until hard, then pack in suitable quantities. Glazed items should be placed in a rigid container for extra protection.

Thaw baked sausage rolls for several hours then reheat for serving. Unbaked sausage rolls should be thawed in the refrigerator overnight. Then bake as directed above.

Cream puffs

Once the pastry is made these are very easy to make. Serve them for afternoon tea or at a coffee morning. Alternatively double the ingredients and make them for a buffet supper party.

Makes 8 cream puffs

4 oz./100 g. flaky or puff pastry	1 tablespoon castor sugar
icing sugar	2 tablespoons raspberry jam
for the filling:	
¼ pint/1½ dl. double cream	

Roll out the pastry on a lightly floured working surface to a rectangle about ¼ inch (½ cm.) thick and approximately 9 inches (23 cm.) by 6 inches (15 cm.). Trim the edges with a sharp, floured knife and prick the pastry all over with a fork. Cut the pastry in half lengthwise, then cut each strip across, first in half and then into quarters. Allow to rest for about 15–20 minutes.

Arrange the pieces of pastry on a wet baking tray. Place above centre in a very hot oven (425°F., 220°C., Gas Mark 7) for 10 minutes. Lower the heat to hot (400°F., 200°C., Gas Mark 6) and bake for a further 5 minutes. When risen and brown remove from the baking tray and allow to cool.

Half whip the cream, sweeten with the sugar and beat until thick. Split each cooled pastry slice in half using a sharp knife. Spread the base with a little raspberry jam and then top with cream. Replace the top and dredge with icing sugar before serving.

Steak and kidney pie

If the onion is omitted from the pie filling, the steak and kidney can be cooked 1–2 days in advance and kept in the refrigerator ready to use.

Serves 6

8 oz./225 g. flaky pastry	seasoned flour
beaten egg	fat for frying
for the filling:	1 medium onion
1½ lb./¾ kg. lean buttock or	1 pint/6 dl. beef stock or water
chuck steak	pinch dried mixed herbs
4 oz./100 g. ox kidney	salt and freshly milled pepper

Prepare the pastry and leave to rest while preparing the filling. Trim away the fat or gristle from the meat and cut the meat into suitable sized pieces. Snip out any core from the kidney and cut the kidney into neat pieces. Roll the meat and kidney in seasoned flour.

Melt the fat in a frying pan, add the meat and fry gently to brown on all sides. Lift the meat from the pan and place in a saucepan.

Add the peeled and chopped onion, the hot stock, herbs and a good seasoning of salt and pepper. Bring up to the boil then cover and simmer for 1½–2 hours. When the filling is cooked, strain off half the liquid into a small saucepan ready to reheat for the gravy.

Meanwhile roll out the pastry about ¼ inch (½ cm.) thick on a floured working surface. Cover and rest the pastry for 20 minutes. Using a 1½-pint (1-litre) pie dish as a guide, cut out the pastry for the pie top. Use a sharp knife and following the line of the pie dish to cut out the shape. Grease the pie dish rim and use the pastry trimmings to line the rim of the dish. Reserve any extra pastry pieces for the decoration.

Pile the meat, kidney and onion into the pie dish, piling the meat high up in the centre. Place in a pie funnel. Add a little of the meat gravy. Damp the pastry rim and cover the pie with the pastry lid. Press the edges gently together to seal. Trim edges if necessary and, with the back of a knife, knock and scallop the edges of the pie.

From the remaining pastry trimmings, cut the decoration for the pie. Four diamonds to make leaves and three small squares of different sizes to make the rose. Place the squares on top of each other, the largest underneath. Turn over and gather into a ball. Cut a cross on the rounded side and open out to make a rose. Grease a small square of paper on both sides. Place over the hole made in the centre of the pie, with the pastry rose placed neatly on top. Glaze the surface of the pie with the beaten egg. Arrange the leaves in position and glaze these. Place the finished pie on a baking tray.

Place in the centre of a hot oven (425°F., 220°C., Gas Mark 7) and bake for 30–40 minutes. Lower the heat (350°F., 180°C., Gas Mark 4) and bake for another 40 minutes to 1 hour. When baked, remove the rose and paper. Through the hole, pour the hot gravy through a funnel then replace the pastry rose.

Place a paper frill round the outside of the dish before serving.

Puff pastry

Illustrated in colour on page 41

The most difficult pastry of all to make, but by far the most rewarding. Puff pastry rises beautifully and should be used for vol au vents or the smaller bouchées cases, cream horns and many kinds of pâtisserie. It can also be used for pie crusts and sausage rolls.

Makes 8 oz. (225 g.) pastry

8 oz./225 g. plain flour	scant ¼ pint/scant 1½ dl. cold
pinch salt	water
1 oz./25 g. white cooking fat	7 oz./200 g. butter

Sieve the flour and salt into a mixing basin. Add the cooking fat, and, using the fingertips, rub into the mixture. Sprinkle over the water and, with a fork, mix quickly to a rough dough that leaves the sides of the basin clean. Turn the dough out on to a floured working surface and knead thoroughly to get a smooth dough. Place the dough in a polythene bag and put in a cool place to rest for 30 minutes.

Cut the butter in one piece from an 8 oz. (225 g.) block. Make sure the butter is at room temperature and not cold from the refrigerator. Sprinkle the butter with flour and lightly flatten the butter slightly to a neat oblong shape. Roll the rested dough out to a strip about $\frac{1}{2}$ inch (1 cm.) wider than the butter on each side and long enough for the ends to fold into the centre over the butter and slightly overlap. Place the butter in the centre and fold the pastry over to enclose the butter completely. Press the three open edges to seal.

Give the dough a half turn clockwise so that the sealed edges now face the top and bottom. Press the dough across several times to half flatten it out and then roll with short sharp strokes. Never roll the length of the pastry otherwise you force air bubbles to break the surface. Keep the corners square and avoid rolling the dough too thinly otherwise the formation of layers of fat and dough will intermingle and spoil.

Roll the pastry out to an oblong about 3 times as long as it is wide. Mark in three. Fold the bottom third up over the centre third and the top third down over both. Seal the edges with a rolling pin and give a half turn clockwise. The pastry has now had one roll and fold. Roll out the pastry and fold once more, then place the pastry inside a polythene bag and put to rest in a cool place for 20–30 minutes.

Give the pastry two more rolls and folds. Then cover and rest again. Finally another two rolls and folds – a total of six. Wrap and store in a cool place until ready to use. Prepared puff pastry will keep well in the refrigerator for 2–3 days. It must be wrapped in foil or placed in a polythene bag to prevent the surface drying.

A useful trick of the trade is to impress the fingertips in the dough to indicate how many rolls and folds it has had. It's so easy to forget. After the first two rolls and folds mark with two fingers, and so on until the pastry is finished when it should show 6 imprints.

A very hot oven (425°F., 220°C., Gas Mark 7) is the correct temperature for puff pastry. Recipes using this pastry will need a wetted baking tray. The high fat content and baking temperature causes this pastry to scorch quickly and a wetted baking tray helps to prevent it.
Freezer note: Raw puff pastry dough freezes well. Freeze in 8 oz. (225 g.) quantities ready for use. Allow to thaw for 1–2 hours at room temperature or overnight in the refrigerator. As a rule, baked puff pastry items are not frozen, the baked pastry is too fragile.

Vol au vent cases

Vol au vents are quite simple to make if directions are followed carefully. They fall over or tip to one side during baking usually when the pastry has been unevenly rolled, or they have been assembled carelessly.

Makes 6 cases

8 oz./225 g. puff pastry   beaten egg to glaze

Roll out the pastry to about $\frac{1}{4}$ inch ($\frac{1}{2}$ cm.) thickness. Lightly flour a board or baking tray and put the pastry on it. Take care not to turn the pastry over at this stage. Leave in a cool place, if possible in the refrigerator for about 30 minutes or until the pastry is firm.

Stamp out an even number of circles using a floured 3-inch ($7\frac{1}{2}$-cm.) round cutter. From this quantity of pastry you should get 12 circles. Using a palette knife, transfer half the circles on to a wetted baking tray. Prick them well with a fork and brush with beaten egg. Cut out the centre from the remaining 6 circles, using a 2-inch (5-cm.) round cutter. Lift these rings, taking great care not to pull them out of shape, and *turn them over* on to the pastry circles. Glaze the tops with beaten egg.

Place above centre in a very hot oven (425°F., 220°C., Gas Mark 7) and bake for 15–20 minutes until well risen. Reduce the oven heat to hot (400°F., 200°C., Gas Mark 6) and bake for a further 10 minutes or until the cases are crisp and brown. Before using the vol au vent cases for savoury fillings, scoop out a little of the softer inside pastry with a teaspoon to allow for a more generous portion of filling.
Freezer note: Vol au vent cases can be cut, shaped and then frozen unbaked. Freeze the prepared cases uncovered on a flat tray. When firm, transfer to a waxed container or stack in freezer bags. When required, they can be transferred to a baking tray and allowed to thaw for 1–2 hours at room temperature or overnight in the refrigerator. Brush with egg and bake as above.

Tarte Française

Either canned or fresh fruits can be used to fill this pastry case. For a special occasion, spoon a layer of confectioner's custard in the base before topping with the apricots. This would certainly be essential if fresh fruit such as strawberries were used. Where other fruits are used, glaze with an appropriately flavoured jam.

Serves 6

8 oz./225 g. puff pastry	2 heaped tablespoons apricot
beaten egg to glaze	jam
for the filling:	1 tablespoon lemon juice
1 (16 oz./450 g.) can apricot	toasted flaked almonds
halves	

Roll the pastry out on a lightly floured working surface to an oblong about $\frac{1}{4}$ inch ($\frac{1}{2}$ cm.) thick, and approximately 14 inches (36 cm.) long by 6 inches (15 cm.) wide. Trim the edges neatly with a sharp floured knife. Dust the surface of the pastry lightly with flour and fold the strip in half lengthwise. Cut a rectangle from the centre of the pastry leaving a border of about 1 inch ($2\frac{1}{2}$ cm.) all round. You will now have a smaller pastry rectangle and a large pastry border. Unfold the pastry border and set aside.

Roll out the remaining piece of pastry to an oblong the same size as the border. Place this on a baking tray which has been rinsed with cold water and prick all over with a fork. Brush the edges of the pastry with a little beaten egg and arrange the pastry border on top. Trim the edges to fit, then, using a sharp knife, flute the edges of the pastry and score a criss-cross design on top of the border. Brush the pastry all over with a little beaten egg and allow to rest in a cool place for 15–20 minutes. Place just above centre in a hot oven (425°F., 220°C., Gas Mark 7) and bake for 20 minutes. Remove from the oven and allow to cool.

Drain the apricots from the can and arrange neatly in the baked pastry case. Sieve the apricot jam into a saucepan and add the lemon juice. Stir over low heat to blend the ingredients, then bring up to the boil. Draw off the heat and, while still hot, brush the fruit with the apricot glaze. Sprinkle with toasted almonds and allow to cool. Serve cut in slices.

Jalousie à la confiture

On various occasions use different flavours of jam or mincemeat to give variety to this recipe. A savoury cheese filling is also very good.

Cuts into 6 slices

4 oz./100 g. puff pastry	beaten egg to glaze
1–2 tablespoons raspberry jam	icing sugar

Roll out the puff pastry to a rectangular shape, about 8–9 inches (20–23 cm.) long and 6–7 inches (15–18 cm.) wide. Fold the pastry in two lengthways. Unfold and cut the pastry lengthwise to one side of the fold mark. Take the smaller of the two pieces and turn over on to a wetted baking tray. Spread the centre with raspberry jam and brush the edges with beaten egg.

Take the remaining larger piece of pastry and fold into two lengthways. With the folded edge towards you, mark lines ½ inch (1 cm.) in from either end and ¾ inch (1½ cm.) in from the top. Use these guiding lines, cut into the pastry with a sharp knife. This method of cutting the pastry makes the familiar slatted appearance down the centre.

Unfold the cut piece of pastry over the base covered with jam. Seal all round and knock back the edges like a pie edge with a knife. Brush with beaten egg and allow to rest for 10–15 minutes.

Place above centre in a hot oven (425°F., 220°C., Gas Mark 7) and bake for 20–25 minutes or until well risen and brown. Dust with sifted icing sugar and pass under a very hot grill just to glaze the surface.

Allow to cool and cut in slices when ready to serve.

Cream horns

These are essentially tea time pastries that need to be eaten with a fork. They look pretty among other cakes. Bake the cream horns in advance but do not fill them too long before serving otherwise the pastry may lose some of its crispness.

Makes 12 cream horns

8 oz./225 g. puff pastry	*to decorate:*
beaten egg to glaze	chopped angelica or glacé
½ pint/3 dl. double cream	cherries
1–2 tablespoons castor sugar	

Roll the pastry out on a lightly floured working surface to an oblong about 12 inches (31 cm.) long by 8 inches (20 cm.) wide. Using a sharp floured knife, trim the edges of the pastry, then cut the pastry in long strips about ½ inch (1 cm.) wide and 12 inches (31 cm.) in length.

Brush the strips of pastry with water. Take them, one at a time, and starting at the pointed end of a cream horn tin, working towards the open end wrapping each strip *wet side inside* round the tins. Each layer should slightly overlap the previous one. Put the covered tins on wetted baking trays and place them with the pastry ends underneath, to prevent them from unrolling during baking. Set aside to rest in a cool place for 15–20 minutes.

Brush with egg and place just above centre in a very hot oven (425°F., 220°C., Gas Mark 7) and bake for 15–20 minutes or until well risen and brown. Remove from the heat and while still hot, gently pull out each pastry horn tin – give each one a gentle, but sharp, twist to loosen it. Leave until cold.

Half whip the cream and then add the sugar to sweeten. Whip until thick and light. Spoon or preferably pipe the cream into the pastry horns – using a piping bag and a large star tube. Decorate with a little chopped angelica or tiny slice of glacé cherry.

Mince pies

Mince pies can be made using a rich shortcrust pastry, flaky or puff pastry depending on the kind of mince pies you like.

Makes 12–14 pies

8 oz./225 g. puff pastry	*to decorate:*
4 oz./100 g. mincemeat	icing sugar
beaten egg to glaze	

On a floured board, roll the pastry out thinly and allow to rest for 15–20 minutes. Using a 2–2½-inch (5–6-cm.) round cutter, stamp out 24–28 circles of pastry. Line 12 tartlet tins, or as many as needed, with half the pastry circles. Place a teaspoon of mincemeat in the centre of each. Damp the edges of the pastry lids with a little beaten egg and place over the filled tartlet tins. Gently press the pastry edges together to seal.

Cut one or two slits in the top of each pie. Brush with a little beaten egg. Place fairly high up in a very hot oven (425°F., 220°C., Gas Mark 7) and bake for 20 minutes or until well risen and brown.

Serve warm, dredged with icing sugar.

Advance preparation: Flaky or puff pastry can be made 1–2 days in advance and kept in the refrigerator ready for use.

Freezer note: These pies can be made well in advance of Christmas if liked, and kept in the freezer. If this is to be done, place the prepared but unbaked pies, still in the tins, in the freezer and freeze until firm. Remove the tins and pack the pies in boxes. Seal and store. To use them, simply take out the number of pies required and reseal the package. Place the pies in the original tins and allow to stand for 1½ hours at room temperature or overnight in the refrigerator. Bake as directed above.

Make good use of the trimmings

After making certain recipes, particularly vol au vents, there is always a quantity of puff pastry trimmings left over and these can be used. Gather up the pastry trimmings carefully. Place them flat layer on flat layer – don't just screw them up. If possible enclose the smaller pieces between larger pieces. Re-roll the trimmings out and give the pastry one, or if necessary two, more rolls and folds to form a piece of pastry that you can use. Wrap and rest the pastry before using.

Eccles and Banbury cakes

puff pastry trimmings
for the filling:
½ oz./15 g. butter, melted
2 oz./50 g. cleaned currants

½ oz./15 g. chopped mixed peel
½ oz./15 g. brown sugar
¼ level teaspoon mixed spice or
    cinnamon

Roll out the pastry trimmings very thinly. Leave to rest for 10 minutes. Mix the melted butter, currants, chopped peel, sugar and spice for the filling and set aside.

Cut out rounds of the pastry about 3½–4 inches (8–10 cm.) in diameter. Damp the edges with water and place a small teaspoon of filling in the centre of each.

Gather up each Eccles cake like a little bag, pinching well to seal. Turn over, with the seal underneath, and roll each one to a circle about 3 inches (7 cm.) wide. The fruit should begin to show through. Make 2–3 slashes through the top layer and chill until ready to bake.

Gather up each Banbury cake like a pasty, with the join running over the top and down the centre. Turn them over and flatten out first with the palm of the hand and then with the rolling pin. Roll Banbury cakes into an oval until the fruit begins to show through. Make 2–3 slashes through the top layer and chill until ready to bake.

Arrange on a baking sheet and place in the centre of a hot oven (425°F., 220°C., Gas Mark 7) and bake for about 15–20 minutes or until crisp and golden.

Choux pastry

Choux pastry is a completely different type of pastry. The liquid and fat are brought to the boil in a saucepan and the sieved flour added. Use a good strong plain flour and take care to add all the liquid mixture in the pan, while still boiling. The eggs added to the recipe are responsible for the puffed, well risen appearance of baked choux pastry. The eggs should be very thoroughly beaten in to get a light pastry.

A piping bag and piping tubes are really essential for good results when making eclairs and cream buns. Choose a large savoy piping bag in nylon or cotton and select a large plain tube ½ inch (1 cm.) in diameter. To use the bag, place the tube inside at the nozzle end, fold back a cuff around the top of the bag. Spoon in the choux pastry mixture level with the cuff. Turn the cuff back up and gather the top together within the hand. The bag is ready to use. Hold the bag vertical and squeeze out bulbs of the mixture for buns. For piped eclair mixtures, hold the bag at an angle of 45 degrees.

Choux pastry

Success with choux pastry depends on gradually and thoroughly beating in the eggs. Texture is important, the mixture should not be too soft to pipe and the amount of egg added does depend on the size of eggs used.

Makes 4 oz. (100 g.) pastry

4 oz./100 g. plain flour
2½–3 oz./65–75 g. margarine
¼ pint/1½ dl. cold water

pinch salt
1 level teaspoon castor sugar
3–4 eggs (see recipe)

Sift the flour on to a square of greaseproof paper and put in a warm place. Cut up the fat and place in a medium sized saucepan along with the water, salt and sugar. Place over a moderate heat and, once the butter is melted, bring up to a quick boil.

Immediately tip in the flour all at once, while the pan is still on the heat. Then draw the pan off the heat and beat the mixture well with a wooden spoon for about 1 minute until it leaves the sides of the pan clean. Allow the mixture to cool, until the hand can be comfortably held against the sides of the pan.

Lightly beat the eggs. Add them a little at a time to the paste in the pan. Beat each addition of egg in very thoroughly before adding any more. When ready, the paste will appear thick and glossy and should be stiff enough to hold its shape when piped. If necessary to get the right consistency an extra egg yolk can be added.

At this stage the mixture can stand until ready to use.

A very hot oven is required for choux pastry (425°F., 220°C., Gas Mark 7) unless otherwise directed.

Cream buns

Cream buns go soft or collapse after baking if they are not dried out thoroughly before removing from the oven. They can be filled with fresh cream or with confectioners' custard (page 185).

Makes 12 buns

4 oz./100 g. choux pastry
beaten egg to glaze
for the filling:
½ pint/3 dl. double cream
1 oz./25 g. castor sugar
few drops vanilla essence

for the coffee icing:
3 tablespoons strong black
    coffee (see recipe)
1 oz./25 g. castor sugar
6 oz./175 g. icing sugar

Prepare the choux pastry mixture according to the basic recipe. Spoon into a large nylon or cotton piping bag, fitted with a 2-inch (5-cm.) plain piping tube. Pipe out the mixture in bulbs, about 2-inches (5-cm.) across, on to a greased baking tray. Allow about 6 buns per tray and do not pipe too closely together. Brush each one with a little beaten egg and mark with the back of a fork.

Place in the centre of a hot oven (425°F., 220°C., Gas Mark 7) and bake *undisturbed* for 20 minutes. Prick a small hole in each one with the tip of a sharp knife and return to the oven for a further 5 minutes, to dry out completely. Allow to cool before filling.

Partly whip the cream, add the sugar and vanilla essence and whip until thick. Make a small slit in the side of each choux bun. Using a piping bag and small tube, pipe the cream into the buns to fill them.

Measure the black coffee (use 1 teaspoon instant coffee to 3 tablespoons hot water) into a saucepan. Add the sugar and heat gently until the sugar has dissolved. Draw off the heat and add the sieved icing sugar. Beat well to get a smooth icing. Dip the rounded sides of each filled choux bun into the warm icing. Drain for a moment and then turn right side up.

Allow the icing to set before serving.

OVERLEAF **Twelve point guide to good pastry**
The explanatory captions to these photographs appear on pages 8 and 9.

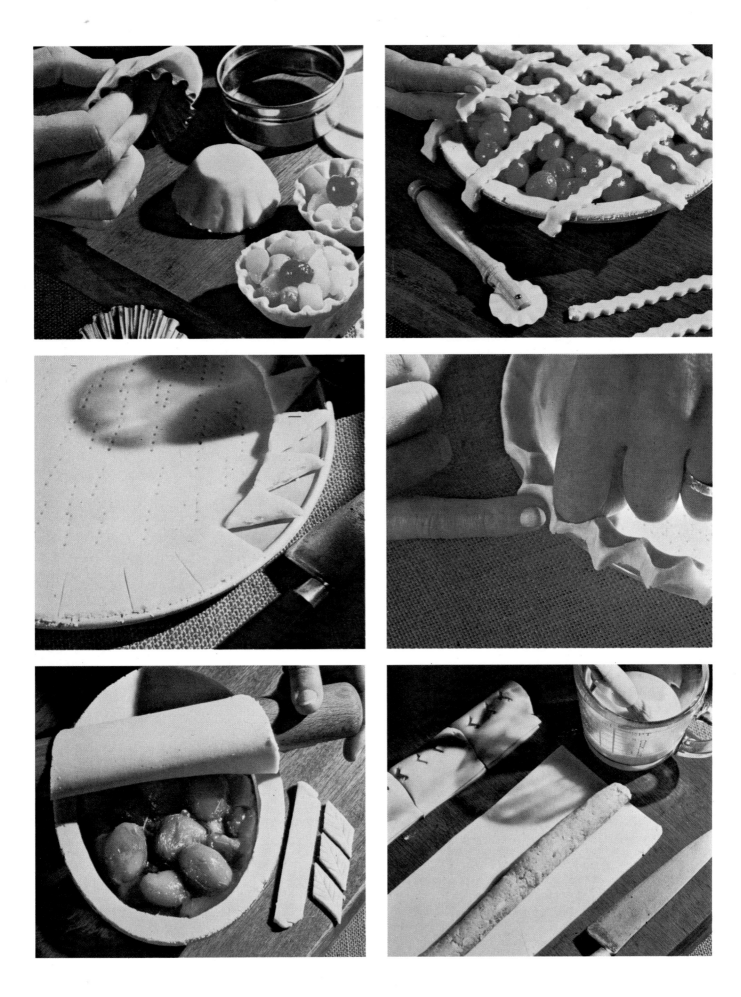

Eclairs

The flat base of each baked eclair is the side used by bakers for dipping in the chocolate icing, this gives the finished goods a much smarter appearance.

Makes 14–16 eclairs

4 oz./100 g. choux pastry	*for the chocolate icing:*
beaten egg to glaze	1 rounded tablespoon cocoa
for the filling:	powder
½ pint/3 dl. double cream	1 oz./25 g. castor sugar
1 oz./25 g. icing sugar	3 tablespoons water
few drops vanilla essence	6 oz./175 g. icing sugar

Prepare the choux pastry according to the basic recipe. Spoon the mixture into a cotton or nylon piping bag, fitted with a ½-inch (1-cm.) plain tube. Pipe out 3-inch (7½-cm.) lengths of the mixture on to greased baking trays. Allow about 6 eclairs per tray and do not pipe too close together. Brush each one with beaten egg.

Place above centre in a preheated hot oven (425°F., 220°C., Gas Mark 7) and bake *undisturbed* for 20 minutes. Prick a small hole in the side of each one with the tip of a sharp knife and return to the oven for a further 5 minutes so that they dry out completely. Allow to cool before filling.

Lightly whip the cream, add the sugar and vanilla essence and whip until thick. Make a small slit in the side of each eclair. Using a piping bag and small tube, pipe the cream into the eclairs to fill them.

Measure the cocoa powder, castor sugar and water into a saucepan. Choose a saucepan wide enough for the eclairs to be dipped into the prepared icing. Stir over a low heat to dissolve the sugar and then bring up to the boil. Draw off the heat and add the sieved icing sugar. Beat well to obtain a smooth icing. Dip the flat base of each filled eclair into the warm icing. Allow any surplus icing to run off. Put the eclairs aside until the icing is set firm.

Arrange in paper cases and serve.

Gougère au fromage

Serve gougère warm and cut in slices, as an appetiser with drinks.

Serves 6–8

4 oz./100 g. choux pastry	egg and milk to glaze
4 oz./100 g. Gruyère cheese, grated	

Prepare the choux pastry according to the basic recipe, omitting the addition of the sugar. Once prepared, beat in all but 1 oz. (25 g.) of the grated cheese.

Butter two baking trays and then dust with flour. Tap the trays sharply to knock off any loose flour. Using a saucepan lid, bang on to the trays to mark out 2 circles, which will act as guides for piping the mixture. Fill a large nylon or cotton piping bag, fitted with a ½-inch (1-cm.) plain nozzle, and spoon in the mixture.

Pipe a circle of the choux pastry mixture on to the trays following the guiding lines. If necessary, pipe round a second time on top of one of the circles to use up all the mixture. Brush the surface of each with egg and milk and sprinkle with remaining cheese. Place in the centre of a hot oven (425°F., 220°C., Gas Mark 7) and bake for 30 minutes. Loosen the baked gougère and remove from the trays. Cut in slices and arrange on a plate for serving.

Advance preparation: The pastry for the mixture can be made in advance and then piped out and baked when required.

Suet pastry

Suet pastry is simple and quick to make. Always prepare the filling for puddings before making up the pastry. Once made, the pastry should be rolled out and used.

To steam suet puddings

Have the steamer ready with water simmering in the pan underneath. If a proper steamer is not available, the pudding can be steamed in a saucepan. Stand the pudding in the pan on an old saucer, rounded side up, with just enough boiling water in the pan to reach one third of the way up the side of the pudding basin. Cover the pan with a tightly fitting lid and steam gently for the required time. Water should be topped up occasionally with extra *boiling* water.

A quicker method is to pressure cook the suet pudding. Place the pudding in the pressure cooker on the trivet base. Add ¼ pint (1½ dl.) boiling water for every ¼ hour cooking time, plus ½ pint (3 dl.) extra. Put on the lid without the pressure knob and place over moderate heat. Leave to steam gently for 15 minutes, this allows the pudding to start rising.

Place the pressure knob in position and bring up to 5 lb. (2¼ kg.) pressure. Reduce heat, hold at pressure and cook for 35 minutes if enamel or aluminium basins are used. Allow an extra 10 minutes if china or oven glass bowls are used.

When cooking time is complete, take the cooker off the heat. Allow to reduce pressure slowly by itself. This will take about 10–15 minutes. The pudding inside will keep hot and in perfect condition until ready for serving.

Suet pastry quantities

Pastry quantities refer to quantity of flour in the recipe. Other ingredients should follow in correct proportions.

Dumplings	4 oz. (100 g.) pastry	8 dumplings
Suet puddings	8 oz. (225 g.) pastry and 1½ lb. (700 g.) filling	for a 2-pint (1¼-litre) basin
	6 oz. (175 g.) pastry and 1 lb. (450 g.) filling	for a 1½-pint (1-litre) basin
	4 oz. (100 g.) pastry and 12 oz. (350 g.) filling	for 1-pint (½-litre) basin

Suet pastry

Suet pastry is easy to make as there is no 'rubbing in', the ingredients are simply mixed together. For a light suet pastry, which is very good in dessert recipes, substitute 2 oz. (50 g.) of the flour in the recipe with 2 oz. (50 g.) fresh white breadcrumbs.

Makes 8 oz. (225 g.) pastry

8 oz./225 g. self-raising flour	4 oz./125 g. shredded beef suet
½ level teaspoon salt	about ¼ pint/1½ dl. water

Sift the flour and salt into a mixing basin. Add the suet and stir to mix. Add the water and, using a fork, stir and mix to a soft scone-like dough but firm enough to be rolled out.

Turn on to a lightly floured working surface and knead very lightly to make a dough.

Use this pastry immediately.

Steak and kidney pudding

A steak and kidney pudding is served in the basin. Have ready a clean white napkin that can be pinned around the outside of the pudding before serving.

Serves 4

1½ lb./¾ kg. lean stewing steak	½–1 oz./15–25 g. dripping or lard
4 oz./100 g. ox kidney	salt and freshly milled pepper
1 onion	¾ pint/½ litre water
seasoned flour	8 oz./225 g. suet pastry

Cut away any fat or gristle from the meat and cut the meat into suitable sized pieces. Remove any core from the kidney and cut the kidney into pieces. Peel and chop the onion. Roll the meat and kidney in seasoned flour to coat.

Melt the dripping or lard in a saucepan, add the meat and fry to seal on all sides. Add the chopped onion and a good seasoning of salt and pepper. Pour in sufficient water just to cover the meat and bring up to the boil. Cover and simmer for 1 hour to partly cook the meat. Strain off most of the liquid and reserve for the gravy.

Meanwhile prepare the suet pastry according to the basic recipe and knead to a round. Roll out on a lightly floured surface to a circle large enough to line a 2-pint (1–1¼-litre) pudding basin with about ½ inch (1 cm.) to spare all round. Cut out a

quarter section of the circle and set this aside for the top. Well grease the pudding basin.

Damp one of the cut edges of the pastry. With floured hands, lift the pastry into the basin, taking care not to stretch it. Press gently into the shape of the basin, working with the knuckles and fingertips from the bottom upwards. When the basin is lined, there should be about ½ inch (1 cm.) of pastry to spare at the top. Press the cut edges together until the join disappears.

Spoon the meat mixture into the basin and add 2–3 tablespoons of the gravy to moisten. Roll out the reserved piece of pastry to a circle to fit the top. Steak and kidney pudding is served in the basin, therefore, the excess pastry edges must be turned in over the filling before the lid is placed on the pudding. Damp the rim of pastry round the pudding and place the lid over the top. Press the edges gently together to seal. Cover the pudding with double thickness greased, greaseproof paper and tie tightly. Steam briskly for 2½–3 hours. Refill the pan with boiling water as required.

Serve the pudding with a clean napkin pinned around the basin. Reheat the reserved cooking liquor and serve as extra gravy.

Fruit pudding

Use other fruits to a total of the quantity given here. Try a mixture of soaked dried fruits or apple only with a little lemon rind to flavour.

Serves 6

8 oz./225 g. suet pastry	8 oz./¼ kg. blackberries
1 lb./½ kg. apples	4–6 oz./100–175 g. castor sugar

Make the pastry according to the basic recipe and knead to a round. Roll out on a lightly floured working surface to a circle large enough to line a 2-pint (1–1¼-litre) pudding basin with about ½ inch (1 cm.) to spare all round. Cut out a quarter section of the circle and set this aside for the top. Well grease the pudding basin.

Damp one of the cut edges of the pastry. With floured hands, carefully lift the pastry into the basin, taking care not to stretch it. Press gently into the shape of the basin, working with the knuckles and fingertips from the bottom upwards. When the basin is lined, there should be about ½ inch (1 cm.) of pastry to spare at the top. Press the cut edges together until the join disappears.

Peel, core and slice the apples, and pick over the blackberries. Pack the fruit into the basin, spooning the sugar into the centre. Add 1 tablespoon of water. Roll out the reserved piece of pastry to a circle to fit the top. Damp the top edges of the pudding and place the lid over the top. Fruit puddings are turned out of the basin, therefore, the overlapping edges around the rim should be turned in over the pastry lid. Press on top gently. Cover the pudding with double thickness greased, greaseproof paper and tie tightly. Steam briskly for 2 hours. Refill the pan with boiling water as required. Turn out and serve with custard sauce.

OVERLEAF **Filet de boeuf en croûte (page 94)**
Cut the puff pastry into two pieces, making one two-thirds larger than the other.
Place the second piece of pastry over the top and seal it to the pastry already round the meat.
Decorate with pastry leaves and brush with beaten egg.

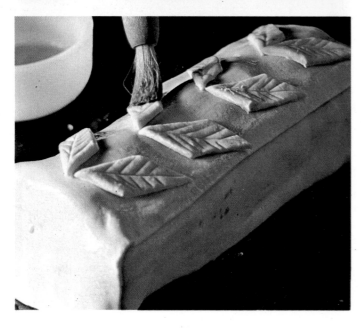

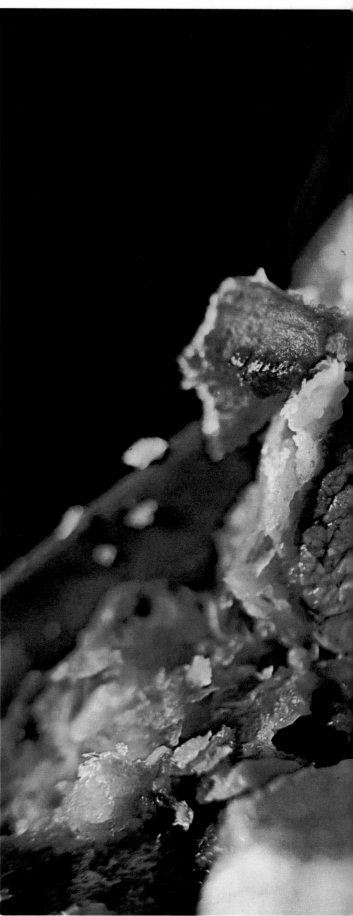

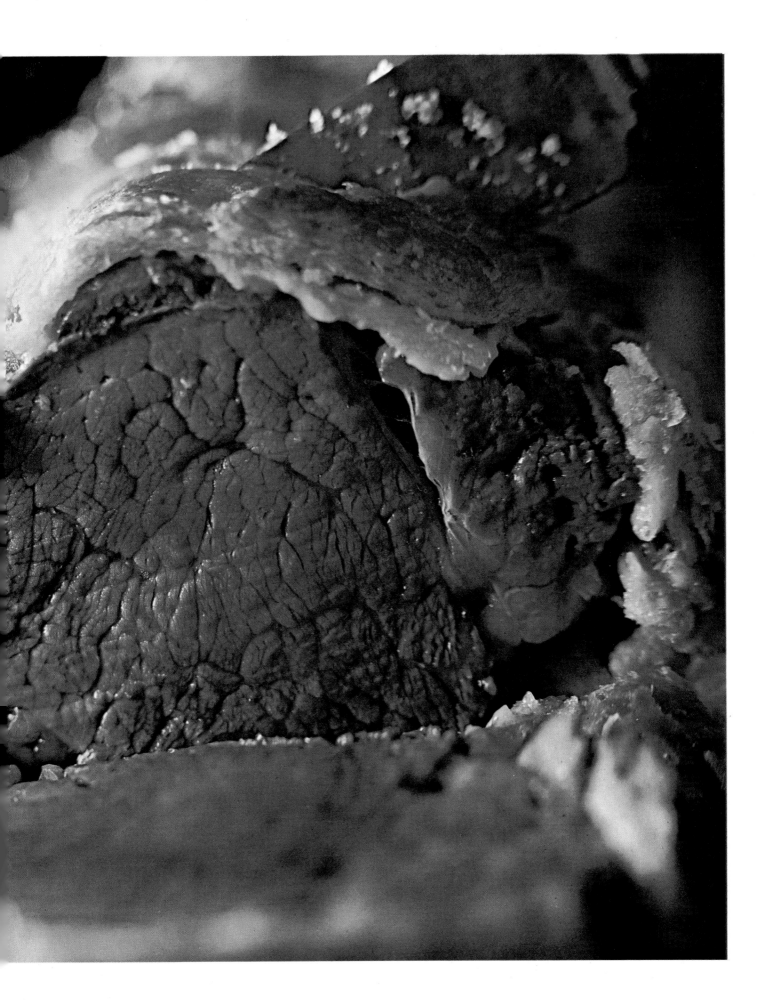

Apple and mincemeat layer pudding

This same pudding can be made with jam or marmalade. Use 3 good tablespoons of the chosen jam instead of the apple filling. Use one spoonful at the base instead of the golden syrup.

Serves 6

12 oz./350 g. cooking apples	1 tablespoon golden syrup
2 good tablespoons mincemeat	8 oz./225 g. suet pastry
1–1½ oz./25–40 g. soft brown sugar	

Peel, core and cut the apples into small dice. Mix them with the mincemeat and brown sugar. Well grease a 2-pint (1–1¼-litre) pudding basin and put the golden syrup in the bottom. Set aside while preparing the suet pastry.

Make the suet pastry according to the directions in the basic recipe. Divide the pastry into 3 unequal portions. Pat out the smallest piece of pastry to a circle to fit the bottom of the basin. Place in the basin and cover with half the apple filling. Pat out the second piece of pastry and put in the basin to cover the apple layer. Add the rest of the apple filling. Finally, cover with the last piece of pastry, patted out to a circle large enough to cover the top of the pudding and form a lid. Cover with double thickness greased, greaseproof paper and tie tightly. Steam briskly for 2½ hours. Refill the pan with boiling water as necessary.

Turn out and serve with a hot, sweet custard.

Savoury dumplings

Dumplings are made using a basic suet pastry mixture. Variations in flavour can be made by adding additional ingredients.

Prepare 4 oz. (100 g.) of suet pastry according to directions in the basic recipe (page 23). Turn the dough out on to a floured working surface and cut into 6–8 equal portions. Using lightly floured fingers, roll each portion into a ball. Roll each dumpling lightly in flour to coat the outside, then shake away any excess flour.

Add the dumplings to a simmering casserole or stew, placing them on top of the meat. Take care not to submerge the dumplings in the liquid. Recover the pan or casserole and continue cooking for 15–20 minutes, or until the dumplings are well risen and cooked through.

Herb dumplings: Prepare as above, adding 1 tablespoon finely chopped parsley and a good pinch of mixed herbs to the sifted flour. Serve with any meat or game stew.

Lemon dumplings: Prepare as above, adding the finely grated rind of ½ lemon to the sifted flour. Serve with oxtail stew.

Bacon dumplings: Prepare as above, adding 2 rashers bacon, trimmed and finely chopped, and 1 teaspoon finely grated lemon rind to the sifted flour. Serve with liver casserole.

Mustard dumplings: Prepare as above, sifting 1 teaspoon dry mustard with the flour and add ½ teaspoon dried mixed herbs with the suet. Serve with beef stew.

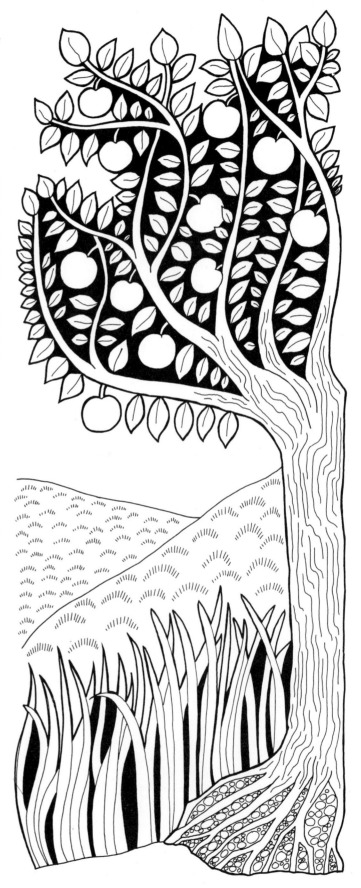

Cheese dumplings: Prepare as before, sifting a pinch of mustard with the flour and adding 2 oz. (50 g.) finely grated cheese along with the suet. Serve with vegetable soup.

Hot watercrust pastry

This is one of the few pastries where warmth is essential. The warm, prepared pastry is moulded to a shape and then filled and baked. Either a raised pie mould or a 6-inch (15-cm.) cake tin with a loose base can be used. Raised pie moulds have no base and need to be set on a baking tray before using. They are usually an oval shape with ridged or patterned sides and held closed with clip rings or hinges, held in place with a pin. These are used because they are decorative. A cake tin is an alternative and makes an attractive round pie.

Hot watercrust pastry

When the saucepan of fat and liquid is boiling, bring the bowl of flour to the pan rather than the other way round. The liquid must be boiling when it is poured into the dry ingredients.

Makes 12 oz. (375 g.) pastry

12 oz./375 g. plain flour	¼ pint/1½ dl. mixed milk and
1 level teaspoon salt	water
4 oz./125 g. white cooking fat	

Sift together the flour and salt into a mixing basin. Put in a warm place. Measure the cooking fat and mixed milk and water into a saucepan. Place over moderate heat and, when the fat has melted, bring up to a brisk boil. Pour at once into the centre of the warmed flour.

Beat well with a wooden spoon, until the mixture clings together in a ball, leaving the sides of the basin clean. Turn the mixture on to a clean working surface and knead thoroughly to a smooth dough.

Place the dough under the warm, upturned basin and leave to rest for 15–20 minutes before using.

Raised pork pie

Where possible choose lean pork fillet to make the filling for this pie. Raised pork pie is excellent served cold in summer with a salad.

Serves 6

12 oz./375 g. hot watercrust	lard
pastry	*to glaze:*
2 lb./1 kg. lean pork	beaten egg
1 small onion	
¼ teaspoon powdered sage	2 level teaspoons powdered
1 level teaspoon salt	gelatine
freshly milled black pepper	½ pint/3 dl. stock

Prepare the hot watercrust pastry and place under an upturned basin to stand for 15 minutes. Trim the pork and cut into neat pieces. Peel and finely chop the onion and add to the meat along with the sage, salt and pepper. Mix the ingredients well.

Heavily grease with lard the inside of a 6-inch (15-cm.) round cake tin with a loose base. Cut off a piece of pastry for the lid and replace under the basin to keep warm. Knead the remaining pastry out to a circle about ½ inch (1 cm.) thick and place in the base of the tin. Using the knuckles, press the pastry from the centre to the sides. When the base of the tin is covered, mould the pastry up the sides, using the four fingers of both hands. Make sure there is no thick layer between the base and the sides and that the pastry has not been pressed too thinly on the sides. Bring the pastry up to overlap the edges. Place the filling in the tin.

Roll out the reserved piece of pastry for the lid. Damp the edges of the pie with water and cover with the pastry lid. Press edges well together to seal and cut away excess pastry. Roll the trimmings and cut leaves for decoration. Make a small hole in the centre of the lid. Brush the top of the pie with egg to glaze and arrange on the pastry leaves.

Place in the centre of a hot oven (400°F., 200°C., Gas Mark 6) and bake for 20 minutes. Lower the heat to moderate (350°F., 180°C., Gas Mark 4) and bake for a further 2–2½ hours. During baking, brush with egg to make the crust a shiny brown. After 1½ hours, remove the pie from the tin. Brush the sides with egg and replace in the oven to complete the cooking time.

Allow the baked pie to cool. Dissolve the gelatine in the stock and leave to cool until beginning to thicken and set. Pour the almost jellied stock into the pie through the hole in the top. Leave to stand for several hours until set.

Recipes using eggs and cheese

Eggs and cheese are important in cookery, both for their food value and the part they play in recipes.

Ideally, eggs should be stored in a cool larder rather than the cold refrigerator. Eggs that are very cold are easier to separate, but at this temperature egg whites will not whisk up to good volume. When eggs are to be used in a recipe, allow them to come up to room temperature before using.

Egg yolks left over from a recipe should be carefully placed, whole and unbroken, in a small cup. Cover with cold water to prevent a skin forming on the surface of the yolk. They will keep in the refrigerator for 1–2 days and can be used to enrich milk or custard puddings, or sauces. Left over egg whites should be placed in a basin – take care there are no traces of egg yolk. Cover with a lid and they will keep for a week or more. They can be used in meringues, macaroons, soufflés or desserts. Should you forget how many egg whites are in a particular container, the answer is to very slowly tip the contents into a second container. Individual egg whites hold together and each one will fall out of the container as a whole. If tipped slowly it is quite easy to count them into a new jar. Never be afraid of using ones which have stood in the larder for several days. Egg whites absorb oxygen from the air as they stand and the volume is much greater.

Cooking eggs

There are four basic methods of cooking eggs. Eggs are often prepared by any one of these methods and subsequently used in a recipe. Careful preparation is important and care should be taken not to over-cook eggs.

Fried eggs

Eggs should always be fried gently, a fierce heat will make the egg white tough and crisp round the edges.

Where possible use bacon fat, lard or butter to cook the eggs. Add sufficient to cover the base of the pan to be used for frying.

When the fat is hot, break the eggs into a cup and, holding close to the pan, add the eggs to the hot fat.

Baste while the eggs are frying, to help set the white around the yolks. Remove from the pan with a fish slice, so that the eggs can drain well.

Boiled eggs

Boiled eggs should, in fact, not be boiled but simmered. Fast boiling makes the white tough. It also causes the eggs to bump against each other and the sides of the pan, causing cracking of the egg shell. It is important that eggs to be boiled should not be taken straight from the refrigerator. The rapid change of temperature will cause the shells to crack.

There are two methods that can be used for boiling eggs:

1. Put enough water to cover the eggs into a saucepan and bring to the boil without the eggs. Lower the eggs into the boiling water. Simmer for 3–4 minutes for a soft-boiled egg, 5 minutes for a firm egg and 8–10 minutes for a hard-boiled egg.
2. Put the eggs into cold water and bring the water to the boil. After the water has boiled, cook for 2–3 minutes for a soft-boiled egg, 3–4 minutes for a firm set egg and 6–8 minutes for a hard-boiled egg.

Plunge hard-boiled eggs into cold running water immediately after draining, to stop further cooking. This prevents a dark ring appearing round the yolks of the hard-boiled eggs.

Poached eggs

Poaching means cooking in hot, but not boiling, water. Poached eggs can be cooked without the addition of vinegar or salt to the water.

Use a shallow pan (a frying pan is excellent). Add water to the depth of 1 inch (2½ cm.). Bring the water to the boil, then turn down the heat to a gentle simmer. The water should be as still as possible.

Crack an egg into a cup and slip it quickly into the water. Hold the edge of the cup close to the surface of the water, so that the egg slides in. Never drop the egg in. Cook gently for 3 minutes until the white is set but the yolk still soft.

Remove the egg with a perforated spoon. When poaching more than one egg, take the eggs out in the order that you put them in.

Where poached eggs are included as an ingredient in a recipe, as in the recipe for Oeufs en gelée (page 29), they can be cooked in advance. Drain the poached eggs from the hot water and place immediately in cold water to cover. This arrests the cooking and keeps the eggs moist and soft cooked. Later, when ready to use, drain and place the eggs on a clean teacloth or absorbent kitchen paper to remove any traces of moisture. Then use as required in the recipe.

Scrambled eggs

Scrambled eggs are very easy to make, they should be lightly cooked and served when moist, but not dry. Allow about 1 tablespoon of milk for each egg used, to make the mixture light. A little butter added gives flavour.

Scrambled eggs with herbs

Serves 4

9 eggs	3 tablespoons finely chopped
¼ pint/1½ dl. milk	parsley and chives
1 level teaspoon salt	1 oz./25 g. butter
freshly milled pepper	

Crack the eggs into a mixing basin, add the milk and seasonings and beat well to mix. Add the chopped herbs.

Heat the butter in a heavy pan over low heat. Pour in the egg mixture and cook over low heat. Stir gently, drawing the spoon across the base of the pan to lift the egg mixture up as it sets. Draw off the heat when the mixture is thickened but still moist. *Variation:* Grated cheese or ham can be added to the mixture in place of the herbs.

Oeufs en gelée

Oeufs en gelée are usually turned out of the moulds in which they are set. This is, perhaps, an easier version where they are served in dishes. Use the small china individual soufflé dishes.

Serves 6

6 eggs	1 tablespoon sherry
1 (10½ oz./290 g.) can	4–6 oz./100–175 g. liver pâté
concentrated beef consommé	salt and pepper
few fresh tarragon leaves	

Poach the eggs in simmering water for about 3 minutes. When the whites are set, but the centres still soft, lift them out of the water with a perforated spoon. Place immediately in a bowl of cold water to prevent further cooking. Leave until cold.

Place the consommé in a saucepan and add a few leaves of fresh tarragon for flavour. Heat gently until the consommé is melted. Draw off the heat, add the sherry and allow to cool.

Place a tablespoon of liver pâté in the base of 6 individual soufflé or serving dishes and spread evenly. Drain the eggs and, where necessary, trim neatly. Top the liver pâté with an egg and season with salt and pepper. Pour over sufficient of the cooled consommé to cover each one. Arrange a tarragon leaf on top. Leave in a cold place to set firm.
Advance preparation: Make these up to 12 hours before serving. If chilled in the refrigerator, remove 1 hour before serving.

Eggs stuffed with pâté in cheese sauce

This is a really good hot meal starter. Arrange the eggs in a gratin dish for heating through and serving.

Serves 6

6 eggs	½ pint/3 dl. milk
2–3 oz./50–75 g. liver pâté	salt and freshly milled pepper
1 oz./25 g. butter	2–3 oz./50–75 g. hard cheese,
1 oz./25 g. flour	grated

Place the eggs in a saucepan, cover with cold water and bring up to the boil. Simmer for 8 minutes to hard cook. Drain and cover with cold water to prevent further cooking. Shell the eggs and, while still warm, cut in half lengthways. Tip out the yolks and reserve the egg whites. Mash the egg yolks with the pâté, blending well. Spoon or pipe the mixture back into the egg white halves and arrange in a gratin or serving dish.

Melt the butter in a saucepan and stir in the flour. Cook gently for a moment over the heat, then gradually beat in the milk. Bring up to the boil, stirring well to get a smooth sauce. Season with salt and pepper and add half the cheese. Pour over the filled egg halves, coating them well.

Sprinkle with the remaining cheese and place above centre in a hot oven (400°F., 200°C., Gas Mark 6) for about 10 minutes to heat through thoroughly. Pass quickly under a hot grill to brown and then serve.

Advance preparation: Prepare the eggs and arrange in a serving dish. Cover with a clear wrap which clings to the surface or with foil to prevent drying. Put in a cool place. Prepare the cheese sauce, cover with a circle of buttered greaseproof and leave to cool. When ready to serve, reheat the sauce and pour over the eggs. Sprinkle with cheese and finish as in the recipe.

Eggs stuffed with kipper pâté

Stuffed eggs make an excellent luncheon dish. Serve them with salad and fresh brown bread and butter.

Serves 6

6 eggs	1 tablespoon olive oil
few lettuce leaves	1 small clove garlic, finely
for the stuffing:	chopped
1 kipper	freshly milled pepper
2 oz./50 g. cream cheese	squeeze lemon juice

Place the eggs in a saucepan, cover with cold water and bring up to the boil. Simmer for 8 minutes to hard boil. Drain and cover with cold water to prevent further cooking. Remove the shells and keep the eggs submerged in cold water until required.

Place the kipper in a jug, pour over boiling water to cover and allow to stand for 5 minutes. Drain and then flake the kipper flesh discarding all bones and skin.

Using a wetted knife blade, cut the eggs in half lengthwise. Tip out the yolks into a basin and reserve the whites. Add the kipper flesh to the yolks and pound until smooth using the rounded end of a rolling pin or the back of a wooden spoon. Beat in the cream cheese, oil and garlic. Season with freshly milled pepper and add a squeeze of lemon juice to taste. Beat the mixture as smooth as possible.

Spoon or pipe the mixture into the reserved egg white halves. Arrange filled egg halves in pairs on crisp lettuce leaves.

Serve with thinly sliced brown bread and butter.

Advance preparation: Prepare and stuff the eggs several hours in advance. Cover with clear wrap or foil to prevent the surface from drying. Arrange on crisp lettuce before serving.

Eggs with tomato mayonnaise

This recipe need only be assembled just before serving, if the eggs are hard boiled and kept in cold water and the dressing made in advance.

Serves 6

6 eggs	2 tablespoons tomato ketchup
lettuce leaves	2 tablespoons double cream
paprika pepper	1 teaspoon Worcestershire
for the mayonnaise dressing:	sauce
2 rounded tablespoons	dash Tabasco sauce (optional)
mayonnaise	squeeze lemon juice

Place the eggs in a saucepan, cover with cold water and bring up to the boil. Simmer for 8 minutes to hard boil. Drain and cover with cold water to prevent further cooking. Remove the shells and keep the eggs submerged in cold water until required.

Measure the mayonnaise, tomato ketchup and cream for the dressing into a basin. Add the Worcestershire sauce, Tabasco, if used, and a squeeze of lemon juice. Stir to blend the ingredients, taste and check flavour.

Using a wetted knife blade, cut the eggs in half lengthways. Arrange the egg halves, rounded side up, in pairs on crisp lettuce leaves. Spoon the dressing over each egg and sprinkle with paprika pepper.

Serve with thinly sliced brown bread and butter.

Macaroni cheese

A rich, creamy macaroni cheese makes a delicious lunch or supper dish. There should be plenty of sauce generously flavoured with cheese and a golden crisp cheese crust on top.

Serves 4

4 oz./100 g. macaroni	2 oz./50 g. butter
1 tablespoon white breadcrumbs	salt and freshly milled pepper
½ oz./15 g. butter	4–6 oz./100–175 g. hard cheese,
for the sauce:	grated
1 pint/6 dl. milk	½ level teaspoon made mustard
2 oz./50 g. flour	

Add the macaroni to a large pan of boiling, salted water. Cook until tender, then drain and rinse.

Pour the milk into a bowl, sift in the flour and whisk briskly until smooth and blended. Melt the butter in a saucepan. Add the blended milk and bring up to the boil, stirring all the time. Simmer for 1–2 minutes then draw off the heat. Season well with salt and pepper, add half the cheese and then the mustard. Taste and check the flavour. Add the cooked macaroni and stir well to blend.

Pour the mixture into a deep well-greased pie dish or deep entrée dish. Sprinkle with the remaining cheese and the breadcrumbs. Dot with the butter, cut in small pieces. Place above centre in a moderately hot oven (375°F., 190°C., Gas Mark 5) and heat through for about 15–20 minutes.

Pass under a hot grill if necessary to brown the top and serve with hot toast.

Advance preparation: Prepare the macaroni cheese, sprinkle with cheese and breadcrumbs and dot with butter. About 30 minutes before serving, put to heat through. If the macaroni cheese has been in the refrigerator, the time required for reheating will be a little longer.

Oeufs en cocotte

Eggs prepared in this simple manner make an excellent meal starter or they can be served as a supper dish. When in season, sprinkle chopped fresh chervil or tarragon over them. Allow two per person.

Serves 4

8 eggs	salt and freshly milled pepper
butter	$\frac{1}{4}$ pint/1$\frac{1}{2}$ dl. double cream

Warm 8 cocotte or ramekin dishes and very thoroughly butter each one. Carefully crack an egg into each. Season well with salt and pepper and spoon a tablespoon of cream over each one.

Arrange the ramekin dishes in a large frying pan and pour in hot water to come halfway up the sides of the dishes. Cover the pan and poach very gently for 7–8 minutes. Alternatively, place the dishes in a large roasting tin with water to come half way up the sides of the dishes. Place in the centre of a preheated moderate oven (350°F., 180°C., Gas Mark 4) and cook for 8–10 minutes. The egg whites should be set, but the yolks still runny.

Serve at once in the dishes.

Advance preparation: Collect the ingredients and prepare dishes but do not start this recipe more than about 15 minutes before serving.

Stuffed eggs with anchovy

Soak anchovy fillets in a little milk for 1 hour or so if a less salty flavour is preferred.

Serves 6

6 eggs	*for the stuffing:*
freshly milled pepper	8 canned anchovy fillets
few lettuce leaves	2 oz./50 g. butter
chopped parsley	

Place the eggs in a saucepan, cover with cold water and bring up to the boil. Simmer for 8 minutes to hard boil. Drain and cover with cold water to prevent further cooking. Remove the shells and keep the eggs submerged in cold water until required.

Drain the anchovy fillets and mash eight to a paste with a wooden spoon. Using a wetted knife blade, cut the eggs in half lengthways. Tip out the yolks and sieve them into a mixing basin. Reserve the egg whites. Add the pounded anchovies to the egg yolks along with the creamed butter and a seasoning of pepper. Beat the ingredients very thoroughly to blend.

Spoon or pipe the mixture into the reserved egg white halves.

Arrange in pairs on crisp lettuce leaves. Garnish with any remaining anchovy fillets and sprinkle with chopped parsley.

Serve with thinly sliced brown bread and butter.

Advance preparation: Prepare and stuff the eggs several hours before serving. Cover with clear wrap or foil to prevent the surface from drying. Arrange on crisp lettuce leaves just before serving.

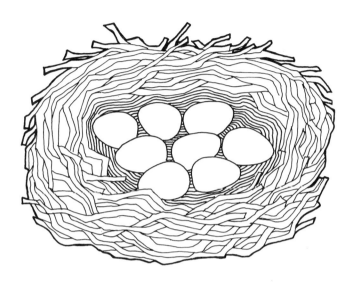

Oeufs à la tripe

Serve this recipe very hot. If necessary turn the mixture into a buttered casserole dish and keep hot in the oven before serving.

Serves 4

4 eggs	1 oz./25 g. flour
2 large onions	$\frac{1}{2}$ pint/3 dl. milk
1 oz./25 g. butter	salt and freshly milled pepper
for the sauce:	pinch nutmeg
1 oz./25 g. butter	1 teaspoon chopped parsley

Hard boil the eggs. Shell and leave submerged in cold water until required. Peel the onions leaving them whole and cut across into thin slices. Add to a pan of boiling water, simmer for 2–3 minutes and then drain well. Rinse out the pan and return to the heat with the 1 oz. (25 g.) butter. When melted, add the onions and cover with a lid. Cook very gently for about 10 minutes or until the onions are tender, but do not allow them to brown.

Meanwhile prepare the sauce. Melt the butter and stir in the flour. Cook gently for a few minutes, then gradually stir in the milk. Beat well after each addition to get a smooth sauce. Season well with salt and pepper and add a pinch of nutmeg. Allow to cook gently for about 5 minutes. When the onions are tender, add the hard-boiled eggs, cut in slices. Pour in the sauce and add the parsley. Toss ingredients gently to blend, check seasoning before serving.

Advance preparation: Hard boil the eggs and leave submerged in cold water. Cook the onions and leave in the pan. When ready to serve, prepare the sauce and reheat the onion. Continue with the recipe as above.

Fried gnocchi

A gnocchi mixture, when egg and breadcrumbed and deep fried, becomes crisp and very appetising. Serve these fried gnocchi with a crisp salad. They make an unusual and inexpensive meal.

Serves 4

1 pint/6 dl. milk	1 level teaspoon salt
1 small onion	pinch cayenne pepper
1 clove	1 tablespoon chopped parsley
1 bay leaf	1 egg
few parsley stalks	browned breadcrumbs
4 oz./100 g. semolina	oil for deep frying
4–6 oz./100–175 g. cheese,	*to garnish:*
grated	parsley sprigs

Measure the milk into a saucepan. Peel the onion, leaving it whole, and stick it with the clove. Add the onion, bay leaf and the parsley stalks to the milk. Heat until almost boiling, then draw off the heat. Cover and leave to infuse for 10–15 minutes.

Remove the flavouring ingredients from the milk and reheat the milk to boiling point. Sprinkle in the semolina, stirring all the time. Cook, stirring well until the mixture is very thick – about 6 minutes. Draw the pan off the heat and stir in the cheese, salt, cayenne pepper and chopped parsley. Spread the mixture out to about 1 inch (2½ cm.) thick and leave until cold.

Cut into fingers, 2 inches (5 cm.) long by 1 inch (2½ cm.) wide. Dip each one first in beaten egg and then in brown breadcrumbs. Pat away any loose crumbs. Place in a frying basket and fry in hot deep oil until crisp and golden brown, about 1–2 minutes. Drain well. Arrange them laying one against the other in a hot serving dish. Garnish with a few sprigs of parsley.

Hot soufflés

Soufflés aren't temperamental – actually they are very easy to make. As a rule, always serve a hot soufflé for a small number of guests. Try one as a main course for a lunch or as a first course for a dinner party. Remember that the basic cream mixture for the soufflé can be prepared in advance. Once the beaten egg whites are folded in, it must be put to bake. Once baked, the soufflé should not be kept waiting but served at once. A hot soufflé goes well with a crisp salad.

A hot soufflé must be prepared and baked with a fair degree of accuracy. There are a few special points to watch:
1. Measure the ingredients accurately and use a large enough saucepan to make the basic cream sauce mix. Remember that the egg whites have to be folded in later.
2. Check the flavour in the basic cream sauce mix. It's easy to alter the flavour at this stage and very difficult later on.
3. As a rule, one extra egg white gives a better result. Beat the whites when ready to fold them in. Beat them until they are stiff but not dry; they should still have a moist sheen.
4. Soufflés are better baked in a medium temperature. A moderate oven (350°F., 180°C., Gas Mark 4) usually gives the best results.

Cheese and parsley soufflé

Use Gruyère or Parmesan cheese in this recipe. Both grate finely and give a good strong flavour.

Serves 2–3

1 oz./25 g. butter	4 oz./100 g. hard cheese, grated
1 oz./25 g. flour	1 tablespoon finely chopped
¼ pint/1½ dl. milk	parsley
salt and freshly milled pepper	4 egg yolks
¼ level teaspoon made mustard	5 egg whites

Melt the butter in a large 1½–2-pint (1–1¼-litre) saucepan over a low heat. Stir in the flour and cook gently for a moment until the mixture lightens in colour and becomes sandy in texture. Gradually stir in the milk, beating well all the time to make a creamy, smooth, fairly thick sauce. Season with salt and freshly milled pepper to taste. Stir in the mustard, cheese and the parsley. Stir until blended and the cheese has melted, then draw off the heat and leave to cool until the hand can comfortably be held against the sides of the pan.

One at a time, beat in the egg yolks very thoroughly. Whisk the egg whites until stiff. Using a metal spoon or spatula, fold in first about a third of the whites. Then add the remainder and fold gently but thoroughly into the mixture.

Pour into a 1½-pint (1-litre) or 6-inch (15-cm.) buttered soufflé dish and spread evenly. Place in the centre of a moderate oven (350°F., 180°C., Gas Mark 4) and bake for 40–45 minutes. The soufflé should be well risen and brown, but still soft in the centre. Serve at once.
Advance preparation: Prepare the basic cream mixture in advance. Fold in the egg whites when ready to bake.

Hot crab soufflé

A can of crab meat from the cupboard provides the flavour in this soufflé. Excellent for a lunch recipe.

Serves 2–3

1 oz./25 g. butter	salt and freshly milled pepper
1 oz./25 g. flour	pinch cayenne pepper
¼ pint/1½ dl. milk	4 egg yolks
2 oz./50 g. hard cheese, grated	5 egg whites
1 (6½ oz./185 g.) can crab meat	

Melt the butter in a large saucepan over a low heat. Stir in the flour and cook gently for a moment until the mixture lightens in colour and becomes sandy in texture. Gradually stir in the milk, beating well all the time to make a creamy, smooth, fairly thick mixture. Stir in the cheese and when blended draw off the heat. Drain and flake the crab meat, discarding any sinews. Stir the crab meat into the sauce along with a seasoning of salt and pepper to taste and a pinch of cayenne. Set the mixture aside until cool enough for the hand to be held comfortably against the sides of the pan.

Beat in the egg yolks very thoroughly, one at a time. Check the flavour. Whisk the egg whites until stiff. Using a metal spoon or a spatula, fold in first about a third of the mixture. Then add the remainder and fold in gently but evenly.

Pour into a 1½-pint (1-litre) or 6-inch (15-cm.) buttered soufflé dish and spread evenly. Place in the centre of a moderate oven (350°F., 180°C., Gas Mark 4) and bake for 40–45 minutes. Serve at once.

Advance preparation: Basic cream mixture can be prepared in advance. Fold in the egg whites when ready to bake.

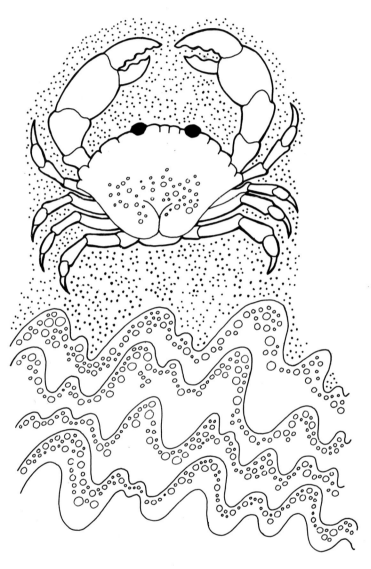

Smoked haddock soufflé

Hot fish soufflés are unusual and very tasty to eat. Use smoked haddock or smoked cod fillet and serve with a tossed green salad.

Serves 2–3

8 oz./225 g. smoked haddock fillet	1 oz./25 g. flour
½ pint/3 dl. milk	salt and freshly milled pepper
slice lemon	pinch nutmeg
few parsley stalks	4 egg yolks
1 oz./25 g. butter	5 egg whites

Cut the fish into pieces and place in a saucepan with the milk. Add a slice of lemon and a few parsley stalks for flavour. Cover and poach gently for about 10 minutes until the fish is tender. Drain and measure out ¼ pint (1½ dl.) of the cooking liquid. Flake the fish, removing any skin and bones.

Melt the butter in a large saucepan over low heat. Stir in the flour and cook gently for a moment until the mixture lightens in colour and becomes sandy in texture. Gradually stir in the reserved milk, beating well all the time to get a smooth, creamy, thick sauce. Season with salt and pepper and add a pinch of nutmeg. Stir in the flaked fish. Draw off the heat and allow the mixture to cool until the hand can be comfortably held against the sides of the pan.

Beat in the egg yolks, one at a time, very thoroughly. Whisk the egg whites until stiff. Using a metal spoon or spatula, fold in first about a third of the whites. Then fold in the remainder gently but thoroughly.

Pour into a 1½-pint (1-litre) or 6-inch (15-cm.) buttered soufflé dish and spread evenly. Place in the centre of a moderate oven (350°F., 180°C., Gas Mark 4) and bake for 40–45 minutes. Serve at once.

Advance preparation: Basic cream mixture can be prepared in advance. Fold in the egg whites when ready to bake.

Spinach soufflé

Spinach and grated Gruyère cheese combine together to make a delicious soufflé that can be served on its own with hot toast and butter.

Serves 2–3

8 oz./¼ kg. fresh spinach	salt and freshly milled pepper
1 oz./25 g. butter	pinch nutmeg
1 oz./25 g. flour	4 egg yolks
¼ pint/1½ dl. milk	5 egg whites
2 oz./50 g. hard cheese, grated	

Wash the spinach in plenty of cold water and pull away the coarse stems and ribs from the leaves. Place the wet spinach in a saucepan with no extra water. Cover and cook gently for about 10 minutes. Drain and then press in a colander to remove any remaining water. Chop the spinach finely.

Melt the butter in a large saucepan over low heat. Stir in the flour and cook gently until the mixture lightens in colour and becomes sandy in texture. Gradually stir in the milk, beating well all the time to make a creamy, smooth, thick sauce. Bring up to the boil. Add the spinach and the grated cheese and cook gently for a further few minutes. Draw off the heat, season with salt and pepper to taste and a pinch of nutmeg. Set aside to cool until the hand can be comfortably held against the sides of the pan.

Beat in the egg yolks very thoroughly, one at a time. Whisk the egg whites until stiff. Using a metal spoon or wooden spatula, fold in first about a third of the egg white. Then fold the remainder gently but evenly into the mixture.

Pour into a 1½-pint (1-litre) or 6-inch (15-cm.) buttered soufflé dish and spread evenly. Place in the centre of a moderate oven (350°F., 180°C., Gas Mark 4) and bake for 40–45 minutes. Serve at once.

Advance preparation: Basic cream mixture can be prepared in advance. Fold in the egg whites when ready to bake.

Omelettes

To make a perfect omelette calls for practice – a flair for knowing just when the omelette is cooked and skill in handling the pan. Omelettes are ideal for snack meals and they go well with salads.

The choice of pan

Either a traditional omelette pan or a good quality frying pan can be used. The pan must be heavy and flat with a smooth surface. The size of the pan to choose is also important. For a single omelette, use 2–3 eggs in a 6½-inch (16-cm.) pan. For 2 servings, use 4–5 eggs in an 8-inch (20-cm.) pan. Quantities larger than these become difficult to handle for open omelettes.

After use, some cooks clean out the pan while still hot, using absorbent kitchen paper and a little salt as an abrasive. Otherwise wipe out the pan with a damp cloth only. Avoid scouring the surface – scratches make an omelette stick. The more an omelette pan is used, the better it becomes. Keep the surface rubbed over with a little olive oil and store the pan in a polythene bag, tied to exclude the air and discourage rusting.

Omelette nature

This omelette or any of the variations would make an excellent lunch or supper dish.

Serves 2

4–5 eggs	salt and freshly milled pepper
1 teaspoon cold water	½ oz./15 g. butter

Break the eggs into a clean basin. (Chef's often use a smooth wooden bowl, which they keep specially for whisking omelettes.) Add the water and a seasoning of salt and pepper. Whisk with a table fork until the mixture is thoroughly blended but not aerated.

Place a heavy based 8-inch (20-cm.) frying pan over medium heat. Add the butter to the hot pan. Have a table fork and a spatula ready.

The minute the butter turns a pale fawn, pour in the egg mixture all at once. Tilt the pan so that the mixture runs over the hot base. Start drawing the edges of the omelette mixture in towards the centre of the pan. Use the table fork for this and, at the same time, tilt the pan so that the liquid egg mixture on the surface runs down on to the pan base. When the omelette has set, but is still moist on the surface, draw the pan off the heat.

Loosen round the edges with the spatula and then tap the pan sharply to loosen the omelette. Shake the pan so that the omelette slides over to the edge of the pan opposite the handle. The edge of the omelette should extend over the rim of the pan. (When preparing a filled omelette, at this stage any hot fillings are added.)

For an unfilled omelette, using the spatula, fold opposite edges of the omelette into the centre. Push the closed omelette right to the edge of the pan. Hold the pan over a heated serving plate. Tip the pan smartly towards you and allow the omelette to fall out on to the plate with the folded edges underneath. Serve at once.

Omelette fines herbes

Add 1 tablespoon very finely chopped mixed fresh parsley, tarragon, chervil and chives to the basic egg mixture before cooking.

Omelette au fromage

Add 2 oz. (50 g.) grated Gruyère or Parmesan cheese to the basic egg mixture. Prepare as instructed in the basic recipe but make a point of serving the omelette moist and lightly cooked.

Omelette parmentier

Peel and cut 1 large potato (about 8 oz./225 g.) into small dice. Fry these in 1 oz. (25 g.) butter and 2 teaspoons oil. Cook gently, tossing the potato until tender and golden brown. Drain from the pan, sprinkle with salt and a little chopped parsley. Add some of the potato to the omelette mixture and serve the remainder as a garnish.

Omelette au lard

Trim away the rind from about 4 rashers of lean bacon and cut the bacon into thin strips. Blanch these in boiling water for about 2 minutes to remove excess salt. Drain and dry. Sauté the bacon strips in a frying pan to draw the fat. When cooked, drain and cool, then add these to the basic egg mixture.

Filled omelettes

The filling for an omelette can vary enormously. Very often the choice of filling is determined by the items available. All fillings must be hot and ready prepared before making the omelette. Add the filling to the omelette when the mixture is cooked, but before folding the edges into the centre.

Omelette provençale

Dip 4 tomatoes into boiling water for 1 minute. Drain and peel away the skins. Halve and remove the seeds and then chop up the tomato flesh. Add 1 clove garlic, peeled and finely chopped, a pinch of dried mixed herbs and a teaspoon of sugar.

Sauté this mixture gently in 1 tablespoon hot oil for about 5 minutes, to eliminate the juices from the tomatoes. Spoon into the cooked omelette, fold closed and serve.

Omelette aux champignons

Wipe clean about 4 oz. (100 g.) small button mushrooms. Trim any stalks evenly and slice the mushrooms finely. Heat about 1 oz. (25 g.) butter in a frying pan, add the mushrooms and sauté gently. They should be just cooked – over-cooking causes the juices to run and the mushrooms to shrivel up. Add to the omelette mixture with a teaspoon of chopped parsley. Fold the omelette closed and serve.

Omelette aux crevettes

Heat about ½ oz. (15 g.) butter in a frying pan and add 4 oz. (100 g.) peeled, fresh or frozen, thawed prawns. Add about 1–2 tablespoons of cream or white sauce. Allow the prawns to heat through. Spoon the mixture into the cooked omelette, fold closed and serve.

Omelette au jambon

Toss about 4 oz. (100 g.) diced, cooked ham in ½ oz. (15 g.) melted butter. When hot, add to the cooked omelette, fold closed and serve.

Omelette lyonnaise

Peel and slice 2 medium onions. Sauté them in 1 oz. (25 g.) butter until tender but not brown – about 5 minutes. Spoon into the centre of the cooked omelette, fold closed and serve.

Open or flat omelettes

These sturdy and filling omelettes are fried open or flat because the addition of bulky ingredients make it impossible to fold them. They are fried on one side in the pan and then can be turned over in the pan with the aid of a palette knife or quickly passed under the grill. These omelettes feature such items as fried potatoes, fried onions, tomatoes, sweet peppers and herbs. They make very substantial supper dishes.

Omelette paysanne

Serves 2

4 large eggs	1 oz./25 g. butter
salt and freshly milled pepper	1 teaspoon finely chopped
2 oz./50 g. streaky bacon	parsley
1 medium-sized potato	pinch chopped chervil

Break the eggs into a basin and add the seasoning. Whisk to mix thoroughly and set aside. Trim the rind from the bacon rashers and cut bacon into strips. Fry in a pan to extract the fat, then remove the bacon from the pan and reserve the drippings. Peel and cut the potato into fine matchsticks strips. Add to the drippings in the pan along with ½ oz. (15 g.) of the butter. Sauté lightly to cook and brown. Add the potato, bacon, parsley and chervil to the omelette mixture.

Melt the remaining butter in a heavy 8-inch (20-cm.) frying pan. Add the omelette mixture all at once, stir for a moment then allow the mixture to set in the pan. When brown on the underside, loosen sides and turn over to brown on the second side. Turn on to a flat plate and serve.

Pizza omelette

Serves 2

4 eggs	1 medium onion
salt and freshly milled pepper	1 tablespoon tomato purée
1 tablespoon cold water	pinch mixed herbs
1 oz./25 g. butter	3 tomatoes
for the topping:	3 oz./75 g. cheese, grated
1 oz./25 g. butter	4 oz./100 g. cooked ham, diced

Crack the eggs into a basin, add the seasoning and water. Mix thoroughly with a fork and set aside while preparing the topping.

Melt the butter in a saucepan. Add the chopped onion, cover and cook gently for 4–5 minutes or until the onion is tender. Add the tomato purée and mixed herbs, cook for a moment and then draw off the heat. Plunge the tomatoes in boiling water for 1 minute. Drain and peel away the skins. Slice and reserve along with the grated cheese and diced ham.

Place the butter in an 8–9-inch (20–23-cm.) heavy frying pan. When melted and bubbling, pour in all the omelette mixture. Stir for a moment, drawing the omelette mixture in towards the centre of the pan. When set underneath but moist on top,

draw the pan off the heat. Cover with the onion mixture, then sprinkle with the diced ham and the sliced tomatoes. Sprinkle the cheese on top.

Place the omelette under a hot grill just long enough for the cheese to melt and brown. Slide out of the pan on to a hot dish and serve.

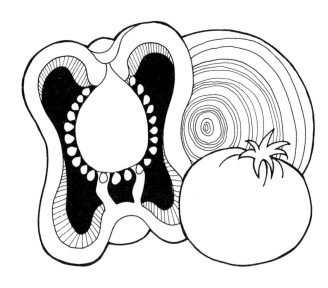

Spanish omelette

Success with a Spanish omelette lies in adding the fried vegetables to the egg mixture *before* making the omelette. Never add the egg to the cooked vegetables in the pan.

Serves 4

8 eggs	1–2 green peppers, according
salt and freshly milled pepper	to size
2 tomatoes	2 tablespoons oil
1 medium onion	2 oz./50 g. butter

Crack the eggs into a basin and whisk thoroughly with a fork. Add a seasoning of salt and freshly milled pepper and set aside while preparing the vegetables.

Peel the tomatoes, remove the seeds and chop the tomato flesh coarsely. Peel and slice the onion. Halve the peppers, remove the hot peppery seeds from inside and shred the pepper flesh. Heat the oil in a frying pan, add the onion and pepper and fry gently for about 8–10 minutes or until they are soft but not brown. Draw the pan off the heat. Add the peppers and onion to the egg mixture leaving behind as much of the oil in the pan as possible. Add the chopped tomato flesh to the egg mixture.

Melt a quarter of the butter in a small frying pan or omelette pan over moderate heat and, when bubbling hot, ladle in a quarter of the egg and vegetable mixture. Fry gently over the heat and as the egg sets at the edge of the pan, draw the mixture back gently with the prongs of a fork and allow some of the mixture on the surface to run underneath. Repeat this several times until the omelette is set but still moist. Serve immediately by sliding the omelette out on to a plate. Repeat the procedure until all four omelettes are made.

Serve with a salad and fried potatoes or hot toast.

Soufflé omelettes

Soufflé omelettes are easier to make than most cooks imagine. They must be cooked slowly over gentle heat. They should take 5 minutes, if not up to 10 minutes, before they are ready. From time to time, lift the sides of the omelette with a spatula to see how it is browning underneath. Keep any fillings very light, the fragile texture of a soufflé omelette will not support bulky ingredients.

Cheese soufflé omelette

A cheese soufflé omelette makes an excellent light luncheon for a busy cook.

Serves 2

3 large eggs	2 tablespoons grated Parmesan
1 tablespoon tepid water	cheese
salt and freshly milled pepper	½ oz./15 g. butter

Separate the eggs, placing the yolks together in a large basin and the whites in a second smaller basin. Add the water, a seasoning of salt and pepper and the cheese to the egg yolks. Using a wooden spoon, stir the egg yolk mixture until blended and creamy. Stiffly beat the egg whites and, using a metal spoon, fold into the egg yolk mixture.

Melt the butter in an 8-inch (20-cm.) omelette or heavy frying pan. When frothing, pour in the egg mixture and spread evenly. Place over a low heat and cook gently for 5 minutes or until the underside is golden brown and the mixture has begun to rise in the pan. Remove the pan from the heat and place under a preheated medium grill for a further 3–4 minutes or until the omelette is set and golden brown on the surface. Using a palette knife, loosen round the sides and fold the omelette in half in the pan. Serve at once.

Cheese and chive soufflé omelette

This makes a light and filling meal. Especially good for those on a diet.

Serves 2

1 (4 oz./100 g.) carton cottage	pinch cayenne pepper
cheese	2 teaspoons chopped chives
3 eggs	½ oz./15 g. butter
salt and freshly milled pepper	

Empty the cottage cheese into a basin and add the yolks of the eggs, placing the whites together in a second basin. Using a wooden spoon, beat the mixture together until thoroughly blended then add a seasoning of salt and pepper, and the cayenne pepper. Stir in the chopped chives. Beat the egg whites until stiff and, using a metal spoon, fold into the mixture.

Melt the butter in an 8-inch (20-cm.) omelette or heavy frying pan. When foaming, pour in the omelette mixture and spread evenly. Cook gently over a low heat; after about 5 minutes the underside will be brown and the mixture will have started to rise in the pan. Remove the pan from the heat and place under a gentle grill and cook for a further 3–4 minutes or until the soufflé is well risen and golden brown on top. Slide on to a hot plate and serve.

Mushroom soufflé omelette

Illustrated in colour on pages 56 and 57

Serves 2

3 eggs	4 oz./100 g. button mushrooms,
salt and freshly milled pepper	trimmed
1 tablespoon tepid water	1 level tablespoon flour
1 oz./25 g. butter	¼ pint/1½ dl. creamy milk
for the mushroom sauce:	salt and pepper
1 oz./25 g. butter	pinch mixed fresh herbs

Prepare the mushroom sauce and have ready. Heat the butter in a pan and add the sliced mushrooms. Fry gently for a few minutes, then sprinkle over the flour, and stir well to absorb the butter. Stir in the milk and bring slowly up to the boil. Season with salt and pepper, and add the herbs. Cover and simmer gently while preparing the omelette.

Separate the eggs, cracking the yolks into a large warmed bowl and the whites into a second basin. Add a seasoning of salt and pepper and water to the yolks. Whisk the yolks until thick, then stiffly beat the whites and fold into the mixture. Heat the butter in an omelette or frying pan until bubbling, then pour in the egg mixture evenly and cook over a gentle heat for about 5 minutes until underside is browned and the omelette begins to rise. Draw off the heat and place under a hot grill for 1–2 minutes to cook the surface. Loosen the sides of the omelette and, using a palette knife, fold one half over on to the other. Hold for a moment to seal the omelette together and then turn out on to a plate. Serve with the mushroom sauce spooned over.

Dessert omelettes

To avoid confusion, especially in a busy hotel kitchen, a chef traditionally marks or 'scores' a dessert omelette in a manner that makes it easily distinguishable from a savoury one. He does this by caramelising the surface of the omelette in a criss cross pattern using a red hot poker. At home, this is not really necessary but it looks attractive and adds a professional touch. All sweet omelettes should be well dusted with sieved icing sugar before serving. To score the omelette, heat a long skewer, preferably over a gas flame or under the grill. When really hot, touch the icing sugar, hold for a second so that it caramelises the sugar. Do this in several places; if the skewer is hot enough in the first instance, you can do the whole job in one process.

Orange soufflé omelette

An alternative delicious filling for this omelette could be hot apricot jam or hot black cherry jam with a tablespoon of Kirsch.

Serves 2

juice ½ orange	finely grated rind ½ orange
2 tablespoons orange marmalade	2–3 drops vanilla essence
3 eggs	½ oz./15 g. butter for frying
1 level tablespoon castor sugar	icing sugar

Measure the orange juice and the marmalade into a saucepan. Heat gently until melted and blended, then keep hot while preparing the omelette.

Separate the eggs, placing the yolks together in one basin and the whites together in a second basin. Add the sugar, grated orange rind and vanilla essence to the egg yolks. Using a wooden spoon, stir well to mix. Beat the egg whites until stiff and, using a metal spoon, fold into the egg mixture.

Melt the butter in an 8-inch (20-cm.) heavy omelette or frying pan. When foaming, pour in the egg mixture and spread evenly. Place over a low heat and cook gently for about 5 minutes. Draw off the heat and place under a preheated medium grill to brown and set the surface. Spread the surface with the orange marmalade sauce. Fold the omelette in half and slip on to a hot plate. Dust with icing sugar and serve at once.

Omelette soufflé Normande

Serves 2

3 eggs	*for the filling:*
1½ tablespoons castor sugar	2–3 dessert apples
grated rind ½ orange	1 oz./25 g. butter
½ oz./15 g. butter	1½ oz./40 g. vanilla sugar
icing sugar	little finely grated lemon rind

Prepare the filling and keep hot. Peel, core and cut the apples into slices. Melt the butter in a frying pan. Add the apple slices and sprinkle with the vanilla sugar. Add a little grated lemon rind. Cover and cook very gently, basting the apples with the sugar as a syrup forms. When the apples are quite tender, put the pan to one side and keep warm.

Separate the eggs, placing the yolks in one basin and the whites into a second larger basin. Add the sugar and orange rind to the yolks and, using a wooden spoon, beat until thick and creamy. Beat the egg whites until stiff and fold into the mixture, using a metal spoon.

Melt the butter in an 8-inch (20-cm.) heavy omelette or frying pan. When frothing, pour in the egg mixture and spread evenly. Cook very gently over a low heat for about 5 minutes. Then place under the grill for a further 2–3 minutes or until the omelette is risen and brown. To serve, slide the open omelette on to a serving dish and make a nick down the centre so that it will fold in half. Spoon in the hot buttery apples and the syrup from the pan. Fold the omelette in half, sprinkle with sugar and serve.

Pancakes

Thin delicate pancakes form the basis of many recipes, both savoury and sweet. They take a little time to prepare, but can be made in advance and are far from being the last minute job.

To make pancakes, ideally one should use the proper pancake pans. These small pans are about 6 inches (15 cm.) in diameter and have shallow sides. They are available in shops specialising in cookery equipment. If you do consider buying one, bear in mind that two pans make the cooking very much quicker than one. A chef, for instance, may have three or four of these pans over the heat at one time. By pouring a little hot fat from one to the other, he can cook a number of pancakes at great speed. The alternative for the home cook could be to use an omelette pan or small frying pan.

Basic pancake batter

Never cook pancakes swimming in a pan full of hot fat. The secret is to cook pancakes in almost no fat at all. An alternative method to the one given here, would be to buy a chunky piece of bacon fat and rub it round the hot pan before pouring in the batter.

Makes 12 pancakes

4 oz./100 g. plain flour	1 egg
pinch salt	½ pint/3 dl. milk

Sieve the flour and salt into a mixing basin and hollow out a well in the centre. Crack the egg into the well and add half the milk. Using a wooden spoon, mix the egg and milk. Keep the liquid in the centre of the basin and gradually draw in the flour from around the sides of the bowl. When all the flour has been incorporated, beat well until small bubbles appear on the surface and the mixture is well aerated. Stir in the remaining milk.

Strain into a jug, cover and leave to stand for 30 minutes, or until ready to use. Stir again before using.

To make pancakes

Melt about 2–3 oz. (50–75 g.) white cooking fat in a small saucepan. Pour a little of the fat into a small heavy pan and heat until smoking hot. Run the fat round the sides of the pan and pour the surplus back into the small pan of melted fat.

Quickly pour about 2 tablespoons of the batter from the jug into the centre of the hot pan. Tilt the pan so that the batter covers the whole of the base, making a very thin pancake. Cook over a moderate heat until the underside is browned – takes about ½ minute.

Shake the pan from time to time and the pancake will loosen when ready. Toss the pancake or turn, using a spatula. The second side takes less time to cook.

To use pancakes immediately

As the pancakes are prepared, stack them neatly between two plates, place over a pan half filled with simmering water. Add the pancakes to the stack as you prepare them. Use as required.

To use pancakes later

This is a method that is particularly useful when the pancakes are to be used in a savoury recipe. Prepare the pancakes and stack them neatly. When cold, wrap in kitchen foil and store in the refrigerator. About 30 minutes before required, unwrap and, using the same piece of foil, rewrap the pancakes again but this time in a loose foil parcel. Put on a baking tray and heat through in a hot oven (400°F., 200°C., Gas Mark 6) for about 20 minutes. Use as required.

To freeze pancakes

Prepare a rich batter, by adding 1 tablespoon oil or melted butter to the basic batter recipe. Prepare pancakes and allow to cool. Stack them neatly, separating each one with a square of greaseproof paper. Wrap in foil or place inside a freezer bag, seal airtight and freeze. To use: allow pancakes to thaw. Then reheat in the oven, wrapped in foil – see above. Use as required.

Savoury pancakes

Savoury pancakes prepared with tasty fillings and delicious sauces are ideal for entertaining. All the work can be done in advance. Pancakes reheat perfectly without becoming tough or dry, so long as there is either sufficient sauce poured over them or they are protected with a sheet of greased kitchen foil.

Serve savoury pancakes with one or more prepared vegetable or with a tossed salad.

Smoked haddock pancakes

Smoked haddock pancakes are excellent for lunch. A little chopped hard-boiled egg is tasty when added to the filling mixture. Serve with a tomato and watercress salad.

Serves 6

12 prepared pancakes	2 oz./50 g. butter
for the filling:	2 oz./50 g. flour
1 lb./½ kg. smoked haddock fillet	salt and freshly milled pepper
	juice ½ lemon
1 pint/6 dl. milk	

Early in the day: Prepare the pancakes as in the basic recipe and stack neatly. Set aside while preparing the filling.

Cut the smoked haddock into pieces and place in a pan. Add half the milk, cover with a lid and poach gently until the fish is tender. Drain and reserve the milk, making it up to 1 pint (6 dl.) with the remaining milk. Flake the smoked haddock, removing any skin and bones. Place the fish in a mixing basin.

Melt the butter in a saucepan over low heat. Stir in the flour and cook gently for 1 minute. Gradually stir in the milk, a little at a time. Bring up to the boil, stirring all the time, until thickened and smooth. Season well with salt and pepper and add the lemon juice to taste.

Pour half the sauce over the smoked haddock. Spoon a little mixture into the centre of each pancake. Roll them up and pack closely together in a buttered, shallow baking dish. Pour over the remaining sauce and cover with a sheet of kitchen foil. Store in a cool place.

About 20 minutes before serving: Remove the foil and place the dish in the centre of a moderately hot oven (375°F., 190°C., Gas Mark 5) and bake for 20 minutes or until bubbling hot and brown. Serve at once.

Lobster pancakes

Serve lobster pancakes with a green salad and a bottle of chilled white wine for a late supper party. Crab meat can be used as a substitute for lobster flesh, if preferred.

Serves 6

12 prepared pancakes	1 teaspoon anchovy essence
for the filling:	1 tablespoon tomato ketchup
2 oz./50 g. butter	1 (8 oz./225 g.) can lobster
2 oz./50 g. flour	lemon juice
1 pint/6 dl. milk	2 oz./50 g. hard cheese, grated
salt and freshly milled pepper	

Early in the day: Prepare the pancakes as in the basic recipe and stack neatly. Set aside while preparing the filling.

Melt the butter in a saucepan over low heat. Stir in the flour and cook gently for 1 minute. Gradually stir in the milk, a little at a time. Beat each addition in well to get a really smooth sauce. Bring up to the boil, stirring all the time until thickened and smooth. Season well with salt and pepper and then stir in the anchovy essence and tomato ketchup. Allow to simmer for 2–3 minutes. Flake the lobster flesh into a mixing basin, taking care to remove any sinews. Add a squeeze of lemon juice and pour half the sauce in. Blend the mixture and spoon into the centre of each pancake. Then roll up and pack the pancakes closely together in a buttered, shallow baking dish. Pour over the remaining sauce. Cover with a sheet of foil and keep cool.

About 20 minutes before serving: Remove the foil and sprinkle the pancakes with the grated cheese. Place in the centre of a moderately hot oven (375°F., 190°C., Gas Mark 5) and bake for 20 minutes or until bubbling hot and brown. Serve at once.

Prawn pancakes

Add a little chopped fresh dill to the sauce in the summer. These pancakes are excellent served as a first course.

Serves 6

12 prepared pancakes	salt and pepper
for the filling:	8–12 oz./225–350 g. prepared
2 oz./50 g. butter	prawns
2 oz./50 g. flour	juice ½ lemon
1 pint/6 dl. milk	

Early in the day: Prepare the pancakes as in the basic recipe and stack neatly. Set aside while preparing the filling.

Melt the butter in a saucepan over low heat. Stir in the flour and cook gently for 1 minute. Gradually stir in the milk, beating well all the time to get a smooth sauce. Bring up to the boil, stirring well all the time until thickened and smooth. Season well with salt and pepper and allow to simmer for 2–3 minutes.

Place the prawns in a mixing basin, add a squeeze of lemon juice and pour in half the white sauce. Blend the mixture and spoon into the centre of each pancake. Roll the filled pancakes up and pack close together in a buttered, shallow baking dish. Pour over the remaining sauce from the pan. Cover with a sheet of kitchen foil and store in a cool place.

About 20 minutes before serving: Remove the foil and place the dish in the centre of a moderately hot oven (375°F., 190°C., Gas Mark 5) and bake for 20 minutes until brown. Serve.

Chicken and mushroom pancakes

Buy 2–3 chicken joints and bake or roast them in the oven to provide the chicken flesh for these pancakes.

Serves 6

12 prepared pancakes	2 oz./50 g. hard cheese, grated
for the filling:	8–12 oz./225 g.–350 g. cooked
3 oz./75 g. butter	chicken
2 oz./50 g. flour	4 oz./100 g. mushrooms, sliced
1 pint/6 dl. milk	pinch dried mixed herbs
salt and freshly milled pepper	

Early in the day: Prepare the pancakes as in the basic recipe and stack neatly. Set aside while preparing the filling.

Melt 2 oz. (50 g.) of the butter in a saucepan over low heat. Stir in the flour and cook gently for 1 minute. Gradually stir in the milk, a little at a time. Beat each addition in well to get a smooth sauce. Bring up to the boil, stirring well all the time, until thickened. Season well with salt and pepper. Stir in half the cheese and allow to simmer for 2–3 minutes.

Dice the chicken flesh and place in the mixing basin. Melt the remaining butter in a frying pan. Add the trimmed and sliced mushrooms and fry quickly for a few moments. Add the mushrooms to the chicken flesh. Add the mixed herbs and half the prepared sauce. Mix the ingredients well and spoon into the centre of each pancake. Roll up the pancakes and pack close together in a buttered baking dish. Pour over the remaining sauce. Cover with a sheet of kitchen foil and leave in a cool place.

About 20 minutes before serving: Remove the foil and sprinkle with the remaining cheese. Place in the centre of a moderately hot oven (375°F., 190°C., Gas Mark 5) and bake for 20 minutes or until bubbling hot and brown. Serve at once.

Dessert pancakes

Liqueurs and fruit feature prominently among dessert pancakes. The recipes are very simple but do require some last minute attention. Prepare these for gay informal occasions when there are just a few guests.

Batter for crêpes

Crêpes are delicate, small pancakes made from a rich batter and used only in dessert recipes. These should be made in a crêpe pan, which is smaller in diameter than a pancake pan. More often, however, the normal pan is used with perfectly good results.

Makes 12 crêpes

4 oz./100 g. plain flour	½ pint/3 dl. milk
pinch salt	1 tablespoon oil or melted
1 egg	butter
1 egg yolk	

Sift the flour and salt into a mixing basin and hollow out the centre. Add the egg, egg yolk and half the milk. Using a wooden spoon, stir the liquid ingredients, gradually drawing in the flour from around the sides of the bowl. Beat well to make a smooth batter. Beat in the remaining milk and, just before using, stir in the oil or melted butter. Pour the batter into a jug, ready for use.

Cook the pancakes following the method given in the basic recipe (page 38).

Crêpes Grand Marnier

Serves 4

12 prepared pancakes	juice 2 oranges
for the sauce:	juice ½ lemon
1 oz./25 g. butter	3–4 tablespoons Grand
2 oz./50 g. castor sugar	Marnier

Have the pancakes ready-prepared and hot. Melt the butter in a large frying pan over moderate heat. Stir in the sugar and cook gently to a golden caramel brown. Stir in the strained orange and lemon juice and stir until the caramel is dissolved. Drop each pancake, in turn, open flat into the pan. Fold in three and push to the side of the pan when adding the next. When all the pancakes are in the hot sauce, add the liqueur. Flambé and shake the pan so that the flames spread well.

Serve at once with the sauce spooned from the pan.
Advance preparation: Make pancakes in advance, see page 38. Wrap in foil. Reheat when ready to make the recipe.

Crêpes aux confitures

Serves 4

12 prepared pancakes	*for the filling:*
1–2 oz./25–50 g. butter, melted	4–5 tablespoons sieved strawberry or other jam
icing sugar (see recipe)	lemon juice, if liked

Have the pancakes ready-prepared and hot. Warm the jam gently for the filling, add a squeeze of lemon juice if liked to thin the jam and sharpen the flavour. Spread each pancake with a little jam and roll up. Place on a buttered dish. Brush the pancakes with melted butter. Dust with icing sugar and slip the dish into a hot oven for 2–3 minutes, or pass under a hot grill to glaze.

Serve with cream.
Advance preparation: Make pancakes in advance, see page 38. Wrap in foil. Reheat when ready to make the recipe.

Crêpes with bananas

Serves 4

12 prepared pancakes	*for the filling:*
squeeze lemon juice	4 large ripe bananas
icing sugar (see recipe)	juice ½ lemon
	¼ pint/1½ dl. double cream

Have the pancakes ready-prepared and hot. Mash the bananas and stir in the strained lemon juice. Lightly whip the cream and fold into the mixture. Spoon a little of the banana filling on to each pancake and roll up. Arrange in a hot serving dish and squeeze over a little extra lemon juice for flavour. Dust with icing sugar and serve.
Advance preparation: Make pancakes in advance, see page 38. Wrap in foil. Reheat when ready to make the recipe.

Crêpes creole

Serves 4

12 prepared pancakes	1 (15 oz./425 g.) can crushed pineapple or pineapple pieces
1–2 oz./25–50 g. butter, melted	
icing sugar (see recipe)	3 tablespoons Kirsch
for the filling:	
4 good tablespoons apricot jam	

Have the pancakes ready-prepared and hot. Place the apricot jam in a saucepan and add a little of the strained pineapple juice. Stir in the pineapple pieces or crushed pineapple and heat gently. Add 1 tablespoon of Kirsch and draw off the heat.

Place a spoonful of the pineapple mixture in the centre of each pancake, then fold in three. Place in a warm, buttered dish. Brush the pancakes with the melted butter. Dust with icing sugar and slip the dish into a hot oven for 2–3 minutes.

Spoon over the remaining warmed Kirsch, flambé and serve at once.
Advance preparation: Make pancakes in advance, see page 38. Wrap in foil. Reheat when ready to make the recipe.

Puff pastry (page 16)

Knead thoroughly to get a smooth dough.

Place the butter in the centre of the pastry and fold the pastry over completely.

Give the dough a half turn clockwise and, with a rolling pin, press the dough gently to flatten it slightly.

Mark the rolled out dough in three. Fold the bottom third up over the centre third and the top third down over both.

Impress in the dough with the fingertips to remind yourself how many rolls and folds the dough has had.

41

Serving cheese

With crusty bread, fresh butter, some salad and a glass of wine, cheese makes a good meal on its own. To its highly nutritive qualities, cheese adds additional advantages. It is a versatile food that needs no preparation and offers a wide range to choose from. All are suitable for serving as dessert cheeses, some in addition are also excellent to use in recipes.

It is important to recognise and know about the more familiar and most useful cheeses:

British cheese

HARD AND SEMI HARD CHEESES

Cheddar: the most versatile and widely used English cheese. It should have a close, creamy texture and rich nutty flavour. Much of today's Cheddar is factory produced and sold rindless, but there are a few farmhouse-made Cheddars and they are worth finding. Mature Cheddar cheese has the best flavour and should be 6–9 months old before it is sold. Serve as a dessert cheese and use in recipes.

Cheshire: the oldest of our English cheeses. A rich, hard cheese with a sharper flavour than Cheddar, and one that is consistently good. Usually red or white and very occasionally blue. Serve as a dessert cheese, very good with celery, or use in cooking. A useful all-purpose cheese.

Leicester: a flaky, moist, open textured cheese. Serve as a dessert cheese, its rich russet colour enhances any cheese board. Can also be used in cooking, especially for sauces and in particular for Welsh rarebit.

Wensleydale: a mild, flaky textured cheese. Usually a pale parchment colour. A dessert cheese that is very good with fruit. Traditionally eaten with apple pie.

Caerphilly: a creamy white, mild flavoured cheese which is very easy to digest. A mild all-purpose cheese that is excellent with salads and fruit and very good to take on a picnic.

Derby: a close textured cheese with a distinctive honey colour. This cheese is sometimes flavoured with sage, when it is known as Sage Derby. The cheese is streaked with green. A dessert cheese and a good choice at Christmas.

Lancashire: this has a crumbly texture and is light in colour with a mild flavour. Very good to use in recipes as it melts quickly and has a good flavour. The one to choose for toasted cheese.

Double Gloucester: a West Country cheese. A golden crumbly cheese with a delicate creamy flavour. Should be matured for the best flavour. A dessert cheese but also delicious served with fresh bread and butter for a snack.

BLUE VEINED CHEESES

Stilton: this is the most famous English cheese and one with a unique flavour. It has a close, crumbly texture but should be creamy white with blue veining. White Stilton is less mature – a moist crumbly cheese without the flavour of the veining.

Use a knife to cut layers off a half Stilton. Do not scoop out the inside, this practise produces a greater area for drying up and for mould to develop. Essentially a dessert cheese, Stilton is traditionally served with port.

SOFT CHEESES

Caboc: a buttery, smooth textured double cream cheese from Scotland. Rolled in pinhead oatmeal. Sold in individual portions and very perishable.

Crowdie: a mild cheese with a rough open texture made from soured milk. Crowdie has a mild flavour but with a bite. It should be blended with a little cream and can be flavoured with chives, chopped parsley or carraway seeds. Very good with oatcakes.

Cottage cheese: a curd cheese made from separated milk with cream and salt added. Has a mild, bland taste. Very good to use in salads and recipes.

Full fat soft cheese: best known are the foil wrapped packets of cream cheese. There are other varieties, often with flavours added. Serve fresh as a spread, or use plain types in dips or in some dessert recipes.

French cheese

HARD AND SEMI HARD CHEESES

Tommes: a cheese made in the hills of Savoie. A round cheese that is made in various sizes. Sometimes covered with a crust of grape pips remaining from wine making. A firm, rich cheese with a creamy texture and a delicious flavour.

Port-Salut: a semi hard round cheese with a bright orange rind. It has a rich, pungent flavour which comes from ripening. A delicious and very popular dessert cheese.

Reybier spécialité au noix: this is a pasteurised cheese spread which is sold as a large or small round cheese. The outside is studded with walnut halves and it has a very good flavour. Looks pretty on a cheese board.

BLUE VEINED CHEESES

Roquefort: a blue veined French cheese. Made from ewe's milk, it has a strong, slightly salty flavour. A dessert cheese but can also be used to add flavour to cheese mixtures for cocktail snacks and in salad dressings for the more acid flavoured salad greens like endive or chicory.

Bleu d'Auvergne: another French blue cheese of the Roquefort type, but is less piquant in flavour. An excellent dessert cheese.

SOFT CHEESES

Camembert: a round or half mooned boxed cheese, which has a strong, unique flavour and a characteristic smell. It should be bought when ripe and the rind should be lightly scraped before serving.

Brie: a flat round cheese, similar in texture and colour to Camembert. Often displayed in shops on a straw mat. Brie has a delicate flavour and should be eaten when ripe. Unripe Brie has a chalky, insipid flavour.

Coulommiers: a type of Brie, but sold in round boxes like Camembert. When ripe, it has a delicious nutty flavour.

Livarot: another famous Normandy soft cheese. It has a strong rich flavour and a reddish brown rind.

Pont l'Evêque: one of the richest soft French cheese and one much acclaimed by connoisseurs. Easily recognised by its square shape and buff coloured rind.

Fromage au poivre: a full fat soft cheese, the outside of which is studded with crushed black peppercorns. The peppercorns add to the flavour and should be eaten.

Boursin: a full fat soft cheese flavoured with garlic and herbs.

Petit suisse: an unsalted French cream cheese. Cylinder shaped and wrapped in thin paper. This cheese is delicious eaten with castor sugar and fresh strawberries.

Demi-sel: as its name suggests, a slightly salted cream cheese. Foil wrapped and good for spreading.

Swiss cheese

HARD AND SEMI HARD CHEESES

Gruyère: a Swiss cheese, pale yellow in colour with a strong mature flavour and aroma. It is similar to Emmental but the holes are smaller and less frequent. Gruyère is an excellent cheese for cooking although expensive. A piece bought keeps very well. In recipes the flavour is excellent.

Emmental: a Swiss hard cheese. The cheese has a slight flavour of walnuts and the holes or 'eyes' vary between the size of a cherry and a walnut. Exported Emmental has the trademark 'Switzerland' in red on the rind.

Italian cheese

HARD AND SEMI HARD CHEESES

Parmesan: a very hard Italian cheese with a characteristic black coating. The matured cheese has the best flavour. Usually grated and used in cooking or for sprinkling on food, especially pasta.

BLUE VEINED CHEESES

Gorgonzola: a blue veined Italian cheese with a very pungent flavour.

Dolcelatte: an Italian veined cheese which is milder in flavour than Gorgonzola. Sold foil wrapped, it has a creamy texture and a delicate flavour.

SOFT CHEESES

Ricotta: a rich Italian cream cheese. It rather resembles cottage cheese and can be used in much the same way. Used in pasta recipes, particularly canneloni and lasagne.

Mozzarella: a round white cheese made from cow's milk. Very good eaten fresh in salads with an oil or vinegar dressing. Also sliced and used as a topping for pizza.

Bel Paese: a sweet, mild semi soft Italian cheese. It has a light colour and a soft rubbery texture. A very popular cheese with a delicious flavour.

Dutch cheese

HARD AND SEMI HARD CHEESES

Edam: a Dutch cheese easily recognized by its round shape and bright red waxed surface. Mildly salty in flavour with a rather solid texture. A good cheese for sandwiches and snacks.

Gouda: a hard round cheese, flat in shape made from full cream milk. A good cheese to use in cooking. The Dutch use this for fondue.

Leiden: a cheese similar to Gouda but with the added flavour of cumin seeds.

Kernham: a round cheese with a high butterfat content. It has a soft texture something like St. Paulin.

BLUE VEINED CHEESES

Bluefort: a creamy, blue veined Dutch cheese. It has a pleasant pungent smell and slightly salty taste.

Danish cheese

HARD AND SEMI HARD CHEESES

Samsoe: a firm textured Danish cheese with round shiny holes. It has a mild, sweet nutlike flavour and is very popular in Denmark. A versatile cheese, serve as a breakfast cheese or for snacks or picnics.

Harvati: a full flavoured Danish cheese with a piquante after taste. It has an open texture with numerous irregular holes. Serve as a dessert cheese or for cocktail snacks.

Esrom: a soft mellow and buttery Danish cheese, with almost no rind and what there is can be eaten. It has a slightly aromatic taste and a butterlike texture with numerous irregular holes. Serve as a dessert cheese.

BLUE VEINED CHEESES

Danablu: a pure white cheese with a creamy consistency and delicate blue veining. It has a distinctive flavour and is a popular after-dinner cheese.

Mycella: this has a golden yellow colour with green veining. It has a soft texture and a delicate and delicious flavour. Milder than Danablu.

Selecting cheese for entertaining

When selecting cheese for a cheese board, choose from all types. Make the selection interesting, varied and attractive in appearance. Whether the cheese course in a menu is served before or after the dessert is entirely a personal decision. If a good wine is served along with the main course, cheese served before the dessert offers a chance to finish the wine. Provide guests with a small cheese plate or dessert plate and a small knife and fork. The cheese in this case is eaten alone and is appreciated for its flavour and for the way it complements the wine.

Storing cheese

Some varieties of cheese are more perishable than others. As a rule, buy all cheese in small quantities at a time, especially soft cheeses of the Camembert type and blue veined cheese such as Roquefort. Hard or semi-hard cheeses will keep for days or even weeks in a cool airy larder. They should be lightly wrapped in waxed paper or foil to prevent the surfaces from drying out. Cheese should not be subjected to rapid changes of temperature, but if the use of the refrigerator is essential, the wrapped cheese should be put in a polythene bag or closed container and placed in the least cold part of the refrigerator. Take them out about 30 minutes before serving.

Cheese such as Brie or Camembert should not be put in the refrigerator. Their storage time is short, only 2–3 days.

Fish with flavour

Unfortunately, these days the fish on the average fishmonger's slab is not as varied as it might be, for there are many fish to choose from. Fish is more expensive than it used to be (Dover sole, lobsters and scallops for example are almost in the luxury class), which is a pity for it discourages many from cooking and serving a source of food that is highly nutritious and very good to eat.

Certain types of fish are suitable for particular kinds of recipes. White fish are good for poaching or baking and serving with sauces, whereas the oily fish are usually grilled or fried. The recipes in this chapter will give you some super new ways of cooking your favourite fish.

Buy fish that is very fresh and cook the same day.

Salt water fish

Cod
Cod is one of our most abundant sea water fishes and is available all year round, although it is best during the winter months from October to February. Cod is sold in fillets, which are cut lengthwise from the fish and can be bought in portions up to the weight required. The fish can also be cut across to give cutlets, sometimes called steaks, which are round in shape. The flesh of cod is firm and white, it is most often poached and served with a sauce and can be used in many made-up dishes. Cod's roe is delicious poached and then sliced and fried.

Haddock
Haddock is a little more expensive than cod, but it has a better flavour. It is available all year round and, like most white fish, is best during winter months particularly from November to February. Haddock is usually sold filleted. In Scotland, the small inshore fish are sold whole and these are particularly popular. Haddock can be poached and served with a sauce or used in made-up fish dishes. Haddock roes are sold during the early months of the year and these can be poached and then fried.

Hake
A salt water relation of the cod and is used in similar ways. The flesh of hake is very white and tender and is easily digestible, making it a good choice for children and invalids. Hake is in season all year round but best in winter months.

Halibut
A very large fish which is rarely seen whole in the shops. Halibut is cut up into steaks which are marvellous for grilling, frying or poaching. The flesh of halibut is firm textured and it has a very good flavour. It is a filling fish, so buy rather less than with other white fish. Halibut is quite an expensive fish, available all year round but best from July to March.

Plaice
Plaice is abundant all round the British coast and is in season all year round, although tends to be rather thin and full of roe in the spring. Plaice is a flat fish and easily recognised by the orange spotted, brown skin. Usually skinned and filleted, the fillets can be poached or egg and breadcrumbed and fried. Although plaice can be used in recipes calling for sole, it has a softer flesh and does not really match up to the flavour of the more expensive sole.

Rock salmon
A fish that has many local names and an unattractive appearance. For this reason, it is skinned, filleted and cut in portions before sold. Rock salmon has a firm white flesh and is the fish to choose for dishes requiring long cooking times, such as fish soups or stews.

Skate
Skate is a curious looking fish, of which only the wings are sold. Best during winter months from October to March. The flesh is moist with a pink tinge, the smaller skate being the better in flavour. When buying, select thick pieces cut as near the centre of the fish as possible. Serve poached, with butter.

Sole
An expensive and very fine white fish. The most famous is the Dover sole. Lemon sole are slightly smaller and lighter in colour, being a rich yellow brown whereas a Dover sole is a very deep shade of dark brown and grey. Sole has a firm textured flesh with a particularly good flavour. It can be fried or grilled on the bone, filleted and poached or cooked in many other ways.

Turbot
Turbot is a highly prized fish with a delicate flavour. The turbot spawns in autumn and is therefore at its best during summer months. Turbot is large and usually sold in cutlets or steaks, which can be grilled or poached. Turbot is a good choice for summer menus, being excellent cold or in mousses, pâtés or salads.

Whiting
A common fish that is cheap and available all year round. Whiting can be bought whole or filleted and should be used fairly soon after purchase. The flesh is very light textured, particularly easy to digest – so it is ideal for small children and invalids.

Oily fish

Eel
The fresh water eel is the one that has a tender, oily flesh and is the eel used in recipes. Eel should be alive when purchased, the fishmonger will skin them for you. Eel may be used in pieces and fried, or poached and served cold in jelly.

Herrings
Fresh herrings can be bought all the year round but they tend to tail off for spawning from March to May. They are particularly plentiful in October and November. Herrings are highly nutritious and can be prepared in many ways. Herrings can be grilled or fried whole, or boned and fried. They are also excellent baked in a vinegar and water mixture to make soused herrings.

Mackerel
Mackerel must be very fresh when bought. The flesh has an oily, slightly savoury, taste. Mackerel should be grilled or fried.

Mullet
There are two types of mullet, the grey mullet and the red mullet. Grey mullet is a fresh or coastal water fish, it has a silvery blue skin and is most plentiful in the autumn. Grey mullet should be gutted and cleaned before cooking. Red mullet is a sea fish with an attractive red colour. The finest red mullet are caught in the Mediterranean. A firm fleshed fish with a delicious flavour and in season during the summer months, Leave red mullet ungutted and cook whole. Grill or fry, or bake in buttered paper envelopes.

Popular freshwater fish

Salmon
English and Scotch salmon are in season from February to August. It is expensive to buy but has a very fine flavour. Salmon can be bought in a large piece for poaching, or in cutlets which are delicious grilled or fried.

Sea trout or salmon trout
This fish is no relation to the salmon but is from the trout family. It is similar to salmon in appearance with a silvery skin and a pink flesh. A salmon trout weighs usually between $2\frac{1}{2}$–3 lb. ($1\frac{1}{4}$–$1\frac{1}{2}$ kg.) and is usually cooked whole; poached, grilled or baked in foil.

Smelt
A small, delicately flavoured freshwater fish found mainly in river estuaries. Not so readily available now since polution of rivers has considerably reduced their numbers.
   They can be shallow fried or grilled.

Trout
There are all kinds of trout, the largest freshwater ones being in the lakes of Switzerland. The best known here is the Rainbow trout, a species originally from America, now farmed on an extensive scale to provide fresh trout all year round. The common river trout or brown trout is a game fish and is available during the fishing season and obtained only locally.

Smoked fish

Bloaters
These are whole, dry salted herring which are lightly smoked. Owing to the light smoking, bloaters do not keep as well as kippers and should be eaten soon after purchase. They can be grilled or fried.

Buckling
Buckling are smoked herring, but unlike kippers they are smoked whole, unsplit. Smoking is at a higher temperature so that the flesh is lightly cooked. Buckling can be treated like smoked trout and served raw. Lift away the skin and serve with lemon wedges and thinly sliced brown bread and butter.

Kippers
Kippers are split, lightly brined and smoked herring. The flesh should be firm and moist. They can be grilled, fried or poached. Kippers can also be bought as boned kipper fillets.

Smoked cod
Larger fish are filleted and then smoked. Smoked cod fillet is less expensive than smoked haddock fillet and it can be used in place of smoked haddock in recipes. The roe of the cod is sold smoked and is very tasty. Scoop the roe out of the skin and blend with freshly milled pepper and lemon juice. Serve with toast or on savoury biscuits. Smoked cod roe can also be used in made up dishes.

Smoked eel
Buy whole, smoked eel or smoked eel fillets. Serve raw with lemon and brown bread and butter.

Smoked haddock
These are smaller haddock, split and smoked whole, and are often called Finnan haddock, although strictly speaking this term should apply only to the very fine smoked haddock that comes from Findon near Aberdeen. Larger haddock are filleted and smoked, then sold as smoked haddock fillet. Poach in water or milk. Smoked haddock can be used in many recipes.

Smoked salmon

Different grades of smoked salmon are sold, from the most expensive Scotch smoked salmon downwards. Smoked salmon should be very thinly sliced. Allow about 2 oz. (50 g.) per person and arrange the smoked salmon flat on a plate. Serve with lemon and brown bread and butter.

Smoked sprats

These are smoked whole fish. Grill or fry to cook and serve hot as a meal starter.

Smoked trout

This is the smoked whole fish which is always served raw. It can be used in pâtés or mousse and is very good served as a meal starter, served with lemon and brown bread and butter. Lift away the skin before serving.

Smokies

These are small haddock which are smoked closed and unfilleted. It is usually grilled with a pat of butter inside. The flaked flesh is very good added to scrambled egg. Arbroath smokies are considered the finest and are excellent served as an hors d'oeuvre. Allow 1 per person and lift away the skin. Serve with lemon and brown bread and butter.

Shellfish

Crab

Crab is usually sold cooked by the fishmonger. Cock crabs are the best buys, be guided by the narrow tail flap underneath. Crabs produce two types of meat, the white meat from the legs and claws and the brown meat from the centre of the body. A crab of 2–2½ lb. (1–1¼ kg.) will serve four and with advance notice the fishmonger will prepare or 'dress' the crab for you. Otherwise see recipe section (page 51).

Crawfish

This is a large salt water shellfish similar to the lobster but easily recognisable because the crawfish has no claws. Crawfish are very popular on the Continent. The flesh is firmer and there is more of it than in a lobster, but it is generally accepted that the lobster has the finer flavour of the two. Prepare and use in the same way as lobster. Quick frozen crawfish tails are available and are delicious thawed and grilled with butter.

Dublin Bay prawns

Dublin Bay prawns look like small miniature lobsters. They are the same species as the French langoustine. The tail holds the fleshy edible part and 'scampi' is the accepted term for this. Usually sold cooked, sometimes in their shells, but most often shelled and quick frozen. Allow 3–4 oz. (75–100 g.) shelled scampi per person. The most popular way of serving them is to coat with egg and breadcrumbs and deep fry, but scampi are also delicious served in sauces.

Lobster

Lobster is generally sold cooked by the fishmonger. Choose a lobster that feels heavy for its size, the tail should be resilient and spring back when straightened and released. The average weight for a lobster is between 1–1½ lb. (½–¾ kg.) which is sufficient for two servings. In season from March to October. For preparation see recipe section (page 63).

Mussels

Scrub mussels thoroughly and wash in several changes of cold water. Pull away the mossy piece on the shell known as the 'beard'. Discard any with broken shells or ones that remain open. Mussels, like oysters, should be alive when purchased and they must be cooked the day they are purchased. Sold in pints and quarts, on average allow 1 quart (1 litre) of mussels for two servings. When cooking mussels, never add salt, only a little finely milled pepper. While cooking, mussels open up and produce a fair amount of salty liquid themselves. Choose a pan large enough to give them a few shakes while cooking and to allow them to open up. Any mussels that remain closed after cooking should be discarded.

Oysters

The season for oysters is from September 1st to April 31st. Natives, that is Colchester, Whitstable or Helford oysters, are sold within this season. Others sold outside the season are imported. On account of the high prices they command, oysters are usually served just as they are – open in the half shell with lemon, brown bread and butter and cayenne pepper if wished. Sold and eaten by the dozen or half dozen, oysters must be fresh and, since they are eaten raw, the shells tightly closed. Give your fishmonger sufficient warning and he will open them for you. They will be packed with the deep shell underneath to retain the oyster liquor.

Prawns

The prawn is like the shrimp in appearance but larger. The best come from the cold waters of the North Sea. They are sold cooked and unshelled by the pint, or peeled and quick frozen by weight. When picked, 1 pint (½ litre) yields about 3 oz. (75 g.) edible prawn. Allow about 2 oz. (50 g.) shelled prawn per person. Very good served shelled with tarragon mayonnaise and brown bread and butter. Also used extensively in recipes.

Scallops

In season during the cold winter months from October to March. Allow 1 large or 2 smaller scallops per person. The fishmonger will open the scallops and remove the greyish surrounding frill or 'beard', the only inedible part. The beige or coral coloured piece of fish is the roe and is very tender and delicious. The firmer, white fleshed part is very similar to lobster in texture and flavour. Ask the fishmonger for the deep half shells. They are useful and decorative as a serving dish for the cooked fish. Scallops can be fried or grilled as kebabs, excellent with bacon, or poached and served in a sauce.

Shrimp

There are two kinds of shrimp. The brown shrimp, which are more plentiful and netted in large numbers close to the shores, and the pink shrimp which are caught further out. The pink shrimp is considered the finest of the two. Both are very good and have a more delicate flavour than the larger prawn. Shrimp can be bought cooked and unshelled by the pint. When picked, 1 pint (½ litre) yields about 3½–4 oz. (75–100 g.) edible shrimp. Allow about ½ pint (¼ litre) unshelled shrimp per person. Usually eaten shelled with lemon and brown bread and butter.

 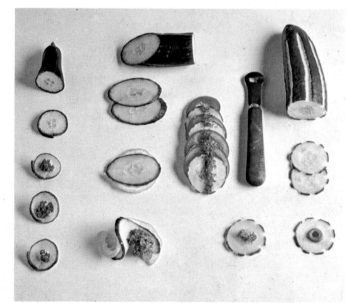
 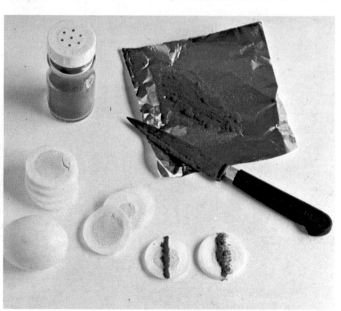

Mussel soup

Those who like mussels will find this soup particularly good. Serve in large soup plates or bowls with crusty French bread and an extra plate for the mussel shells.

Serves 4

1 quart/1 litre mussels	2 oz./50 g. butter
1 pint/½ litre water	2 oz./50 g. flour
1 small onion	2–3 tablespoons single cream
½ pint/3 dl. dry white wine	2 tablespoons finely chopped
salt and freshly milled pepper	parsley

Scrub and clean the mussels in several changes of cold water. Remove the beards with a knife and discard any mussels with broken shells and those that remain open. Place the mussels in a large saucepan with the cold water, cover and bring up to the boil. Simmer for 2–3 minutes or until the mussels have opened, then strain and reserve the cooking liquor. Discard any mussels that have not opened. Carefully remove the open half of the shells from the remaining mussels. Set the mussels and reserved cooking liquor aside.

Finely chop the onion, place in the saucepan and add the white wine. Bring to the boil and simmer for about 5 minutes. Add the reserved mussel liquor and season to taste with pepper and only a little salt. On a flat plate, blend the butter and flour together to make a 'beurre manie'. Add this mixture in pieces to the hot liquid in the pan. Stir to blend the ingredients, then bring up to the boil, stirring until evenly thickened. Stir in the cream and the reserved mussels. Heat through for a few moments but do not boil. Sprinkle with chopped parsley and serve.

Potted salmon

Potted salmon is usually made in small quantities and is an excellent way of using up any left over pieces of cooked salmon, partly from the head and tail end of a whole fish. The mixture keeps well for 4–5 days in the refrigerator. Marvellous for a snack and very good for picnics.

Serves 4

8 oz./225 g. cooked salmon	salt and freshly milled pepper
3 anchovy fillets	pinch ground mace
4–5 oz./100–150 g. butter	

Flake the salmon flesh, removing any bones and skin. Pound the anchovies well, then add the salmon flesh and pound the two together. Add all but 1 oz. (25 g.) of the butter and beat very thoroughly until the mixture is creamy. Season with a little salt, some freshly milled pepper and a pinch of mace. Taste and recheck the seasoning.

Savoury garnishes
The explanatory captions to these garnishes appear on page 66.

Spoon into a small china pot and spread evenly. Melt the remaining butter and pour over the surface. Chill for several hours.

Serve with hot toast.

Advance preparation: Make potted salmon 1–2 days in advance of serving. The mixture keeps well and improves with keeping.

Smoked cod's roe pâté

Made this way, smoked cod's roe pâté is very tasty. A little goes a long way. Use the mixture as a filling for celery stalks for cocktails and with hot toast as a meal starter.

Serves 6

1 complete smoked cod's roe,	2 tablespoons olive oil
about 12 oz./350 g.	freshly milled black pepper
1 small clove garlic	¼ pint/1½ dl. double cream
juice ½ lemon	

Split open the two halves of the roe and scoop the flesh out into a bowl. Remove the papery coating of the garlic and crush. Add the garlic and gradually beat in the lemon juice and oil. Season with freshly milled pepper and beat well to get a soft mixture. If small lumps of the roe remain, rub the mixture through a coarse sieve and beat again. Lightly whip the cream and fold into the mixture. Spoon into a serving dish and spread evenly. Chill for several hours.

Serve with hot toast and butter.

Advance preparation: Make this recipe up 1–2 days before serving and chill in the refrigerator. The mixture keeps well for a week.

Tomatoes stuffed with prawns

For these you require the larger Continental tomatoes, only these can hold a sufficient portion of filling. Although readily available on the Continent, these tomatoes are only imported in limited quantities to this Country. They can be found in specialist greengrocers.

Serves 4

4 large tomatoes	4 tablespoons tarragon
salt	mayonnaise
12 oz./350 g. prepared prawns	1 teaspoon chopped parsley

Cut a slice from the top of each tomato for a lid. Cut out the centre stalk and set lids aside. Scoop out the seeds and pulp from the tomatoes. Sprinkle the insides with salt and leave upside down to drain.

Blend the prawns, mayonnaise – use the tarragon-flavoured variety – and parsley together. When ready to serve, spoon a generous filling of prawns into each tomato and top with the lid. Garnish with a sprig of parsley.

Serve with a little crisp lettuce.

Advance preparation: Scoop out the tomatoes. Prepare the prawn and mayonnaise filling and chill. Assemble the recipe when ready to serve.

Smoked trout pâté

This is a particularly good recipe for a meal starter. The texture is rather soft when newly prepared and it is better to make it up the day before required, to give the mixture a chance to firm up. Keeps well in the refrigerator for up to 1 week.

Serves 4

2 smoked trout	juice ½ lemon
¼ pint/1½ dl. soured cream	freshly milled pepper
1 (4 oz./100 g.) carton cottage cheese	

Skin and flake the smoked trout into the goblet of an electric blender. Add the soured cream and the sieved cottage cheese. Add the lemon juice and a good seasoning of freshly milled pepper. Cover and blend to a purée. Turn into a small dish and chill for several hours or overnight.

Serve with hot toast.

Advance preparation: Make up 1–2 days in advance of serving.

Egg and breadcrumbed scallops with anchovy butter

Served this way scallops make a delicious start to a meal. Use small fresh scallops and have them removed from the shell or use frozen, thawed small Queen scallops. Serve the scallops hot and the anchovy butter very chilled.

Serves 4

8–12 scallops, according to size	toasted breadcrumbs
seasoned flour	oil for deep frying
1 egg, lightly mixed	anchovy butter (page 65)

Trim the scallops and roll in seasoned flour. Dip in the lightly beaten egg and then coat all over in toasted breadcrumbs. At this stage, keep chilled until ready to fry.

When ready to serve, fry the scallops in hot deep oil for about 5 minutes. Turn them once for even browning. When golden and cooked, drain well.

Serve at once topped with a slice of chilled anchovy butter.

Advance preparation: Make the anchovy butter well in advance. Egg and breadcrumb the scallops and chill in the refrigerator. Fry when required.

Devilled crab

If liked use 1 lb. (½ kg.) frozen thawed crab meat in this recipe instead of freshly prepared crab. In this case, pack the mixture in small ramekin dishes or scallop shells for serving.

Serves 4

2 small dressed crabs	2 tablespoons finely grated Parmesan cheese
2 oz./50 g. butter	2 teaspoons French mustard
2 shallots, peeled and finely chopped	dash anchovy essence
2 tablespoons brandy	dash Worcestershire sauce
4 tablespoons thick cream	pinch cayenne pepper
4 tablespoons fresh white breadcrumbs	salt and pepper

Remove the crab meat from the shells (page 51), rinse the shells and set aside.

Heat the butter in a small saucepan, add the shallot and cook gently for 5 minutes until the shallot is soft but not brown. Place the crab meat in a small mixing basin, add the brandy and work to a fine paste with a wooden spoon. Stir in the sautéed shallot, cream, half the breadcrumbs and half the cheese. Add the French mustard, anchovy essence, Worcestershire sauce, cayenne pepper and salt and pepper to taste.

Pack the mixture into the reserved crab shells and sprinkle with the remaining cheese and breadcrumbs. Place on a baking tray, put in the centre of a hot oven (400°F., 200°C., Gas Mark 6) and cook for 5–10 minutes to heat through before serving.

Advance preparation: Prepare the mixture and pack into the shells or dishes. Keep chilled. Reheat when ready to serve. If necessary, allow a little extra time to heat through.

Baked avocado and crab

Avocados served hot are unusually good. Choose a hard cheese for the topping – Parmesan or Gruyère are both ideal.

Serves 6

3 ripe avocado pears	pinch mixed herbs
½ lemon	lemon juice to taste
for the filling:	*for the topping:*
1 oz./25 g. butter	1 oz./25 g. butter
1 level tablespoon flour	2 heaped tablespoons fresh white breadcrumbs
⅓ pint/2–2½ dl. milk	1 tablespoon grated cheese
salt and freshly milled pepper	
8 oz./225 g. fresh or frozen white crab meat	

Halve the avocados and remove the stone. Rub the flesh with the cut side of a lemon and set aside while preparing the filling.

Melt the butter in a saucepan and stir in the flour. Simmer for 1 minute over low heat, then gradually stir in the milk. Beat well to get a smooth sauce and bring up to the boil. Simmer for a few moments, then season well with salt and pepper and draw off the heat. Stir in the crab meat, pinch herbs and lemon juice to taste. Fill the avocado halves and shape into a dome.

Melt the butter for the topping over low heat and, using a fork, stir in the breadcrumbs and then add the cheese. Sprinkle the topping over the avocados. Put the avocados in a buttered baking dish, place in a moderately hot oven (350°F., 180°C., Gas Mark 4) and bake for 15 minutes. Serve hot.

Advance preparation: Prepare crab filling and the buttered crumbs for the topping. When ready to heat through, cut open avocados, fill and top with crumbs. Bake and serve.

Grapefruit with prawns

A pleasant light starter to serve. If the grapefruits are on the small side, add a few drained, canned grapefruit segments.

Serves 6

3 grapefruit	1 (¼ pint/1½ dl.) carton soured cream
8 oz./225 g. prepared prawns	
3–4 crisp lettuce leaves	*to garnish:*
for the dressing:	paprika
4 rounded tablespoons mayonnaise	

Cut each grapefruit in half across the centre and loosen the segments. Remove the segments from each grapefruit half and put into a basin. Strain the grapefruit pieces away from the juice. Use the juice for another purpose and mix the grapefruit segments with the prawns. Chill well.

Remove the white pith from the inside of the grapefruit shells. Snip round the edges of each one with scissors to make a decorative edge. Set the shells aside for serving. Wash and shred the lettuce and keep fresh with a sprinkling of water, cover in the refrigerator.

When ready to serve, mix together the mayonnaise and soured cream. Place a little shredded lettuce in each grapefruit shell. Toss the grapefruit and prawns in the mayonnaise dressing and pile the mixture into each serving shell.

Sprinkle with paprika and serve with thinly sliced brown bread and butter.

Advance preparation: Prepare the grapefruit shells and the filling. Keep chilled, then assemble when ready to serve.

Skate with caper sauce

Skate is always served very simply. Rarely is it cooked at home by any other method than poaching.

Serves 4

about 2 lb./1 kg. wing of skate	*for the caper sauce:*
½ pint/3 dl. water	2 oz./50 g. butter
½ lemon, sliced	juice ½ lemon
1 small bay leaf	1 tablespoon capers
2 peppercorns	1 tablespoon finely chopped
1 small onion	parsley
¼ level teaspoon salt	

Rinse the skate, cut into suitable sized pieces and place in a saucepan with the water, lemon slices, bay leaf, peppercorns, onion slices and salt. Bring slowly just up to the boil, then cover with a lid and poach very gently for 15–20 minutes. Drain the fish from the liquid and arrange on a warm serving dish.

Place the butter for the sauce into a saucepan. Heat until melted and beginning to brown. Add the lemon juice, capers and parsley. Pour over the fish and serve.

Advance preparation: Rinse and cut up the skate but cook when ready to serve.

Crab quiche

Most shellfish, particularly crab, prawns or lobster, make a delicious quiche. Serve for lunch or supper; shellfish quiche is particularly delicious for a buffet supper party.

Serves 4–6

4 oz./100 g. quiche pastry	¼ pint/1½ dl. single cream
(page 13)	salt and freshly milled pepper
for the filling:	1–2 oz./25–50 g. hard cheese,
6 oz./175 g. crab meat	grated
2 eggs	

On a lightly floured working surface, roll out the pastry to a circle large enough to line an 8-inch (20-cm.) quiche tin. Line the tin and trim the edges. Sprinkle the crab meat for the filling over the base of the quiche and set aside.

Whisk together the eggs and cream and season well with salt and pepper. Strain over the crab filling and sprinkle the quiche with the cheese. Place above centre in a moderately hot oven (375°F., 190°C., Gas Mark 5) and bake for 40 minutes.

Serve warm with salad.

Advance preparation: Make up quiche and bake as directed. Reheat in a moderate oven (350°F., 180°C., Gas Mark 4) for 10 minutes when ready to serve. Two or more of these are excellent for a supper party and can be reheated together.

Dressed crab

Prepare dressed crab and serve for a summer lunch or take on a picnic. Delicious with lettuce and fresh tomatoes.

Serves 3–4

1 medium sized cock crab	mayonnaise
(2–2½ lb./1–1¼ kg.)	1 hard-boiled egg
seasoning to taste	chopped parsley
lemon juice or vinegar	*to garnish:*
fresh white breadcrumbs	lettuce and tomato wedges

Wipe the crab with a damp cloth. Place on its back with the tail facing towards you and remove the claws and legs by twisting in towards the body with a circular motion. To separate the body from the shell – place the fingers on the shell and the thumbs under the tail flap and push upwards until the body breaks away from the shell. The fishmonger will do this on request. Reverse the shell so that the head is facing you. With the thumbs, press on the mouth downwards and forwards so that the mouth and stomach bag come away all in one piece. Discard these.

With the handle of a plastic spoon, ease round the inside of the shell to loosen the soft brown meat. Turn all this meat into a mixing basin, leaving the shell clean. Using the handle of a knife, tap sharply over the false line around the shell cavity. Press down and it will neatly come away. Scrub and dry the shell and oil lightly.

From the body of the crab, remove the 'dead men's fingers' and tail flap and discard. Remove the brown meat and add to the basin. Scoop out of the leg sockets as much white meat as possible and put this meat in a second basin. Remove the meat from the large claws by twisting off the first part of the joint and scooping out the meat. Then tap sharply round the broadest part of the claw until the shell cracks apart. Empty both into the white meat basin.

Mash the brown meat with seasonings of salt, pepper, lemon juice or vinegar to taste and, if liked, add enough fine white breadcrumbs to stiffen the texture. Pile the brown meat into either side of the shell. Flake the white meat, moisten with a little mayonnaise and arrange in the centre between the dark meat. Garnish with sieved yolk of hard-boiled egg, chopped white of egg and chopped parsley. Stand the shell on a 'bracelet' made by joining the legs into a circle. This will hold the shell steady and make serving easier. Garnish with the lettuce and tomato wedges.

Advance preparation: Prepare the dressed crab several hours in advance of serving and chill until required.

Tarte aux pommes (page 13)

Line a tart tin with pastry and prick the surface with a fork.
Peel, core and cut the apples into chunks, reserving the peelings
and cores to make apple juice. Place the apple pieces, sugar,
butter, water, lemon juice and cloves in a saucepan and heat
to simmering.
Arrange thinly sliced dessert apples over the surface of the tart.
Dredge the surface of the tart with icing sugar and pass the tart
under a hot grill to caramelise the edges of the apple slices.

Scampi provencale

The term provençale always implies the use of garlic and tomatoes among other ingredients in a recipe. In most recipes where tomatoes are used, a little sugar is added to counteract their slightly acid flavour.

Serves 4

1 lb./½ kg. prepared scampi	salt and freshly milled pepper
1 onion	1 level teaspoon castor sugar
1 clove garlic	1 rounded teaspoon cornflour
2 tablespoons oil	1 tablespoon water
1 (15 oz./425 g.) can tomatoes	chopped parsley
3 tablespoons white wine	

Rinse the scampi and pat dry or allow frozen scampi to thaw. Peel and chop the onion and garlic. Heat the oil in a saucepan, add the onion and fry gently for about 5 minutes until soft but not brown. Stir in the garlic and scampi and sauté for 1–2 minutes. The scampi flesh will firm up. Add the tomatoes, wine and a seasoning of salt and pepper and the sugar. Bring up to the boil and simmer for about 5–6 minutes.

Blend the cornflour with the water and stir into the sauce. Cook for a further few minutes, stirring all the time until the sauce has thickened and is boiling. Draw the pan off the heat, check seasoning and add the parsley.

Serve with plain boiled rice.

Advance preparation: Assemble and prepare ingredients but do not cook until ready to serve.

Trout with tarragon

Illustrated in colour on page 64

Tarragon adds a delicious flavour to this recipe for trout. Choose a heavy lidded frying pan for cooking the fish.

Serves 4

4 fresh trout	½ lemon, thinly sliced
4–5 tablespoons water	salt and freshly milled pepper
1 wine glass dry white wine	fresh parsley and tarragon
1 tablespoon finely chopped onion	½ pint/3 dl. single cream

Clean the trout or ask the fishmonger to do this, but leave on the heads. Rinse the trout, handling them carefully and place in a large shallow pan. Add the water and wine. Sprinkle with the onion, add the thinly sliced lemon and a good seasoning of salt and pepper.

Wash the parsley and tarragon, select curly tops from the parsley and strip leaves from the tarragon. Using a sharp kitchen knife, chop both parsley and tarragon together finely. Sprinkle about half of the mixture over the fish.

Bring the contents of the pan just to the boil, then lower the heat and poach the fish gently for 10–15 minutes. Do not turn the fish over, but cover with a lid while cooking.

When cooked, lift the fish gently from the pan on to a large, hot serving dish. Raise the heat and continue to cook the fish liquor quickly, to reduce it to about half in quantity. Stir in the cream and reheat until hot and almost boiling. Strain over the trout, sprinkle with remaining chopped parsley and tarragon before serving.

Advance preparation: Assemble ingredients but do not cook until ready to serve.

Scampi in curry sauce

This is a delicious way of serving scampi – keep the recipe for a special occasion. Use a 1-lb. (½-kg.) packet of frozen scampi and allow to thaw slowly in the unopened packet. Drain away the watery liquid before using the scampi.

Serves 4

2 small onions	1 tablespoon sweet chutney or apricot jam
1 tablespoon olive oil	juice ½ lemon
1 level tablespoon curry powder	1 oz./25 g. butter
1 level tablespoon flour	1 lb./½ kg. prepared scampi
¼ pint/1½ dl. stock or water	1–2 tablespoons double cream
1 rounded teaspoon tomato purée	

Peel and finely chop one of the onions. Heat the oil in a saucepan, add the onion and fry gently for about 5 minutes. Keep the pan covered so that the onion becomes tender but not brown. Stir in the curry powder and fry gently for a few moments to draw out the flavour. Stir in the flour. Gradually add the stock or water and stir until the mixture comes to the boil. Add the tomato purée, chutney or jam and the lemon juice. Simmer for about 5 minutes, then draw off the heat and strain the sauce.

Peel the remaining onion and chop finely. Heat the butter in a frying pan and add the onion. Fry gently to soften the onion, then add the prepared scampi. Toss the scampi in the hot butter and fry gently for a few moments. When ready, the scampi flesh will firm up and become whiter looking in colour – takes only a few minutes. Add the strained curry sauce, stir to blend with the scampi and bring up to the boil. Simmer for a few moments, then draw off the heat. Stir in the cream and serve with hot, plain boiled rice.

Advance preparation: Prepare the curry part of the sauce in advance and keep ready to use. After this the recipe is very quick to cook and should be finished when ready to serve.

Sautéed trout with bacon

Trout and bacon together provide a wonderful combination of flavours that is not nearly widely enough appreciated.

Serves 4

4 trout	1½–2 oz./40–50 g. butter
seasoned flour	4–8 bacon rashers

Clean and gut the trout. Roll in seasoned flour and add to the hot butter melted in a frying pan. Fry gently for 3–4 minutes on each side. After turning the fish, add the trimmed bacon rashers and cook these for 3 minutes each side. If there is insufficient room in the frying pan, the bacon may be grilled.

Serve with the butter from the pan.

Advance preparation: Assemble the ingredients. Fry and cook when ready to serve.

Flake the salmon and place in the pastry case. Melt the butter in a saucepan and add the onion. Cover and fry gently for a few minutes until the onion is tender but not browned. Drain the onion and sprinkle over the salmon. Mix together the eggs and cream and season with salt and pepper. Pour over the salmon to fill the quiche. Place in the centre of a hot oven (375°F., 190°C., Gas Mark 5) and bake for 45 minutes or until the filling has set.

Serve warm with a tossed salad.

Advance preparation: Prepare and bake the quiche as directed above. Reheat in a moderate oven (350°F., 180°C., Gas Mark 4) when ready to serve.

Rollmops

Herrings prepared in this manner should be allowed to cool in the cooking liquor overnight. They can be prepared up to 24 hours in advance. Prepare as many at one time as will be required. For the first course, serve one per person with a little brown bread and butter. For a main dish, serve 1½–2 per person with a salad.

Serves 4

4 herrings	1 bay leaf
salt and freshly milled pepper	*to garnish:*
4 tablespoons malt vinegar	lettuce leaves and lemon wedges
¼ pint/1½ dl. water	

Wash the herrings under cold water and scrape away any loose scales with a knife. Leave the fin on the back of each herring and trim off the others with scissors. Cut off the head and tail. Slit the herrings lengthwise and remove the roes. Place each herring, in turn, cut side down on a working surface and press sharply along the backbone to loosen. Turn the fish over and carefully pull away the bone. Rinse well under cold water.

Sprinkle a seasoning of salt and pepper inside each fillet. Then roll up starting at the tail end. Pack closely together in a baking or pie dish. When rolled, the fin left on the back opens out and looks attractive. The herrings should be packed with the end of each fillet underneath and the fin facing upwards. Mix the vinegar and water and pour over the herrings, the liquid should just cover the herrings. Add the bay leaf.

Cover with a lid or buttered paper and place in the centre of a moderate oven (350°F., 180°C., Gas Mark 4) and bake for 45 minutes. Remove from the heat and allow to cool in the liquid.

Drain and serve with a crisp, washed lettuce leaf and a lemon wedge for garnish.

Advance preparation: Prepare and bake these as directed above a day in advance. They will keep in the refrigerator for 1–2 days.

Salmon quiche

Use any left over cooked salmon to make this delicious quiche. Really delicious for a picnic, or for a summer lunch or supper with salad.

Serves 4

4 oz./100 g. quiche pastry (page 13)	½ oz./15 g. butter
for the filling:	1 small onion, peeled and sliced
8 oz./225 g. cooked salmon, flaked	3 eggs
	½ pint/3 dl. single cream
	salt and freshly milled pepper

Roll the pastry out on a floured working surface to a large enough circle to line an 8-inch (20-cm.) quiche tin, or flan ring set on a baking tray. Line the tin with the pastry and trim the edges neatly.

OVERLEAF **Mushroom soufflé omelette (page 36)**
Heat the butter in a pan and add the sliced mushrooms. Fry gently then sprinkle over the herbs and flour.
Stir in the milk and bring to the boil.
Pour the whisked egg mixture into an omelette pan containing melted butter.
Spoon the mushroom sauce over the omelette.

Old fashioned fish pie

Use smoked fish or a mixture of smoked and fresh fish to vary this recipe.

Serves 4

1 lb./½ kg. haddock or cod fillet	salt and pepper
½ pint/3 dl. milk (see recipe)	1 lb./½ kg. potatoes
1–2 hard-boiled eggs	melted butter (see recipe)
1 oz./25 g. butter	1 tablespoon grated Parmesan
1 oz./25 g. flour	cheese

Place the fish in a greased pie dish, add about half the milk and cover with greased paper or a lid. Bake in the centre of a moderately hot oven (375°F., 190°C., Gas Mark 5) for 10–15 minutes. Strain and, reserving the milk in which the fish has been cooked, make up to ½ pint (3 dl.) with remaining milk. Bone and flake the fish and place in a well buttered 1½-pint (1-litre) pie dish along with the sliced hard-boiled eggs.

In a saucepan, melt the butter and stir in the flour. Cook over a low heat for 1–2 minutes but do not allow to brown. Gradually add the milk and season well with salt and pepper. Stir the sauce continuously until smooth, thickened and boiling. Pour over the fish and tap the dish gently so that the sauce coats all the fish through to the bottom.

Boil, then mash the potatoes, season with salt and pepper and beat until smooth with a nob of butter and a little milk. Spoon over the fish, spread evenly then rough up with a fork. Brush with a little melted butter and sprinkle with the Parmesan cheese.

Place high up at the top of a hot oven (400°F., 200°C., Gas Mark 6) until well heated and the top is golden brown and crisp – takes about 20 minutes.

Advance preparation: Prepare the fish sauce, top with potato, brush with butter and sprinkle with cheese several hours in advance. Keep chilled. Reheat when required for serving, if necessary allowing a little extra time to heat through.

Salmon mousse

Use canned salmon or tuna fish for this recipe. The mousse is delightful served for a light lunch with a tossed salad and crusty French bread and butter.

Serves 4–6

¼ pint/1½ dl. water	pinch paprika pepper
½ oz./15 g. powdered gelatine	1 teaspoon Worcestershire sauce
¼ pint/1½ dl. stock (use water	1 teaspoon onion juice
and ¼ chicken stock cube)	(see recipe)
¼ pint/1½ dl. mayonnaise	1 (16 oz./450 g.) can salmon
2 tablespoons lemon juice	¼ pint/1½ dl. double cream
salt and freshly milled pepper	

Measure the water into a small saucepan, sprinkle in the gelatine and set aside to soak for 5 minutes. Place over a low heat and stir until the gelatine has dissolved and the mixture is clear. Draw the pan off the heat and stir in the stock. Set aside to cool until just warm.

Measure the mayonnaise, lemon juice, seasoning of salt and pepper, paprika and Worcestershire sauce into a mixing bowl. Add the onion juice – for this finely grate a small onion on to a saucer and scoop out the juice, using a teaspoon. Strain in the warm gelatine mixture and blend ingredients well. Drain the salmon from the can, discard any skin and bone. Flake and mash the flesh with a fork. Fold the salmon flesh into the mixture, adding the lightly whipped cream. Pour into a 1½-pint (1-litre) wetted mould. Chill until set firm.

To unmould, loosen the edges of the mixture with the tip of a knife. Dip the mould into water, hot as the hand can bear, for 1 minute then invert on to a plate and serve.

Advance preparation: Make the mousse up to 24 hours before serving for the best flavour. If chilled in the refrigerator, take out at least 1 hour before serving.

Sole Veronique

Ask the fishmonger to remove the dark and light coloured skin from both the sole. He will then fillet the fish for you. Bring home the skin and bones for the fish stock.

Serves 4

2 (1¼ lb./generous ½ kg.) sole	¼ pint/1½ dl. dry white wine
salt and freshly milled pepper	4 oz./100 g. green grapes
1½ oz./40 g. butter	1 level tablespoon flour
1 shallot	¼ pint/1½ dl. double cream
squeeze lemon juice	
¼ pint/1½ dl. fish stock	
(see recipe)	

Season the fillets of sole and fold each one in half. Select a frying pan with a lid for poaching the fish. Using a good ½ oz. (15 g.) of the butter, well grease the pan. Peel and finely chop the shallot and sprinkle in the pan. Arrange the sole in the buttered pan, sprinkle with lemon juice and season again with salt and pepper. Cover and set aside while making the fish stock.

Place the fish bones and skin in a saucepan. Add water to cover, a seasoning of salt and pepper and a squeeze of lemon juice. Bring to the boil and simmer gently for 20–30 minutes. Then strain, measure out ¼ pint (1½ dl.) and reserve.

Add the white wine and fish stock to the sole fillets. Cover with a buttered paper and the pan lid. Poach the fish gently for about 10 minutes or until the fish is tender – it should feel firm and look white. Draw the pan off the heat, and lift the fish out on to a hot serving dish. Halve and deseed the grapes and arrange at either end of the dish. Keep hot in the oven.

Strain the fish liquor into a saucepan. Reduce the liquor in the pan by about half by rapid boiling. Meanwhile, blend the remaining butter with the flour to make a *beurre manie*. Draw the reduced liquor off the heat and stir in the cream. Add the 'beurre manie' in pieces and stir until melted. Replace over the heat and bring up to the boil, stirring continuously to get a smooth sauce. Check seasoning. Pour over the sole fillets and serve.

Advance preparation: Cook the fish and prepare the sauce. Pour over the fish several hours in advance. Keep chilled. When ready to serve, heat through in a moderate oven (350°F., 180°C., Gas Mark 4) for about 15 minutes. Then serve.

Baked herrings with mustard butter

Herrings are rich and the spicy, sharp flavour of mustard goes well with them. This is a very clean and easy way of cooking them.

Serves 4

4 fresh herrings
3 oz./75 g. butter
2 level teaspoons made mustard

squeeze lemon juice
salt and freshly milled pepper

Cut away the heads and tails from the herrings and slit along the belly of each. Turn over on to a clean working surface and press firmly down the backbone to loosen it from the flesh. Turn the fish over and, beginning from the tail end, lift the backbone away from the herring flesh.

Cream the butter until quite soft and then beat in the mustard, a little lemon juice and a seasoning of salt and pepper. Spread this mixture over the inside of each herring and fold closed. Wrap each herring in a square of buttered foil to make a parcel. Place in the centre of a moderately hot oven (375°F., 190°C., Gas Mark 5) and bake for 25–30 minutes. Serve with the juices from the parcel.

Advance preparation: Prepare and bone herring and make the mustard butter in advance. Spread the mustard inside the herrings, cover and chill for a few hours in advance. Wrap and bake when ready to serve.

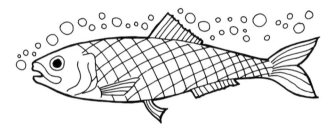

Devilled soft roes

Soft herring roes are a great delicacy. Take care, when handling, not to break the very thin membrane surrounding them or they will lose their shape.

Serves 4

¾–1 lb./350–450 g. soft herring
  roes
1 level tablespoon flour
1 level teaspoon curry powder
salt and freshly milled pepper
2 oz./50 g. butter

dash Worcestershire sauce
dash vinegar
4 slices hot buttered toast
to garnish:
paprika and parsley

Separate the herring roes, rinse and carefully pull away the 'thread'. Mix together the flour, curry powder and a seasoning of salt and pepper. Dip the roes in the flour to coat them. Add to the hot butter, melted in a frying pan, and fry gently for about 3–5 minutes. Turn to brown them evenly. Add a dash of Worcestershire sauce and a little vinegar. Cook for a further moment; the roes should be just set but not crisp. Serve on hot buttered toast. Garnish with paprika and a sprig of parsley and serve.

Advance preparation: Assemble the ingredients, but cook only when ready to serve.

Baked halibut in cider with tomatoes

Halibut is a fish with a fine, delicate flavour and a firm flesh. Ask the fishmonger to cut two whole steaks across the halibut and then cut each one in half to make four pieces.

Serves 4

4 (about 1½ lb./¾ kg.) halibut
  cutlets
salt and freshly milled pepper
1 lemon
1 tablespoon cooking oil

1 onion
1 clove garlic
½ pint/3 dl. dry cider
8 oz./225 g. tomatoes
1 tablespoon chopped parsley

Arrange the halibut pieces closely together in a buttered, large shallow baking dish. Sprinkle with salt, freshly milled pepper and the juice of ½ lemon. Slice the remainder of the lemon and arrange these over the top.

Heat the oil in a small saucepan, add the finely chopped onion and sauté gently until softened – about 5 minutes. Add the chopped garlic, crushed with salt – remove any outer papery coating before chopping, and sauté for a further few moments. Draw the pan off the heat and stir in the cider. Pour this over the fish. Arrange the tomatoes, cut in slices, over the top and sprinkle with the chopped parsley. Cover with a buttered paper and place in the centre of a moderate oven (350°F., 180°C., Gas Mark 4) and bake for 45 minutes.

Advance preparation: Assemble the ingredients but do not prepare the recipe until ready to cook and serve.

Lobster mornay

Any recipe using lobster is expensive. Serve this recipe for a special occasion with a tossed salad.

Serves 4

2 cooked lobsters (about 1½ lb./
  ¾ kg. each)
1 oz./25 g. butter
1 oz./25 g. flour
½ pint/3 dl. milk

salt and freshly milled pepper
4 oz./100 g. Gruyère cheese,
  grated
2–3 tablespoons cream
2 tablespoons sherry

Split each lobster open down the back and remove the flesh from both the body and the claws. Cut up the flesh coarsely and set aside ready for use. Wipe the shells clean and reserve.

Melt the butter in a saucepan and stir in the flour. Cook gently for a few minutes, then gradually stir in the milk, beating well all the time to get a smooth sauce. Bring up to the boil stirring all the time, then simmer for 2–3 minutes. Season with salt and freshly milled pepper and stir in half the cheese. Add the cream, sherry and reserved lobster meat and heat through gently for about 3–4 minutes.

Divide the mixture equally and pile into the reserved lobster shells. Sprinkle with the remaining cheese and place under a hot grill to brown.

Serve at once.

Advance preparation: Prepare the ingredients, but do not assemble and cook the recipe until ready to serve.

Kidneys with Béarnaise sauce (page 77)

Remove the core and skin from the kidneys and slice into each kidney on the rounded side, cutting almost through.
Open out the kidneys and skewer in pairs. Brush the kidneys with oil.
Chop tarragon leaves and shallot for the Béarnaise sauce.
Whisk the egg mixture for the sauce until thick and light, then add the melted butter, lemon juice and chopped parsley.
Spoon Béarnaise sauce into the centre of each kidney.

Halibut with lemon sauce

Halibut is an expensive fish and one to choose for a special occasion. The delicate flavour of the fish goes well with the lemon sauce and it looks pretty too.

Serves 4

4 halibut steaks (about 6 oz./ 175 g. each)	1 oz./25 g. flour
¼ pint/1½ dl. water	½ pint/3 dl. mixed milk and fish liquor
pinch salt	salt and pepper
½ small onion	juice 1 small or ½ large lemon
½ lemon, cut in slices	1 egg yolk
1 small bay leaf	2 tablespoons single cream
few parsley stalks	*to garnish:*
2 peppercorns	chopped parsley
for the lemon sauce:	
1 oz./25 g. butter	

Place the halibut steaks in a buttered baking dish. Measure the water into a saucepan and add the salt, sliced onion, lemon slices, bay leaf, parsley stalks and peppercorns. Bring up to the boil, cover with a lid and simmer for 5 minutes. Strain the liquor over the fish.

Cover the dish with a buttered paper and place in the centre of a moderate oven (350°F., 180°C., Gas Mark 4) and bake for 40–45 minutes. When ready, the fish flesh will look white and flake away from the bone. Strain the cooking liquor away from the halibut steaks. Discard all pieces of lemon, onion and parsley stalks. Make the liquor up to ½ pint (3 dl.) with milk for the sauce. Keep the fish warm.

Melt the butter in a small saucepan over a low heat. Stir in the flour and cook for 1 minute. Gradually stir in the mixed milk and fish cooking liquor. Beat well all the time to get a smooth sauce and bring up to the boil. Season well with salt and freshly milled pepper and stir in the lemon juice. Simmer for 1–2 minutes. Blend together the egg yolk and cream, stir into the sauce and draw off the heat. Recheck the seasonings and sharpness of sauce, add a little more lemon juice if liked. Pour over the halibut steaks.

Sprinkle with chopped parsley and serve.

Fish creole

This recipe has a spicy flavour and a delicious crunchy cheese topping. The fish used can be cod, haddock, hake, halibut or 4 large plaice fillets.

Serves 4

1½ lb./700 g. cod fillet	pinch dried oregano
1 oz./25 g. butter	*for the topping:*
1 onion	1 oz./25 g. butter
1 clove garlic	2 tablespoons fresh white breadcrumbs
1 lb./½ kg. tomatoes	1 oz./25 g. Parmesan cheese
1 green sweet pepper	
salt and pepper	

Rinse the fish fillets and skin them. If plaice fillets are used fold them in halves. Arrange the fish in a well buttered fireproof dish.

Melt the butter. Peel and chop the onion, crush and chop the garlic. Add these to the hot butter and sauté gently until soft but not brown. Meanwhile plunge the tomatoes into boiling water for 1 minute. Drain and peel away the skins. Halve, then remove the inner seeds and chop the tomato flesh coarsely. Halve, deseed and shred the green pepper. Add the tomato and green pepper to the saucepan along with a seasoning of salt and pepper and the oregano. Cover and cook gently for about 5–10 minutes. Pour the vegetable mixture over the fish.

Melt the butter for the topping in a saucepan and draw off the heat. Add the breadcrumbs and toss, using a fork, until the crumbs are buttery. Add the grated cheese and sprinkle this mixture on top of the vegetables. Place in the centre of a hot oven (400°F., 200°C., Gas Mark 6) and bake for 30 minutes or until the fish is tender and the topping crisp and brown.

Advance preparation: Prepare vegetables and buttered crumbs for the topping. Assemble the recipe and cook when required.

Poached salmon with cucumber sauce

Cutlets or steaks of salmon are often grilled but can also be poached. Choose a shallow ovenproof dish, large enough for the salmon cutlets to lie flat.

Serves 4

4 salmon cutlets	1 oz./25 g. butter
1 pint/6 dl. water	1 oz./25 g. flour
1 level teaspoon salt	½ pint/3 dl. milk
½ small onion, thinly sliced	salt and freshly milled pepper
juice ½ lemon	lemon juice
few parsley stalks	2–3 tablespoons single cream
for the cucumber sauce:	
½ cucumber	

Place the salmon cutlets in a well buttered, shallow baking dish. Measure the water, salt, onion slices, lemon juice and parsley stalks into a saucepan. Bring up to the boil and simmer for 5 minutes. Strain over the salmon cutlets in the dish; this *court bouillon* should just cover the fish.

Place in the centre of a moderate oven (350°F., 180°C., Gas Mark 4) and cook gently for 15–20 minutes. To test for readiness, press the centre of the cutlets near the bone. The flesh should feel firm and flake slightly.

Meanwhile, prepare the sauce. Peel and slice the cucumber in half lengthwise. Remove the centre seeds and chop up the flesh coarsely. Melt the butter in a saucepan and add the cucumber pieces. Cover with a lid and cook over low heat for about 5 minutes until the cucumber is soft.

Sprinkle in the flour and stir to mix, then gradually stir in the milk. Bring up to the boil, stirring all the time. Season well with salt and pepper, then lower the heat and simmer gently for 2–3 minutes. When ready to serve, draw the pan off the heat and add lemon juice to taste. Check seasoning and stir in the cream or extra milk to make a fairly thin sauce.

Lift the cooked salmon carefully from the baking dish and drain each slice well. Arrange in a hot serving dish and coat with the hot cucumber sauce.

Advance preparation: Prepare the sauce in advance but do not stir in the lemon juice or cream. Cover with buttered paper to prevent a skin forming. When ready to serve, put the salmon cutlets to cook. Reheat the sauce, stir in the lemon juice and cream and serve.

Fresh lobster

Once prepared and ready to serve, the empty head of each lobster half can be filled with a little Russian salad or a few sprigs of fresh parsley to make an attractive presentation. Lobster picks should be provided to get the flesh out of the claws.

Serves 4

2 cooked lobsters (about 1½ lb./¾ kg.) each	cucumber and parsley sprigs mayonnaise for serving

Each lobster must be split in half, allowing one half per person. Put each lobster in turn on a chopping board, with the open side of the shell downwards. Press flat along the board and, using a large sharp knife, press the tip of the knife into the centre of the head – be guided by the natural line which runs along the centre of the head. Pressing the knife hard down, first cut right down the centre of the back, dividing the lobster equally in two. Then turn the lobster round and cut the head completely in half. Separate the two halves and repeat the procedure with the second lobster. Give the claws a quick twist so that they come away from the body.

Lift out the tail flesh from the lobster half. Remove the vent, found running down the back of the flesh. Remove the stomach bag, found in the head of the lobster. Wash out the shells. Replace the tail flesh in the shell. Crack the claws so that they can be easily opened, but do not remove the flesh from the claws.

Arrange each lobster half on a serving plate and garnish with thinly sliced cucumber. Place a sprig of parsley in the head. Serve with mayonnaise – green mayonnaise is particularly good with fresh lobster – and with thinly sliced brown bread and butter.

Advance preparation: Keep lobster in a cool place. Split and prepare when ready to serve.

Salmon salad

If you have no fish kettle with a perforated tray to hold the fish, use a deep baking tin and tie the fish in muslin to support it when lifting out after cooking.

Serves 6–8

tail end of salmon (about 2½–3 lb./1¼–1½ kg.)	1 level teaspoon salt
lettuce, tomato, asparagus and hard-boiled egg to garnish	1 carrot
to poach the fish:	½ onion, stuck with a clove
¼ pint/1½ dl. dry white wine or cider	1 small bay leaf

Rinse the salmon in cold water and scrape off the scales, working from the tail end towards the head, using the back of a knife.

Measure the dry white wine or cider into the fish kettle. Add the salt, scraped carrot, onion and bay leaf. Place in the fish and add sufficient water to cover. Bring just to boiling point. Lower the heat so that the water is just simmering. Cover with a lid or foil and cook very gently for 15 minutes. Draw off the heat and *leave the fish to cool in the liquor.*

Carefully lift the fish out of the pan. Gently peel away the skin. Serve on a bed of lettuce and surround with slices of tomato, asparagus tips and slices of hard-boiled egg.

Serve with mayonnaise.

Advance preparation: Cook the salmon and leave to cool overnight in the liquor. This way the flesh remains moist and tender. Assemble the salad shortly before serving.

Cod's roe à la meunière

Cod's roe can be bought already boiled and it is then ready to slice and fry. Otherwise cook fresh cod's roe following the method here.

Serves 4

1 lb./450 g. fresh cod roe	2–3 oz./50–75 g. butter
1 lemon	chopped parsley
1 teaspoon salt	lemon wedges
seasoned flour	

Roll the fresh cod roe not too tightly in a piece of muslin. Secure the loose ends with string. Put the wrapped roe in a large pan and cover with cold water. Add a slice cut off the end of the lemon and the salt. Bring slowly to the boil and simmer for about 45–50 minutes. Draw the pan off the heat and leave the roe to cool in the liquid.

Next day (or when roe is cold) slice the roe into rounds about ½ inch (1 cm.) thick. Coat lightly in seasoned flour. Heat the butter in a frying pan until it froths but without allowing it to brown. Put in the slices of roe and fry gently for a few minutes each side until brown.

Lift the roe from the pan on to a hot serving dish. Increase the heat under the pan until the butter browns lightly. Add a good squeeze of lemon juice. Pour over the roes and scatter with chopped parsley.

Serve with lemon wedges or tartare sauce.

Advanced preparation: Cook cod roe in advance. Flour roe slices ready for frying and chill. Fry when required.

Trout with tarragon (page 54)

Clean the trout, leaving on the head.
Strip leaves from the tarragon sprigs and chop finely.
Poach the trout gently in the cooking liquor.
Remove the fish to a hot serving dish. Stir cream into the
reduced cooking liquor. Reheat and strain over the trout.

Sauces for fish

White sauce

The liquid for mixing a white sauce can be made up of some of the milk used for poaching or baking the fish at an earlier stage. This gives the sauce extra flavour.

Makes ½ pint (3 dl.) sauce

1 oz./25 g. butter	½ pint/3 dl. milk (see recipe)
1 oz./25 g. flour	salt and freshly milled pepper

Melt the butter in a heavy saucepan over a gentle heat. Stir in the flour and cook gently for a minute until the mixture lightens in colour. Remove from the heat. Cool for a moment, then gradually stir in the milk. If using part hot liquid from poaching fish and part cold to make up the amount, always stir in the hot liquid first – this blends in more smoothly and quickly. Stir in the cold liquid afterwards.

When all the liquid is added, return the pan to the heat. Bring up to the boil, stirring all the time, and cook gently for 2–3 minutes.

Season with salt and pepper to taste and the sauce is ready.

Parsley sauce: Stir in 2–3 heaped tablespoons finely chopped parsley and a squeeze of lemon juice into the cooked sauce.

Cheese sauce: Stir 2–3 oz. (50–75 g.) grated cheese into the cooked sauce. Stir over the heat for 1–2 minutes until the cheese has melted. Add a small pinch of mustard for extra flavour.

Shrimp sauce: Stir about 2 oz. (50 g.) shrimps into the cooked sauce. Add 1 teaspoon lemon juice and 1 teaspoon anchovy essence to taste.

Mornay sauce: Prepare a cheese sauce as suggested and, just before serving, stir in 1 egg yolk mixed with 2 tablespoons cream. Serve at once.

Hollandaise sauce

Make sure the butter used for this sauce is not cold from the refrigerator. Using this method, the sauce can be kept hot for a short while before serving.

Serves 4

juice ½ lemon	4 oz./100 g. butter
1 teaspoon water	salt and freshly milled pepper
2 egg yolks	

Put the lemon juice and water into a small basin and place over a saucepan of hot water. Add the egg yolks and ½ oz. (15 g.) butter. Whisk until the marks of the whisk show. Remove from the heat and whisk in the remainder of the butter in small pieces. Check seasoning and serve.

Advance preparation: Hollandaise sauce does not suit being made in advance. Using this method, leave the sauce to stand over the pan of hot water, *drawn off the heat*, for a short while before serving.

Flavoured butters

Flavoured butters are always served with grilled or fried foods. Prepare the butter and shape well in advance of serving, so that it chills well and will slice easily.

Parsley butter

2 oz./50 g. butter	2 teaspoons lemon juice
2 teaspoons finely chopped parsley	salt and pepper

Cream the butter with the parsley and lemon juice. Season well. Spoon into a square of greaseproof paper or foil and form into a long roll about ½ inch (1 cm.) thick. Twist the ends like a cracker. Chill well.

Cut into thick slices and serve.

Mustard butter

2 oz./50 g. butter	1 teaspoon lemon juice
1 tablespoon French mustard	

Beat the butter, mustard and lemon juice together. Spoon into a square of greaseproof paper or foil and form into a long roll about ½ inch (1 cm.) thick. Twist the ends like a cracker. Chill well.

Cut into slices for serving.

Anchovy butter

4 anchovies	freshly milled pepper
2 oz./50 g. butter	

Soak the anchovy fillets. Drain and pound to a purée. Beat into the butter with a seasoning of pepper. Spoon into a square of greaseproof paper or foil and shape into a roll about ½ inch (1 cm.) thick. Twist the ends like a cracker. Chill well.

Cut into slices for serving.

Tomato butter

2 oz./50 g. butter	1 teaspoon tomato purée

Blend the butter and tomato purée. Spoon into a square of greaseproof paper or foil and form into a long roll about ½ inch (1 cm.) thick. Twist the ends like a cracker. Chill well.

Cut into slices for serving.

Savoury garnishes

Illustrated in colour on page 48

Parsley

Choose bright green parsley with tight leaves. Nip the curly heads off the stalks, wash and shake or pat dry in a tea towel. These tops may be snipped off and used as a garnish, alone or placed in the centre of an onion ring, or sprigs may be chopped. To chop it, place parsley sprigs in a small bunch on a chopping board and use a sharp knife without a serrated edge. To chop parsley correctly, use the 'heel' of the knife, as opposed to the tip. This cuts parsley coarsely. For fine chopping, hold the tip of the knife with fingers of left hand, keep tip on board and chop with right hand, swinging knife backwards and forwards over parsley, chopping until required fineness. Parsley is best stored unchopped. Sprinkle with cold water, place in a polythene bag and it will keep fresh in a refrigerator for up to one week. Use parsley to garnish all meat dishes and casseroles.

Tomatoes

These should be firm and ripe. Skins may be removed, if liked. Simply nick skin with a sharp knife, plunge into boiling water for 1 minute. Drain and peel off skins. Sliced tomatoes make a simple and effective decoration. Place tomato, stalk end to the table surface, and slice downwards. Keep slices in correct order so they retain the tomato shape and lay flat. Sprinkle with finely chopped parsley. Place a straight line of parsley across the slices. Alternatively, tomatoes may first be cut in half, then into quarters. Dip the centre edge in finely grated Parmesan cheese or finely chopped parsley. Tomato lilies are cut using a small, sharp-pointed kitchen knife. Push tip of knife into centre of a tomato at an angle. Work round the tomato, placing the knife at opposite angles of each cut and taking care to cut into the centre each time. When completed, lift the two halves apart. Use tomatoes on cold meat or salads.

Gherkins and red pimento

Bottled gherkins and canned pimentos (better known as Spanish sweet peppers) make a colourful garnish and are easily stored in a refrigerator. Before using, drain gherkins from the vinegar in the bottle. Gherkin fans are easily prepared with a small, sharp knife. Cut gherkins lengthways into three or four slices, leaving stalk end whole. Press flat, spreading out slices to a fan shape. These fans can be made even prettier if thin slivers of pimento are slipped in between each slice.

Pimento is canned in whole pieces and should be drained and opened out flat. Either cut into simple squares or diamond shapes with a knife or cut out pretty shapes with a small cutter. The correct garnish cutters come in many tiny shapes. Use gherkins and pimentos on open sandwiches and cocktail snacks.

Cucumber

This can be peeled or cut, using a crimper (shown in photograph) used to cut away strips of peel. Draw the crimper from the stalk end of the cucumber towards you in a straight line. Cut next line, keeping it straight, about $\frac{1}{8}-\frac{1}{4}$ inch $(\frac{1}{4}-\frac{1}{2}$ cm.) away. Slice the cucumber. Place a slice of stuffed olive or sprig of parsley in the centre of each slice. Try alternating slices of cucumber and tomato in a row with chopped parsley.

Cucumber may also be used unpeeled and sliced at an angle. Try placing one of these slices over a slice of lemon, cut through both from outer edge to centre, making one cut. Twist both edges in opposite directions; add a parsley sprig. The stalk end of cucumber is useful for cucumber cones. Slice thinly, then cut each slice to the centre only. Turn edges, overlapping to make a cone. To store cucumber, stand it, stalk end downwards, in a glass of water – cover the cut end with kitchen foil. Add cucumber to salads of cold fish or shellfish dishes.

Lemon

This may be cut using the same crimper as for cucumber. Cut lengthways – makes pretty lemon slices – garnish the centre with sliced stuffed olive or chopped parsley. Or ring the edge of lemon in chopped parsley to make a pretty border. A lemon looks prettiest when cut with a crimper in a circular fashion, working from one end of the lemon, round the fruit to the opposite end. Then cut lengthways into wedges. Dip the centre edge in chopped parsley.

A lemon left plain may be sliced to make lemon butterflies. Cut slices in half, then cut each half to centre into quarters but leave centre segments attached. Gently open out and garnish with parsley sprigs. Lemon twists can be made by cutting plain lemon slices once into the centre and then twisting the two edges in opposite directions.

Use a stainless steel knife to cut lemons, as acid in fruit discolours steel knives and lemon flesh. Use lemon on any fish or veal recipe.

Paprika pepper

This is bright red and mainly used in cookery because of its colour. It should not be confused with cayenne pepper which is also bright red but has a very hot and pungent flavour. The uses of paprika pepper are limited: attractive lines of paprika can be used as a garnish on egg slices or lemon wedges. Tip pepper out on to a square of kitchen foil or greaseproof paper. Then, using a knife, pick up evenly along knife edge as much pepper as you wish to use in the decoration. Tip quickly over food, making a straight line. This procedure can be used with very finely chopped parsley and the two used together make a pretty contrast. Paprika pepper comes in jars with shaker tops. If you store in a dry cupboard, it will last for months. Use paprika over vegetables in white sauce and mayonnaise dishes.

Everyday recipes using meat and poultry

To provide main meals for family menus all the year round is no easy task for any cook. Meat is likely to be one of the most expensive items on the shopping list. Luckily, all cuts of meat can be used most satisfactorily. Choose the more expensive cuts for roasting, grilling or frying and the less expensive cuts for pies, stews and delicious casseroles. Cuts of meat that are cheaper are not necessarily inferior in quality. They have been taken from the same carcass as the more expensive joints, but probably from the fore-quarters of the animal. The expensive 'prime' cuts come from the least muscular part of the animal, in other words the part that does the least work. The less expensive cuts usually have a high proportion of bone, fat and muscle fibre. They need careful slow cooking, but have just as much protein as the more expensive cuts.

Poultry, particularly chicken, holds an important place in our menus. Most chickens are very tender and can be cooked by any method — roasting, grilling, frying or casseroling. The rather bland flavour of chicken makes it an excellent medium for spicy, well flavoured sauces.

When planning everyday meals, variety and attractive presentation are all important. Nothing dulls the appetite more than constant repetition.

How much meat to buy

When buying boneless meat – that is steak, stewing or braising steak, liver, mince or boned and rolled joints – allow 4–6 oz. (100–175 g.) of meat per person. Meat with an average amount of bone – a roasting joint or steak – allow 6–10 oz. (175–275 g.) per person. For meat with a large amount of bone – such as neck of lamb – allow 10–12 oz. (275–350 g.) per person.

Beef

Look for a firm, moist but not wet surface on the meat and a good red colour. There should be marbling of fat through the flesh in prime quality cuts. This marbling in beef is most important as it is a sign of quality and maturity. They are thin threads of fat between muscle fibres, which run through the flesh of the animal. Marbling opens out the meat during cooking and keeps it moist and tender. Where this is present on a mature animal, there will also be a better covering of fat. Fat is important too because it helps prevent drying out of the meat during hanging and cooking. The correct hanging of beef is also highly important for tenderness. Any butcher who values his customers will provide good meat, which is correctly hung.

Cuts of beef

Shin: A coarse grained and very gelatinous cut of meat. Excellent for stock or soups. If cooked slowly, it makes an excellent stew or casserole with a delicious gravy.
Topside: An excellent cut of meat for braising or pot roasting. It can also be roasted but is not considered one of the prime roasting joints. Topside can also be cut into what is sometimes called buttock steak and sold for stewing beef.
Silverside: A cut from the buttock of the animal. Silverside is usually salted by the butcher. Soaked and boiled, it can be served hot or cold.
Rump: A good quality cut, usually for cutting into steaks.
Sirloin: A very expensive part of the animal and the best cut for roasting, particularly if bought on the bone. If bought on the bone, the chump end adjoining the rump is the best, since it has a section of the undercut including the fillet. More often sirloin is boned and rolled these days, for economy. In this case, the fillet is taken out and sold separately for steaks. The top part of the sirloin can also be cut into sirloin or entrecôte steaks. Less tender than fillet steak, sirloin steak is considered to have a very fine flavour.
Ribs: There are several cuts from the ribs of beef. Those near the sirloin are the best. Fore rib or wing rib are good for roasting. Ribs, boned and rolled, make an excellent, less expensive, roast.
Shoulder steak: Usually cut into pieces for stewing or pies and sold as chuck steak.
Brisket: Rather a fat cut, very good fresh and pot roasted. If salted by the butcher, it should be soaked and then boiled.
Flank: This can be salted and boiled or used fresh, cut up for stews or casseroles.

Steak cuts

Steak varies tremendously in size, shape and tenderness. It can be one of the most expensive cuts of meat but, on the other hand, the meat is lean and there is little waste. Generally speaking, steaks should be cut no thinner than 1 inch (2½ cm.) thick otherwise it is almost impossible to control the degree of cooking, which is very important. Prime quality steak can be eaten rare without being tough, but the cheaper the cut and the poorer the quality, the more it needs cooking. Steak has more flavour and is most tender when undercooked. When overcooked, the protein in the flesh shrinks and becomes hard. Unlike casseroling or roasting (where the meat is cooked in a moist heat), steaks are always grilled or fried – a cooking process which tends to dry the meat. For this reason, it pays to buy the best you can afford when selecting a steak.

Fillet steak: Cut from the long narrow muscle which runs along the back bone in the loin area. It is the most expensive and the most tender cut of steak; without bone and no fat or waste. Chateaûbriand steaks are cut from the wide end, the fillet steak from the centre and the Tournedos steaks are cut at the narrow end of the fillet. Ask the butcher to cut the steaks about 1 inch (2½ cm.) thick.
Rump steak: This is the next best known steak – some cooks claim this cut has the most flavour. It is cut from the rump or buttock part of the animal. Rump is usually cut in one large slice from the whole section of meat and then cut into individual portions. When buying, it is best to buy the steak in one large piece, allowing about 3–4 oz. (75–100 g.) per portion. Cook the meat as a whole and then cut up before serving.
T Bone steak: This steak is cut from the sirloin, which lies just towards the front of the animal from the rump. A whole sirloin contains part of the fillet as well as the sirloin. If you are prepared to pay the price, a butcher will cut this particular steak for you. A large slice about 1–2 inches (2½–5 cm.) thick, cut right through the sirloin, is large enough to serve 3 portions. Easily recognised by the 'T' shaped bone which gives this particular steak its name.
Porterhouse steak: This is also a sirloin steak, in fact it is a slice off the sirloin after it has been boned. It is usually cut about ½–1 inch (1–2½ cm.) thick and is easily recognised by the slightly long shape and the layer of fat down one side of the cut.
Frying steak: Steak sold under this label can mean anything. Depends on the prices as to whether it is good or poor quality. Frying steak can be cut from the buttock, top rump, top leg or even skirt.
Minute steaks: These are quick-fry steaks and can also be cut from any part of the animal. They are cut very thin and then beaten flat to make the cooking very quick, hence this name. Easily recognised by the very thin cut of meat.

Lamb

Lamb is a young meat. Look first of all for a pinkish tinge, rather than a reddish tinge, and a firm white fat. Look also for streaky red lines running up the rib bones of the best end of neck or on the shank bone of the leg. Lamb is a meat that is consistently high in quality all year round. New Zealand lamb comes on to the market just after Christmas and is at its best up to the month of June. By this time the English lamb, which starts in spring, is coming in quantity. This is followed by Scottish lamb which has a later season. Then Australian lamb comes into season, taking the market through to Christmas.

Cuts of lamb

Leg: A whole leg weighs from 3½–5 lb. (1½–2¼ kg.). It can be bought in half joints, the fillet end (top half) or the shank end. Whole leg of lamb or the fillet end is best for roasting; the shank end is sometimes used for boiling.

Loin: A very choice cut. Can be bought in the piece, usually about 3–4 lb. (1½–1¾ kg.) or less, for roasting. The individual loin chops are for grilling or frying. The loin chops have a small T bone which can be cut out if liked and the chop tied neatly into a circle to make a 'noisette' of lamb.

Chump chops: Larger than loin chops, with more meat on them, and so more expensive. They are cut from the thick end of the leg and have a small round bone in the centre.

Best end: This can be bought in one piece, usually with 6–7 bones, for roasting. It can also be boned, stuffed and rolled for roasting. Two pieces of best end sewn together are used to make a crown roast. Individual cutlets are cut for grilling or frying. When buying these, make sure they have a good 'eye' of meat.

Shoulder: This weighs 3½–5 lb. (1½–2¼ kg.). It can be bought in half joints, the blade end being more tender than the knuckle end. Whole or half shoulder can be roasted. Whole shoulders can be boned, stuffed and rolled for roasting.

Breast: An inexpensive, tasty joint. It can be boned, stuffed and roasted or braised.

Neck fillet: A small, lean piece of meat cut from the neck. Excellent for stews or casseroles, or for kebabs.

Scrag end and middle neck: These have a good flavour but are a bony cut, therefore proportionally more should be allowed in recipes. Excellent for stews and hotpots. Make sure that it is well cut, because bony splinters can spoil a dish.

Pork

With modern refrigeration, pork can now be eaten at any time of the year. Since the animal is slaughtered at a very young age, all cuts of pork are tender, in fact, all cuts are suitable for roasting. Pork meat should be light in colour with a pinkish tinge. The fat should be white and there should be a reasonable covering of it on the meat. Pork crackling is always a great favourite, therefore when buying a joint make sure the skin is left on – because without this, there is no crackling. Get the butcher to score it for you. This not only helps to ensure crisp crackling but makes it easier to carve.

Cuts of pork

Leg: This is one of the prime cuts of pork and very popular as a roast at Christmas. It is essentially a roasting joint and often the leg is halved to make two smaller joints. The *fillet end* – the fatter upper part of the leg and a delicious lean roast, and the *knuckle end* – the part of the leg narrowing down to the leg bone.

Loin: Another prime cut for roasting. Loin is also cut up to give pork chops for grilling or frying. The loin chops are sometimes sold with the kidney in. The chump end of loin provides chops which are large and meaty.

Belly: An inexpensive cut and very tasty, but fairly fatty. It can be roasted with a stuffing or casseroled; it is sometimes sold cut up into rashers for frying or grilling. It is also sold salted for boiling.

Shoulder: A large roasting joint and particularly good when boned and rolled. Shoulder, however, is often divided into two smaller joints. *Blade* – a delicious roasting joint. It has a bone in the middle and can be roasted on the bone, or with the bone removed and stuffing in its place. Blade can also be braised. *Sparerib* – the other shoulder cut, is a meaty cut which is less expensive and is also excellent for roasting. Sometimes sparerib is cut up and sold as sparerib cutlets or chops. Sparerib is also the cut to buy for the filling for homemade pork pies.

Hand and spring: A large joint for roasting whole, which is cut from the foreleg of the animal. This cut is often divided into *hand*, which can be boned and roasted and *shank*, which is used for casseroles and stews. Both cuts are sold salted for boiling.

Tenderloin: A lean cut found on the inside of the loin bone. It is a choice piece of meat with no bone and practically no waste. It can be sliced and fried, or split, stuffed and roasted. This cut is also referred to as pork fillet but should not be confused with the fillet end of the leg.

Bacon and gammon

Freshly cut bacon and bacon joints should have a pleasant aroma. The lean should be a good pink colour, the fat should be firm and white and free from any yellow marks. Cuts which are cured but not smoked are known as 'green' or 'plain'. They are easily recognised because they have a plain rind, while the smoked have a deep brown rind. The term gammon and bacon are sometimes confusing but both come from the same animal. The gammon is the hind leg or ham of a bacon pig and is cured while still on the pig. Gammon is seldom sold whole, but is cut into smaller gammon joints. The middle cut of a bacon pig is used to produce bacon rashers and the fore or shoulder cuts are referred to as bacon joints.

Bacon and gammon cuts

Briefly, the middle cuts are used to provide the rashers and the fore or shoulder and gammon cuts are used as joints. The method of cutting varies in different parts of the country.

Collar: A whole collar weighs about 8 lb. (3½ kg.). Collar is usually cut into smaller bacon joints. The choicest part is called prime collar, this is boneless and with a high proportion of lean to fat. Collar is less expensive than gammon.

Forehock: The whole forehock, including bone and knuckle, weighs about 8 lb. (3½ kg.). It is a good buy as a large joint for a party. Most shops, however, bone and roll the forehock to sell in smaller joints of about 2–3 lb. (1–1½ kg.). Forehock is cheaper than gammon or collar, it is not so fine textured but is equal to the others in flavour.

THE MIDDLE CUTS

In the North of England and Scotland, 'through cut' rashers, including both prime and streaky bacon, are sold. In Scotland, this bacon is rolled and sliced and is known as Ayrshire roll.

Prime back and long back: These are the best rashers. They are very lean and suitable for frying or grilling.

Wide streaky and thin streaky: The most economical rasher, with lean and fat interspersed in streaks, as the name suggests.

Oyster rashers: A fat rasher, so called because an oyster shaped bone is removed. It is an inexpensive cut.

Flank rashers: This is a very fat rasher, lying between the thin streaky and the gammon. Good for basting when cooking poultry, veal or venison.

GAMMON

A whole gammon weighs about 14 lb. (6 kg.) but is rarely sold as one joint. It is cut into the following smaller joints:

Half gammon: Weighs about 7–8 lb. (3–3¾ kg.) and is suitable to serve for a large buffet supper or wedding. Expensive but very good, with little waste.

Middle gammon: Weighs up to 6 lb. (2¾ kg.). It is boneless and very lean. This is the most prized gammon joint. Very good for buffet supper.

Corner gammon: This joint weighs up to 4 lb. (1¾ kg.) and is a good choice for a family. Boneless and easy to carve.

Gammon slipper: Weighs about 2 lb. (1 kg.) and is chunky and quite lean. An inexpensive small sized joint.

Gammon hock: An inexpensive gammon cut for the average household. Includes a portion of the prime cut and the knuckle. Weighs about 4 lb. (1¾ kg.) including the bone.

Gammon rashers and steaks: These are cut from the middle gammon. Cheaper gammon steaks are cut from the gammon slipper.

Veal

Veal comes from either very young milk-fed calves, in which case the meat is very light and tender, or from older calves which have been grass fed, in which case the meat is darker in colour and considered by many to have a better flavour. Veal, being a young meat, has very little fat but what there is should be very white.

Cuts of veal

Shoulder: Sold on the bone for roasting or can be boned, stuffed and rolled before cooking. This cut can also be used for veal dishes such as stews or casseroles.

Loin: Sold as one piece with the bone, or boned and rolled for roasting. Loin can also be cut up for veal chops for frying or grilling.

Best end of neck: This can be roasted as a joint or cut up into cutlets for grilling.

Fillet: A choice part for roasting, this is the most expensive part of the animal. From this joint are cut the thin slices for veal escalopes to make Paupiettes de veau (page 96) or Veal Parmesan (page 96).

Breast: An economical cut which can be stuffed and rolled, roasted and braised.

Veal shin: Very bony cut but excellent for broths and soups. Have the shin cut across into thick pieces for Osso buco (page 98).

Veal knuckle: The lower part of the leg and very good for jellied stock.

Pie veal: Usually pieces of different cuts, cut up and sold. Use this for veal and ham pie or in a pâté.

Choosing liver and kidney for recipes

Calve's liver: This is the finest liver and by far the most expensive. Choose this for a special occasion and use in recipes to grill or fry.

Lamb's liver: This is less expensive and the best alternative for everyday use. Lamb's liver can be grilled or fried, braised or used in pâtés. Often it is soaked in milk for an hour or so before using – this draws the blood and makes the liver more tender.

Pig's liver: This is cheaper, but has a stronger flavour. Many dislike it grilled or fried, but it is a good choice for pâtés, meat loaves or to use in casserole recipes.

Chicken livers: These are small and very tender. Fry them in butter and serve with bacon or use in kebabs, risotto or in pâté.

Ox kidney: This is cheap and has a strong flavour, it needs careful cooking. Use in steak and kidney pie or pudding.

Lamb's kidney: These are the smallest and the best to use for grilling, frying or in recipes with sauces where the cooking is fairly quick. They are the neatest in shape and are easy to fit on skewers. Where possible, buy lamb's kidneys with the suet still attached. This way you know they are fresh and not frozen. Remove the suet, skin and snip out the core before using.

Pig's kidney: These are similar in shape to lamb's kidneys but larger. Use them in stews and casseroles.

Chicken

Today's chickens are young birds of 9–20 weeks old and have a bland, delicate flavour. They are very tender and it is important not to overcook them. A whole chicken is the best value for money when catering for a family. It takes longer to cook than chicken pieces, but can provide more than one meal. The bone and giblets can be used for making stock and soup. Choose a bird by weight, allowing about 8 oz. (¼ kg.) oven-ready weight per portion. For a family of four, a 2½-lb. (1¼-kg.) oven-ready chicken will provide 1 meal and a 4-lb. (1¾-kg.) bird up to 2 meals.

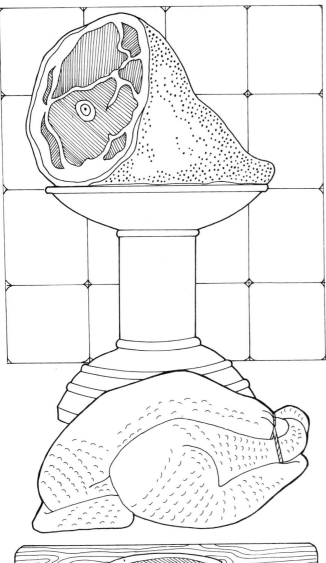

Cut up chicken pieces are the best buy for quickly cooked meals, individual portions and for recipes using jointed chickens. Grilled or fried chicken portions cook in less than $\frac{1}{2}$ hour, but if baked or casseroled they take about 1 hour.

Keep a fresh chicken in the coolest place available. Remove the giblets from inside the bird and place the bird in the refrigerator, where it will keep for up to 2 days. If the chicken is frozen, leave in the protective wrapping and allow to thaw completely before cooking. A frozen whole chicken will take 7–8 hours to thaw and chicken joints will take 3–4 hours. When thawed, cook a whole chicken within 24 hours and cook cut chicken within 12 hours.

How chicken is sold

Chicken: All birds reared by modern methods are known as chicken. Birds reared for table use, weigh from $2\frac{1}{2}$–5 lb. ($1\frac{1}{4}$–$2\frac{1}{4}$ kg.). Sometimes they are referred to as roasting chickens, but this tends to be misleading since they can be cooked by other methods as well. Chicken joints are usually cut from a bird of about 2 lb. (1 kg.) oven-ready weight.

Poussin: These are smaller birds of 1–$1\frac{1}{2}$ lb. ($\frac{1}{2}$–$\frac{3}{4}$ kg.) in weight and only about 4–8 weeks old. They are considered suitable for one, or at the most two persons. They are very tender and excellent for grilling.

Spring chicken: These young chickens are a little older, from 8 weeks to 4 months. They make excellent small roasting chickens and usually weigh between $2\frac{1}{2}$–3 lb. ($1\frac{1}{4}$–$1\frac{1}{2}$ kg.).

Capon: A specially reared and fattened bird which has extra quality and quantity of flesh on the breast. Capons can weigh anything from $4\frac{1}{2}$–7 lb. (2–$3\frac{1}{4}$ kg.) each.

Turkey

Turkey is an economical buy whenever you have a lot of people to feed. In recent years, highly specialised breeding has produced small birds with broad, plump breasts. Turkeys are available fresh usually around Christmas time and frozen, oven-ready nearly all the year round.

Buy a fresh turkey with a plump breast and a white, unblemished skin. In winter time, a freshly drawn turkey will keep for 2–3 days in a cool place. If possible, hang the bird up so that the air circulates and keep it in a cold larder. If small enough, place the bird in the refrigerator. In summer, it is advisable to cook a fresh turkey within 24 hours of purchase. The price per pound ($\frac{1}{2}$ kg.) of a fresh turkey is charged on the undrawn weight.

A frozen, oven-ready bird is sold by the oven-ready weight. Allow a frozen turkey ample time to thaw completely before cooking. Leave the turkey in the protective polythene bag and puncture a hole so that any liquid can drip out. A large bird, over 12 lb. (5 kg.), will require 48 hours to thaw. Up to 12 lb. (5 kg.), a turkey will need 30 hours to thaw. Once thawed, remove from the bag, take out the giblets from inside and wipe the bird dry.

Turkey portions, sliced turkey breast and turkey drum-sticks are excellent for frying or roasting or to use in casserole dishes.

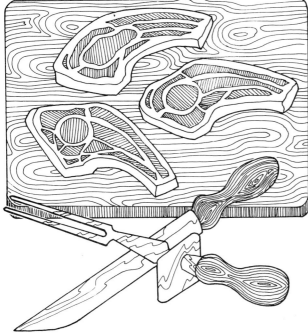

When estimating the size of turkey to buy, allow $\frac{3}{4}$–1 lb. (350–450 g.) oven-ready weight per portion. Take care not to buy a turkey that is too large for your oven. A 14–15-lb. ($6\frac{1}{4}$–$6\frac{3}{4}$-kg.) oven-ready turkey is a good average size.

WEIGHT OF OVEN-READY TURKEY

6–8-lb. ($2\frac{3}{4}$–$3\frac{1}{2}$-kg.) — 7–9 portions
8–10-lb. ($3\frac{1}{2}$–$4\frac{1}{2}$-kg.) — 9–11 portions
10–12-lb. ($4\frac{1}{2}$–$5\frac{1}{2}$-kg.) — 11–13 portions
12–14-lb. ($5\frac{1}{2}$–$6\frac{1}{4}$-kg.) — 13–15 portions
14–16-lb. ($6\frac{1}{4}$–$7\frac{1}{4}$-kg.) — 15–18 portions
16–18-lb. ($7\frac{1}{4}$–8-kg.) — 18–24 portions

Goose

Goose are best from October to around Christmas. Not all butchers take orders for goose at Christmas, so make sure you find a butcher in good time who will take an order for you. As a rule, goose or gosling have a fairly shallow breast and, for the size and weight, comparatively little flesh. Allow a 10-lb. ($4\frac{1}{2}$-kg.) oven-ready bird for 8 people.

Duckling

Duckling are sold from 6–8 weeks old. These young, tender birds are reared on an intensive scale. Frozen, oven-ready duckling are available all year round.

Roasting meat and poultry

A dinner party, friends for the weekend or a family lunch – there's a roast for every occasion. A roast is easy and unfussy to cook; once in the oven, little more attention is required.

A good sized joint of meat always roasts better than a small joint. Where possible, buy a large joint and plan on using the meat for more than one meal. When selecting your joint, remember that the nearer the bone the sweeter the meat and if you can buy the joint on the bone, this is best. A joint of meat that has a good covering of natural fat will roast better, retaining more moisture and flavour. A lean joint should be smeared with fat before placing it in the roasting tin. For best results, meat should be kept out of the hot fat during roasting. Place the meat on a trivet or on a bed of flavouring vegetables. Use carrots or onion, cut into large slices. During roasting the natural sugars in the vegetables caramelise slightly round the edges, giving a flavour and colour to the subsequent gravy. Add a tablespoon of dripping to the tin and place in the joint. In most cases, a hot oven seals the surface of the meat and browns it. The heat is then lowered to allow the joint to cook through. Once the cooking time is complete, allow the roast to stand for 5–10 minutes so that the meat has a chance to 'settle'. The joint will carve more easily and retain more juices this way.

To make the gravy

For a thin gravy, strain off all the fat from the roasting tin, but tip back into the tin any flavouring vegetables or crispy brown

MEAT ROASTING CHART

Beef	15 minutes per lb. ($\frac{1}{2}$ kg.) plus 15 minutes added to total for rare joint. Increase to 20 minutes for well done.	Start in a hot oven (425°F., 220°C., Gas Mark 7) for 15 minutes. Lower to 375°F., 190°C., Gas Mark 5 for remaining time.	Place joint on bed of roasting vegetables. Baste frequently. Serve with gravy, Yorkshire pudding, roast vegetables and mustard or horseradish sauce.
Pork	35 minutes per lb. ($\frac{1}{2}$ kg.) plus 35 minutes added to total. For stuffed joints, allow 40 minutes per lb. ($\frac{1}{2}$ kg.).	Start in a hot oven (425°F., 220°C., Gas Mark 7) for 20 minutes. Lower to 350°F., 180°C., Gas Mark 4 for remaining time.	Ask butcher to score fat. Rub in salt for crisp crackling. Raise heat to 425°F., 220°C., Gas Mark 7 for last 25 minutes to crisp it. Do not baste. Pork must be well done. Serve with apple sauce or baked apples, red cabbage, roast vegetables and gravy.
Lamb	30 minutes per lb. ($\frac{1}{2}$ kg.) plus 30 minutes added to total. For stuffed joints, allow 35 minutes per lb. ($\frac{1}{2}$ kg.) plus 30 minutes.	350°F., 180°C., Gas Mark 4	Best results come from slow cooking of lamb. Rub surface over with a cut clove of garlic. Dredge with flour and rub in for a crisp golden finish. Baste occasionally. Serve with redcurrant jelly or mint jelly, gravy and roast vegetables.
Veal	40 minutes per lb. ($\frac{1}{2}$ kg.) plus 40 minutes added to total.	325°F., 170°C., Gas Mark 3	Protect veal with bacon rashers and slow roast. Baste frequently. Serve with gravy and redcurrant jelly or cranberry jelly.

bits. Add a pint (6 dl.) of stock or vegetable cooking water. Stir and boil briskly until reduced by about half. Taste and correct the seasoning. Strain into a hot gravy boat and skim off any fat that rises to the surface.

For a thick gravy, leave a tablespoon of fat in the roasting tin and stir in a tablespoon of flour. Add the liquid, stirring it in smoothly. Cook and stir for 2–3 minutes after boiling. Taste and correct the seasoning. Strain into a hot gravy boat.

Sauces and accompaniments for roast meats

The accompaniments with a roast are all important – Yorkshire pudding and mustard or horseradish sauce go with beef, mint sauce with lamb, apple sauce with pork and cranberry sauce with veal. Or there are other delectable extras, such as hot fruits – try hot pineapple slices with roast lamb, hot orange slices with roast veal or baked apples with pork.

Yorkshire pudding

Serves 4 (makes 1 large or 8 individual puddings)

2 oz./50 g. plain flour
pinch salt
1 egg

$\frac{1}{4}$ pint/1$\frac{1}{2}$ dl. liquid (3 parts milk and 1 part water)

Sift the flour and salt into a mixing basin. Add the egg and about half the mixing liquid. Using a wooden spoon, beat the egg and liquid gradually drawing in the flour from around the edges – work from the centre of the basin to the sides – and mix to a smooth batter.

Add the remainder of the liquid gradually, stirring all the time. Beat well for a few minutes until thoroughly aerated. Then cover the bowl with a cloth and leave to stand for 1 hour, or until required. Stir again before using because the starch grains tend to settle at the bottom.

Yorkshire pudding may be cooked in a sheet of tartlet tins or bun tins, a Yorkshire pudding tin, small roasting tin or an ovenproof glass dish. If using a large container, put a tablespoon of dripping or fat in the dish and heat thoroughly at the top of the oven for a few minutes. Pour in the stirred batter and replace on the top shelf of a preheated hot oven (425°F., 220°C., Gas Mark 7) and cook until well risen – about 30–40 minutes.

If using small tartlet or individual bun tins, grease 8 thickly and heat them thoroughly in the oven. Pour the batter into each tin, using a jug, and fill each fairly full. Bake as before until crisp and golden – about 12–15 minutes. Serve at once.

Cranberry sauce

Serves 4–6

6 oz./175 g. castor sugar
$\frac{1}{4}$ pint/1$\frac{1}{2}$ dl. water

8 oz./225 g. fresh cranberries

Measure the sugar and water into a saucepan. Stir over a low heat to dissolve the sugar. Wash the cranberries, removing any soft berries, and pick out the stalks. Add the berries to the pan and bring to the boil. Simmer gently for about 10 minutes until the berries are quite tender. Serve warm with roast veal.

Mint sauce

Serves 4–6

1 good handful fresh mint
1–2 teaspoons castor sugar

1 tablespoon boiling water
2–3 tablespoons vinegar

Wash the mint and strip the leaves from the stem. Chop the leaves finely and place in a small mixing basin or teacup. Add the sugar and then the boiling water. Stir to dissolve the sugar, then pour in the vinegar. Prepare this sauce when ready to serve, as the mint discolours if left to stand too long.

Serve with roast lamb.

Horseradish sauce

Serves 4–6

about 2 oz./50 g. fresh horse-radish root
$\frac{1}{4}$ pint/1$\frac{1}{2}$ dl. double cream
1 tablespoon lemon juice or vinegar

1 level teaspoon castor sugar
$\frac{1}{4}$ level teaspoon made mustard
pinch salt

Scrub and scrape the horseradish root, then grate it finely. Lightly whip the cream, stir in the lemon juice or vinegar, sugar, mustard, salt and horseradish.

Serve with roast beef.

Apple sauce

Serves 4–6

1 lb./$\frac{1}{2}$ kg. cooking apples
2 tablespoons water
1 clove
pinch ground cinnamon

juice $\frac{1}{2}$ lemon
2 level tablespoons castor sugar
$\frac{1}{2}$ oz./15 g. butter

Peel, core and slice the apples. Place in a saucepan with the water and the clove. Cover and simmer gently for about 10 minutes until the apples are quite soft. Draw the pan off the heat and beat to a purée with a wooden spoon. Add the cinnamon, lemon juice, sugar and butter and stir over the heat until the ingredients are blended.

Serve hot with roast pork.

Poultry such as chicken or turkey, which have a very lean and rather dry flesh, need some protection during roasting. Streaky bacon rashers or kitchen foil can be used. Goose or duckling, on the other hand, are very fatty and require no protection.

Chicken	Allow 20 minutes per lb. (½ kg.) plus 20 minutes added to total.	375°F., 190°C., Gas Mark 5	Avoid overcooking chicken, by checking weight of the bird. Calculate the time from oven-ready weight. Stuff body and breast cavity. Protect with bacon rashers. Baste frequently. Serve with gravy, bread sauce, bacon rolls and chipolata sausages.
Turkey	Allow 25 minutes per lb. (½ kg.) up to 12 lb. (5½ kg.). Over 12 lb. (5½ kg.) allow 20 minutes per lb. (½ kg.).	325°F., 170°C., Gas Mark 3	Slow roasting gives best results. Add about 2 lb. (1 kg.) to the oven-ready weight to allow for stuffing, when calculating cooking time. Stuff breast and body cavity. Protect breast with rashers and loosely cover bird with kitchen foil. Serve with gravy, cranberry sauce and chipolata sausages.
Duckling	Allow 25 minutes per lb. (½ kg.).	350°F., 180°C., Gas Mark 4	Rub skin with salt and prick all over. Place in roasting tin with 2 tablespoons cold water – no fat required. Stuff body cavity only. Serve with gravy and apple sauce.
Goose	Allow 20 minutes per lb. (½ kg.) plus 20 minutes added to total.	Start in hot oven (400°F., 200°C., Gas Mark 6) for 30 minutes. Lower heat to 375°F., 190°C., Gas Mark 5 for remaining time.	Rub skin over with flour and prick skin with fork. No fat required in tin. Cover with foil for first 45 minutes. Stuff body cavity only. Serve with apple sauce and gravy.

Stuffings for poultry

A stuffing helps to keep poultry moist during cooking. It soaks up flavour from the bird, makes the roast more interesting and helps to increase the number of portions.

When stuffing poultry, never pack the stuffing too tightly – the breadcrumbs used expand during cooking and room should be allowed for this. A stuffing should be moist but not wet. Stuffing deteriorates quickly and should not be made or put inside the poultry until ready to cook.

To make breadcrumbs
Depending on the type of stuffing, breadcrumbs can form a major ingredient. In most cases, bread that has been allowed to stale for a day or so can be rubbed through a coarse grater to obtain crumbs. Those who own a liquidiser will find the task even easier. Remove the centre cap in the lid of the goblet. Switch the machine on, drop the pieces of bread through the hole on to the moving blades. Do only a little at a time and frequently empty the machine. Breadcrumbs can be made in advance and will freeze very well. Weigh out amounts suitable for using in recipes and freeze in polythene freezer bags.

Sausagemeat stuffing

Sufficient for a 10–12-lb. (4½–5½-kg.) oven-ready turkey

2 lb./1 kg. pork sausagemeat	½ oz./15 g. butter
8 oz./225 g. streaky bacon	1 level teaspoon powdered sage
1 large onion	

Place the sausagemeat in a basin. Trim and chop the bacon into small strips. Peel and chop the onion. Fry the bacon and onion in the melted butter until tender but not brown. Add to the sausagemeat with the powdered sage and mix well.

Use to stuff the body cavity of the turkey.

Cranberry stuffing

A colourful stuffing with a distinctive flavour and one which is very good in chicken. Double the quantities to stuff the breast of a turkey.

For a 4-lb. (1¾-kg.) oven-ready chicken

3 level tablespoons castor sugar	½ small onion
3 tablespoons water	2 rounded tablespoons finely chopped parsley
4 oz./100 g. fresh cranberries	finely grated rind ½ lemon
4 oz./100 g. fresh white breadcrumbs	salt and freshly milled pepper

Measure the sugar and water into a saucepan. Stir over a low heat until the sugar has dissolved. Add the washed cranberries and bring up to the boil. Cook briskly until the skins pop – takes about 5 minutes. Lower the heat and simmer for a further 5 minutes until the berries are quite tender.

Measure the breadcrumbs, chopped onion, parsley, lemon rind and a seasoning of salt and pepper into a basin. Using a fork, stir in the cooked cranberries and mix well.

Spoon the stuffing into the body of the chicken.

Sage and onion stuffing

A traditional stuffing for duck or goose. If you have fresh sage, substitute a tablespoon of chopped fresh sage for the powdered sage in the recipe.

For a 4–5-lb. (1¾–2¼-kg.) oven-ready duckling

1 large onion	½ level teaspoon salt
3 oz./75 g. fresh white	freshly milled pepper
breadcrumbs	1 oz./25 g. butter, melted
1 level teaspoon powdered sage	

Peel and slice the onion. Place in a saucepan and cover with cold water. Bring to the boil and simmer until tender – takes about 30 minutes. Drain and chop coarsely.

Measure the breadcrumbs, sage, salt and pepper into a basin. Add the chopped onion and mix well. Using a fork, stir in the melted butter.

Use to stuff the body cavity of the duckling.

Chestnut stuffing

Use 1½ lb. (700 g.) dried chestnuts, soaked in cold water overnight, in place of the fresh chestnuts in this recipe. Treat them as peeled fresh chestnuts. Alternatively use 1 (15 oz./425 g.) can chestnut purée and omit the initial stages of peeling, cooking and sieving the chestnuts.

Sufficient for a 10–12-lb. (4½–5½-kg.) oven-ready turkey

2 lb./¾ kg. fresh chestnuts	1 egg
milk or stock	2 oz./50 g. butter, melted
4 oz./100 g. fresh white	2 tablespoons milk
breadcrumbs	salt and freshly milled pepper
grated rind ½ lemon	

Slit the skins on the flat side of the chestnuts. Place in boiling water and simmer for 10 minutes. Drain and remove the skins. Replace the chestnuts in the pan and cover with milk or stock. Simmer for 20 minutes or until tender. Drain and rub the nuts through a coarse sieve to make a purée.

Put the chestnut purée in a basin and add the breadcrumbs, grated lemon rind, mixed egg, melted butter, milk and seasoning. Mix all the ingredients well to blend.

Use to stuff the body cavity of the turkey.

Parsley and thyme stuffing

Often referred to as veal forcemeat. This is a traditional stuffing for the breast of a turkey but is also good in chicken.

Sufficient for a 10–12-lb. (4½–5½-kg.) oven-ready turkey

8 oz./225 g. white breadcrumbs	grated rind ½ lemon
3 oz./75 g. shredded beef suet	2 rashers back bacon, finely
2 tablespoons chopped parsley	chopped (optional)
salt and freshly milled pepper	1 egg, lightly mixed
1 teaspoon dried thyme	

Measure the breadcrumbs, suet, chopped parsley, salt and pepper, thyme, lemon rind and bacon, if used, into a mixing basin. Using a fork, stir in sufficient beaten egg to bind the ingredients together.

Recipes to grill and fry

Both grilling and frying are simple and quick methods of cooking. Both depend on food that cooks quickly and evenly and therefore has to be of good quality. In most cases, high heat should be used initially to brown and seal the food, then a more gentle heat used to cook the food through.

Choice and preparation for grilling

Steak

Only the best cuts of meat are suitable for grilling – cheaper cuts tend to become dry and tough when cooked by this quick method. *Fillet* – which should always be cut in fairly thick slices by the butcher; *Rump* – which is best bought in one large piece and then cut into portions after grilling; *Porterhouse* – which is cut individually; many cooks say this is more reliable as far as tenderness goes than any other steak.

Trim away any excess fat from around the meat, season both sides with freshly milled pepper (salt draws juices) and brush all over with oil or melted butter. Steak should be cooked under a high heat to seal in the juices – then reduce the heat and cook under a low heat, according to the thickness of the meat, first on one side and then the other. Take care not to prick the meat while turning. When the meat is ready, a good cook can tell by the 'feel' of the meat. Press the centre of the meat with a forefinger, if the flesh gives easily under pressure, the meat is rare – very red with the centre still raw. If the flesh resists, but is still a little soft, it is medium rare – red in the centre and cooked round the edges. If the meat feels firm then the steak is cooked right through.

Lamb

Choose from the following – best end of neck cutlets, loin chops, chump chops. Check there are no splintered pieces of bone, especially in the neck cutlets. Trim the fat away neatly at the top of the neck cutlet bones and serve garnished with a cutlet frill.

The larger loin chops of lamb can be boned, the butcher will do this or you can prepare them yourself. Using a sharp knife, cut the bone out of the chop. Curl the chop, wrapping the thinner part round the centre piece of meat. Wrap each boned chop with a thin bacon rasher and secure with a skewer or cocktail stick. Season with pepper and brush both sides with oil or melted butter and grill. For extra flavour, sprinkle with a pinch of dried thyme, pressing it well in before grilling.

Pork

Choose loin chops – sometimes the larger ones have a kidney included as well. Trim fat neatly and, using a small knife, cut slits at ½ inch (1 cm.) intervals on the fat down the outer edge on a pork chop. This helps to prevent the chops curling out of shape while grilling.

Season with freshly milled pepper or Jamaica pepper. Pork chops have a delicious sharp sweet flavour if rubbed over with equal parts castor sugar and dry mustard – about 1 teaspoon is sufficient for 4 chops – the sugar makes them brown nicely too.

Veal

Loin chops or neck cutlets. Trim chops neatly as for lamb and season with freshly milled pepper.

Chicken

Choose cut chicken joints or small, halved 'poussin'. It is not necessary to remove the skin from chicken joints before cooking; simply trim away any loose pieces. Ask the butcher to halve the poussin for you. Season with salt and pepper then brush both sides with melted butter or oil – add crushed rosemary or thyme if liked.

Lambs' and calves' kidneys

Lambs' or calves' kidneys are the most suitable. Of the two, lambs' kidneys are smaller, more readily available and less expensive. To prepare the kidneys, remove all the protective fatty tissue from the outside, snip away any core and remove the skin around the kidney. Slice into each kidney on the *rounded* side, cutting *almost* through, but not quite. Open out the kidneys and skewer in pairs on kitchen skewers. Unless skewered, kidneys will curl up too much while cooking. Brush over with oil and season with salt and freshly milled pepper.

Bacon and gammon rashers

Back rashers are the leanest. Trim away the rind before grilling; no additional fat is needed. Gammon rashers are usually cut about ¼ inch (½ cm.) thick. Trim away any rind with a sharp pair of scissors and nick the fat at intervals to prevent buckling while cooking. If you like a mild flavour, soak gammon rashers in cold water or milk for about 2 hours; drain and pat dry.

Arrange bacon rashers for grilling with the fat part of each covering the lean part of the next rasher.

Sausages

These need no preparation. Simply place them closely together in the grill pan, brush with oil to help even browning; do not season.

COOKING TIMES FOR GRILLED MEATS

	Rare	Medium done	Well done
Steak			
¾ inch (2 cm.) thick	3–5 minutes	9–10 minutes	14–15 minutes
1 inch (2½ cm.) thick	6–7 minutes	10 minutes	15 minutes
1½ inches (3½ cm.) thick	10 minutes	12–14 minutes	18–20 minutes
Lamb		12 minutes	14 minutes
Pork and veal chops (must be well done)			15 minutes
Chicken joints and poussin			20–25 minutes
Kidneys			6–8 minutes
Bacon		2–3 minutes	4 minutes
Sausages			10 minutes

Mixed grill

To prepare a mixed grill successfully, the order of cooking individual items is important. Those that take the longest are placed under the grill first so that everything is ready at the same time.

Serves 4

4 lamb cutlets	4 open mushrooms
4 lambs' kidneys	oil or melted butter for brushing
8 oz./225 g. chipolata sausages	salt and freshly milled pepper
4 tomatoes	1 bunch watercress

Wipe the cutlets and trim away excess fat. Scrape away the fat about 1 inch (2½ cm.) down from the top of the bone. Remove any fat from around the kidneys, pull away the skin and, using scissors, snip out the core. Slice through the kidneys but do not cut in half. Slice the tomatoes in half, wash and peel the mushrooms and cut the stalks level with the caps.

Preheat the grill until hot and brush the trivet in the pan with oil or butter. Arrange the tomato halves in the base of the grill pan and season with salt and pepper. Season the cutlets and brush with melted butter or oil. Arrange the meat on the trivet over the tomato. Grill under high heat, turning the meat to seal both sides. Lower the heat and continue cooking. Cutlets need about 12 minutes, sausages need 8–10 minutes and the kidneys need 6–8 minutes. Brush all the food with oil or butter while grilling, turn sausages several times and kidneys once. Towards the end of the cooking time, add the mushrooms.

Serve with a garnish of well washed watercress.

Fried pork fillet with onions

Onions require gentle slow frying to make them tender and golden brown. They are delicious served with fried pork fillet.

Serves 4

1–1½ lb./½–¾ kg. pork fillet	3 rounded teaspoons castor
seasoned flour	sugar
1 lb./½ kg. onions	juice ½ lemon
3 oz./75 g. butter	

Using a sharp knife, trim away any fat, skin and sinew from the outside of the pork fillet. Cut the meat across into 2-inch (5-cm.) pieces. Place each slice on end, that is with one cut side facing upwards. Place each piece, one at a time, between two squares of wetted greaseproof paper and beat with a rolling pin until quite thin and flat. The wetted paper prevents the meat from sticking to either the board or the pin. Dip each piece of pork into seasoned flour and set aside ready for frying.

Peel and slice the onions. Melt 2 oz. (50 g.) of the butter in a frying pan. Add the onions, cover with a lid and fry gently until the onions are soft and tender – takes about 15 minutes.

Blend the sugar and lemon juice in a small basin. Remove the pan lid and stir in the sugar and lemon mixture. Continue to fry a little more quickly until the onions have browned – the addition of the sweet sour mixture gives the onions a delicious flavour.

Meanwhile, melt the remaining butter in a frying pan. Add the pieces of pork fillet and fry gently for 3–5 minutes, turning the pieces to brown on both sides. Draw the pan off the heat and serve the pork fillet with the hot onions.

Kidneys with Béarnaise sauce

Illustrated in colour on pages 60 and 61

Grilled specialities are very popular in France. Use the proper French flat skewers in preference to twisted meat skewers. Most large kitchen equipment stores should have them – buy ones at least 6–8 inches (15–20 cm.) long.

Serves 4

8 lambs' kidneys	2 tablespoons water
oil for brushing	2 egg yolks
salt and pepper	1 oz./25 g. butter, melted
for the Béarnaise sauce:	juice $\frac{1}{2}$ lemon
little chopped fresh tarragon	little chopped fresh parsley
10 turns of the pepper-mill	*to garnish:*
1 shallot, finely chopped	fresh watercress
1 tablespoon wine vinegar	

To prepare the kidneys, remove all protective fatty tissue from the outside, cut away any core and peel off the skin. Slice into each kidney on the rounded side, cutting almost through but not quite. Cutting kidney from this side keeps the shape well rounded. Open out the kidneys and skewer in pairs on four skewers.

Remove the grid from a grill pan and brush the base of pan with cooking oil. Brush kidneys with the oil and place open sides downwards on the grill pan. Put under a moderately hot grill and cook for 8 minutes. Season well with salt and freshly milled pepper and turn kidneys over. Grill for a further 2–3 minutes.

Meanwhile, prepare the Béarnaise sauce. Strip a few leaves from tarragon and chop finely. Place in a small saucepan with the pepper, shallot and vinegar. Use a plain enamel or stainless steel saucepan – a copper one would react with vinegar and discolour sauce. Heat gently until the vinegar has boiled away, but take care not to burn shallot. This initial reduction gives a special flavour and sharpness to the final sauce.

Add the water and egg yolks to the saucepan over low heat and, using a small hand whisk, whisk the mixture until thick and light. If the heat is too high, the egg mixture will overcook. Whisk over heat only until the mixture has thickened, then draw pan off heat and beat for a further few minutes. Gradually beat in the melted butter, then add a squeeze of lemon juice and a little finely chopped parsley. This sauce will stand quite well for a short time. In order to keep it warm, place the base of the pan in a pan or shallow roasting tin of hot, not boiling, water.

Serve the kidneys with a garnish of fresh watercress and straw potatoes, and spoon Béarnaise sauce into the centre of each kidney. Serve extra sauce separately.

Kebabs of lamb

Any cut of meat used for kebabs must be lean and tender. The best cut of meat to use for this recipe would be neck fillet of lamb.

Serves 4

1$\frac{1}{2}$ lb./$\frac{3}{4}$ kg. lean lamb	salt and freshly milled pepper
2 small onions	oil (see recipe)
4 oz./100 g. small mushrooms	1 teaspoon Worcestershire sauce
1 bay leaf	

Trim any fat or skin from the meat, then cut into chunky 1-inch (2$\frac{1}{2}$-cm.) pieces. Peel the onions, cut into quarters and separate the pieces. Wash and trim the mushroom stalks level with the caps. Place the meat and onion in a shallow dish together with the crushed bay leaf. Season well with salt and pepper and sprinkle with oil and the Worcestershire sauce. Leave for 1 hour to marinate, turning occasionally.

Thread the pieces of meat on to 4 skewers, alternately with pieces of onion and mushrooms. Roll the kebabs in the oil in the dish, coating well, then place under a hot grill. Cook, turning once, for 6–8 minutes.

Serve the kebabs with plain boiled rice and a tossed salad.

Fried liver with mushrooms and herbs

A quick recipe and an effective way of making fried liver interesting to serve and eat. Omit the garlic if preferred.

Serves 4

1 lb./$\frac{1}{2}$ kg. lamb's liver, cut in	8 oz./$\frac{1}{4}$ kg. button mushrooms
thin slices	1–2 tablespoons finely chopped
seasoned flour	parsley
2 oz./50 g. butter	juice $\frac{1}{2}$ lemon
1 clove garlic	

Trim the slices of liver and dip both sides of each piece in seasoned flour. Melt the butter in a frying pan, add the liver and fry gently to brown on both sides. Cook for about 2–3 minutes then remove the liver from the pan and keep hot.

Peel and finely chop the garlic. Trim and slice the button mushrooms. Add the garlic, mushrooms and parsley to the hot fat remaining in the pan. Fry gently for about 3–5 minutes. Then draw the pan off the heat. Squeeze over the lemon juice and spoon the mixture over the liver. Serve at once.

Grilled gammon rashers with pineapple

A delicious extra to this recipe is to place a thin slice of cheese under the pineapple. Grill until the cheese has melted and the pineapple is hot.

Serves 4

4 gammon rashers, about	1 oz./25 g. butter
$\frac{1}{4}$ inch/$\frac{1}{2}$ cm. thick	1 (8 oz./225 g.) can pineapple
soft brown sugar	rings

Trim any outer rind from the gammon rashers and snip the fat at $\frac{1}{4}$ inch ($\frac{1}{2}$ cm.) intervals. Rub the fatty parts with sugar and place a small piece of butter on each rasher.

Place under a preheated hot grill and grill for 5 minutes. Turn, rub the fat with sugar and baste with the dripping in the pan. Grill the second side for 2–3 minutes.

Drain the pineapple rings from the can and place one ring on each rasher. Return under the grill for a few moments until the pineapple is heated through. Serve hot.

Pork chops with piquante sauce

The sharp piquant flavour of this sauce goes well with fried pork chops and makes a pleasant change from apple sauce. Choose lean pork chops, preferably without any kidney.

Serves 4

4 pork chops	1 large onion
salt and freshly milled pepper	1 teaspoon concentrated tomato
flour (see recipe)	purée
1 oz./25 g. butter	¼ pint/1½ dl. dry white wine

Trim the chops and season both sides with salt and pepper, then dip both sides in a little flour. Shake away any surplus flour. Melt the butter in a frying pan, add the chops and fry gently, turning to brown them on both sides. Cook until tender – time depends on the size of the chops, but about 15 minutes should be sufficient. Keep the heat fairly low, the chops should be golden brown and not too dark in colour.

When cooked, lift the chops from the pan to a hot serving dish and keep hot. Finely chop the onion, or cut the onion in quarters and pass through a Mouli grater. The more finely the onion is chopped, the better the appearance and flavour. Add the onion to the hot fat remaining in the frying pan. Stir and cook for a moment until the onion begins to soften, then add the tomato purée and white wine. Stir to blend and bring up to a simmer. Cover the pan with a lid and simmer gently for about 15 minutes. Since there is a relatively small amount of liquid in the pan, take care to cook gently and keep the pan covered so that the sauce does not evaporate too rapidly. Taste, the sauce should be sharp in flavour. Add a pinch of sugar if too acid. Spoon the sauce over the chops and serve.

Hamburgers

These hamburgers are inexpensive to make and tasty to eat. Any left over are delicious served cold with mustard and a salad.

Serves 4

1½ lb./700 g. minced beef	1 egg
1 small onion	salt and freshly milled pepper
2 thin slices white bread	seasoned flour
2 tablespoons milk	2 oz./50 g. butter

Place the minced beef in a mixing basin. Peel and finely chop or grate the onion and add to the meat. For a less strong flavour, place the chopped onion in a saucepan, cover with boiling water and simmer for about 5 minutes. Drain and add to the meat. Trim the crusts from the bread. Place the bread in a basin and add the milk. Allow the bread to soak for a few minutes, then squeeze away the excess moisture. Add the bread to the meat along with the egg and a seasoning of salt and pepper – allow about 1 teaspoon of salt.

Mix the ingredients together by hand. Squeeze the mixture together and beat thoroughly. Turn the mixture out on to a board and divide into 8 equal portions. Using floured hands, shape to a round and then flatten out to a hamburger shape. Dip each one in seasoned flour on both sides and they are ready to fry.

Melt the butter in a frying pan. When frothing, add the hamburgers and brown quickly on both sides. Lower the heat, cover the pan with a lid and fry gently for 25–30 minutes. Turn the hamburgers once for even browning. When cooked, lift from the pan on to a hot serving dish.

Pour away the fat from the pan, leaving only the dripping and dark bits. Replace the pan over the heat and allow to get quite hot. Quickly pour about ½ teacup of cold water into the hot pan. Shake the pan so that the water swirls around and forms a gravy. Pour over the hamburgers and keep hot until ready to serve.

Fried liver with aubergines

For the best flavour, liver should be thinly sliced and very quickly fried – prepare and fry the aubergines first. The combined flavour of the two go particularly well together.

Serves 4

1 lb./½ kg. lamb's liver, cut	oil for frying
in slices	squeeze lemon juice
seasoned flour	*to garnish:*
2 large aubergines	chopped parsley
salt	

Trim the liver and dip both sides in seasoned flour. Peel and slice the aubergines. Place in a colander with a little salt sprinkled between the slices and leave for 30 minutes to draw the moisture. Press well to extract juices and pat the aubergines dry.

Pour sufficient oil into a large frying pan to just cover the base. Heat and add the slices of aubergine. Fry gently, turning to brown the slices on both sides. Fry for about 5 minutes until tender then remove from the pan and keep hot. Add more oil, if necessary, to fry all the aubergine.

Add the liver slices to the pan and fry quickly for about 2 minutes on each side. Squeeze the lemon juice over the cooked liver and sprinkle with the chopped parsley. Lift from the pan and serve with the aubergines. Pour over the juices from the pan.

Spatchcock of chicken

Spatchcock is a term applied to small birds, split down the back and grilled. Poussin or small spring chickens are ideal for this method of cooking, the flesh of the chicken must be young and tender.

Serves 4

2 small poussin	8 lean bacon rashers
2 oz./50 g. butter	*to garnish:*
salt and freshly milled pepper	watercress

Using a sharp knife, cut each bird down the back bone so that they lie flat. Place the inside upwards on the grill pan and spread the surface of each one liberally with the butter. Season with salt and freshly milled pepper. Place under a preheated hot grill and cook for 20–25 minutes, turning after 10 minutes. Baste the second side with the melted butter in the grill pan and sprinkle with salt and pepper.

About 5 minutes before the cooking time is complete, place the trimmed bacon rashers alongside the chicken. When cooked, separate the two halves using a pair of scissors or poultry shears. Serve garnished with the bacon rashers and washed watercress.

Kebabs of pork
with spiced orange sauce

This unusual and delicious sauce goes very well with pork. Choose pork tenderloin for kebabs, it is a cut which is very lean and easy to handle.

Serves 4

1½–2 lb./¾–1 kg. pork tender-loin	concentrated orange juice
2 small onions	4 tablespoons Worcestershire sauce
for the spiced orange sauce:	juice 1 lemon
6 oz./175 g. soft brown sugar	1 level teaspoon made mustard
1 (6¼ fl. oz./2 dl.) can frozen,	1 level tablespoon cornflour

Trim away any fat or skin from the meat and then cut the meat into neat pieces. Peel the onions, cut into quarters and then separate into pieces. Thread the pieces of meat on to 4 skewers, alternating with pieces of onion, then prepare the sauce.

Measure the sugar, concentrated orange juice, Worcestershire sauce, lemon juice and mustard into a saucepan. Place over a low heat and stir to dissolve the sugar. Draw the pan off the heat and brush the kebabs liberally with some of the sauce as a baste. Place under a hot grill and cook, turning once, for about 6–8 minutes.

Meanwhile, blend the cornflour with a little water to make a smooth paste and stir into the sauce remaining in the pan. Replace the pan over the heat and bring up to the boil, stirring to thicken evenly. Serve as a sauce, with the grilled kebabs arranged on a bed of saffron rice.

Swedish meatballs

Where possible, shape the meat balls about 1 hour in advance of cooking, so that they keep their shape better when frying.

Serves 4

1 lb./½ kg. lean steak	1 egg
2½ oz./65 g. butter	1 level teaspoon salt
1 medium onion, finely chopped	freshly milled pepper
3 slices white bread, from a small loaf	pinch ground cloves
4 tablespoons milk	6 tablespoons stock

Trim away any fat from the meat and pass the meat twice through the fine blade of a mincer. Melt ½ oz. (15 g.) of the butter in a small saucepan. Add the onion, cover with a lid and sauté gently for 5 minutes or until the onion is soft. Trim the crusts from the bread slices and place the bread in a bowl. Add the milk and leave to soak for 5 minutes. Then add the egg and mix together with a fork to make a soft purée. Add the bread mixture, the onion with any butter in the pan, the salt, pepper and ground cloves to the meat. Mix thoroughly to make a smooth, soft mixture. Using oiled fingers, shape into 20 small meatballs.

Melt the remaining butter in a large frying pan and add all the meatballs. Fry over a moderate heat for about 6–8 minutes, shaking the pan to brown them on all sides and prevent them from sticking. Draw the pan off the heat and lift the meatballs out on to a serving dish. Pour away excess fat in the pan and add the stock. Bring to the boil and simmer for a few minutes to reduce the stock slightly. Check seasoning, pour over the meatballs. Serve with cranberry sauce or jelly.

Recipes that are cooked slowly

Long, slow simmering encourages flavours to mellow and blend together. This is one of the reasons why a casserole always has such a good flavour. Gentle cooking encourages the less expensive meats to become tender, it imparts flavour to chicken and offers a method of serving meat and poultry that requires no last minute preparation or fuss. Serving times are not critical where casseroles are concerned. Once cooked they can be served when it suits you.

Barbecue chicken casserole

This is an ideal recipe to make in advance. It reheats very well. The spicy flavour mellows and is particularly good after about 24 hours.

Serves 4

4 chicken joints	1 teaspoon Worcestershire sauce
2 oz./50 g. butter	4 level tablespoons soft brown
2 medium onions	sugar
1 green pepper	juice $\frac{1}{2}$ lemon
1 tablespoon oil	1 ($2\frac{1}{2}$ oz./65 g.) can
1 level teaspoon salt	concentrated tomato purée
freshly milled pepper	$\frac{1}{2}$ pint/3 dl. water
2 level teaspoons made mustard	

Trim the chicken joints neatly. Heat the butter in a frying pan, add the chicken and fry until golden brown on all sides. Lift the pieces of chicken from the pan and place in a casserole.

Peel and slice the onions. Deseed and shred the green pepper. Add the oil to the fat remaining in the frying pan. Add the onions and green pepper and cook gently for about 5 minutes, until the vegetables are soft but not brown. Measure the salt, a seasoning of pepper, the mustard, Worcestershire sauce, sugar, lemon juice, tomato purée and water into a basin. Blend well and then add to the softened onions and green pepper in the frying pan. Stir to mix, bring up to the boil and simmer for a few minutes. Draw off the heat and pour over the chicken joints. Cover the casserole, place in the centre of a moderate oven (350°F., 180°C., Gas Mark 4) and cook for 1 hour.

When ready, spoon the chicken joints out on to a serving dish. Skim off any fat from the surface of the sauce and then pour the sauce over the chicken.

Advance preparation: The recipe can be made in advance. Reheat in a moderate oven (350°F., 180°C., Gas Mark 4) until bubbling hot and heated through – about 30 minutes.

Hot pot of lamb

This recipe, from the North of England, provides both meat and vegetables cooked together and serves as a meal on its own.

Serves 4

2 lb./1 kg. middle neck of lamb	2 sticks celery
seasoned flour	1 leek
1 oz./25 g. dripping or white	salt and freshly milled pepper
cooking fat	$\frac{1}{4}$ level teaspoon mixed herbs
$1\frac{1}{2}$ lb./$\frac{3}{4}$ kg. potatoes	$\frac{3}{4}$ pint/$\frac{1}{2}$ litre stock (see recipe)
2 medium onions	chopped parsley
2 carrots	

Wipe the meat and cut away the bones. Put the bones in a saucepan and cover generously with cold water. Bring up to the boil and allow to simmer while preparing the vegetables.

Trim away the fat from the meat and cut the meat into neat pieces. Roll in seasoned flour and then fry in the hot dripping to brown and seal on all sides. Peel and slice the potatoes about $\frac{1}{4}$ inch ($\frac{1}{2}$ cm.) thick. Reserve half the nicest slices for the top and place the remainder in the base of a casserole dish. Peel and chop the onions, peel and thinly slice the carrots. Wash, trim and slice the celery. Wash and slice the leek. Mix all the vegetables together with a good seasoning of salt and pepper and the herbs. Arrange layers of seasoned vegetables and meat in the casserole, beginning and ending with a layer of vegetables. Top with the reserved potato slices, arranging them neatly in overlapping circles on top. Measure out about $\frac{3}{4}$ pint ($\frac{1}{2}$ litre) of the bone stock and pour into the casserole, the stock should barely cover the vegetables. Cover with a buttered paper and a tight fitting lid. Place in the centre of a moderate oven (350°F., 180°C., Gas Mark 4) and cook for 2–$2\frac{1}{2}$ hours.

About 30 minutes before serving, remove the paper and lid from the casserole. Brush the potatoes with a little melted dripping and sprinkle with salt. Raise the oven heat to hot (400°F., 200°C., Gas Mark 6) and return the casserole to the oven, placing it above centre. Do not cover with the lid, but allow the potatoes to crisp and brown slightly. Sprinkle with chopped parsley before serving.

Advance preparation: This recipe will keep hot nicely. It is not advisable to make in advance and reheat because of the quantity of vegetables.

Casserole of lamb

Young lamb has a sweet, delicious flavour. On the whole, cuts of lamb are usually grilled or roasted because the meat is very tender. This also means that casserole of lamb is reasonably quickly cooked and ideal for combining with the young spring vegetables.

Serves 4

4 double cutlets of lamb	8 oz./$\frac{1}{4}$ kg. young carrots
salt and pepper	1 lb./$\frac{1}{2}$ kg. new potatoes
1 oz./25 g. butter	*to garnish:*
2 onions, finely sliced	chopped parsley
$\frac{1}{2}$ pint/3 dl. stock, use water and	
a stock cube	

Trim the chops neatly, cutting away any excess fat. Season well with salt and pepper. Melt the butter in a frying pan, add the chops and brown well on both sides. Lift the meat from the pan and place in the base of a casserole dish. Add the onions to the hot fat in the pan and fry gently until soft. Add these to the casserole, together with the stock and a good seasoning of salt and pepper. The stock should only just cover the pieces of lamb.

Peel and scrape the carrots and scrape the new potatoes. Cut the potatoes in half if large but where possible select small ones that can be left whole. Add these to the casserole and sprinkle with salt. Cover with a lid and place in the centre of a moderate oven (350°F., 180°C., Gas Mark 4) and cook for $1\frac{1}{2}$ hours. Sprinkle with chopped parsley and serve.

Advanced preparation: This recipe will keep hot without spoiling.

Beef stew with herb dumplings

A beef stew with old fashioned dumplings is nourishing and filling on a cold winter's day. Other flavours for dumplings are suggested on page 26.

Serves 4

1½–2 lb./¾–1 kg. lean stewing steak	*for the dumplings:*
8 oz./¼ kg. small onions	4 oz./100 g. self-raising flour
8 oz./¼ kg. carrots	pinch salt
seasoned flour	1 level teaspoon dried mixed herbs
1 oz./25 g. dripping or white cooking fat	2 oz./50 g. shredded beef suet
1½ pints/1 litre beef stock or water	1 tablespoon finely chopped onion
salt and freshly milled pepper	about 3–4 tablespoons water

Trim away any fat from the meat and cut the meat into neat pieces. Peel the onions, leaving them whole, and scrape and slice the carrots. Toss the meat in the seasoned flour. Reserve the extra seasoned flour for making the gravy later in the recipe. Heat the fat in a frying pan, add the meat and fry quickly to brown on all sides. Remove the meat from the pan and place in a medium sized saucepan. Add the prepared onions and the carrots to the meat.

If necessary add a little extra fat to the frying pan and then add a tablespoon of the reserved seasoned flour. Stir over the heat until the flour begins to brown and cook gently until fairly dark in colour. This gives colour and flavour to the gravy. Gradually stir in the hot stock. Stir well, scraping up all the bits from the base of the pan and bring up to the boil. Check seasoning and if necessary add salt and pepper. It is important at this stage that the gravy has a good flavour and colour. Strain into the saucepan over the meat and vegetables. Cover with a lid, bring to a simmer and cook gently for 2½–3 hours or until the meat is quite tender.

About 35 minutes before the end of the cooking time, prepare the dumplings. Sift the flour and salt into a basin. Add the mixed herbs, suet and onion. Mix well and sprinkle in the water. Using a fork, stir to a soft, but firm enough to handle, dough. Turn out on to a floured working surface and divide the dough into 6 or 8 pieces. With floured hands, roll each piece into a ball. Coat very lightly with flour and add the dumplings to the stew. Place the dumplings on top of the nearly cooked meat – do not submerge them in the liquid. Cover and cook for the last 30 minutes.

Serve the stew with the dumplings.

Advance preparation: The beef stew can be made in advance and reheated. The dumplings should be cooked only when ready to serve.

Swiss steak

Serves 4

1½ lb./¾ kg. piece lean braising steak	2 large onions
2 level tablespoons flour	1 clove garlic
½ level teaspoon salt	1 green pepper
freshly milled pepper	1 lb./½ kg. tomatoes or
1 oz./25 g. beef dripping or white cooking fat	1 (15 oz./425 g.) can tomatoes

Trim the meat neatly. Mix together the flour, salt and a good seasoning of pepper. Lay the meat on a board and sprinkle with half the flour mixture. Rub or pound the flour thoroughly into the surface of the meat. Turn the pieces and repeat the procedure until all the flour is used up. Cut the meat into four neat pieces.

Melt the fat in a large frying pan, add the meat and fry over a moderate heat for about 15 minutes to brown thoroughly on all sides. Meanwhile, peel and chop the onions and peel and finely chop the garlic. Peel, deseed and chop the green pepper. Nick the skins on the fresh tomatoes, place together in a bowl and cover with boiling water. Allow to stand for 1 minute, then drain and peel away the skins. Slice the tomatoes coarsely and add to the meat together with the other vegetables. If canned tomatoes are used they should be added at this stage. Lower the heat, cover the pan with a lid and simmer very gently for about 2 hours or until the meat is quite tender.

When ready to serve, lift the meat and vegetables from the pan, arrange in a serving dish. Check seasoning in the gravy, strain over the meat and serve.

Stuffed green peppers

Green peppers are very versatile, they add colour and flavour to casseroles and make the most marvellous cases for meat or savoury stuffings.

Serves 4

4 even-sized green peppers	2 tomatoes
1–2 oz./25–50 g. Parmesan cheese, grated	1 rounded tablespoon flour
for the filling:	2 teaspoons Worcestershire sauce
½ oz./15 g. white cooking fat	2 tablespoons tomato ketchup
1 large onion	¼ pint/1½ dl. stock or water
1 clove garlic	salt and freshly milled pepper
¾–1 lb./⅓–½ kg. lean minced beef	

Where possible, select squat round peppers that will stand upright. Using a small sharp knife, cut neatly round the stem of each pepper. Draw it out, together with the seeds from inside. Place the peppers together in a bowl. Cover with boiling water and allow to stand for 5 minutes. Then drain the peppers upside down and set aside while preparing the filling.

Melt the fat in a saucepan, add the chopped onion and fry gently for a few minutes until soft. Remove the outer papery coating from the garlic and then mash the garlic to a purée with a little salt. Add the garlic to the onion along with the minced beef. Continue to fry gently until the meat is well browned.

Scald the tomatoes, peel away the skins and remove the seeds. Chop the tomato flesh coarsely and add to the meat. Sprinkle in the flour and stir thoroughly. Add the Worcestershire sauce, tomato ketchup and stock or water. Season well with salt and pepper and stir over a low heat for about 5 minutes or until the sauce is thick.

Arrange the peppers neatly in a well buttered fireproof dish. Spoon the meat mixture evenly into the peppers. Sprinkle the tops of each lavishly with Parmesan cheese. Add about 2 tablespoons of water to the dish. Place the peppers in the centre of a moderate oven (350°F., 180°C., Gas Mark 4) and cook for 35–40 minutes. Serve hot.

Advance preparation: Prepare the stuffing and fill the peppers in advance. Keep chilled and put to bake when required.

Liver and bacon casserole

Liver and bacon casserole is a good recipe for a busy day. A little sliced onion can be fried with the bacon if liked – it gives extra flavour to the gravy. This recipe works equally well for smaller portions.

Serves 4

4 lean bacon rashers	1 oz./25 g. butter
1 lb./½ kg. lambs' liver, cut in thin slices	½ pint/3 dl. stock
seasoned flour	salt and pepper

Trim the rind from the bacon rashers and cut the rashers in half. Place these in a dry frying pan and fry gently until the fat runs and the rashers are lightly cooked. Lift the rashers from the pan and place in a casserole dish. Trim the liver and pull away any skin. Dip both sides of each piece in seasoned flour.

Add the butter to the hot bacon fat and when melted and frothing, place in the slices of liver. Fry the liver over moderate heat to brown and seal on both sides. Place the liver in the casserole along with the bacon.

To the hot fat remaining in the frying pan, add about 1 level tablespoon of the seasoned flour. If necessary add about ½ oz. (15 g.) extra butter to absorb the flour and stir the mixture over the heat until it becomes a nutty brown colour. Gradually stir in the hot stock. Stir constantly over the heat until the mixture thickens to make a gravy. Season to taste with salt and pepper. Draw off the heat.

Strain the gravy into the casserole and cover with a lid. Place in the centre of a moderate oven (350°F., 180°C., Gas Mark 4) and cook for 30–40 minutes. Serve from the dish.
Advance preparation: This casserole can be made in advance and reheated without spoiling.

Boeuf en daube

Illustrated in colour on pages 88 and 89

This is a French country casserole of beef, vegetables, wine and herbs, simmered in a slow oven for 4–5 hours. Fresh tomatoes may be used instead of tomato purée, but whatever the variation the result is always richly delicious.

Serves 6

3 lb./1 kg. 400 g. piece shoulder or skirt of beef	bouquet garni
6 oz./175 g. streaky unsmoked bacon, cut in one piece	½ bottle dry red wine
1 lb./½ kg. carrots, peeled and sliced	3 oz./75 g. butter
1 lb./½ kg. onions, peeled and sliced	1 clove garlic (optional)
6 black peppercorns	¾ pint/4½ dl. stock or water plus stock cube
2 level teaspoons salt	1 (2½ oz./65 g.) can tomato purée
	1 tablespoon finely chopped parsley

Trim off the fat and cut the meat into thick slices or large cubes. Trim away the rind from the bacon and dice. Place the meat and bacon in a large mixing basin with the prepared vegetables, peppercorns, salt and bouquet garni made as follows: using fine string or thick spread, tie together in a bundle one bay leaf, a sprig of dried thyme and a few fresh parsley stalks. Leave a long piece of string or thread hanging from the bouquet garni, so that it may be easily removed after cooking. Pour the red wine over meat and vegetables and leave to marinate for 3 hours, turning meat occasionally. The purpose of marinating raw meat in red wine is to add flavour and help soften fibres.

Drain the meat and vegetables from marinade, reserving liquor. Using half the butter, fry the meat pieces until brown, then add the rest of the butter and fry the mixed vegetables. Remove the papery coating of the garlic clove and crush with salt. Add to the vegetables while frying. It is preferable to add garlic at this stage, if liked, but the garlic may be omitted. In a large casserole, arrange a base using half of the vegetables, then top with meat and finally with remaining vegetables. Strain the marinade over the top and add the bouquet garni. Add the stock to the frying pan. Place the pan over the heat and bring to the boil, then stir in the tomato purée. Pour the liquid over the meat in the casserole and add the parsley. Cover and place in centre of a slow oven (300°F., 150°C., Gas Mark 2) and cook for 4–5 hours.

The long, slow cooking makes the meat really tender and the juices rich and full of flavour. When cooked, the meat will have a reddish appearance. Check the seasoning and remove the bouquet garni.

This casserole can be rather rich in fat because of the bacon, which is added to give extra flavour, so skim off as much fat as possible with a spoon.
Advance preparation: This dish can be cooked in advance and reheated when ready to serve.

Braised lambs' tongues

Lambs' tongues are very tasty and inexpensive. They can be cooked in a pressure cooker for 30 minutes at 15 lb. (9 kg.) pressure, which cuts down cooking time considerably.

Serves 4

4 lambs' tongues	*for the sauce:*
8 oz./¼ kg. carrots, scraped and sliced	½ pint/3 dl. cooking liquor (see recipe)
2 large onions, peeled and sliced	½ oz./15 g. butter
1 pint/6 dl. water or stock	1 level tablespoon flour
	salt and pepper

Wash the tongues and place in a deep saucepan, on a bed of the prepared carrots and onions. Add the water or stock. Bring up to the boil then lower the heat, cover with a lid and allow to simmer gently for 1½–2 hours.

When tender, lift out the tongues, remove the skins and the core at the back of the tongue. Reserve the carrots, a little of the onion and the cooking liquor, which should be strained and measured. Replace the carrots, onions and sliced lambs' tongues in the saucepan. Reduce the strained liquor by boiling rapidly until about ½ pint (3 dl.). Melt the butter in a pan over moderate heat. Stir in the flour and allow to cook gently until the mixture is dark brown. Gradually stir in the reduced stock, a little at a time. Bring to the boil, season if necessary and simmer for 5 minutes. Pour over the lambs' tongues and heat through thoroughly.

Serve with creamed potatoes and Brussels sprouts or other green vegetables.
Advance preparation: This casserole will reheat without spoiling and can be made in advance.

Oxtail casserole

Choose a good sized oxtail; one should be enough to serve four persons. Start this recipe well in advance, oxtail needs a long, slow cooking time. Serve with mashed or creamed potatoes.

Serves 4

1 oxtail, cut in joints	1 rounded tablespoon flour
2 pints/generous 1 litre water	salt and freshly milled pepper
bouquet garni	1 level teaspoon curry powder
2 large onions	1 (2½ oz./65 g.) can concentrated
2 carrots	tomato purée
1 leek	chopped parsley
1 oz./25 g. dripping or white	
cooking fat	

Place the oxtail joints in a saucepan and add the water and a bouquet garni of thyme, bay leaf and parsley stalks. Bring up to the boil, cover with a lid and simmer the oxtail very gently for about 2 hours. Strain off the liquor and let it cool, then skim off the heavy layer of fat. Make the liquor up to 1 pint (½ litre) with water if necessary.

Peel and slice the onions and scrape and slice the carrots. Trim the leek, cut through to the centre and wash well in cold water. Shred the leek finely and place all the prepared vegetables in the base of a large casserole. Place the pieces of oxtail on top.

Melt the fat in a saucepan. Stir in the flour and cook gently, stirring from time to time, until the mixture is a nutty brown colour. Stir in a seasoning of salt and pepper, the curry powder and tomato purée. Gradually stir in the 1 pint (½ litre) of reserved oxtail cooking liquor. Bring up to the boil, stirring all the time. Pour over the oxtail and vegetables in the casserole. Cover and place in a moderate oven (325°F., 170°C., Gas Mark 3) and cook for 1½–2 hours. The oxtail meat should fall way from the bones. Sprinkle with chopped parsley and serve.

Advance preparation: Oxtail casserole reheats very well. Oxtail can be boiled and left overnight to cool in the liquid. Remove the fat from the surface and measure out the stock. Continue with the recipe. When cooked it keeps hot without spoiling or can be reheated.

Casserole of beef with onions, tomatoes and sweet peppers

In this beef recipe, the juices come from the mixture of vegetables cooked with the meat. The flavour is very good.

Serves 4

4 oz./100 g. streaky bacon	1 lb./½ kg. onions
rashers	4 green sweet peppers
1½ lb./¾ kg. lean braising steak	1 lb./½ kg. tomatoes
2 oz./50 g. butter	salt and freshly milled pepper

Trim the bacon rashers and use to line the base of a casserole dish. Trim the meat and cut into cubes. Arrange the meat over the bacon in the casserole.

Melt the butter in a frying pan. Peel and slice the onions and halve, deseed and shred the green peppers. Add the pepper and onion to the hot butter and fry gently for about 10 minutes or until the vegetables are soft. Scald the tomatoes and peel away the skins. Slice the tomatoes thickly.

Spoon the onion and pepper over the meat and top with the slices of tomato. Season well with salt and pepper and cover the casserole with a lid. Place in the centre of a moderate oven (325°F., 170°C., Gas Mark 3) and cook for 2 hours. No extra liquid is required as sufficient will be made from the tomatoes.

Serve with the vegetables and juice from the casserole.

Advance preparation: Prepare the recipe in advance and reheat. It also keeps hot without spoiling.

Casserole of pork with apples and prunes

Apples, prunes and onions all make this casserole an unusual and very attractive dish to serve. Pork combines well with the fruit flavours.

Serves 4

4 lean pork chops	8 large tenderised prunes
salt and freshly milled pepper	$\frac{1}{2}$ level teaspoon powdered sage
1 oz./25 g. lard or dripping	about $\frac{1}{2}$ pint/3 dl. liquid, use
2 medium cooking apples	part cider or light ale and
2 medium onions	part water.

Rub the pork chops with salt and pepper. Melt the fat in a frying pan, add the pork chops and seal on both sides. Fry to brown them and then remove from the pan.

Peel and slice both the apples and the onions. Arrange a third of them in the base of a casserole dish. Blanch the prunes for 3 minutes in boiling water. Halve and remove the stones. Place half the prunes on the bed of apples and onions and arrange the pork chops on top. Sprinkle with the sage and a seasoning of salt and pepper. Cover with remaining apples and onion and the remainder of the prunes on top. Pour over the liquid. Cover with buttered paper and a lid. Place in the centre of a moderate oven (350°F., 180°C., Gas Mark 4) and cook for 2 hours.

Check the level of the liquid after about $1\frac{1}{2}$ hours and if necessary add a little more. When ready, the casserole should be juicy, but most of the liquid should have been absorbed or evaporated.

Sprinkle with chopped parsley before serving.

Advance preparation: This casserole will keep hot without spoiling; it is not advisable to make it in advance.

Pasta

Pasta, in its various forms, can provide a wide range of satisfying meals that are ideally suited to the colder weather. Economical too, since the majority of dishes call for little more than a tasty sauce and some cheese.

How to cook pasta

Use a large saucepan with plenty of boiling, salted water. Add the pasta slowly so that the water remains as close to the boil as possible. To cook long spaghetti, hold a handful of the pasta at one end and dip the other end in the fast boiling water. As the spaghetti softens, coil it round the inside of the pan until all the spaghetti is immersed. Boil all pasta fast to keep it moving, and keep the pan uncovered.

Add a tablespoon of oil to the water when cooking larger pasta, particularly lasagna or canneloni. The oil helps prevent the pieces of pasta from sticking together while cooking – particularly important where lasagna is concerned.

Pasta should be cooked until tender but still slightly chewy – the Italians call this 'al dente'. To test, lift a strand of pasta from the pan with a fork against the sides of the pan, it should break easily and cleanly. The cooking time will depend on the type and thickness of the pasta used. Quick cooking varieties may take as little as 2 minutes for quick cooking egg noodles, or as long as 7 minutes for quick cooking macaroni. The standard

Melt the butter in a saucepan. Trim and chop the bacon rasher and fry lightly in the hot butter. Add the sliced onion and carrot and fry gently for a further 5 minutes. Wash and quarter the tomatoes and add to the ingredients in saucepan. Cover and allow to cook gently for about 5 minutes or until the tomatoes are soft and juices have been drawn out.

Stir in the stock, flour blended with a little water, seasoning of salt and pepper, sugar and lemon juice. Cover with a lid and simmer for 30 minutes. Draw off the heat and rub the sauce through a sieve. Discard the skin and pips and reheat the sauce. Check seasoning and use as required.

Advance preparation: Make the sauce in advance. Strain, check seasoning and reheat when ready to use.

Meat sauce for pasta

This is a sauce to serve with spaghetti or tagliatelle. Serve with the sauce mixed in; do this by lifting and turning the spaghetti in the sauce with two forks – never stirring; or serve the sauce separately. Either way, hand round a bowl of grated Parmesan cheese.

Makes 1 pint (6 dl.) sauce

2 tablespoons oil	freshly milled pepper
1 medium onion	1 (2½ oz./65 g.) can concentrated
1 clove garlic	tomato purée
1 lb./½ kg. lean minced beef	pinch dried mixed herbs
1 lb./½ kg. fresh tomatoes	¾ pint/½ litre stock
2 level tablespoons flour	1 wine glass red wine
1 level teaspoon salt	

Heat the oil in a medium sized saucepan. Peel and finely chop the onion, peel the garlic and crush to a purée with a little salt. Add the onion to the hot oil, cover and cook gently for about 5 minutes until the onion is soft but not brown. Stir in the minced beef and the crushed garlic. Continue to fry gently for a moment, to seal the meat. Stir to brown the mixture on all sides.

Scald the tomatoes and peel away the skins. Cut tomatoes in half and scoop out the seeds. Stir the flour, salt, pepper, tomatoes, tomato purée and mixed herbs into the meat mixture. Add the stock and red wine. Bring to the boil. Lower the heat and simmer gently for 40–45 minutes. Stir occasionally to prevent the sauce sticking and add a little extra stock if necessary. The final consistency should not be too thick. Check seasoning and use as required.

Advance preparation: Make the sauce in advance. Check the seasoning and keep chilled. Reheat when ready to use.

Lasagna

Made up dishes, such as lasagna with layers of meat sauce and canneloni with various stuffings, take more time to prepare but they make excellent party dishes because they can be assembled in advance and then reheated for serving.

Serves 6

8 oz./225 g. lasagna	1 pint/6 dl. meat sauce
1 tablespoon oil	(page 84)
8 oz./225 g. ricotta cheese	3–4 oz./75–100 g. Parmesan
1 egg	cheese, grated

Add the lasagna to a pan of boiling salted water (with 1 tablespoon oil added) and boil for 15–20 minutes or until tender. Drain in a colander and separate the pieces.

Meanwhile, mix the ricotta cheese with the egg and have the meat sauce ready made. Spoon a little of the meat sauce into the base of a large shallow baking dish. Cover with a layer of lasagna, spoon over a layer of ricotta cheese and sprinkle with a little Parmesan cheese. Repeat the procedure ending with a layer of meat sauce. Sprinkle with the remaining Parmesan cheese.

Heat through in a moderate oven (350°F., 180°C., Gas Mark 4) and cook for 30–40 minutes or until bubbling hot and browned. Allow to stand for 5 minutes before serving.

Serve with a tossed salad.

Advance preparation: Make the meat sauce, cook the pasta and assemble the lasagna. Keep chilled and put to reheat when ready to serve.

Canneloni stuffed with chicken and spinach

If flat squares of canneloni are used, the filling should be rolled up inside each one.

Serves 6

12 canneloni shells	1 onion, peeled
for the filling and sauce:	1 bay leaf
1 lb./½ kg. fresh or	2 oz./50 g. butter
8 oz./225 g. frozen spinach	2 oz./50 g. flour
8–12 oz./225–350 g. cooked	salt and freshly milled pepper
chicken	3–4 oz./75–100 g. Parmesan
1 pint/6 dl. milk	cheese, grated

Start by preparing the filling and sauce. Wash and prepare the spinach. Place in a saucepan and cook for 10 minutes – water clinging to the leaves is sufficient moisture. Drain well, chop finely and reserve. Frozen spinach needs only to be thawed and chopped if necessary. Chop or mince the chicken flesh finely. Put the milk to infuse with an onion and bay leaf for 10–15 minutes. Meanwhile, melt the butter in a large saucepan and stir in the flour. Cook very gently for a few moments but do not allow to brown. Gradually stir in the strained milk, beating well all the time. Gradually bring up to the boil and add salt and pepper to make a well-seasoned white sauce. Simmer for about 15 minutes.

Add sufficient of the sauce to the spinach and chicken to make a moist stuffing. Add about 3 oz. (75 g.) of the Parmesan cheese to the sauce remaining in the pan and stir well to make a cheese sauce. Add the canneloni shells to boiling, salted water and cook for 15 minutes or until just tender – take care not to over-boil as once broken they are difficult to fill. Drain and cool for a few minutes. Stuff each shell with spinach and chicken filling. It is easier to do this with a large nylon piping bag and a plain nozzle about ½ inch (1 cm.) wide.

Check the flavour in the sauce and spoon a little into the base of a large shallow serving dish. Arrange the stuffed shells neatly in the dish. Pour over remaining sauce and sprinkle with the remaining grated cheese. Place above centre in a moderate oven (350°F., 180°C., Gas Mark 4) and heat through for 20–30 minutes or until bubbling hot and brown. Serve with salad.

Advance preparation: Prepare and stuff the canneloni. Cover with the sauce when ready to reheat. Place in the oven as above and heat through when ready to serve.

Party recipes using meat and poultry

Gather a collection of suitable recipes for entertaining, but make frequent additions to the list so that the menus are imaginative and never monotonous. A menu is usually planned around the main course, so consider it carefully. Choose a main course that suits the season of the year, one that suits the occasion and the time available for preparation. Something as simple as roast pheasant is as good a party dish for an autumn menu, as the Chicken Marengo would be for a spring dinner. The quality of ingredients is important — buy the best and use wine, herbs and cream, where possible, to make the recipes taste superb.

Choosing game

Young, tender game should always be roasted. Older birds can successfully be made into casseroles, pies or pâtés.

All game should hang for a period of time. The purpose of hanging being to make the flesh tender. The period of hanging depends on the type of game and the weather. Game will naturally hang longer in cold weather. Pheasant can be hung for a week or more if the weather is cold. When a tail feather can be pulled out fairly easily, it is a good indication that the bird is ready. Partridge requires only to be hung for about 3 days. Unlike other game, partridge should never be allowed to become too high in flavour. Hare should be hung for 7–8 days in a cool place and can hang longer if the weather is very cold. Hare should hang by the hind legs, with a polythene bag tied over the head to catch the blood. The blood is often used in recipes to thicken and enrich the sauce. Water birds, such as wild duck, should be eaten fresh. They have an oily flesh which soon becomes rancid.

Not until the game is ready to cook should it be plucked and drawn. At this stage, most butchers will do the job for you if you are a regular customer, he will usually charge a small fee. Game purchased from the butchers will have been hung and be ready to cook.

Game can be kept in the home freezer. It must be hung before freezing and cannot be hung afterwards. It is important not to allow game to become too high in flavour when it is to be frozen. Separate out and label young birds for roasting and older birds for casseroling. Young birds can be identified by their supple feet and the short sharp spur at the back of the leg. The birds should be plucked, drawn and tied into a neat shape. Place in a polythene bag, exclude all the air. Tie tightly and place in the freezer. When ready to use, thaw slowly overnight in the refrigerator.

Pheasant (available 1st October – 1st February)
One pheasant will serve four portions. The cock bird is larger than the hen, but the hen is fatter and the flesh more succulent.

Place a large nut of butter inside the bird and cover the breast with bacon rashers. Roast on a trivet or bed of vegetables in the centre of a hot oven (425°F., 220°C., Gas Mark 7). After 10 minutes, reduce the oven heat to 400°F., 200°C., Gas Mark 6. Baste frequently and roast a tender young bird for 40–45 minutes. About 10 minutes before the cooking time is complete, remove the bacon rashers and baste the bird. Dredge the breast with flour, baste again and return the bird to the oven to brown.

Grouse (available 12th August – 10th December)
One grouse will usually serve two portions, according to size. Place a nob of butter inside each trussed bird and tie a fatty bacon rasher over the breast. Roast in a hot oven (400°F., 200°C., Gas Mark 6) for about 30–40 minutes. Baste frequently. Remove the bacon rashers and baste the birds 10 minutes before cooking time is completed. Dredge with flour and baste again. Return to the oven to brown. When cooked, cut the grouse in half lengthwise with game shears and remove the back bone.

Serve the two portions with thin gravy and trimmings.

Partridge (available 1st September – 17th February)
Allow one bird per person and roast exactly as for Grouse, allowing about 30 minutes cooking time.

Hare (available 1st August – last day in February)
The best cut of hare for roasting is the saddle, the leg joints are usually casseroled. Hare should be marinated before cooking. This draws the blood and makes the flesh less rich and more tender. The marinade can be used in the gravy.

Marinate the hare in red wine with 1–2 tablespoons olive oil, a bay leaf, sliced onion and freshly milled pepper. Leave for several hours and then drain. Lard the back with strips of bacon fat or tie with bacon rashers. Roast in a hot oven (425°F., 220°C., Gas Mark 7) for 45 minutes–1 hour. When ready, pour the marinade over and leave in the oven for 2–3 minutes. Remove the hare, strip away the bacon rashers and keep the hare hot. Add stock to the pan and thicken the gravy in the same manner as roast venison, below.

Serve with the gravy and redcurrant jelly.

Venison (Buck available June – September)
(Doe available November – February)
Cuts of venison for roasting can be taken from the fore-quarters or saddle, which is a very sweet meat, or from the hind quarters which is considered more tender. The meat is very dry and so must be protected with bacon rashers, a flour and water paste or as in Scotland, with mutton fat which is considered the best to combine with the flavour of venison.

Rub venison with salt and cover with streaky bacon rashers. Place in a covered roasting tin or cover with a protective layer of foil. Roast as for beef, that is allowing 20 minutes per lb. ($\frac{1}{2}$ kg.) plus 20 minutes. When cooked, lift the meat from the tin and keep hot in the oven while preparing the gravy.

Pour away the fat from the tin and add $\frac{1}{2}$ pint (3 dl.) stock or water. Bring up to the boil, stirring to pick up the bits. In a basin, blend 2 teaspoons of flour with water to make a paste and stir in a little hot stock. Return to the tin and stir until boiling. Taste for seasoning.

Serve with redcurrant jelly and the gravy.

Wild duck (available 1st September – 17th February)
Allow one bird to two portions. Pack one or two pieces of orange inside the bird. Spread the skin with softened butter. Roast in a hot oven (425°F., 220°C., Gas Mark 7), basting often, for about 25–30 minutes. Wild duck should not be overcooked.

Serve with a thin gravy and orange salad.

OVERLEAF **Boeuf en daube (page 82)**
Cut the meat into thick slices and prepare the vegetables.
Add the marinated vegetables and meat to a large casserole, starting with a layer of vegetables, the meat, then the remaining vegetables.
Add the stock with tomato purée to the casserole. Cover and cook in the oven.

Sugar baked gammon with spiced peaches

Wherever possible, prepare these peaches 24 hours before serving. This allows the spiced flavours to mellow and blend. Check the weight of the gammon joint before soaking so that you can calculate the cooking time.

Serves 6

1 piece corner gammon, about 2½–3 lb./1¼–1½ kg.	3 tablespoons wine vinegar
demerara sugar	4 oz./100 g. castor sugar
few whole cloves	6–8 cloves
for the spiced peaches:	1-inch/2½-cm. piece stick
1 (15 oz./425 g.) can peach halves	cinnamon

Cover the gammon with cold water and leave to soak for several hours or overnight. Drain and place skin side down in a saucepan, recover with fresh cold water and bring up to the boil. Allowing 20 minutes per lb. (½ kg.) plus 20 minutes over, simmer the joint for half the cooking time.

Lift the gammon from the pan and, using a sharp knife, strip away the rind. Score the fat in a criss-cross fashion and coat the entire surface with demerara sugar. Press a few cloves over the surface. Place the gammon in a roasting tin and put in the centre of a moderate oven (350°F., 180°C., Gas Mark 4) and bake for the remaining cooking time. When cooked, allow the gammon to cool.

Serve sliced with the spiced peaches.

For the spiced peaches, drain the peaches from the can and reserve the syrup. Place the fruit in a basin and measure ¼ pint (1½ dl.) of the peach syrup into a saucepan. Add the vinegar, sugar, cloves and cinnamon stick. Stir over a low heat until the sugar has dissolved, then bring up to the boil. Simmer for a moment, then pour the hot syrup over the fruit. Allow to stand, preferably over 24 hours, until cold.

Advance preparation: Prepare peaches well in advance. Cook and glaze gammon early in the day or the day before.

Fricadelles

Fricadelles are delicious, tender little morsels of veal smothered in a rich tomato sauce. They can be made using the cheaper cuts of veal; after trimming and mincing, the meat should weigh at least 10–12 oz. (275–350 g.).

Serves 4

1 lb./⅓–½ kg. lean veal	¼ level teaspoon pepper
1 oz./25 g. pork fat or shredded suet	pinch ground mace or nutmeg
1 small onion	¼ pint/1½ dl. water or veal stock
2½ oz./65 g. white bread, with crusts removed	seasoned flour
4 tablespoons milk	2 oz./50 g. butter
1 heaped teaspoon finely chopped parsley	½ pint/3 dl. tomato sauce (page 84)
pinch thyme	*to garnish:*
1 level teaspoon salt	chopped parsley

Trim away fat or any skin from veal and put through the fine blade of a mincer with the pork fat and quartered onion. (If suet is used, simply mince veal and onion and stir in the suet.) Slice the bread, put into a bowl and spoon the milk over. Leave to soak for about 30 minutes.

Put the minced meat, fat, onion, parsley, thyme and a seasoning of salt, pepper and mace or nutmeg into a bowl. Squeeze excess moisture from the bread and add the bread to the meat. Using the fingers, squeeze all ingredients together to get a light, smooth texture. Gradually work in water or stock, about a tablespoon at a time. It is important not to add the liquid too quickly, or the mixture will become sloppy. Squeeze well after each addition of liquid until it is completely absorbed.

Measure two good rounded tablespoons of seasoned flour on to a plate. Flour the hands well. Scoop out the meat mixture in teaspoonfuls and mould into small balls about the size of a small walnut. Melt the butter in a heavy frying pan until it just begins to froth. Drop in the meat balls and fry until lightly browned on all sides. Lift out into a hot ovenware dish.

Meanwhile, have the prepared tomato sauce hot in a saucepan. Pour over the meat balls. Cover with a lid or foil and cook in a moderate oven (350°F., 180°C., Gas Mark 4) for 15–20 minutes. Sprinkle with chopped parsley and serve.

Advance preparation: These can be cooked in advance. Reheat in a moderate oven (350°F., 180°C., Gas Mark 4) until bubbling hot.

Roast duckling and orange sauce

Illustrated in colour on pages 120 and 121

Always insist on a young duckling. Ducks mature rapidly and reach their prime between 9 and 12 weeks, when a good sized one weighs up to 5 lb. (2 kg. 250 g.). The quality of fresh duckling is often difficult to judge. Although they are a little more fatty, frozen, oven-ready birds are a good, reliable buy.

Serves 4

1 oven-ready duckling, about 5 lb./2 kg. 250 g.	*for the orange sauce:*
salt	5 level tablespoons granulated sugar
for the stuffing:	2 tablespoons water
6 oz./175 g. fresh white breadcrumbs	2 tablespoons vinegar
1 level teaspoon salt	2 oranges
1 rounded tablespoon chopped parsley	1 tablespoon orange marmalade
1 level teaspoon dried sage	½ pint/3 dl. giblet stock (see recipe)
1 orange	4 level teaspoons cornflour
2 oz./50 g. butter, melted	*to garnish:*
1 egg	watercress

Thaw the duckling, if necessary, overnight and remove the giblets from the body cavity; wipe a fresh bird with a damp cloth. Remove any fat visible at openings and rub a little salt into the skin. To prepare the stuffing, measure the breadcrumbs, salt, parsley and sage into basin. Finely grate the orange rind and add to the mixture with strained orange juice, melted butter and egg. Mix lightly.

Spoon the stuffing into the duckling. Using a skewer, close the tail or 'parson's nose' and place the stuffed bird in roasting tin. Duckling is a very fatty bird and needs no extra fat when roasting. Simply put 2 tablespoons of water in the roasting tin and place in the centre of a moderate oven (350°F., 180°C., Gas Mark 4) and roast for 25 minutes per lb. ($\frac{1}{2}$ kg.). There is no need to baste the bird while roasting; the salt rubbed into the skin will cause the duckling to turn a delicious rich brown colour. To check that the duckling is completely cooked, pierce the flesh with a sharp skewer or knife tip – the juices should be clear. Place the giblets in a saucepan, cover with cold water and bring to boil. Simmer gently for about 30 minutes to make giblet stock.

Meanwhile prepare the orange sauce. Measure the granulated sugar and water into a small saucepan, stir over a moderate heat until the sugar has dissolved and the mixture becomes a caramel colour. Draw the pan off the heat and add the vinegar – take care, as vinegar boils furiously at this stage. Reboil, stirring to dissolve the caramel. Remove segments from one of the oranges. Reserve the flesh from this orange. Squeeze the juice from remaining orange into the liquid caramel in the saucepan. Stir in the orange marmalade together with $\frac{1}{2}$ pint (3 dl.) strained giblet stock. Cover with a lid and simmer the contents gently for about 30 minutes and strain.

Select the peel from one of the oranges and, using a sharp small knife, slice away white pith inside. Then carefully slice the zest thinly, lengthwise, into thin slivers. The sauce will look and taste better if the peel is really thin. Cover the peel with cold water and bring to the boil. Drain and recover with cold water. Bring to the boil a second time then lower the heat and simmer gently for 20 minutes or until quite tender. The initial boiling helps remove the bitter flavour from the peel and the second boiling cooks it thoroughly. When ready, drain and set aside for adding to the sauce. In a small teacup, thinly blend the cornflour with about 1 tablespoon cold water. Stir this into the sauce and reheat, stirring until thickened and boiling. Add the drained, cooked rind and reserved orange segments. Heat through.

Remove the cooked duckling from the roasting tin on to a hot serving platter. Spoon some orange sauce over it, garnish with watercress and serve the remaining sauce separately. When serving, add a little orange stuffing from the body to each portion and spoon over extra orange sauce.

Advance preparation: The sauce can be made in advance and reheated. Roast the duckling when the dish is required.

Beef goulash

Paprika gives the flavour to goulash, which is delicious served with hot creamed potatoes or buttered noodles. This recipe also freezes very well.

Serves 6

2 lb./1 kg. lean stewing steak	salt and freshly milled pepper
2 lb./1 kg. onions	1 level tablespoon flour
1 oz./25 g. dripping	$\frac{3}{4}$ pint/$\frac{1}{2}$ litre beef stock
1–2 cloves garlic	2 teaspoons concentrated
1 level teaspoon caraway seeds	tomato purée
1 rounded tablespoon paprika	2–3 tablespoons natural yoghurt
pepper	

Wipe the meat, trim neatly and discard the fat. Cut the meat into strips about 1$\frac{1}{2}$–2 inches (3$\frac{1}{2}$–5 cm.) long. Peel and slice the onions. Melt the dripping in a saucepan, add the meat and fry gently until brown.

Pound the garlic with the caraway seeds. Add to the meat together with the paprika and onions. Season with salt and pepper, cover the pan and cook over a very low heat for 1 hour. Shake the pan occasionally and stir once or twice. At this stage, there is no liquid in the pan, only the juices from the onion. Take care to cook the contents very gently and, where possible, place a simmering mat under the pan.

Sprinkle in the flour and stir to blend. Gradually add the stock and then the tomato purée. Bring up to the boil and simmer for a further hour. Stir occasionally and, when cooked, check the flavouring. Turn into a heated serving dish and just before serving, stir in the yoghurt.

Advance preparation: The flavour of goulash improves on reheating. Prepare not more than 24 hours in advance of serving. Refrigerate and reheat in a moderate oven (350°F., 180°C., Gas Mark 4) until bubbling hot before serving.

Pork chops in sweet and sour sauce

Pork is a rich meat that goes particularly well with sweet and sour sauce and with fruits. The initial short roasting time given in this recipe allows the pork to loose some of the fat and the resulting sauce is well flavoured and not greasy.

Serves 6

6 pork chops	4 tablespoons vinegar
1 oz./25 g. white cooking fat	3 oz./75 g. soft brown sugar
for the sauce:	1 tablespoon soy sauce
1 (12 oz./350 g.) can pineapple	$\frac{1}{4}$ level teaspoon salt
chunks	2 level tablespoons cornflour

Trim the pork chops and place in a roasting tin with the white cooking fat. Place just above centre in a hot oven (400°F., 200°C., Gas Mark 6) and brown for about 15 minutes, turning once.

Drain the pineapple from the can and reserve the syrup – making it up to $\frac{1}{2}$ pint (3 dl.) with water. Combine the liquid with the vinegar, sugar, soy sauce and salt. Measure the cornflour into a saucepan and moisten with a little of the liquid, mixing to a smooth paste. Stir in the remaining liquid and cook over a moderate heat until thickened and boiling. Add the pineapple and draw the pan off the heat.

Drain off excess fat from the roasting tin, then pour the sauce over the chops, coating each one thoroughly. Cover with a square of kitchen foil and replace just above centre in a moderately hot oven (375°F., 190°C., Gas Mark 5) and bake for a further 45–50 minutes – according to the thickness of the chops – basting once or twice with the sauce.

Advance preparation: Have pork chops ready for cooking and sauce made in advance. Put to cook in time for serving.

Chicken Kiev

In a restaurant, the waiter will always pierce the hot chicken pieces to release the butter. When serving this at home, warn guests so that they can do it themselves carefully.

Serves 4

2 spring chickens, about 2 lb./1 kg. each
squeeze lemon juice
salt and freshly milled pepper
2 oz./50 g. butter (see recipe)
little finely chopped parsley
seasoned flour
1 egg, lightly beaten
fresh white breadcrumbs
oil for deep frying
to garnish:
watercress

Using a sharp knife, first cut away the chicken legs (these should be set aside for use in another recipe). Next make an incision along either side of the breast bone and carefully cut away both breasts from each chicken, keeping them in one piece. Remove the skin and any small bones at the wing end. Place each piece of chicken in turn between wetted squares of greaseproof paper and, using a rolling pin, beat them out flat. Take care not to tear or break the flesh – the wetted squares of paper helps to prevent this. Sprinkle the inside of each with a little lemon juice and season with salt and freshly milled pepper.

Have ready for each breast fillet, a torpedo shape of well chilled butter. Allow about $\frac{1}{2}$ oz. (15 g.) per portion. Roll each piece of butter in a little finely chopped parsley and place each one in the centre of a breast fillet. Make sure that the butter is lying lengthwise. Turn in both ends of the chicken fillet over the butter and fold over the sides to make a parcel. Roll first in seasoned flour, then dip each one in lightly beaten egg and finally in breadcrumbs. Press the coating on well and set aside for at least 2 hours to chill before frying.

When ready to serve, fry in hot, deep oil for 6–8 minutes or until golden. Drain and serve at once with a garnish of watercress.

Advance preparation: It is advisable to prepare Chicken Kiev well in advance of serving so that the rolled chicken breasts have a chance to set and chill thoroughly. Fry only when ready to serve.

Whole curried chicken

The longer the chicken cooks the better the flavour; in this particular recipe the chicken should be overcooked to the extent that it almost falls apart when served.

Serves 6

1 (4–5 lb./2–$2\frac{1}{4}$ kg.) oven-ready chicken
for the stuffing:
4 oz./100 g. long grain rice
1 oz./25 g. butter
1 small onion
2 level teaspoons curry powder
$\frac{1}{2}$ level teaspoon salt
for the curry sauce:
$1\frac{1}{2}$ oz./40 g. butter
1 small onion
3 level tablespoons curry powder
1 rounded tablespoon plain flour
1 pint/6 dl. chicken stock
1 tablespoon mango chutney
1 rounded tablespoon soft brown sugar
juice $\frac{1}{2}$ lemon
$\frac{1}{2}$ level teaspoon salt

Wipe the chicken, remove the bag of giblets and set aside while preparing the stuffing. Add the rice to a pan of boiling salted water, stir well, reboil and cook rapidly for 8 minutes. Meanwhile, melt the butter in a small pan. Peel and chop the onion. Add to the pan and fry gently until the onion is soft but not brown. Stir in the curry powder, then the drained cooked rice and season with salt. Stir the ingredients to blend, then spoon into the body cavity of the bird. Skewer the chicken closed and place in a large casserole dish.

Melt the butter for the curry sauce in a medium-sized saucepan. Peel and chop the onion, add to the pan then cover and cook gently for 5 minutes until the onion is soft but not brown. Stir in the curry powder and cook for a further 5 minutes to bring out the flavours and oils. Then stir in first the flour and gradually the stock. Bring up to the boil and add the remaining ingredients. Cover with a lid and simmer gently for 30 minutes. Draw off the heat and strain the sauce over the chicken in the casserole dish.

Cover the casserole with a lid and place in the centre of a slow oven (325°F., 170°C., Gas Mark 3). Cook gently for about 3–4 hours, basting occasionally.

Serve with the stuffing.

Advance preparation: Plan to serve this recipe when cooked, although it will keep hot without spoiling for a little time.

Roast duckling with peaches

On average, a good-sized duckling will serve four generous portions but rarely will one bird be large enough to serve six. For this number, it is better to roast two duckling simultaneously. Check the weight of the birds before cooking.

Serves 6

2 (4–$4\frac{1}{2}$ lb./$1\frac{3}{4}$–2 kg.) oven-ready duckling
salt
$\frac{3}{4}$ pint/$\frac{1}{2}$ litre giblet stock
1 (15 oz./425 g.) can peach halves
salt and freshly milled pepper
1 oz./25 g. butter
1 level tablespoon flour
to garnish:
watercress

Wipe the duckling and rub a little salt into the skin. Prick the surface of the breast all over with a fork. Place the ducklings together in a large roasting tin and add 2 tablespoons of water – no extra fat is required. Place in the centre of a moderate oven (350°F., 180°C., Gas Mark 4) and roast, allowing 25 minutes per lb. ($\frac{1}{2}$ kg.), for about $1\frac{1}{2}$ hours. Place the giblets in a saucepan, cover generously with cold water. Add a seasoning of salt (half an onion, a bay leaf and a few peppercorns too if you like) and bring up to the boil. Simmer for 30–40 minutes, then strain and reserve for the stock.

When cooked, remove the duckling from the pan. Joint each bird into four and arrange in a serving dish along with the peach halves, drained from the can. Replace in the oven while preparing the gravy and allow to heat through thoroughly. Pour away the duck drippings from the pan, leaving behind the dark duck drippings. Add the hot stock and stir well to pick up all the bits. Half Madeira and stock or half wine and stock can be used instead. Bring up to the boil and season well with salt and pepper. Blend the butter and flour on a plate to make a beurre manié. Add in pieces to the pan, then stir until the gravy has thickened. Check the flavour – strain over the duckling and peaches. Serve garnished with watercress.

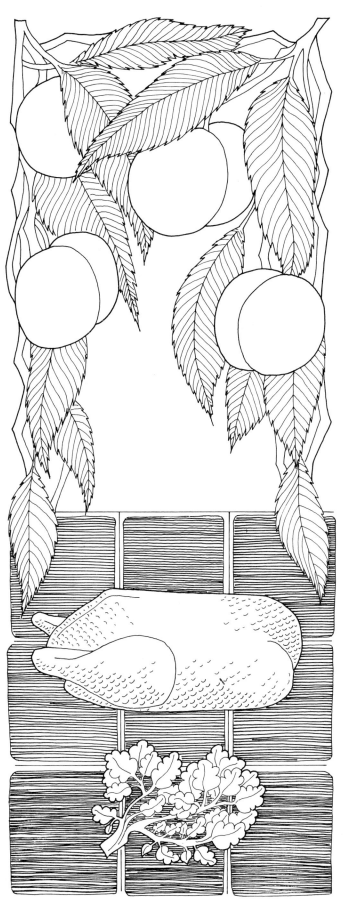

Tarragon chicken

For this recipe, you will need a large saucepan or a large fireproof casserole that can be placed over direct heat.

Serves 6

4 level teaspoons dried tarragon	½ pint/3 dl. chicken stock
2 tablespoons lemon juice	½ pint/3 dl. double cream
6 chicken joints	*to garnish:*
2 oz./50 g. butter	chopped parsley
salt and freshly milled pepper	

Before starting the recipe, measure the dried tarragon into a small bowl and add the lemon juice. Leave to soak for 30 minutes.

Wipe and trim the chicken joints. Melt the butter in a large saucepan, add the chicken joints and brown them slowly and evenly on all sides. If necessary, brown them half at a time, taking the first few out once sufficiently browned to make room for the last ones. When the chicken is well browned, this should take about 10–15 minutes, place all the pieces in the pan together. Season well with salt and pepper and pour over the tarragon and lemon juice. Add the hot stock and the cream. Cover with a lid and simmer gently for 45–55 minutes or until the chicken pieces are quite tender.

Lift out the chicken on to a hot serving plate. Strain the sauce and pour over the chicken. Sprinkle with chopped parsley and serve.

Veal Cordon Bleu

In this recipe the veal is stuffed with a slice of Gruyère cheese and ham. Buy the escalopes unflattened, so that a pocket can be cut in each one. It is important to cut the pocket in the meat while the meat is fairly thick. It is impossible to do so after the veal has been beaten out thinly.

Serves 6

6 veal escalopes	fresh white breadcrumbs
6 thin slices Gruyère cheese	3 oz./75 g. butter
3 slices ham	2 tablespoons oil
1 large egg	*to garnish:*
salt and freshly milled pepper	lemon
juice ½ lemon	

Using a sharp knife, cut into the side of each escalope making a pocket into the centre of the meat. Place the escalopes of veal, one at a time, between two sheets of wetted, greaseproof paper. Using a rolling pin, beat the meat out thinly. The wetted paper prevents the meat from sticking to either the board or the pin. Place a slice of Gruyère cheese and half a slice of ham inside each pocket. Trim the escalopes neatly and press flat.

Arrange the veal in a shallow dish. Beat the egg, a seasoning of salt and pepper and a squeeze of lemon juice. Pour over the veal and leave to marinate for about 15 minutes, turning the pieces to coat on both sides.

Drain the escalopes from the egg and then dip both sides in the white breadcrumbs. Shake away any loose crumbs and press the remainder on firmly. Heat the butter and oil in a frying pan and add the veal. Fry gently for about 10 minutes, turning once to brown on both sides. Drain and serve hot with a garnish of lemon.

Advance preparation: Beat out and prepare veal escalopes ready for frying. Chill in the refrigerator. Fry when ready to serve.

Chicken with paprika sauce

Paprika gives a lovely colour and a delicious flavour to the sauce in the recipe. Some paprika powders are stronger than others – use with care.

Serves 4

1 oven-ready chicken, about 3 lb./1½ kg.	4 ripe tomatoes
salt and freshly milled pepper	2 green peppers
1 oz./25 g. butter	¼ pint/1½ dl. single cream
1 onion	juice ½ lemon
1 level tablespoon paprika	1 level tablespoon flour
¼ pint/1½ dl. chicken stock or water	

Joint the whole chicken into eight pieces (page 102). Season the chicken pieces with salt and pepper.

Melt the butter in a large frying pan and add the finely chopped onion. Sauté gently until the onion is soft but not brown. Stir in the paprika and then the stock. Add the chicken pieces to the pan. Allow the mixture to come to the boil, then lower the heat and simmer gently. Meanwhile, nick the skins on the tomatoes, place in a basin and cover with boiling water. Allow to stand for 1 minute, then drain and peel away the skins. Halve, deseed and chop the tomato flesh. Halve, deseed and shred the green peppers. Blanch in boiling water for 1 minute, then drain. Add the tomatoes and green pepper flesh to the chicken. Cover the pan and allow to simmer gently for 1 hour, turning the pieces of chicken occasionally.

Lift the pieces of cooked chicken out on to a hot serving dish. Pour the single cream into a small basin and stir in the lemon juice to sour it. Sift the flour over the surface and then whisk to blend together – there should be no lumps. Stir into the hot liquid in the pan. Cook over a moderate heat, stirring all the time, until the mixture has thickened and is boiling. Simmer for 1 minute, then draw the pan off the heat. Check seasoning and pour the sauce over the chicken.

Serve with plain boiled rice or boiled new potatoes.
Advance preparation: This chicken recipe will keep hot in the oven without spoiling. Spoon on to an ovenproof serving dish, cover with foil and keep hot in the oven (325°F., 170°C., Gas Mark 3).

Filet de boeuf en croûte

Illustrated in colour on pages 24 and 25

This classic French recipe is dramatic in appearance, but in fact quite simple to prepare. All the work can be done in advance.

Serves 6

2–3 lb./1–1½ kg. piece beef fillet	8 oz./225 g. puff pastry (see recipe and page 16)
2½ oz./65 g. butter	little beaten egg for glazing
salt and pepper	*to garnish:*
4 oz./100 g. button mushrooms	watercress
pinch mixed herbs	

Ask the butcher to cut the piece of meat from the thick end of the fillet. He will charge you for the untrimmed joint. Then ask him to trim off excess fat and skin if possible. During initial roasting the skin shrinks and sometimes causes the joint to curl into a difficult shape to cover. If the skin has not been removed, then score it with a sharp knife.

Melt 2 oz. (50 g.) of the butter in a large roasting tin, over a low heat. Add the fillet and turn to coat in the butter. Season with salt and pepper and brown on all sides. Place in the centre of a hot oven (425°F., 220°C., Gas Mark 7) and roast quickly for 15 minutes. This makes a rare joint in the finished recipe. For those who prefer well cooked meat, increase this initial roasting by a further 10 minutes. Remove the meat from the pan and allow to cool.

Wash and trim the mushrooms and fry quickly in the remaining ½ oz. (15 g.) butter. Stir in the mixed herbs, draw off the heat and allow to cool.

Roll the puff pastry out to a rectangle about ¼ inch (½ cm.) thick, at least 1 inch (2½ cm.) longer than the beef fillet and three times as wide. If you are inexperienced at rolling out puff pastry or are using bought ready-made pastry, increase the amount used to 12 oz. (350 g.). Using a sharp knife, cut the pastry into two pieces, making one two-thirds larger than the other. Spoon the mushroom mixture down the centre of the larger piece and lay the beef fillet on top. Using lightly floured fingers, press the pastry up the sides of the beef and fold ends up neatly. Lift the meat, at this stage, on to a wetted baking tray. Roll the remaining strip of pastry gently to make it longer by half again. Brush edges with water and lift over on to the joint to cover the top and either end, sealing it against the pastry already round the joint.

Brush the joint all over with a little beaten egg and decorate the top with any pastry trimmings. Place the meat just above centre in a hot oven (400°F., 200°C., Gas Mark 6) and bake for 35–40 minutes, or until the pastry is golden brown. Garnish with watercress.

To serve, using a sharp knife, cut into 1 inch (2½ cm.) thick slices.
Advance preparation: Partly roast the beef and allow to cool. Make pastry well in advance. The meat can be covered with pastry, ready for baking, 2–3 hours in advance.

Pâté de campagne

Illustrated in colour on the jacket

Pig's liver is not the kind to choose for frying, but is ideal to use in pâtés or terrines. Belly of pork supplies the necessary fat to keep the recipe moist. Serve this pâté as a starter or with French bread and salad for a light lunch recipe.

Serves 6

6 oz./175 g. streaky bacon rashers	1 clove garlic
8 oz./225 g. pig's liver	1 level teaspoon salt
8 oz./225 g. belly of pork	freshly milled pepper
1 medium onion	pinch mixed herbs
3 slices stale white bread	1 large egg

Trim the rinds from the bacon rashers and flatten the rashers by pressing and stretching along a chopping board with the flat side of a knife blade. Use these to line a 1½-pint (1-litre) oval pie dish. Allow any ends to overlap. If liked, bay leaves can be placed in the base of the dish.

Remove the skin from the pig's liver and cut the rind from the pork. Cut the liver and pork into pieces. Peel the onion and cut into quarters, and trim the crusts from the slices of bread. Pass the liver, pork, onion and bread through the coarse blade of a mincer. Place the mixture in a bowl. Add the peeled clove of garlic, which has been crushed with a little of the salt. Add the remaining salt, a seasoning of pepper, the herbs and the egg. Mix the ingredients thoroughly together.

Spoon into the prepared dish and spread evenly. Cover with a buttered paper and place the dish in a larger shallow roasting tin. Fill the tin with ½ inch (1 cm.) cold water. Place in the centre of a moderate oven (325°F., 170°C., Gas Mark 3) and cook for 1½ hours. Cool under a heavy weight, preferably for 24 hours. Turn out and serve sliced.

Advance preparation: Pâté is best made the day before serving and chilled overnight.

Hot gammon with orange sauce

Hot gammon goes particularly well with an orange sauce. This is a good recipe for a dinner party.

Serves 6

1 (3 lb./1½ kg.) piece of gammon corner	¾ pint/½ litre stock, use water and chicken stock cube
for the sauce:	1 teaspoon concentrated tomato purée
1 medium onion	
1 carrot	3 oz./75 g. castor sugar
2 rashers streaky bacon	3 tablespoons wine vinegar
1 oz./25 g. butter	2 oranges
1 oz./25 g. flour	salt and pepper

Soak the gammon in cold water to cover for several hours or overnight. Drain and place in a large saucepan with fresh cold water to cover. Bring up to the boil, then lower the heat and simmer gently allowing 20 minutes per lb. (½ kg.) and 20 minutes extra. Top up with boiling water when necessary, to keep the gammon covered.

While the gammon is cooking, prepare the orange sauce. The sauce may be reheated at a later stage when the gammon is ready to serve. Peel and finely chop the onion and carrot. Trim and cut the bacon rashers into small pieces. Melt the butter in a saucepan, add the vegetables and bacon and fry gently until the onion is soft and beginning to brown. Stir in the flour and then continue to cook gently, stirring occasionally, until the mixture is a nutty brown colour – takes about 15 minutes. Gradually stir in the hot stock and bring up to the boil, stirring all the time. Add the tomato purée and allow to simmer very gently while preparing the rest of the sauce.

Measure the sugar into a saucepan and stir over a moderate heat until melted and turned to caramel. At first the mixture will become lumpy but eventually the sugar will dissolve and turn golden. Draw off the heat and cool for a few moments, then add the vinegar. Take care as the mixture will boil up rather fiercely. Thinly pare the rind from the oranges and set aside. Strain the juice and add to the caramel away from the heat. Replace the saucepan over the heat and bring up to the boil, stirring to dissolve the caramel, which at this stage will have become a lump in the base of the pan. Check the seasoning in the brown sauce and then strain into the orange mixture. Stir to blend and draw off the heat.

Finely shred the pared orange rind, place in a saucepan and cover with cold water. Bring up to the boil, then strain and return the peel to the pan. Recover with cold water and bring up to the boil again, lower the heat and simmer for about 20 minutes until the peel is tender. Strain and add to the orange sauce.

When the gammon is cooked, drain from the water and, using a sharp knife, strip the skin off the rind.

Serve the gammon carved in slices with the hot orange sauce.

Advance preparation: Prepare orange sauce in advance and reheat for serving. Cook gammon in time for serving. Keep hot for a short while in the oven (325°F., 170°C., Gas Mark 3), well covered with foil to prevent surface drying.

Herb baked chicken

A coating of buttery breadcrumbs and herbs gives these chicken joints a delicious crisp crust. They can be prepared and put to bake without further attention, no basting or turning is required. Serve them warm with a tossed salad.

Serves 4

4 chicken joints	2 teaspoons dried mixed herbs
1 egg	salt and freshly milled pepper
seasoned flour	little grated lemon rind
4–5 oz./100–150 g. fresh white breadcrumbs	2 oz./50 g. butter
1 tablespoon finely chopped parsley	

Trim the chicken joints and remove the skin. Lightly mix the egg and pour into a shallow dish. Spoon a little seasoned flour on to a plate. Measure the breadcrumbs into a basin. Add the parsley, dried mixed herbs, a seasoning of salt and pepper and a little grated lemon rind. Melt the butter over a low heat, then add to the breadcrumb mixture all at once. Using a fork, stir and toss the breadcrumbs gently until they are all buttery and the ingredients are well mixed.

Roll the chicken joints first in seasoned flour, then in beaten egg and finally in the buttered crumbs. Pat the coating of crumbs on firmly to give a firm even covering. Place the chicken pieces in a buttered roasting tin, space them a little apart so that they do not touch. Place above centre in a hot oven (400°F., 200°C., Gas Mark 6) and bake for 45 minutes. When ready, the covering should be crisp and golden brown. Test the chicken joints by piercing with the tip of a sharp knife – there should be no pink juices. Lift the pieces out on to a serving platter. Serve warm with salad.

Veal Parmesan

The addition of Parmesan cheese to the coating of breadcrumbs gives these veal escalopes a crisp, flavoursome covering. Ask the butcher to beat the escalopes flat for you.

Serves 4

4 veal escalopes	1 oz./25 g. Parmesan cheese,
seasoned flour	grated
1 egg, lightly mixed	2 oz./50 g. butter
salt and freshly milled pepper	juice ½ lemon
2 oz./50 g. fresh white	*to garnish:*
breadcrumbs	parsley sprig

Trim the escalopes neatly and dip both sides of each in seasoned flour. Shake off any excess flour and dip the meat into lightly mixed egg, seasoned with salt and pepper. Drain from the egg and then place at once into the mixed white breadcrumbs and Parmesan cheese. Coat all the escalopes in this way, pressing the coating of crumbs on lightly. Set aside until ready to fry.

Melt the butter in a frying pan. Add the escalopes to the hot butter and fry for about 8–10 minutes. Turn occasionally for even cooking and to brown on both sides.

Lift the veal out on to a hot serving plate. Add a squeeze of lemon juice to the butter in the hot pan and shake over the heat to mix. Strain the butter over the veal.

Garnish with a sprig of parsley and serve.

Advance preparation: Coat escalopes and chill in refrigerator until ready to use. Fry when ready to serve.

Spring chicken with peas

Serves 6

2 spring chickens, weighing	1 lettuce heart
about 2½ lb./1¼ kg. each	12 spring onions
salt	¼ pint/1½ dl. water
2 oz./50 g. butter	1 level tablespoon castor sugar
for the peas:	½ level teaspoon salt
¾–1 lb./⅓–½ kg. shelled, fresh	freshly milled pepper
peas	2 oz./50 g. butter

Wipe the chickens and season with salt. A large casserole dish is needed to hold the two chickens. Preheat the oven to hot (400°F., 200°C., Gas Mark 6). Melt the butter in the casserole dish in the hot oven, add the chickens and brown on all sides – if the casserole dish is flameproof, it's quicker to do this initial browning on the top of the stove than in the oven. Cover the casserole with the lid and replace in a moderate oven (350°F., 180°C., Gas Mark 4) and braise for 1 hour.

In the meantime, shell the peas. Wash the lettuce and shred, wash the onions, trimming away the tops and base of each and leaving the bulb whole. Measure the water, sugar and seasoning into a saucepan and bring up to the boil. Add the peas, lettuce, onion and butter to the pan. Cover with a lid and bring gently up to the boil, shaking the pan occasionally. Pour the entire contents of the saucepan over the chickens in the casserole. Recover and replace in the oven for a further 30 minutes or until the chickens are quite tender.

When cooked, lift the chickens from the casserole and serve in portions with the peas and juices from the dish.

Advance preparation: Prepare and cook chickens. Keep hot, if necessary, in a moderate oven (325°F., 170°C., Gas Mark 3).

Using wine in recipes

Wine is used in cooking for the flavour it contributes. Where possible, use in a recipe the same wine as that to be served with the meal. Any bottle of wine can be opened in the afternoon to extract some wine for using in the recipe. Leave a red wine uncorked to stand and warm at room temperature. Press the cork back in a white wine and, about 1 hour before the meal, chill the wine in the refrigerator.

You may prefer to keep small half bottles of inexpensive red and white wine in the larder for cooking. Avoid using remainders left over from bottles and which have been kept indefinitely. If a little wine is left over from a meal, pour it into a smaller bottle and cork it tightly. The more air you manage to exclude the better. Never keep wine that has been opened too long, it is better to drink it. After a short time standing open, wine will develop a sharp disagreeable flavour and should be thrown away. Wine that is undrinkable should never be used in a recipe.

Paupiettes de veau

Illustrated in colour on page 101

Ask the butcher to beat the veal escalopes out thinly. This recipe is excellent for a dinner party.

Serves 6

6 veal escalopes	*for the stuffing:*
6 rashers streaky bacon	8 oz./225 g. pork fillet
2 oz./50 g. butter	1 small onion
2 onions	1 clove garlic
4 carrots	1 tablespoon finely chopped
¼ pint/1½ dl. dry white wine or	parsley
stock	salt and pepper
8 oz./225 g. tomatoes	2 heaped tablespoons fresh
8 oz./225 g. button mushrooms	white breadcrumbs
few olives, stoned	½ lightly beaten egg
¾ pint/½ litre rich brown sauce	dry white wine or brandy
(page 98)	

Trim away any skin or loose pieces from around the meat and set aside the prepared escalopes while making the stuffing.

Trim the pork fillet, discard any fatty tissues and cut into pieces. Pass through the coarse blade on a mincer into a mixing basin, along with the peeled and quartered onion and garlic, crushed with salt. Add the parsley, a good seasoning of salt and pepper, breadcrumbs, lightly beaten egg and enough white wine to mix to a fairly soft consistency.

Spread a little of the stuffing over each veal escalope and roll up from the narrow end of the meat. Trim and stretch the bacon rashers on the working surface, using the flat side of a knife, then wrap a bacon rasher round each veal roll. Veal is a very lean meat and the added protection from the bacon rashers helps keep the meat moist and the colour white. Tie each veal roll in shape.

Melt the butter in a frying pan and add the peeled and sliced onions and carrots. These are used to form a bed of vegetables upon which the veal rolls will braise. Place the meat carefully in the pan, add the wine or stock. Cover the pan with a lid and leave to braise gently for 1 hour.

Meanwhile nick the skin on the tomatoes and plunge into boiling water. Leave for 1 minute then lift out, peel away the skins and quarter the tomatoes. Wash the mushrooms and slice in half – no need to peel the skins from button mushrooms.

Lift the cooked veal rolls from the pan and carefully remove the string and bacon, discarding both. Strain any braising liquid from the pan and discard the braising vegetables. Replace the veal rolls in the pan along with the prepared tomatoes, mushrooms and the olives. Pour in the prepared rich brown sauce and add the braising liquor. Cover the pan with a lid and reheat gently for about 15 minutes. Check seasoning before serving.

Advance preparation: Prepare in advance and keep hot in a moderate oven (325°F., 170°C., Gas Mark 3) or reheat in the oven (350°F., 180°C., Gas Mark 4) until bubbling hot before serving.

Boeuf bourguignonne

A delicious casserole of beef cooked in red wine. This is a good choice for a party as it will keep hot without spoiling.

Serves 6

2½ lb./1¼ kg. lean braising steak	12 button onions
1 oz./25 g. butter	8 oz./225 g. button mushrooms
1 tablespoon oil	salt and freshly milled pepper
1 shallot	1 level tablespoon cornflour
1 clove garlic	2 tablespoons water
¾ pint/½ litre stock	*to garnish:*
¼ pint/1½ dl. red wine	chopped parsley
bouquet garni (see recipe)	

Wipe and trim the meat and cut into cubes. Brown quickly in the hot butter and oil in a large saucepan. Lift the meat from the pan and add the peeled and finely chopped shallot to the hot fat. Cover and fry gently for a few minutes until soft, then stir in the peeled and finely chopped garlic. Replace the meat in the saucepan. Gradually stir in the stock and then the red wine. Bring up to the boil, add a bouquet garni – a few parsley stalks, a sprig of thyme and a bay leaf tied together in a bundle. Cover with a lid and simmer gently for 1 hour.

Meanwhile peel the button onions, leaving them whole. Place the onions in a saucepan and cover with cold water. Bring to the boil and simmer for 5 minutes then drain. Add to the beef and continue to simmer for a further 1–1½ hours or until the meat is tender. About 15 minutes before the cooking time is completed, add the trimmed, whole mushrooms and seasoning. Recover and complete cooking time.

Remove the bouquet garni and spoon the meat, onions and mushrooms into a hot serving dish. Blend the cornflour with the water and stir into the liquid remaining in the pan. Bring up to the boil, stirring all the time, check seasoning and strain over the meat and vegetables.

Sprinkle with chopped parsley and serve.

Advance preparation: Prepare in advance and keep hot in a moderate oven (325°F., 170°C., Gas Mark 3) or reheat in the oven (350°F., 180°C., Gas Mark 4) until bubbling hot before serving.

Rich brown sauce

A rich brown sauce is often used as part of a savoury casserole recipe. Where mushroom caps are included in the casserole recipe, put the stalks into the sauce for extra flavour.

Makes ½–¾ pint/3–4½ dl. sauce

1 oz./25 g. dripping or 2 tablespoons oil	1 oz./25 g. plain flour
2 tablespoons each finely diced carrot and onion	¾–1 pint/4½–6 dl. hot beef stock
finely chopped mushroom stalks (optional)	1 rounded teaspoon concentrated tomato purée
1–2 bacon rashers or bacon trimmings	bouquet garni
	salt and freshly milled pepper

Heat the dripping or oil and add the finely chopped carrot, onion, any mushroom stalks and chopped bacon. Cook gently until the onion just begins to brown – takes about 5 minutes. Stir in the flour and continue to cook gently, uncovered, until the mixture is a dark brown colour. Gradually stir in the stock and bring up to the boil. Add the tomato purée and the bouquet garni. Cover with a lid and simmer gently for 30 minutes. Pass through a strainer, check seasoning and use as required.

Advance preparation: This sauce can be made in advance and reheated ready for use.

Osso buco

Osso buco is particularly good served with a saffron flavoured rice. Ask the butcher to cut the veal into 3-inch (7½-cm.) pieces – you should allow one or two pieces per person.

Serves 4

3½–4 lb./1½–1¾ kg. veal shin or knuckle	¼ pint/1½ dl. dry white wine
seasoned flour	¾ pint/½ litre stock, use water and a stock cube
4 tablespoons oil	1 level teaspoon salt
8 oz./225 g. onions	freshly milled pepper
8 oz./225 g. carrots	finely grated rind ½ lemon
1 clove garlic	1 tablespoon finely chopped parsley
1 (15 oz./425 g.) can tomatoes	
bouquet garni	

Roll the pieces of veal knuckle in seasoned flour. Heat the oil in a large saucepan, add the peeled and chopped onion and the diced carrots. Fry gently until the onions are soft and a little brown.

Add the pieces of veal and the peeled and chopped garlic and brown the veal on all sides – takes about 10 minutes. Add the tomatoes and juice from the can, bouquet garni, white wine, stock, salt and seasoning of freshly milled pepper. Cover and cook gently for 1½ hours. If preferred, the ingredients can all be transferred to a large casserole and cooked in a moderate oven (325°F., 170°C., Gas Mark 3) for 2 hours.

When cooked, remove the bouquet garni and add the finely grated lemon rind. Check the seasoning and sprinkle with the finely chopped parsley.

Serve with rice or noodles.

Advance preparation: Prepare in advance and keep hot in the oven (325°F., 170°C., Gas Mark 3) or reheat in a moderate oven (350°F., 180°C., Gas Mark 4) until bubbling hot before serving.

Chicken hunter style

This recipe is for chicken served in a rich tomato sauce. It can be prepared using six chicken joints.

Serves 6

1 oven-ready chicken, about 4 lb./1¾ kg.	1 wine glass dry white wine
seasoned flour	1 lb./½ kg. tomatoes
2 oz./50 g. butter	½ pint/3 dl. chicken stock
1 tablespoon oil	1 (2½ oz./65 g.) can tomato purée
2 shallots	bouquet garni
1 clove garlic	*to garnish:*
8 oz./225 g. button mushrooms	chopped parsley

Joint the chicken into eight pieces (page 102) and roll them in seasoned flour. Heat the butter and oil in a saucepan. Add the chicken and fry gently to brown on all sides – takes about 10 minutes. Remove the chicken from the pan and keep warm.

Peel and chop the shallots and chop the garlic. Add to the hot fat remaining in the pan and fry for a few minutes. Add the mushrooms. Replace the chicken in the pan, add the wine, the peeled, deseeded and chopped tomatoes. Stir in the stock and tomato purée, add the bouquet garni. Cover with a lid and simmer gently for 30 minutes.

To serve, discard the bouquet garni and lift the chicken and mushrooms into a hot serving dish. Reduce the sauce in the pan, if necessary, then strain over the chicken.

Sprinkle with chopped parsley and serve.

Advance preparation: Prepare in advance and keep hot in the oven (325°F., 170°C., Gas Mark 3) or reheat in a moderate oven (350°F., 180°C., Gas Mark 4) until bubbling hot before serving.

Steak with mustard sauce

A delicious, quick recipe to prepare. A mustard flavour goes well with steak and the tarragon adds extra interest.

Serves 4

4 fillet steaks	pinch pepper
2 oz./50 g. butter	1 tablespoon French mustard
¼ pint/1½ dl. dry white wine	1 level tablespoon dried tarragon
¼ pint/1½ dl. stock	
½ level teaspoon salt	

Trim the steaks. Heat the butter in a large frying pan, add the steaks and brown quickly on both sides. Reduce the heat and cook gently according to taste. Remove from the pan, place on a plate and keep warm.

Add the wine to the frying pan, bring to the boil, stirring all the time and scraping the base of the pan well. Simmer rapidly until almost evaporated, then add the stock and seasoning. Continue simmering until reduced by half – takes about 5 minutes.

Meanwhile, spread the steaks with the mustard and sprinkle with the tarragon. Pour the sauce from the pan over the steaks and serve immediately.

butter remaining in the frying pan. Sauté for a few moments, then stir in the tomato purée and the white wine. Bring up to the boil and simmer for 5 minutes. Add the *strained* brown sauce. Stir to blend, check seasoning and heat through gently. Pour the sauce over the chicken. Sprinkle with chopped parsley and serve.

Advance preparation: Prepare in advance and keep hot in the oven (325°F., 170°C., Gas Mark 3), or reheat in a moderate oven (350°F., 180°C., Gas Mark 4) until bubbling hot.

Chicken with wine, mushrooms and cucumber

Mushrooms and cucumber are the chosen vegetables in this casserole of chicken. A pleasant summer recipe and one that looks pretty when served.

Serves 6

1 oven-ready chicken, about 3–4 lb./1½–1¾ kg.	bouquet garni
salt and freshly milled pepper	1 large cucumber
2 oz./50 g. butter	4 oz./100 g. button mushrooms
¼ pint/1½ dl. chicken stock (see recipe)	¼ pint/1½ dl. single cream
¼ pint/1½ dl. dry white wine	1 rounded tablespoon flour
	to garnish:
	chopped parsley

Joint the chicken (page 102). Cover the chicken giblets and carcass with cold water, add a pinch of salt and boil up for the stock needed in the recipe. Melt the butter in a large frying pan or saucepan. Add the chicken joints and brown, over a low heat, on all sides. Pour away the butter and add the stock, white wine and bouquet garni to the pan. Cover with a lid and leave to simmer very gently for 30 minutes. The chicken should be quite tender. To test – pierce the flesh in one of the shoulder joints with a sharp knife, the juices that run out should be quite clear with no tinges of pink.

Meanwhile, peel the cucumber, cut in half and remove the centre seeds. Cut the cucumber flesh into thin strips about 1 inch (2½ cm.) long. Wipe, trim and slice the mushrooms. Blanch the cucumber by adding to a pan of boiling salted water. Bring back up to the boil, simmer for 1 minute then drain. Set both cucumber and mushrooms aside ready for the sauce.

When the chicken is tender, lift from the pan and arrange in a serving dish and keep hot. Strain the cooking liquid and measure – it should be about ½ pint (3 dl.). Return this to the saucepan, add the sliced mushrooms and simmer for 1 minute. Measure the cream into a small mixing basin and sift the flour over the surface. Whisk to blend the cream and flour together – there should be no lumps. Stir a little of the hot liquid from the pan, blend well and return all to the pan. Cook over a moderate heat, stirring all the time until thickened and boiling. The addition of the flour will prevent the cream from separating. Add the cucumber and seasoning. Allow to simmer gently for 1–2 minutes to heat through ingredients.

Spoon the sauce over the chicken, sprinkle with chopped parsley and serve.

Advance preparation: Prepare in advance and keep hot in the oven (325°F., 170°C., Gas Mark 3) or reheat in a moderate oven (350°F., 180°C., Gas Mark 4) until bubbling hot before serving.

Chicken sauté chasseur

An excellent recipe for a dinner party. The sauce requires careful preparation but once made this dish will keep hot without spoiling.

Serves 6

1 (3½–4 lb./1½–1¾ kg.) oven-ready chicken	1 level tablespoon flour
1 oz./25 g. butter	¾ pint/½ litre chicken stock
salt and freshly milled pepper	bouquet garni
1 tablespoon chopped parsley	4–6 oz./100–175 g. button mushrooms, trimmed
for the chasseur sauce:	2 teaspoons concentrated tomato purée
1 oz./25 g. dripping	1 wine glass dry white wine
½ small onion	
1 small carrot	

Joint the chicken into 6 portions (page 102). Melt the butter in a frying pan and add the chicken pieces, skin side down. Fry quickly to brown, then turn and season with salt and pepper. Lower the heat, cover the pan with a lid and cook gently for 25–30 minutes or until the chicken pieces are tender.

Meanwhile, prepare the sauce. Melt the dripping in a saucepan. Peel and finely chop the onion and carrot. Add to the pan and cook gently for a few minutes until softened. Stir in the flour and continue to cook, stirring occasionally, until the mixture is a nutty brown colour. Stir in the hot chicken stock and bring up to the boil. Add any mushroom trimmings and the bouquet garni. Simmer gently for about 20 minutes to make a well seasoned brown sauce.

Lift the cooked chicken from the pan on to a hot serving dish and keep warm. Slice the mushrooms and add to the hot

Chicken in white wine

Any dry white wine can be used in this recipe but it does taste particularly good with Riesling. As a general rule, you should always drink with the recipe the same wine as that used in the recipe.

Serves 6

1 (3–4 lb./1½–1¾ kg.) roasting chicken	2 tablespoons brandy
2 oz./50 g. butter	1 level tablespoon flour
1 tablespoon oil	sprig fresh thyme
1 carrot	1 bay leaf
2–3 shallots	½ bottle Riesling
1 clove garlic	1 egg yolk
salt and freshly milled pepper	2–3 tablespoons cream

Cut the chicken into 8 joints (page 102). Melt the butter and oil in a large frying pan. Add the chicken pieces and brown gently on all sides for about 10 minutes. Remove from the pan. Peel and slice the carrot and the shallots. Add to the hot fat in the pan and replace the chicken pieces on top. Crush the clove of garlic with a little salt and add this with a seasoning of pepper. Spoon over the brandy and flambé. Shake the pan so that the flames spread over the contents. When the flames have died, sprinkle over the flour and turn the chicken joints. Add the thyme and bay leaf and then pour in the wine. Cover and allow to simmer until the chicken is tender – about 45 minutes.

When cooked, lift the chicken pieces from the pan and keep hot. Strain the liquid and discard the carrot, shallot and herbs. Blend the egg yolk and cream in a basin and stir in a little of the hot liquid. Blend well and return all to the pan. Replace the pieces of chicken in the pan. Allow the chicken in the sauce to heat through thoroughly, but do not boil.

Jambon de bourguignonne

Cooked, chopped ham set in a delicious jelly flavoured with wine, vinegar and parsley is the basis of this recipe. Use a pudding basin for a mould. Buy fresh ham from the grocer or keep a 1 lb. (450 g.) can of good quality cooked ham in the store cupboard.

Serves 4

1 lb./450 g. cooked ham	1 level tablespoon powdered gelatine
½ pint/3 dl. chicken stock	
¼ pint/1½ dl. dry white wine	1 teaspoon tarragon vinegar
freshly milled pepper	4 tablespoons finely chopped parsley
3 tablespoons cold water	

Cut the ham into small pieces and place in a saucepan. Add the chicken stock, white wine and a seasoning of freshly milled pepper. Bring up to the boil and simmer for 2–3 minutes. Meanwhile, measure the cold water into a small cup and sprinkle in the gelatine. Allow to soak for 5 minutes.

Draw the saucepan off the heat and add the soaked gelatine. Stir until the gelatine has dissolved, the heat of the pan should be sufficient to do this. Check seasoning and add the vinegar to taste. Allow to cool until the mixture is beginning to thicken and becomes syrupy. Stir in the finely chopped parsley and immediately pour into a 1½ pint (1 litre) pudding basin or mould. Chill for several hours until set firm.

Unmould and serve cut in slices – this is particularly delicious with French bread and fresh butter.
Advance preparation: Prepare well in advance, the day before if liked. If chilled in the refrigerator, allow to stand at room temperature for 1–2 hours before serving.

Chicken Marengo

Illustrated in colour on pages 104 and 105

This much renowned chicken dish has many variations. This recipe is an easy and tasty version of the original.

Serves 6

1 (4–5 lb./1¾–2¼ kg.) roasting chicken or 6 chicken joints	1 lb./½ kg. tomatoes
	bouquet garni (see recipe)
seasoned flour	½ pint/3 dl. chicken stock (see recipe)
2 oz./50 g. butter	
1 tablespoon oil	1 (2½-oz./65-g.) can concentrated tomato purée
1 lb./½ kg. button onions	
2 shallots	8 oz./225 g. button mushrooms
1 clove garlic	*to garnish:*
2 wine glasses dry white wine	finely chopped parsley

Chicken joints may be used for this recipe, but a whole chicken cut into 6–8 pieces is far more satisfactory. The pieces are neater and there is less bone. See page 102 to joint a chicken.

Cover the carcass and giblets with cold water and simmer for 30 minutes to make the stock. Where chicken joints are used, prepare the stock using a cube.

Dip the joints in seasoned flour and add to the heated butter and oil in a large frying pan, along with the onions, peeled but left whole. Fry gently to brown the onions and chicken pieces on both sides – about 10 minutes. Drain away most of the fat and add the peeled and chopped shallots and the garlic, which has been crushed with a little salt after the outer papery coating has been removed. Fry for only a few minutes, then add the wine and simmer fairly quickly to reduce the wine by about half.

Meanwhile, nick the skins on the tomatoes and place in a mixing basin. Cover with boiling water and allow to stand for 1 minute. Drain and peel off the skins. Cut the tomatoes in half, discard inner seeds and juice, then chop the tomato flesh coarsely. Add to the chicken with a bouquet garni (simply tie together a few washed parsley stalks, a sprig of thyme and a bay leaf), the stock and tomato purée. Cover with a lid and simmer gently for 30 minutes. About 10 minutes before the end of the cooking time, add the trimmed mushrooms, either left whole or sliced. Re-cover and cook until the end of the cooking time.

To serve, discard the bouquet garni and lift the chicken pieces, onion and mushrooms out on to a hot serving dish. Reduce the sauce in the pan a little more, if necessary, then strain over the chicken. Sprinkle with chopped parsley and serve. Garnish with puff pastry crescents, if liked.
Advance preparation: Prepare in advance and keep hot in the oven (325°F., 170°C., Gas Mark 3). Or reheat in a moderate oven (350°F., 180°C., Gas Mark 4) until bubbling hot before serving.

OPPOSITE **Paupiettes de veau (page 96)**
Trim and beat out the veal.
Spread a little stuffing over each escalope and roll up. Wrap a bacon rasher round each veal roll and tie.
Add the wine to the veal rolls and vegetables.

Chicken liver pâté

This delicious pâté keeps well for up to 1 week in the refrigerator. Serve as a first course for a dinner party or as part of a buffet supper menu.

Serves 6–8

2 oz./50 g. butter	salt and freshly milled black
1 large onion, peeled and finely	pepper
chopped	¼ pint/1½ dl. double cream
1 small clove garlic	2 eggs, lightly beaten
4 tablespoons chicken stock	1 level tablespoon cornflour
(use water plus stock cube)	4 tablespoons dry sherry
1 lb./450 g. chicken livers	2 oz./50 g. butter, melted

Melt the butter in a small saucepan, add the onion, crushed garlic and stock. Bring to the boil, simmer gently, covered with a lid, for 10 minutes or until the onion is soft. Trim the livers and add to the onion with a seasoning of salt and pepper. Bring to the boil slowly, then lower the heat, cover with a lid and simmer gently for about 10 minutes. Pass the livers and cooking liquid through a mouli food mill or purée in an electric blender. Pour into a mixing basin and stir in the cream, eggs and the cornflour blended with the sherry. The mixture at this stage is very soft.

Pour into a well greased 2-pint (1-litre) pâté dish. Cover with a lid or foil and place in a shallow baking or roasting tin with cold water 1 inch (2½ cm.) up the sides of the dish. Place in the centre of a moderate oven (325°F., 170°C., Gas Mark 3) and bake for about 2–2½ hours, or until the pâté is quite firm.

Remove from the oven and, when cold, cover the top with melted butter. Leave in a cold larder or chill for at least 24 hours before serving.

Advance preparation: Most pâté recipes improve in flavour the day after making. Prepare this recipe 1–2 days before serving. Keep chilled.

Chicken with cream and asparagus sauce

Out of season, this recipe can be prepared using canned asparagus.

Serves 4

1 (3 lb./1½ kg.) oven-ready	*for the sauce:*
chicken	12 asparagus spears
3 oz./75 g. butter	4 oz./100 g. button mushrooms
¼ pint/1½ dl. dry white wine	¼ pint/1½ dl. single cream
¼ pint/1½ dl. chicken stock	1 level tablespoon flour
salt and freshly milled pepper	
1 tablespoon grated Parmesan	

Joint the chicken into 8 pieces (opposite). Melt 2 oz. (50 g.) of the butter in a frying pan and add the chicken. Fry gently to brown on all sides. Pour away the butter and add the white wine, chicken stock and seasoning to the pan. Cover with a lid and leave to simmer gently for 30 minutes or until the chicken is quite tender.

Meanwhile, wash and scrape the asparagus stems, trim the ends evenly and place the asparagus in a large bowl of salt water.

Bring a pan of water to the boil, lay the asparagus spears in the simmering water and cook gently for 15 minutes or until just tender. Drain well and then trim the spears down the tender green tops and the heads. Melt the remaining butter in a pan and add the trimmed and sliced mushrooms. Sauté gently for 1–2 minutes, tossing the mushrooms so that they cook lightly. Draw off the heat and reserve.

When the chicken is tender, lift the pieces from the pan and arrange them on a hot serving dish. Measure the liquid from the pan – it should be about ½ pint (3 dl.). Pour this into a saucepan. Measure the cream into a small basin and sift the flour over the cream. Whisk thoroughly to blend the flour and cream – there should be no lumps. Stir in a little of the hot liquid, blend well and return to the saucepan. Bring up to the boil, stirring well until thickened. Simmer for a few moments, then check seasoning with salt and pepper. Add the mushrooms and asparagus. Heat through for a moment and then spoon the sauce over the chicken pieces. Sprinkle with the cheese and brown for a moment under a hot grill before serving.

Advance preparation: Prepare asparagus and mushrooms and assemble ingredients. Cook chicken and make sauce when ready to serve. Keep hot for a short while in a moderate oven (325°F., 170°C., Gas Mark 3).

Jointing a chicken

Whenever chicken joints are used in a party recipe, it is generally more satisfactory to joint a whole chicken, than to buy individual chicken joints. The pieces are neater and there is less bone. It is also easier to cook jointed chicken pieces in a pan or casserole, than the more bulky chicken joints.

One rarely joints a chicken less than 2–3 lb. (1–1½ kg.) oven-ready weight. From this size of bird, you will get 6–8 good size pieces of chicken.

With the aid of a sharp knife, joint the chicken as follows:
First cut away the legs from each side of the bird. Cut each leg in half through the joint to make four pieces in all. Turn the chicken so that the breast is facing you and carefully cut down one side of the breast bone. Lifting the chicken flesh away, continue cutting and scraping with the knife to remove all the flesh from the bone and cut through the wing joint to detach the piece from the carcass. Lay the breast flesh flat on the working surface and cut it neatly in half. Repeat this procedure on the second side and cut the piece neatly in half. There are now eight pieces of chicken – four from the breast and four from the legs.

Do not remove the skin from the chicken pieces before cooking unless the joints are to be coated with egg and breadcrumbs or some other coating. The skin gives protection and keeps the flesh moist.

Chicken stock

The carcass of the chicken can be used to make stock for a recipe or for soup. Place the carcass in a saucepan and cover generously with cold water. Add salt, a peeled onion and a bay leaf. Bring up to the boil and simmer for 40–45 minutes. Skim off the fat, check seasoning and use as required.

Serving rice

Rice is most versatile. It combines well with other ingredients, absorbing the flavours of foods in the same recipe and makes an excellent accompaniment to dishes with rich, well flavoured sauces. For all savoury recipes, use a long grain rice of good quality. A cheaper grade often becomes soft and mushy, however carefully cooked.

Hot fluffy rice

This method is most successful when really good quality rice is used. During cooking, the rice grains absorb all the liquid in the pan. Care should be taken to see that the ingredients are accurately measured.

Serves 4

8 oz./225 g. long grain rice   1 pint/6 dl. water
1 level teaspoon salt

Choose a saucepan with a tightly fitting lid and lightly butter the inside – this prevents the rice grains sticking to the pan during cooking. Measure the rice, salt and water into the pan and bring to the boil. Stir once, then lower the heat. Cover with a lid and simmer over a very low heat for 15 minutes, without removing the lid or stirring.

When the rice is ready, the grains will be tender and all the liquid in the pan absorbed. Draw the pan off the heat and allow the rice to stand covered for 10 minutes. Fluff up with a fork and serve.

Buttered rice: Add 1 oz. (25 g.) butter and 1 tablespoon chopped parsley to the cooked rice. Toss with a fork.
Serve with shellfish recipes.

Cheese rice: Add 2 oz. (50 g.) grated Parmesan or Cheddar cheese and 1 oz. (25 g.) butter to the cooked rice. Toss with a fork.
Serve with beef stews or casseroles.

Saffron rice: Warm a good pinch saffron strands in a small basin until crisp. Add a pinch of granulated sugar and pound with the end of a rolling pin to a fine powder. Add 1 tablespoon boiling water and allow to infuse for 10 minutes. Strain the liquid into the cooked rice. Toss with a fork so the rice is evenly coloured and flavoured.
Serve with veal or fish recipes.

Rice ring

A ring or border of rice looks most attractive for serving fish or meat dishes in a sauce and is easy to prepare. While still hot, spoon the cooked rice into a well buttered ring mould. Pack down lightly. Keep in a warm place until ready to serve. Put the serving plate over the mould, turn the right way up and lift the mould away. The rice will remain in a perfect ring on the plate. Spoon the mixture for serving into the centre.

Cooking rice this way requires accurate measurements. When calculating servings allow 2 oz. (50 g.) rice per person.

Rice	Water	Salt
For 2 servings use 4 oz./100 g.	½ pint/3 dl.	½ teaspoon
For 4 servings use 8 oz./225 g.	1 pint/6 dl.	1 teaspoon
For 6 servings use 12 oz./350 g.	1½ pints/9 dl.	1½ teaspoons
For 8 servings use 1 lb./450 g.	2 pints/12 dl.	2 teaspoons

Rice pilaff

Rice can often take the place of potato in a menu. This rice mixture, flavoured with onion and herbs, is delicious served with steaks, grilled chicken, braised beef or casserole recipes.

Serves 4

1 oz./25 g. butter   1 pint/6 dl. stock (use water
1 onion   and chicken stock cube)
8 oz./225 g. long grain rice
1 level teaspoon dried mixed
  herbs

Melt the butter in a saucepan. Peel and finely chop the onion and add to the pan. Cover with the lid and cook the onion gently for about 5 minutes until soft but not brown.

Add the rice and stir to toss in the butter and onions. Add the herbs and stir in the hot stock. Bring up to the boil. Stir once, then lower the heat. Cover with a lid and simmer over a low heat for 15 minutes, without removing the lid or stirring.

When the rice is cooked, the grains will be tender and the liquid in the pan absorbed. Draw the pan off the heat and allow the rice to stand, covered, for 10 minutes. Stir with a fork and serve.

Advance preparation: Use this method for preparing rice to serve for a supper party or a barbecue supper. Soften the onion in the butter and draw off the heat. Stir in the rice and herbs and add the stock cube. Increase the number of stock cubes for a larger quantity of rice – two are required for every 1½ pints (9 dl.) water. Remember that the rice takes the flavour from the stock. When ready to cook, stir in the required quantity of boiling water and cook as above.

OVERLEAF **Chicken Marengo (page 100)**
Cut the chicken into 6–8 joints and dip into seasoned flour.
Skin and chop the tomato flesh coarsely.
Ten minutes before the end of the cooking time, add the mushrooms.

Spanish rice

Spanish rice, with its interesting blend of ingredients, makes a colourful and tasty accompaniment to most fried or grilled foods. It goes particularly well with chicken but can also be served with grilled or fried chops, steak, hamburgers or saus-ages. Check the rice for flavour before serving and, if necessary, season with extra salt and freshly milled pepper. Spanish rice should taste quite savoury.

Serves 4

1 onion	2 level teaspoons castor sugar
1 green pepper	1 bay leaf
1 oz./25 g. butter	6 oz./175 g. long grain rice
1 (15 oz./425 g.) can tomatoes	1–2 oz./25–50 g. Parmesan
½ level teaspoon salt	cheese, grated

Peel and slice the onion. Halve, deseed and finely shred the green pepper. Melt the butter in a saucepan and add the prepared vegetables. Cover with a lid and cook gently for about 5 minutes or until the onion is soft but not brown.

Stir in the contents of the can of tomatoes, salt, sugar and bay leaf. Cover and simmer gently for a further 15 minutes, stirring occasionally. Then draw off the heat.

Meanwhile add the rice to a saucepan of boiling, salted water. Bring back to the boil and cook for 8–10 minutes or until the rice is tender. Drain well. Add the rice to the tomato and onion mixture and stir well. Turn the mixture into a buttered casserole dish and place, uncovered in a moderate oven (350°F., 180°C., Gas Mark 4) for about 15 minutes. This allows the excess moisture to evaporate. Check seasoning, stir with a fork and the rice is ready.

Sprinkle with the grated cheese and serve.

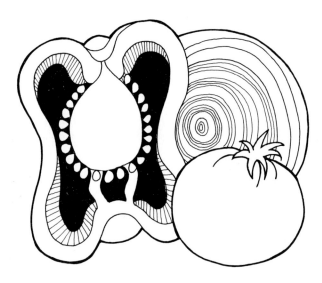

Versatile vegetables

Vegetables require and deserve careful preparation and cooking. They form the basis of delicious soups and provide interesting and unusual meal starters. Vegetables add colour and a variation of texture to a main course, whether in the form of a vegetable dish or a salad.

A wide variety of both our own seasonal and other imported vegetables are available all year round. Buy your vegetables with care, choose those which are firm and fresh. Store in a cool airy place, but not for too long. Better to buy little and often. Remember that the scrubbed and washed varieties must be used up fairly quickly, for they deteriorate more quickly than those which have the soil still on them. Use fresh vegetables within their season and save frozen vegetables to serve when the fresh are not available.

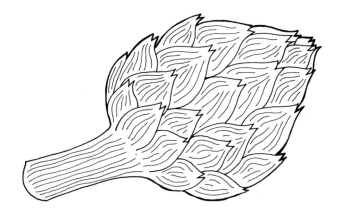

Artichoke (Globe)

Globe artichokes should be a good green colour with tightly clinging, fleshy leaves. When bought, they should have about 6 inches (15 cm.) of stem attached. Globe artichokes deteriorate quickly and should be eaten the day after they are purchased.

Cut off the stem close to the base of the leaves and remove any dry or discoloured leaves from around the outside. Because the leaves are tightly closed, globe artichokes should be soaked in cold salted water to cover for 30 minutes before cooking, to ensure that they are thoroughly cleaned.

Artichoke (Jerusalem)

Jerusalem artichokes are pale, buff looking tubers which grow underground, rather like a potato. All varieties are inclined to be unattractive looking and knobbly, although modern varieties are less knobbly than they used to be. Jerusalem artichokes should not be bought if they are too misshapen because they are difficult to peel.

Scrub well and then peel and plunge immediately into cold water with a squeeze of lemon juice or a few drops of vinegar added. Keep them under the surface of the water to prevent discolouration before cooking.

Asparagus

Green asparagus, grown out of doors, has a short season during May and June of each year. The buds should look bright and green and the stems should be fresh with some white or bleached part showing. Asparagus wilts quickly in warm weather and, once bought, should be kept in the refrigerator or in the coldest corner of the pantry. For made up recipes, buy the thinner sticks or loose asparagus or the grade known as 'sprue'. These are small sticks that are not thick enough to go into the specially selected other grades.

Wash asparagus in cold water and lightly scrape the white part of the stem with a sharp knife. Cut the stems to the same length and soak in cold, salted water for about 10 minutes. Then retie the bundles with the heads together. Asparagus tips cook more quickly than the stems and for this reason they are best cooked upright in water, with the tips peeping over the surface. A tall asparagus kettle is the ideal container to use. Otherwise cook asparagus in bundles upright in a saucepan of boiling water for half the time allowed, then lay them on their sides and cook for the remaining time or until the tips are tender. Take care not to overcook.

Aubergine

The aubergine or eggplant is a native of Asia. It has a deep purple colour and should have a firm, shiny skin with no wrinkles or soft parts.

Cut off the stem and remove the small leaves that surround it. Aubergines can be peeled, if wished. Slice across or cut in dice, or alternatively cut in half lengthwise if they are to be baked or stuffed. Aubergines are often sprinkled with salt and left to stand for 30 minutes before using, to draw out the excess moisture. Drain away any liquid, rinse in cold water and pat dry before using.

Beans (Broad)

Broad beans are widely cultivated in this country and grow well in cold areas. The soft, greyish kidney shaped beans are enclosed in a furry lined pod. When young and newly in season, the beans are very tender. As they grow older, they develop a tough outer skin that can be removed after cooking.

Pod the beans when ready to cook.

Beans (French)

French beans have a shorter season than other beans and a great part of the crops are grown under glass. These hot house varieties appear in early spring, with the outdoor grown varieties following on in summer. French beans are generally more expensive than the other types of beans. They should be fine and thin and carefully sorted out to the same length and size. French beans should be young and tender. They should snap when broken and the pods firm and juicy.

French beans should be topped and tailed and left whole.

Beans (Runner)

These sturdy beans come into season in later summer and continue to autumn. The pods should have a fresh, crisp looking appearance and the developing seeds inside should be reasonably small. A runner bean when snapped open should break clean, thus indicating that it is not stringy.

Top and tail runner beans. It should not be necessary to string young beans early in the season. Older beans will need strings removed from each side of the bean with a sharp knife. Runner beans should be shredded finely – a bean slicer, the small inexpensive gadget with a few sharp blades set across a small square, is most useful for this.

Beetroot

Early beetroots are available in summer months, particularly June. Maincrop varieties come in September for winter months. Fresh beetroot should be a good dark colour without any withered parts. Any leaves attached to early beetroot should be fresh looking. In all cases, the skin should be unbroken.

Twist off or cut off the beetroot tops about 1 inch (2½ cm.) above the root, so that the skin remains unbroken and therefore will not bleed when boiled. Beetroot are cooked untrimmed and the skins removed after boiling.

Broccoli

Purple sprouting broccoli is the best known of the types of broccoli available. It has a number of small purple or green heads. In spring, a green sprouting broccoli known as Calabrese is available. Both these have a delicate flavour and should be cooked with care.

Remove the outer leaves and trim the stalks. Soak broccoli in cold salted water for 30 minutes before cooking, to draw out any insects.

Brussels sprouts

Brussels sprouts are best when still small and firm, and are considered better after the first frosts. If the weather stays warm, sprouts are inclined to become 'blown' and rather open. Sprouts should have a good fresh green colour.

Trim the base and remove any outer loose leaves. Make a deep cross in the stalks. Wash well and leave to soak for 10–15 minutes in cold salted water. Drain and rinse.

Cabbage (Spring, green and white)

Cabbage, in one form or another, is available all year round. The varieties vary according to the season. Spring cabbage, those with small or almost no heart, are often known as spring greens. These give way to the hearted green cabbage and the white summer varieties. Winter cabbage is hardy and darker green in colour. Any cabbage purchased should look fresh enough to eat raw.

Separate the leaves of spring greens, discarding any tough or damaged outer leaves. Wash well. Roll spring cabbage up in bundles and shred with a sharp knife. With green, summer and winter types of cabbage, trim off the base of the stalk and remove any very tough outer leaves. Quarter the cabbage heart and slice out the thick centre stalk. Shred the cabbage evenly across the leaves. Wash in cold salted water and drain well.

Cabbage (Red)

Red cabbage comes into season in the autumn, it goes particularly well with sweet and sour flavour and is often cooked with apples and onions. Red cabbage recipes go well with rich meats such as pork, goose, duck and most game.

Trim off the base of the stalk and remove any tough outer leaves. Quarter the cabbage heart and slice out the thick centre stalk. Shred the cabbage evenly across the leaves. Rinse in cold salted water and drain well before using.

Carrot

According to the time of year, either new or maincrop carrots will be available. Carrots should be tender throughout with no woody core. The colour should be bright and clear. Bunched new carrots should not show any green at the crowns.

Trim the top and base from each carrot. Scrape new carrots and peel maincrop ones. Small new carrots can be cooked whole. Maincrop varieties are usually sliced or cut in dice.

Cauliflower

When buying cauliflower, choose one where the curds are hard and close together. The stalks should be clean and white.

Trim the stalks evenly and remove all but the very smallest inner green leaves. If the cauliflower is to be cooked in sprigs, separate the heart into even sized pieces.

Celeriac

Celeriac is known also as celery root. It is a variety of celery which has a large bulbous edible root, resembling a turnip. It is a rough skinned, brownish looking vegetable and can be anything from the size of an apple to a coconut.

Peel celeriac fairly thickly and then slice or dice. The flavour of celeriac goes well with strong flavoured game and it is often combined with potato.

Celery

Home grown celery is only available during winter months. Imported celery with green stalks appears during the spring and summer. Celery can be purchased washed or unwashed according to your own preference. The unwashed celery tends to keep the freshest.

Trim off the root and leaves. Remove any very coarse outer stalks. These can be kept for the stock pot, or used in soups or casseroles. The celery leaves are very good for adding flavour to soups and stews. Divide the heart of celery into 3–4 portions. Tie the celery in a bundle, using 1-inch ($2\frac{1}{2}$-cm.) gauze.

If celery is to be served raw, scrub and chill the stalks in the refrigerator for a few hours beforehand.

Chicory

Chicory should be very fresh, otherwise it is inclined to have a slightly bitter flavour. The close packed leaves on the head of the chicory should be white with edges of faintest yellow. There should be no green, which would indicate that the chicory has been in the light too long and is probably an old sample.

Trim a slice from the base and remove any damaged outer leaves.

Courgettes

Courgettes are grown from a variety of the marrow family, the fruit of which is picked when immature. When buying courgettes, they should be not more than about 6 inches (15 cm.) long. They should be straight in shape and a fresh green colour.

It is not necessary to peel courgettes. The skin however has a slightly bitter flavour and because of this, courgettes are usually blanched before use. Wash, trim the ends and slice the courgettes thickly. Add to boiling water, reboil and simmer for 1–2 minutes. Then drain and use as required.

Fennel

Fennel which is eaten as a vegetable is the Florence Fennel and a native of Italy, where it is one of the staple vegetables known as Finocchio. It is a thick set, low growing plant with solid white stems which are swollen at the base. It has a slightly aniseed flavour. When buying, look for fresh looking bulbs with the tops evenly trimmed.

Separate the fresh fennel stalks and shred in a salad or cook.

Leeks

Leeks are a most versatile vegetable. They have a delicate, more discreet flavour than the onion. Leeks can be used raw in salad, they give a subtle flavour to soups and they can be served as a vegetable in their own right. Leeks should be fresh looking with no yellow leaves. Small leeks are ideal for cooking whole and are often sold in bundles. Larger leeks are usually sold loose.

Leeks are a gritty vegetable and need careful preparation. Trim off the root and the green tops leaving about 2 inches (5 cm.) of leaf above where the outside leaf divides. Slice the leek lengthwise to the centre and to within about 1 inch (2½ cm.) of the base. Wash well under running cold water to clean thoroughly. Where leeks are to be simmered and served as a vegetable on their own, it is advisable to retie the prepared leeks in bundles with 1-inch (2½-cm.) gauze. This helps retain the shape during cooking.

Marrow

The ideal size for a marrow is between 9–12 inches (23–31 cm.) long. It is generally wise to avoid buying any very large samples. Apart from the surplus of seeds, these larger marrows tend to be tasteless.

Peel the marrow and cut into thick 1½–2-inch (4–5-cm.) slices. Remove the seeds from the centre of each slice with a spoon. Marrow can be steamed in rings when subsequently stuffed. If it is to be served in a sauce, the flesh is usually diced.

Onion

Onions are one of the oldest known vegetables. There are many varieties ranging from the very small pickling onions to the larger Spanish onion. Shallots are not so pungent in their flavour as onions and are often preferred for this reason. Shallots are useful in salads and in recipes where a small amount is added for flavour, and where onion might be too strong. With the exception of spring or salad onions which are sold fresh, all onions sold are dry. In other words, they have been uprooted and hung to get rid of the moisture in the surface skin. This way they store well.

Cut a slice from the top and base of each onion and peel away the outer brown skin. Try to avoid peeling away more layers of onion flesh, since most of the goodness in an onion lies just under the brown, feathery surface skin. Where a large quantity of smaller pickling or button onions have to be peeled, cut a slice from the top and base and put the onions all together in a basin. Pour over boiling water to cover. Leave to stand for 5 minutes, then drain. You should find that the brown skins slip off quite easily.

Parsnip

Parsnips should feel firm and be free from blemishes. Scrub and peel, then cut in fingers or thick slices.

Peas

Peas should taste sweet and tender and the pods should snap open under gentle finger pressure. They should look green and fresh and rustle when the greengrocer picks them up. Avoid overfat pods, in these the peas are inclined to be tough.

Shell peas when ready to cook.

Potato

There are many varieties of both early and maincrop potatoes. Always buy best quality potatoes – firm, well shaped and free from blemishes. Avoid green potatoes and any which are sprouting. Maincrop potatoes keep better than new potatoes, nevertheless only buy amounts that can be conveniently stored and keep them away from the light. New potatoes should be bright and in small quantities. Select those on which the soil is moist rather than dry. If the skins rub off easily, then the potatoes are very fresh.

There are two types of potatoes, Reds and Whites. The chief red varieties are King Edwards, Red King, Redskin and Kerr's Pink. These cook soft and are excellent for creaming, roasting or baking in their jackets. White potatoes include Majestic, Arran Peak, Dr. McIntosh and Golden Wonder, all of which are good to choose for boiling and chipping as they cook firm and keep their shape.

New potatoes should be scrubbed and maincrop potatoes peeled.

Salsify

Salsify is a vegetable more widely known on the Continent than in the United Kingdom. Salsify is sometimes called oyster plant, it has a very delicate flavour. The roots should be long and tapered, brownish looking on the outside but with a white flesh inside.

They should be scrubbed and then scraped and peeled. Place immediately in cold water with a few drops of lemon juice added to prevent discolouration. Cut in short lengths ready to cook.

Spinach

Spinach must be very fresh. Leaves should be crisp and a bright green colour, never limp or with any yellow parts. Some varieties of spinach have a stronger flavour than others. The summer varieties are particularly tender and mild in flavour.

Wash spinach thoroughly in 2–3 lots of cold water. Drain and pull away the stalks and coarse centre rib. Spinach should be packed dripping wet into the saucepan and needs no other water for cooking than that which is clinging to the leaves.

Swede

Swedes can be cooked on their own but tend to be used along with other vegetables in soups or casseroles.

Using a knife, cut away the tough outer skin, then cut into slices or dice before cooking.

Sweet corn

Sweet corn or corn on the cob is easily perishable and should be cooked soon after purchase. For this reason, the outer leaves are not removed by the greengrocer. The 'silks' or 'tassel' at the top of the cob should be black when the corn is ripe. The cobs should be well rounded and plump and the corn a creamy colour and fresh looking.

Trim the stalk level with the cob and remove the outer leaves and the silks. Cook the cobs whole. Many cooks prefer not to add salt to the water but to sprinkle the corn with salt after cooking. There is a theory that salt added to the cooking water makes the corn tough.

Sweet pepper

Sweet peppers should be fresh, with smooth shiny skins, showing no wrinkles. They can be bright green or red in colour, although the most commonly found are the green variety.

Sweet peppers have hot spicy seeds inside and these should

be removed. Where the peppers are to be kept whole for stuffing, cut round the stalk end with a sharp knife and draw out the whole seed box. Shake, rinse or poke out any further seeds from inside. Where peppers are to be shredded, cut the peppers in half lengthwise and remove the seeds. Then shred the peppers across. Whole peppers are often blanched before using, to remove any slightly acid flavour in the flesh. Place the deseeded pepper cases together in a large basin. Pour over boiling water to cover and leave to stand for 5 minutes. Drain the peppers upside down. For use in salads or hors d'oeuvre, the peppers are sometimes skinned before using. When this is done, the flesh looks even greener and more attractive. Blister the pepper skins either by placing the peppers under a hot grill and turning them round, or roasting them over a gas flame. Once the skins blister and split, plunge peppers into cold water and peel off skin.

Turnip

There are several varieties of turnips both early and maincrop. The early turnips have a sweet flavour and a very white flesh. The large maincrop turnips are more yellow in colour.

Peel maincrop turnips and then cut in slices or dice. Smaller early turnips can be cooked whole and the skins slipped off afterwards.

Vegetable	Allow for 4 servings	Method of cooking	Cooking time
Artichokes (Globe)	1 head per person	Trim and soak in salted water. Cook in boiling, salted water until leaves will pull out easily. Drain upside down. Serve hot with melted butter or cold with French dressing.	20–40 minutes
Artichokes (Jerusalem)	1½–2 lb./ ¾–1 kg.	Peel and cook in boiling, salted water with lemon added. Drain and serve with melted butter or white sauce. Peel, blanch for 5 minutes. Drain and roast around a joint.	30 minutes 30–40 minutes
Asparagus	Approx. 8–10 stems per person	Scrape stems, trim and tie in loose bundles. Cook in boiling, salted water, upright with tips above water for 10 minutes, then lying down in pan for remaining 10 minutes. Untie bundles. Serve hot with melted butter or cold with mayonnaise.	20 minutes
Aubergines	1½ lb./ ¾ kg.	Slice then sprinkle with salt. Leave to stand for 30 minutes. Drain well. Dip in seasoned flour, fry in oil or butter.	5–8 minutes
Beans (runner)	1–1½ lb./ ½–¾ kg.	Top and tail. Slice thinly and cook in boiling, salted water. Drain well. Serve with butter. Any left over are very good in salads.	10–15 minutes
Beans (broad)	2 lb./ 1 kg.	Pod and cook in boiling, salted water. Drain and serve with butter. Young tender samples can be cooked – pods included.	10–15 minutes
Beans (French)	1–1½ lb./ ½–¾ kg.	Top and tail. Leave whole and cook in boiling, salted water. Drain well. Serve with butter.	15–20 minutes
Beetroot	1–1½ lb./ ½–¾ kg.	Scrub and cook whole in boiling, salted water. Drain and peel off skins. Cut into cubes or slice. Serve hot in white sauce or cold in vinegar for salads.	1–2 hours (depending on size)
Broccoli	1½–2 lb./ ¾–1 kg.	Trim and soak in salt water. Cook in boiling, salted water. Drain well. Serve hot with butter or hollandaise sauce.	10 minutes
Brussels sprouts	1½ lb./ ¾ kg.	Trim and remove loose leaves. Cut a cross in stalk of larger ones. Cook in boiling, salted water. Drain. Serve with butter.	10–15 minutes
Cabbage	1 lb./½ kg.	Trim, quarter and remove core. Shred finely. Soak in salted water. Cook in small amount of boiling, salted water with pan covered. Turn cabbage occasionally to cook evenly. Drain and press well. Serve with butter and good seasoning of pepper. A pinch of nutmeg is also good with cabbage.	15 minutes
Cabbage (red)	1 lb./½ kg.	Remove outer damaged leaves, quarter and core. Casserole or cook in covered pan with extra ingredients.	2–4 hours (according to recipe)

Vegetable	Allow for 4 servings	Method of cooking	Cooking time
Carrots	1–1½ lb./½–¾ kg.	Trim and peel old carrots or scrape new. Leave whole or slice and cook in boiling, salted water with bay leaf added. Drain and toss in butter. Sprinkle with chopped parsley or mint.	15–20 minutes
Cauliflower	1 large or 2 small heads	Trim and remove outer green leaves. Cook whole in boiling, salted water. Head down in a pan. Drain and serve with white or cheese sauce. Break heads into sprigs of even size. Cook in boiling, salted water. Drain and serve with melted butter or use cold in salads.	15–20 minutes 10 minutes
Celeriac	1–1½ lb./½–¾ kg.	Scrub then peel thinly. Slice or dice. Cook in boiling, salted water or stock until tender. Drain and serve with melted butter or in white sauce, or mash to a purée.	20 minutes
Celery	1 head per person	Wash, scrub and cook in boiling, salted water. Serve in white, parsley or cheese sauce. Trim, blanch for 5 minutes in boiling water. Braise in stock in moderate oven (350°F., 180°C., Gas Mark 4). Serve with braising liquor.	½–1 hour 1–1½ hours
Chicory	1–2 heads per person	Cut a slice from the base. Remove outer damaged leaves. Cook in boiling, salted water. Serve in cheese or white sauce. Prepare and cook in boiling, salted water for 15 minutes or until just tender. Drain and leave until cold. Roll in seasoned flour and fry in butter.	20 minutes 5 minutes
Courgettes	1 lb./½ kg.	Wash, trim ends but do not peel. Leave whole or slice thickly. Blanch in boiling water for 2–3 minutes. Drain and fry in butter.	15–20 minutes
Fennel	1 head per person	Trim and remove outer leaves. Cook whole in boiling, salted water. Drain. Serve in white or cheese sauce.	20–30 minutes
Leeks	1½ lb./¾ kg.	Remove outside leaves. Trim green tops and slice from base. Open out and clean. Cook in boiling, salted water. Drain. Serve with white sauce or cheese sauce, or cold in oil and vinegar dressing. Remove outside leaves. Trim tops and clean. Shred finely. Gently fry in butter in covered pan.	20 minutes 15 minutes
Mange-tout	1 lb./½ kg.	Wash, top and tail. Cook in boiling, salted water and drain. Serve tossed in melted butter.	5–8 minutes
Marrow	1½ lb./¾ kg.	Peel, remove inner seeds and dice flesh. Blanch for 2 minutes in boiling water. Drain and cook with butter in a casserole in a moderate oven (350°F., 180°C., Gas Mark 4). Serve with parsley or cheese sauce poured over.	30 minutes
Mushrooms	8–12 oz./225–350 g.	Wipe, leave whole or slice, and fry in butter. Season afterwards to avoid drawing juices. Wipe, leave whole and brush with oil and grill.	3–4 minutes 3–5 minutes
Onions	1½ lb./¾ kg.	Peel, blanch whole in boiling water for 5 minutes. Place in casserole with butter and cook in moderate oven (350°F., 180°C., Gas Mark 4). Serve with white sauce poured over. Peel, blanch in boiling salted water for 5 minutes. Drain, dry and roast in dripping round a joint.	1 hour ¾–1 hour

Vegetable	Quantity	Method	Time
		Peel and slice thinly. Dip in egg white and then in seasoned flour. Fry in hot deep fat. Drain well.	2–3 minutes
Parsnips	1½ lb./¾ kg.	Peel and cut in quarters. Boil in salted water. Drain. Toss in butter.	30–40 minutes
Peas	2 lb./1 kg.	Pod. Cook in boiling, salted water with mint and sugar added. Drain. Serve with butter.	15–20 minutes
Potatoes	1½–2 lb./ ¾–1 kg.	Peel old potatoes. Scrub or scrape new ones. Place old potatoes in cold, salted water and bring to the boil. Cook until tender. Drain and serve whole or mash. For creamed potato, beat mashed potato with a knob of butter and add a little milk. Season with salt and pepper. Add new potatoes to boiling, salted water. Cook until tender. Drain. Serve with melted butter and chopped parsley, chives or mint added.	20–30 minutes 15–20 minutes
		Choose even-sized main-crop potatoes and scrub. Bake near top of the oven (400°F., 200°C., Gas Mark 6) until soft when squeezed. Cut a cross in the top of each one and top with butter or soured cream and chives. For a soft outside, rub potatoes with butter and wrap in foil.	1–1¾ hours
Salsify	1½ lb./ ¾ kg.	Scrape roots and cut into short lengths. Place in water with vinegar added. Cook in boiling, salted water until tender. Serve in cheese or white sauce.	30 minutes
Spinach	2 lb./1 kg.	Wash well in several waters. Remove mid ribs and stems. Cook spinach in water clinging to the leaves, in covered pan. Drain well and press out all moisture. Reheat in butter.	10–15 minutes
		Cook until tender. Drain and press well then chop to a purée. Reheat with a little cream and season with nutmeg.	10–15 minutes
Swedes	1½ lb./¾ kg.	Peel and slice or cut in dice. Cook in boiling, salted water until tender. Drain and mash with salt, butter and plenty of pepper.	1 hour
Sweet corn	1 head per person	Remove leaves and silky threads. Add to boiling, salted water and cook until tender. Drain and serve with salt and melted butter.	15 minutes
Sweet pepper	1 per person	Cut peppers in half and remove inner seeds. Shred finely and fry in butter to soften. Very tasty mixed with sliced onions.	10 minutes
Tomatoes	1–2 per person	Choose even-sized tomatoes and cut in half. Brush with oil and season with salt, pepper and sugar. Grill.	5–10 minutes
		Prepare as above and place in buttered baking dish. Cook in oven (350°F., 180°C., Gas Mark 4) until tender.	15 minutes
Turnips	1½ lb./¾ kg.	Peel maincrop varieties and slice or dice. Cook in boiling, salted water until tender. Drain and mash with butter and seasoning.	20–30 minutes
		Cook new turnips whole, unpeeled in boiling, salted water. Remove skins after cooking. Serve turnips in butter or in white sauce.	30–40 minutes

Chervil soup

Chervil soup is a Belgian speciality. It is essentially a spring soup made using leeks, often with asparagus stalks added for flavour. The chervil is added at the last minute, since prolonged cooking spoils both the colour and flavour.

Serves 4

1 small onion	1½ pints/scant 1 litre
2 leeks	chicken stock
8 oz./¼ kg. potatoes	salt and freshly milled pepper
1 stick celery	about 1½ oz./40 g. fresh chervil
1 oz./25 g. butter	

Peel and finely chop the onion. Split the leeks, wash well and then shred finely. Peel and cut the potato into dice and scrub and shred the celery. Melt the butter in a saucepan. Add the onion and leeks and sauté gently for few minutes to soften but not brown the vegetables. Add the potato and celery and cook for a further few minutes. Stir in the stock and bring up to the boil. Cover and simmer gently for 30 minutes or until the vegetables are tender.

Draw the soup off the heat and pass the vegetables and liquid through a 'mouli' soup mill, or blend to a purée in a liquidiser. Return the soup to the pan, check seasoning with salt and pepper and reheat. Finely chop the chervil, stir into the soup and serve. *Note:* Chervil is a herb with a delicious, slightly aniseed, flavour. It is as easy to grow as parsley. Most large seed merchants have it listed in their catalogues.

Spanish summer soup

Illustrated in colour on the jacket

The use of a blender is rather essential when making this recipe. The combination of flavours from the blended fresh vegetables is delicious. For a party, serve extra finely chopped tomato, green pepper, cucumber and small, diced croûtons to sprinkle in the soup.

Serves 6

2 (15 oz./450 g.) cans peeled tomatoes	4 tablespoons olive oil
6 spring onions	1½ pints/9 dl. chicken stock
½ cucumber	salt and freshly milled pepper
2 green peppers	1 level teaspoon castor sugar
1 small clove garlic	3 tablespoons wine vinegar
1 thick slice white bread	1 tablespoon chopped parsley

Empty the contents of the cans of tomatoes into a large basin. Trim and chop the spring onions. Peel and chop the cucumber. Halve, deseed and shred the green pepper. Peel the clove of garlic and crush to a pulp with a little salt. Trim the crusts from the bread, soak the bread in about 2–3 tablespoons cold water for a few minutes, then squeeze out the moisture. Add the bread and oil to the vegetables in the basin.

Ladle the ingredients, half at a time, into the glass container of an electric blender. Cover and blend only for a few seconds to a coarse purée. Then pour the purée into a large bowl. Stir in the cold chicken stock. Season to taste with salt and pepper and stir in the sugar and vinegar. Chill for several hours.

Serve in chilled soup bowls and sprinkle with chopped parsley. *Advance preparation:* Make several hours in advance and chill well before serving. Prepare vegetables and croûtons for garnish and keep in small polythene bags ready for serving.

Sorrel soup

Sorrel has a pleasant, slightly astringent, flavour that makes a very refreshing soup. Sorrel is usually combined with either lettuce or spinach, using equal parts of each. This is partly to temper the flavour and also because sorrel looses its colour on cooking and the addition of either lettuce or spinach helps to balance this.

Serves 6

1 oz./25 g. butter	8 oz./225 g. sorrel and lettuce
1 small onion	leaves, mixed
8 oz./¼ kg. potatoes	salt and pepper
1½ pint/9 dl. stock	

Melt the butter in a saucepan. Peel and chop the onion and add to the pan. Fry gently for about 5 minutes or until the onion is soft and tender but not brown. Peel and dice the potatoes and add to the pan. Toss in the onion flavoured butter and then stir in the stock. Bring up to the boil, lower the heat and simmer for about 15 minutes or until the potato is tender.

Meanwhile wash the sorrel and lettuce leaves in several changes of cold water. Pull away the coarse stem and mid ribs from the leaves. Add the leaves to the pan and bring back to the boil. Allow to simmer for 10 minutes then draw off the heat. Pass the soup through a mouli soup mill or blend to a purée in an electric blender. Check seasoning with salt and pepper and reheat before serving.

Advance preparation: Sorrel soup can be made in advance. The flavour noticeably mellows on reheating and it tastes even better the second day.

Cucumber and mint soup

A refreshing summer soup. Serve very cold to emphasise the subtle mint flavour.

Serves 6

2 cucumbers	1 rounded tablespoon flour
1 bunch (about 12 stalks) fresh mint	$\frac{1}{2}$ pint/3 dl. milk
	salt and freshly milled pepper
1 oz./25 g. butter	1 ($\frac{1}{4}$ pint/1$\frac{1}{2}$ dl.) carton soured
1 small onion	cream
$\frac{3}{4}$ pint/$\frac{1}{2}$ litre chicken stock	

Cut about 2 inches (5 cm.) off one of the cucumbers and set aside for the garnish. Peel both cucumbers, cut in half lengthways, remove seeds and chop the flesh coarsely. Strip the mint leaves from the stems and wash. Chop the leaves coarsely – there should be enough to fill a $\frac{1}{2}$ pint (3 dl.) measure.

Melt the butter in a saucepan. Peel and chop the onion, add to the pan and sauté gently until the onion is soft but not brown. Add the cucumber and the mint. Stir to mix, then add the chicken stock. Bring to the boil, cover and simmer for 20 minutes.

Blend the flour with the milk. Stir or whisk well – there should be no lumps. Stir into the soup and bring up to the boil. Simmer for 2–3 minutes, then draw off the heat. Pass the soup through a mouli soup mill or purée in an electric blender. Allow to cool and season. Stir in the soured cream and then chill well.

Garnish with thin slices of cucumber, cut from the reserved cucumber, and serve.

Advance preparation: Make well in advance and chill thoroughly before serving.

Potage Parisien

Illustrated in colour on page 125

A mixture of leeks and potatoes makes a very pleasant flavoured soup. Serve hot for the family or chilled for a party. Add a dash of Worcestershire sauce to give the soup extra piquancy when served cold.

Serves 6

1 lb./$\frac{1}{2}$ kg. leeks	1 level teaspoon salt
1 onion	freshly milled pepper
2 medium potatoes	2–3 tablespoons single cream
2$\frac{1}{2}$ oz./65 g. butter	1–2 tablespoons finely chopped
2$\frac{1}{2}$ pints/1$\frac{1}{4}$ litres stock	chives or parsley

Trim the base of the leeks and cut the green tops down to about 1 inch (2$\frac{1}{2}$ cm.) of the white stem. Split each leek lengthways to the centre and wash well under running cold water to remove any grit or dirt. Shred the leeks finely. Peel and chop the onion. Peel the potatoes and cut into large dice. Melt 2 oz. (50 g.) butter in a large saucepan and add the prepared leeks and onion. Cover and cook very gently for about 5 minutes until the vegetables are tender but not browned. Add the potatoes and then stir in the stock. Bring up to the boil and simmer for about 20 minutes.

Draw off the heat and pass the vegetables and liquid through a mouli soup mill or blend in an electric liquidiser to make a purée. Return the soup to the pan and check seasoning. Bring almost to the boil then stir in the remaining butter, the cream and chopped herbs. Serve hot.

To serve the soup cold: Omit the addition of the last $\frac{1}{2}$ oz. (15 g.) butter and instead increase the cream to $\frac{1}{4}$ pint (1$\frac{1}{2}$ dl.). Chill well before serving.

Advance preparation: Make the soup in advance ready to reheat, or put to chill if serving cold.

Minestrone

Use a well flavoured broth when making minestrone. Use stock from boiling a bacon joint or water made up to the correct quantity using beef stock cubes. Use more or less vegetables according to how substantial you wish the minestrone to be.

Serves 4

1–2 carrots	2 large tomatoes
1–2 sticks celery	1 small leek
1 onion	1 teacupful shredded cabbage
1 small turnip	or sprouts
1 medium potato	1 oz./25 g. spaghetti or quick
2 tablespoons oil	cooking macaroni
1 clove garlic	salt and pepper
1$\frac{1}{2}$ pints/scant 1 litre hot stock	grated Parmesan cheese

Peel and slice the carrot. Wash and shred the celery. Peel and chop the onion, peel and cut the turnip and the potato into small dice. Heat the oil in a large saucepan and add the carrot, celery, onion, turnip and potato. Add the skinned and finely chopped garlic. Sauté the vegetables for a few minutes until slightly softened, but not brown. Stir in the hot stock and bring up to the boil. Cover and simmer for about 15–20 minutes or until the vegetables are almost tender.

Skin, halve and deseed the tomatoes. Chop up the tomato flesh. Wash and finely shred the leek. Add the leek, tomato flesh, shredded cabbage or sprouts to the soup. Bring back to the boil, then add the spaghetti (break long spaghetti into smaller pieces) or the macaroni. Simmer gently without a lid for a further 10–15 minutes.

Check seasoning and serve the minestrone with plenty of grated Parmesan cheese for sprinkling over the top.

Advance preparation: Minestrone can be made and reheated – but the soup is best newly cooked.

French onion soup

Onions tend to hold the heat and care should be taken not to serve this soup boiling hot.

Serves 4–6

1 lb./½ kg. onions	¼ pint/1½ dl. cold water
1 oz./25 g. butter	4 slices French bread
2 pints/generous 1 litre stock	butter
½ level teaspoon salt	1–2 oz./25–50 g. Gruyère
1 oz./25 g. flour	cheese, grated

Peel and slice the onions. Melt the butter in a fairly large saucepan and add the onions. Cover and allow to cook gently for about 30 minutes until the onions are soft and transparent looking. Remove the lid and continue frying the onions, stirring occasionally until they are a golden brown colour. Stir in the stock and salt. Recover and simmer for a further 30 minutes. In a small basin, blend the flour and the cold water together. Whisk or stir well to blend thoroughly. Stir into the soup and continue stirring until the soup has come back to the boil. Simmer for 2–3 minutes then draw off the heat.

Meanwhile, butter both sides of each slice of French bread, then heap a little of the grated cheese on one side of each slice. Arrange the slices of prepared bread on a greased baking sheet. Place in a moderately hot oven (350°F., 180°C., Gas Mark 4) until the bread is crisp and the cheese melted.

Have ready the hot soup tureen or individual heated serving dishes. Place the pieces of hot bread in the base, or one in each if individual dishes are used. Pour the soup over.

Serve with a little extra grated cheese for sprinkling on top.
Advance preparation: Make this soup in advance. Butter the bread and top with cheese but do not brown until ready to serve. Reheat the soup, pour over and serve.

Spinach soup

The best soup is made using spinach freshly picked from the garden. This recipe is quick and easy to prepare. It has a pleasant flavour and is thickened by the addition of a small amount of potato.

Serves 6

1 oz./25 g. butter	8 oz./¼ kg. fresh spinach
1 medium onion	salt and freshly milled pepper
8 oz./¼ kg. (1 large) potato	
1½ pints/scant 1 litre chicken stock	

Melt the butter in a saucepan. Peel and finely chop the onion and add to the pan. Fry gently for about 5 minutes until the onion is soft and tender but not brown. Peel and dice the potato and add with the chicken stock. Bring up to the boil, lower the heat and simmer gently for about 15 minutes or until the potato is tender.

Meanwhile, wash the spinach in plenty of cold water and pull away the stalk and centre rib from the leaves. Add the spinach to the pan, bring back to the boil and simmer for 10 minutes. Draw off the heat and either pass the soup through a mouli soup mill or blend to a purée in an electric blender. Return the soup

to the pan, season to taste with salt and pepper and reheat before serving.
Advance preparation: Spinach soup can be made in advance and reheated.

Avocado pears stuffed with cream cheese

A pretty and most original way of serving avocado pears that makes an excellent first course. Prepare early in the day so that they are well chilled before slicing.

Serves 6

3 ripe avocado pears	1 oz./25 g. butter, melted
2 (3 oz./75 g.) packets full fat cream cheese	6 tablespoons vinaigrette dressing
2 tablespoons double cream	*to garnish:*
salt and freshly milled pepper	watercress
1–2 teaspoons chives or parsley	

Cut the avocado pears carefully in half round the middle (do not cut lengthwise) and remove the stones. Soften the cream cheese by beating in the cream and then season with salt and pepper. Add the chives or parsley and beat well with a wooden spoon. Fill the cavity of each avocado half evenly with the cream cheese. Brush the cut edges of the avocado with melted butter and seal the fruit together again. Place in the refrigerator and leave for several hours so that the butter becomes quite firm and the two halves are firmly sealed together.

When ready to serve, peel the skin away from each avocado with a vegetable parer. Slice the avocado into ¼-inch (½-cm.) thick slices across the fruit. At the base and top of the fruit no cream cheese will show, but the centre slices (where there is normally a cavity for the stone) will show a ring of avocado filled with cream cheese. Divide the slices up between six servings – arrange the filled slices on top. Spoon a little vinaigrette dressing over each and garnish each one with a sprig of watercress.

Serve with thinly sliced brown bread and butter.
Advance preparation: Prepare the avocados and chill well in advance. Do not slice until ready to serve.

OPPOSITE **Mustard pickle (page 188)**
Clean, prepare and cut the vegetables into suitably sized pieces for eating, breaking the cauliflower into sprigs.
Prepare the mustard sauce and add the drained vegetables, which have been soaked in brine.
Pack the vegetables into jars and pour over sufficient sauce to cover.

Courgettes à la grecque

Vegetables cooked à la grecque can be served as a first course. Pass round plenty of French bread to mop up the juices.

Serves 4

2 lb./¾ kg. courgettes	1 teaspoon coriander seeds
¼ pint/1½ dl. olive oil	2 bay leaves
½ pint/3 dl. dry white wine and	1–2 sprigs thyme
water, mixed	2 cloves garlic, peeled
salt and freshly milled pepper	

Trim either end of the courgettes, leave them unpeeled and slice fairly thickly. Add to a pan of boiling, salted water. Reboil, simmer for 2–3 minutes and then drain. This 'blanching' helps to preserve the green colour and removes any bitter flavour in the skins.

Measure the oil, wine and water, a seasoning of salt and pepper, the coriander seeds, bay leaves, thyme and garlic into a large saucepan. Bring just up to the boil, then cover with a lid and simmer for 5 minutes. Add the prepared courgettes, recover and cook gently for 10–12 minutes or until the courgettes are tender.

Draw the pan off the heat and, using a perforated spoon, carefully lift the vegetables out on to a serving dish. Replace the pan over the heat and boil briskly for about 5 minutes to reduce the wine mixture. Pour over the courgettes and leave until quite cold.

Advance preparation: Make this recipe well in advance so that the mixture is quite cold before serving. Prepared this way, the vegetables keep for 1–2 days.

Swiss rosti

'Rosti' should be made with potatoes that have been boiled the day before. Do not use potatoes that are inclined to break up and become floury. Serve rosti hot with grilled or fried bacon, sausages or fried eggs. Also delicious served hot with cold sliced chicken, turkey or ham and salad.

Serves 4

2 lb./1 kg. even sized potatoes	2 level teaspoons salt
2 oz./50 g. butter	freshly milled pepper

Scrub the potatoes and place in a saucepan. Cover with cold water, bring up to the boil and cook for about 5–7 minutes or until barely tender. Drain and leave until cold. Peel away the potato skins and coarsely grate the potatoes on to a plate.

Melt the butter in a large heavy frying pan. Add the grated potato, sprinkling it with the salt and a seasoning of pepper. Fry the mixture over moderate heat for about 15 minutes; as the potato browns underneath turn, using a spatula, so that the crispy brown underneath comes on top allowing more potato to brown underneath. Towards the end of the cooking time, press the potato down gently and allow to become quite crisp and brown on the underneath. When ready to serve, loosen the 'rosti' and place a round serving plate over the pan. Invert the 'rosti' on to it and serve.

Advance preparation: Prepare potatoes ready for grating in advance. Do not cook 'rosti' until ready to serve.

Stuffed aubergines

Choose plump aubergines that are even in size. Prepared this way, they make a tasty and unusual start to a meal.

Serves 6

3 aubergines	1 level teaspoon dried mixed
salt	herbs
4–6 tablespoons oil	salt and freshly milled pepper
1 oz./25 g. butter	*for the topping:*
2 medium onions	2 oz./50 g. butter
6 tomatoes	2 oz./50 g. fresh breadcrumbs
1 clove garlic	2 oz./50 g. hard cheese, grated

Cut the aubergines in half lengthwise. Using a knife, cut them around the edges and slash across the middle. Sprinkle the cut surface with salt and leave them for 30 minutes upside down to drain. Then dry them well.

Heat the oil in a frying pan. Add the aubergines, placing them face down in the pan. Fry gently for about 8 minutes or until tender, turning them once or twice. When brown, remove the aubergines from the pan and scrape the flesh from the shell. Retain the shells and chop up the flesh coarsely.

Melt the butter in a saucepan. Peel and finely shred the onions. Add to the pan and cook gently until soft but not brown. Blanch and peel the tomatoes. Halve and remove the seeds, then chop the tomato flesh coarsely. Add the tomato flesh, the chopped garlic, herbs, a seasoning of salt and pepper and the aubergine flesh to the pan. Fry gently for about 5 minutes. Then draw the pan off the heat.

Spoon the mixture into the aubergine skins. Melt the butter for the topping and, using a fork, stir in the breadcrumbs. Sprinkle the buttered crumbs over the filled aubergines and sprinkle with the cheese. Place under a hot grill to brown, then serve.

Advance preparation: Prepare aubergine mixture and fill the shells. Top with breadcrumbs and cheese and set aside. When ready to serve, reheat in a moderate oven (350°F., 180°C., Gas Mark 4) for 15 minutes, then brown under a grill and serve.

Tomatoes with guacamole

Guacamole is a delicious mixture made using avocado pears. On its own it can be served as a dip with crisp raw vegetables. In this recipe the guacamole is used to fill tomatoes for a first course.

Serves 6

12 even sized tomatoes	2 tablespoons olive oil
salt	2 tablespoons lemon juice
for the filling:	2 teaspoons finely chopped
2 ripe avocado pears	onion
1 small clove garlic	freshly milled pepper
salt	Tabasco sauce to taste

Wipe the tomatoes and cut a slice off the top of each one. Scoop out the inside of each one with a teaspoon. Sprinkle each tomato with salt and leave upside down to drain. Remove the centre stalk from each tomato lid. Reserve the lids.

Cut each avocado in half, remove the stone and scoop out the flesh. Peel the garlic clove and crush with a little salt. Mash the avocado with a fork and mix in the garlic, oil, lemon juice, onion and a seasoning of pepper. No extra salt will be required if it has been included with the garlic. Mix thoroughly and season to taste with Tabasco sauce. Cover the bowl and place in the refrigerator until required.

Spoon the guacamole generously into the tomato shells. Replace the lids and serve – allowing 2 per person.

Advance preparation: Prepare tomato cups and guacamole mixture and chill. Keep avocado mixture covered with film wrap or foil to prevent discoloration. Fill tomato shells when required for serving.

Croquette potatoes with almonds

Potato croquettes are ideal for a dinner party, they can be prepared ready for frying well in advance of serving. They also keep well in the home freezer.

Serves 6

2 lb./1 kg. potatoes	flour
½ oz./15 g. butter	flaked almonds for coating
salt and freshly milled pepper	oil for deep frying
2 eggs	

Peel the potatoes, place in a saucepan with sufficient salted water to cover. Bring to the boil, then simmer for 15–20 minutes or until tender, but do not over cook. Drain the potatoes well, return to the hot pan and dry thoroughly over low heat for a few moments. Pass the potatoes through a sieve to get rid of all the lumps – for croquettes, mashing the potatoes is not sufficient.

Rinse out the pan and then return to the heat with the butter. Warm over a low heat just to melt the butter. Draw off the heat and add the potatoes. Beat well to mix and add a good seasoning of salt and freshly milled pepper. Separate the eggs and beat the yolks into the potato mixture. Place the whites in a shallow dish.

Turn the potato mixture out on to a lightly floured working surface, shape neatly and then divide into 24 equal portions. Dust the potato with flour and then, using lightly floured hands, roll each portion of potato into a ball about the size of a small apricot. Lightly beat the egg whites with a fork just to break them up. Roll each potato first in the egg whites and then in either flaked almonds or toasted breadcrumbs.

When ready to serve, fry the potatoes in hot, deep oil, a few at a time. Turn the potatoes in the hot oil so that they brown evenly. Drain on absorbent paper, then keep warm until ready to serve.

Advance preparation: The croquettes can be prepared in advance, but they should be fried only when ready to serve.

Golden roast potatoes

To be sure of tender roast potatoes with a crisp, golden surface every time, blanch, then toss the potatoes in seasoned flour before roasting. Thick slices or fingers of parsnip are also very good cooked this way.

Serves 6

2 lb./1 kg. potatoes	2 oz./50 g. dripping or
seasoned flour	white cooking fat

Scrub and peel the potatoes. Cut in halves or quarters if large. Blanch in boiling water for 5 minutes only, then drain at once. Toss in a little seasoned flour to coat the potatoes lightly all over. Melt the fat in a roasting tin. Put the potatoes in and turn them in the fat to coat them all over. Place in a moderately hot oven (375°F., 190°C., Gas Mark 5) or place above a roast and bake for 45 minutes. Turn and baste once or twice until crisp, golden and cooked.

Lyonnaise potatoes

Lyonnaise potatoes are worth making properly. They should never be prepared using left-over boiled potatoes, which break up when fried. Prepared using the method given here, the potato slices become crisp and remain unbroken. Serve with grilled sausages, fried eggs, cold ham or fried chicken.

Serves 4

1½ lb./¾ kg. potatoes	salt and freshly milled pepper
1½–2 oz./35–50 g. bacon fat	1 teaspoon tarragon vinegar
or butter	chopped parsley
1 large onion, finely sliced	

Peel the potatoes and cut into ¼-inch (½-cm.) thick slices. Blanch for 5 minutes only in boiling water and then drain. Melt 1½ oz. (35 g.) fat in a frying pan and add the onion. Cook gently for 5–8 minutes or until the onion is soft but not brown. Remove the onion from the pan and reserve for adding later.

If necessary add the remaining ½ oz. (15 g.) fat to the hot fat in the pan and add the potato slices. Fry gently until cooked and beginning to brown. Turn the potatoes and shake the pan occasionally. Cook the potatoes in batches if the pan is small.

When the potatoes are tender and golden, add the onion to the pan. Season well with salt and pepper and sprinkle over the vinegar. Fry for a moment longer, then sprinkle with chopped parsley and serve.

Advance preparation: Slice and blanch the potatoes. Do not fry until ready to serve.

OVERLEAF **Roast duckling and orange sauce (page 90)**
Prepare the stuffing and bind with orange juice, melted butter and egg.
Place the duckling in a roasting tin and close the tail of the bird with a skewer.
Add the orange flesh to the sauce.

Creamed potatoes

A good dish of smooth, creamed potatoes requires careful preparation. Creamed potatoes go well with any recipe that has a sauce or gravy. For a special occasion, finely chopped chives, parsley or spring onions may be added or a little grated orange rind is particularly good when served with a beef casserole.

Serves 4

1½ lb./¾ kg. potatoes (preferably a floury type)
salt and freshly milled pepper

1 oz./25 g. butter
about ¼ pint/1½ dl. hot milk

Scrub and peel the potatoes and cut up any large ones. Place in cold salted water, bring to the boil and cook gently for 15–20 minutes or until tender. Drain and return to the hot pan for a minute to dry off. Press (don't rub or stir) the potatoes through a sieve into a warm bowl. Add a good seasoning of salt and pepper, the butter and half the hot milk. Beat well with a wooden spoon, adding more milk as required to produce a smooth creamy consistency.

Advance preparation: Creamed potatoes can be prepared ready for serving. To keep them hot, cover the bowl with a plate or pan lid and place the bowl over a saucepan of simmering water until ready to serve.

Chipped potatoes

A chef's well known secret for chips that are really crisp outside and soft inside, is to fry them twice. The first frying in fat that is not too hot but enough to cook the chips through without browning them. The second frying is very quick, at a high temperature to brown and crispen them.

Serves 4

2 lb./1 kg. large potatoes   salt

Select large potatoes if you want good sized chips. Peel and then slice about ¼ inch (½ cm.) thick. Keeping the potato shape, turn slices on their sides and cut again to make fingers or chips, discard any small trimmings. Soak the chips for 20–30 minutes in cold salted water to draw out some of the starch. Drain and dry thoroughly in a cloth before frying. This is important, wet chips coming in contact with very hot fat could cause dangerous spluttering and the finished chips will be soggy.

Never fry chips without a basket, it should be possible if necessary to remove them quickly from the hot fat. No more than half fill the chip basket, the water in the chips causes the hot fat to foam up. Too many chips in the basket could make the fat overflow the pan, if this does happen lift out the basket quickly. Fry gently, shaking the basket occasionally for even cooking. Cook only until chips are tender, test a chip with the tip of a knife blade – it should feel soft. Drain on plenty of absorbent paper and set aside for the final frying.

When ready to serve, heat the fat until very hot and plunge in the basket of chips. Fry quickly until brown, then drain, sprinkle with salt and serve.

Advance preparation: Using this method, the initial frying of the chips can be completed well in advance. They need only to be plunged into hot fat for browning just before serving.

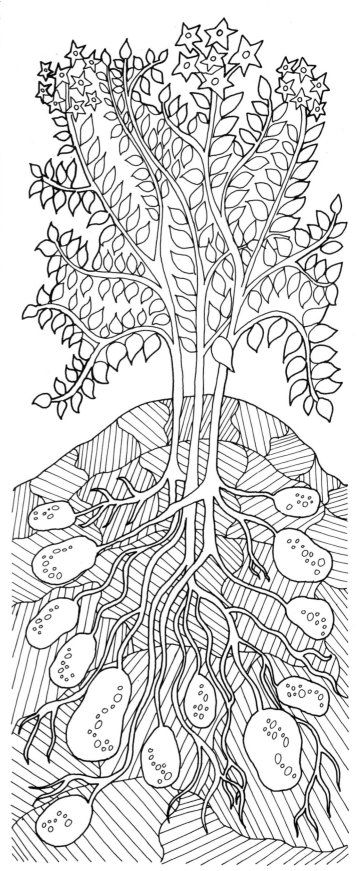

Quick fried asparagus

This unusual, in fact Oriental, method of cooking asparagus is one of the quickest ways of serving fresh asparagus as a vegetable. Buy the less expensive, thinner green sticks.

Serves 4

1–1½ lb./½–¾ kg. fresh asparagus	2 tablespoons water
3 tablespoons olive oil	salt

Wash the asparagus then snap off and discard the woody base of the stalks. Line up several stalks on a cutting board and, using a sharp knife, cut across the asparagus on the extreme bias making slices about ¼ inch (½ cm.) thick. This should give thin slanting slices about 1 inch (2½ cm.) long.

Measure the oil and water into a saucepan, cover with a lid and bring up to the boil. Add the asparagus and a seasoning of salt. Recover and cook over a moderate heat, shaking the pan occasionally, for about 5 minutes. Draw the pan off the heat and test the asparagus – the pieces should be tender-crisp. Serve at once.

Advance preparation: Assemble ingredients and cook when ready to serve.

Spinach cream

This is an attractive and unusual way for serving spinach as a vegetable. Spinach goes well with veal or pork recipes.

Serves 6

2 lb./1 kg. fresh spinach	2 eggs
1 oz./25 g. butter	1 tablespoon single cream
1 oz./25 g. flour	pinch ground or a little grated
½ pint/3 dl. milk	nutmeg
salt and freshly milled pepper	

Tear away coarse stems and wash the spinach in plenty of cold water. Reserve about 6 nicely shaped leaves. Drain the rest and pack into a large saucepan. Boil over moderate heat until the spinach is quite soft – the water on the leaves will provide quite sufficient liquid. Drain and purée, whether by passing through a coarse sieve or blending on an electric liquidiser. Return to the saucepan and dry off a little over the heat.

Meanwhile, prepare a sauce by melting the butter in a saucepan over low heat. Stir in the flour and cook gently for 1 minute. Gradually stir in the milk, beating in each addition well to get a smooth sauce. Bring up to the boil and simmer for 2–3 minutes. Draw off the heat, season well with salt and pepper and stir in the spinach purée, the eggs, cream and nutmeg.

Plunge the reserved spinach leaves into boiling water for 2 minutes to soften, then use to line a well buttered 6-inch (15-cm.) soufflé or round baking dish. Pour in the spinach mixture. Any spinach leaves overlapping the edge of the dish should be turned inwards over the top of the mixture. Place the dish in a large roasting tin containing ½ inch (1 cm.) cold water. Place in the centre of a moderate oven (350°F., 180°C., Gas Mark 4) and bake for 45 minutes to 1 hour. Allow to cool for 5 minutes before turning out, then serve as a vegetable.

Advance preparation: Prepare spinach and mould ready to bake. Put to bake when ready to serve, allowing the longer cooking time.

Aubergine and tomato ragoût

This blend of aubergines and tomatoes goes well with any casserole dish or with steak or chops. Choose fresh aubergines that have a smooth shiny skin and no wrinkles.

Serves 6

3 medium aubergines	1 lb./½ kg. tomatoes
salt	freshly milled pepper
1 oz./25 g. butter	2 level teaspoons castor sugar
2 large onions	2 bay leaves
1 clove garlic	pinch dried mixed herbs

Peel and cut up the aubergines. Sprinkle with salt and allow to stand in a colander under a weight for about 30 minutes, to draw out some of the moisture. Drain away any juices that have formed, rinse the aubergines and pat dry.

Melt the butter in a saucepan. Peel and slice the onions and add to the pan. Fry gently for about 5 minutes until the onion is soft and not brown. Crush the garlic with salt and add to the pan. Add the aubergines and toss to mix with the butter and onions. Scald the tomatoes and peel away the skins. Quarter the tomatoes and add to the pan. Season with pepper and add the sugar, bay leaves and mixed herbs. Cover the pan with a lid and continue to simmer, stirring occasionally, for 40–45 minutes. Remove the pan lid towards the end of the cooking time, to allow extra juices to evaporate. When ready, the aubergines should be quite tender and the mixture fairly thick with most of the liquid evaporated. Check the seasoning before serving.

Advance preparation: Assemble ingredients and put to cook when ready to serve.

Sweet and sour red cabbage

Success with red cabbage depends on getting the right sweet-sour flavour combination. Add extra sugar if necessary, the cabbage must taste sweet enough. Serve with pork, duck or game.

Serves 4–6

about 1½ lb./¾ kg. red cabbage	salt and freshly milled pepper
1 large cooking apple	1 level tablespoon sugar
1 medium onion	¼ pint/1½ dl. dry cider
1 oz./25 g. butter	juice ½ lemon

Remove any outer damaged leaves from the red cabbage, then quarter and cut away the core. Shred across the leaves very finely. Peel, core and chop the apple. Peel and chop the onion. Melt the butter in a saucepan. Add the cabbage, onion and apple and fry gently for about 5 minutes, stirring all the time. Add a seasoning of salt and pepper, the sugar and cider. Cover with a close fitting lid and simmer very gently for 1–1¼ hours. Check once or twice during cooking and give the cabbage a stir. A little more cider or water may be added if necessary, but the liquid should have almost evaporated by the time the cabbage is tender. Check seasoning, stir in lemon juice to taste and serve.

Advance preparation: Red cabbage is ideal for dinner parties. It keeps hot without spoiling and reheats very well. Keep hot or reheat in a casserole in the oven.

Creamed cabbage

This is an unusual and extremely tasty way to serve white cabbage as a hot vegetable.

Serves 4

1 small or ½ large white cabbage, about 1½ lb./¾ kg.	salt and freshly milled pepper
1 small onion	1 level tablespoon flour
2 oz./50 g. butter	¼ pint/1½ dl. single cream or milk
¼ pint/1½ dl. boiling stock or water	pinch nutmeg

Remove any outer damaged leaves and cut the cabbage into quarters. Remove the hard core and shred the cabbage finely Peel and chop the onion.

Melt half the butter in a large saucepan, add the onion and cook gently for about 5 minutes until the onion is tender but not brown. Add the cabbage, the boiling stock and a seasoning of salt and pepper. Bring up to the boil, cover and cook gently for about 15 minutes until the cabbage is tender.

Melt the remaining butter in a large saucepan and stir in the flour. Cook gently for 1 minute, then gradually stir in the cream. Stir until thickened and boiling. Season well with salt and pepper and add the nutmeg. Drain the cooked cabbage and add to the cream sauce. Add a little extra milk if necessary, the mixture should not be thick. Toss well to mix, check seasoning again, heat through and serve hot.

Serve with roast beef or lamb, or with grilled sausages, chops or hamburgers.

Advance preparation: Prepared this way, cabbage keeps hot without spoiling. Keep hot over a saucepan of simmering water.

Courgettes with parsley butter

A simple and effective way of serving courgettes. Prepared this way, they go particularly well with grilled fish or with fried veal or pork escalopes.

Serves 4

1 lb./½ kg. small courgettes	1 tablespoon finely chopped parsley
salt and freshly milled pepper	
2 oz./50 g. butter	squeeze lemon juice
1 teaspoon olive oil	

Trim either end from the courgettes and if small leave unpeeled, if large peel along the ridges. Slice fairly thickly and then add to a pan of boiling, salted water. Reboil and simmer for 2 minutes and drain. This helps preserve the pleasant green colour of the courgettes and removes any bitter flavour.

Add the drained courgettes to half the melted butter and the oil in a frying pan. Season well with salt and pepper, cover with a lid and sauté very gently for about 15 minutes or until tender. Meanwhile, cream together the remaining butter, parsley and lemon juice. When courgettes are cooked, draw the pan off the heat, add the parsley butter, shake the pan only to melt the butter and serve at once.

Advance preparation: Blanch the courgettes ready for frying. Put to cook when ready to serve.

Peas with lettuce

Fresh peas cooked like this are delicious served with lamb, veal or chicken recipes. The amount of water may vary – starchy peas absorb more.

Serves 4

2 lb./1 kg. fresh peas	salt and freshly milled pepper
heart 1 lettuce	1 level teaspoon castor sugar
8–10 spring onions	1 slightly rounded teaspoon cornflour
1 oz./25 g. butter	
¼ pint/1½ dl. water	

Shell the peas and wash and shred the lettuce. Wash the spring onions, trim off the base and green tops leaving the white onion bulbs. Put the lettuce and onions into a saucepan with the butter and water. Bring to the boil, add the peas, a seasoning of salt and pepper and the sugar. Cover with a lid and simmer gently for 15 minutes.

Stir in the cornflour, blended with 2–3 tablespoons water, and bring up to the boil, stirring gently until thickened. Serve the entire contents of the pan.

Advance preparation: Assemble ingredients. Cook when ready to serve.

Fennel in cream sauce

Fennel makes an excellent hot vegetable, it has a pleasant taste of aniseed and should be treated very much like celery in cooking.

Serves 4

4 medium or 2 large heads fennel	¼ pint/1½ dl. cream
for the cream sauce:	salt and freshly milled pepper
1½ oz./40 g. butter	squeeze lemon juice
1 oz./25 g. flour	chopped parsley or 'fines herbes'
scant ½ pint/scant 3 dl. milk	

Trim the base of the fennel and the green stalky tops level with the bulb. Leave small heads of fennel whole and cut large ones in half lengthways. Place in a saucepan and cover with boiling water. Add salt and simmer for 15–20 minutes depending on the size of the fennel. It should feel tender when pierced with a sharp knife. Drain and place the fennel in a hot buttered serving dish.

Meanwhile, melt 1 oz. (25 g.) of the butter for the sauce and stir in the flour. Cook gently for a few moments, then gradually stir in the milk. Beat well all the time to get a smooth sauce. Cook for a few minutes, then stir in the cream and draw off the heat. Season to taste with salt and pepper and add lemon juice. Beat in the remaining butter to get a smooth consistency.

Pour the hot sauce over the fennel and sprinkle with chopped parsley or chopped 'fines herbes' before serving.

Advance preparation: Prepare fennel and make the sauce, without adding cream, in advance. Cook fennel, reheat sauce and stir in cream. Pour over fennel and serve.

OPPOSITE **Potage Parisien (page 115)**
Trim and split the leeks lengthwise and wash.
Shred the leeks finely.
Dice the potatoes and add to the saucepan.
Add the remaining ingredients to the liquidised vegetables.

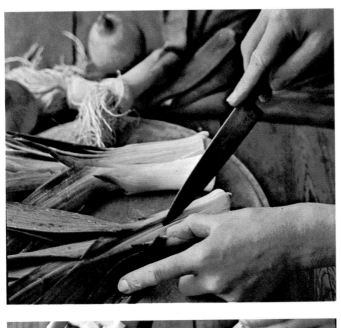

Baked stuffed marrow

Stuffed vegetables offer a wonderful opportunity for using up left-over meat. If meat is short, include 1–2 finely chopped bacon rashers and fry lightly with the onion.

Serves 4

1 small marrow	¼ pint/1½ dl. stock
butter	(use water and stock cube)
2 oz./50 g. cheese, grated	8–10 oz./225–275 g. cooked
breadcrumbs	meat
1 large tomato	1 level teaspoon curry powder
for the stuffing:	salt and freshly milled pepper
1 small onion	pinch mixed herbs
1 oz./25 g. butter	1 teaspoon Worcestershire sauce
1 oz./25 g. flour	

Peel and then cut the marrow into rings about 1½ inches (3½ cm.) wide. Scoop out the seeds and then blanch the rings in boiling, salted water for 5 minutes. Drain and arrange in a buttered baking dish. Keep warm while preparing the filling.

Peel and chop the onion. Melt the butter in a saucepan, add the onion and cook gently over low heat until the onion is soft. Stir in the flour and then the stock. Bring up to the boil, stirring until thickened and smooth. Draw off the heat and mix in all the remaining ingredients.

Fill the marrow rings with the filling. Cover with a buttered paper and place in the centre of a moderate oven (350°F., 180°C., Gas Mark 4) and bake for 30 minutes or until the marrow is tender. Remove the paper. Sprinkle with a little grated cheese and a few breadcrumbs. Top with a slice of tomato and a generous nob of butter. Return to the oven, uncovered and bake for a further 10 minutes before serving.

Advance preparation: Blanch marrow rings. Prepare stuffing and fill the marrow. Put to bake when ready to serve.

Glazed new carrots

Only new carrots should be cooked this way, they are tender and young and cook quickly. All the flavour is retained as the carrots are served in a buttery glaze. Sprinkle with fresh mint when available later in the season.

Serves 4

1 lb./½ kg. new carrots	1 level teaspoon castor sugar
1 oz./25 g. butter	1 teaspoon chopped parsley
salt and freshly milled pepper	

Scrub and scrape the carrots and cut into even slices about ¼ inch (½ cm.) thick. Put into a saucepan with the butter, a seasoning of salt and pepper and the sugar. Add cold water just to cover the carrots. Bring up to the boil, cover with a lid and simmer gently for 15–20 minutes until tender.

Remove the lid and boil briskly until the liquid has almost evaporated and only the butter remains in the pan. Watch the pan towards the end of the time, the carrots should not be allowed to brown. Draw off the heat, add the parsley and toss in the butter glaze. Turn into a hot dish and serve.

Advance preparation: Prepare carrots and put in pan with water, sugar and butter. Cook when ready to serve.

Salads

Salads are seasonal all year round. When summer ingredients become scarce and more expensive, make use of the winter vegetables. The firm heart of ordinary green cabbage, white and red cabbage, large sprouts or leeks can be shredded to provide the necessary greens. Keep salads interesting with such additions as shredded green pepper, sliced mushrooms, crisp fried and crumbled bacon rashers, diced carrots and chopped parsley.

Beetroot
Buy them already cooked. Slice off the skins using forefinger and thumb and thinly slice or dice the flesh. Serve separately in vinegar or add it last to a salad, as the colour stains lettuce.

Cabbage
Quarter the cabbage and cut away hard centre core. Wash leaves in cold, salted water, then drain and shred.

Carrots
Scrub to remove any dirt. Always use new, young carrots, cut into thin matchsticks or grate. Pare off very thin layers lengthwise to make carrot curls for a garnish. Leave them in iced water to go crisp and curl up.

Cauliflower
Break cauliflower into small heads. Wash well and use uncooked.

Celery
Separate stalks from the head of celery, scrub clean. Trim off base and tops and then shred finely.

Chicory
Cut a thin slice from the base of the head. Separate the leaves and wash in cold water. Shake and leave whole or shred.

Cress, watercress and chives
Wash very thoroughly under running water. Use the tops of cress and watercress only, snip off cress with scissors and, using fingers, pinch off upper parts of watercress. Pick out the greenest leaves of chives and chop finely.

Cucumber
Wash thoroughly and peel thinly, or flute the skin by running the prongs of a fork down the length. Slice thinly across.

Garlic
Only the merest suspicion should be used in salads. Best way is to crush a clove of garlic and rub it round the inside of the salad bowl or dish, then discard the clove.

Green pepper
Slice in half lengthwise and remove seeds and core. Then shred flesh and use it raw. If liked, skins can be blistered and peeled. Shred flesh and toss in French dressing.

Leeks
Trim off base and top green part, leaving on the white stalk and about 1 inch (2½ cm.) of the green part. Cut lengthwise with a knife to the centre only and then wash under cold running water to remove all grit. Shred finely.

Lettuce and curly endive

Select crisp, fresh heads and wash in plenty of cold water. The best way is to dip the head up and down in cold water, this draws out all the dirt by suction. Break apart and separate the leaves, tear lettuce into smaller pieces if liked, but never cut with a knife. Shake the leaves in a colander or salad basket, or pat dry in a clean tea towel. Choose from round lettuces or the long crisp Cos variety. Select heads of endive that are crisp and fresh looking. Endive has a slightly bitter taste, it goes particularly well with strong flavoured dressings.

Mushrooms

Select small button mushrooms. Wash in cold water and trim the ends of the stalks. Slice thinly downwards and use raw.

Onions

Ordinary onions should be peeled and sliced into rings. Cover with vinegar for several hours before using – this way they soften slightly. Spring onions should be well washed, then trim off roots and top parts of the green. Use whole or slice into rings.

Radishes

Wash thoroughly and trim off tops and tails. Add to a salad, sliced or whole, or make pretty radish roses – using a small sharp knife, slit the radish down from the tail end about 4–6 times to form petals. Take care not to cut right through. Leave in iced water to open out.

Tomatoes

Wash and cut into slices or quarters. Or cut into attractive tomato lilies, by making zig zag cuts round the middle of each tomato with a sharp knife and separate into neat halves. Sliced tomatoes topped with chopped spring onions or chives are delicious in French dressing.

Mayonnaise

When making mayonnaise, avoid using eggs that are cold from the refrigerator. This often causes a mayonnaise to curdle. Lemon juice can be used instead of vinegar and for those who dislike the strong flavour of olive oil, a lighter salad oil can be used instead.

Makes ¼ pint/1½ dl.

1 egg yolk	2 teaspoons wine vinegar
pinch dry mustard	¼ pint/1½ dl. olive oil
salt and freshly milled pepper	1 tablespoon boiling water

Place the egg yolk in a deep mixing basin. Add the mustard, a seasoning of salt and pepper and the vinegar. Measure the oil into a jug. Whisk the egg and seasoning to blend, then begin to add the oil very slowly. Whisk all the time and as the mayonnaise mixture begins to thicken, add the oil a little more quickly. The oil should be poured directly on to the whisk so that it is immediately incorporated into the mixture. By the time all the oil is added, the mixture will be very thick. Whisk in the boiling water, this gives the mayonnaise a light colour and a slightly softer consistency.

Store in a cool place.

French dressing

A French dressing is sometimes fairly sharp in flavour and for those who dislike this, a good pinch of castor sugar can be added with the seasonings at the beginning of the recipe.

Makes ¼ pint/1½ dl.

salt and freshly milled pepper	2 tablespoons wine vinegar
¼ teaspoon French mustard	6 tablespoons olive oil

Place a good seasoning of salt and pepper in a basin. Add the mustard and the vinegar and stir to dissolve the seasonings. Add the olive oil. For a thin dressing, stir the ingredients to mix. For a thicker dressing, whisk the ingredients very thoroughly until the mixture becomes emulsified and slightly thickened.

Various flavoured vinegars can be used to give the dressing a different taste. Alternatively chopped parsley, chervil, chives or finely chopped shallot or garlic can be included.

Courgette and tomato salad

Any combination of vegetables looks pretty in a salad. Tomatoes and courgettes contrast attractively in colour and the flavours combine well.

Serves 4–6

1 lb./½ kg. courgettes	1 tablespoon chopped parsley
1 lb./½ kg. tomatoes	4–6 tablespoons prepared
1 small onion	French dressing (above)

Wash the courgettes, trim either end but leave whole. Place in a saucepan, cover with boiling water and bring up to the boil. Simmer for about 10 minutes or until just tender but still firm. Drain and slice thickly and leave until cold.

Meanwhile, scald the tomatoes, drain and peel away the skins. Slice the tomatoes thickly and add to the cooled courgettes with the chopped onion, chopped parsley and French dressing. Toss ingredients gently to mix before serving.
Advance preparation: Prepare this salad and toss vegetables in the dressing. Chill for several hours before serving.

Avocado pear and lettuce salad

This salad is particularly good served with cold ham or chicken.

Serves 4

1 round lettuce	3–4 tablespoons prepared
½ cucumber	French dressing
1 ripe avocado pear	1 box cress

Remove outer bruised leaves from the lettuce. Wash remaining leaves, tear away hard stalks and place the leaves in salad bowl. Add the peeled, sliced cucumber. Peel the avocado pear, halve and remove centre stone. Slice the flesh and add to the salad with the prepared French dressing. Toss well to mix and garnish with the snipped, washed cress.
Advance preparation: Wash and prepare greens but do not cut avocado. Prepare salad and toss in dressing just before serving.

Danish cucumber salad

Danish cucumber salad is quite different from any other. The sliced cucumber is marinated in a sweet-sour mixture. It goes very well with most fried foods and particularly with roast lamb.

Serves 4

½ cucumber	1 oz./25 g. sugar
2 level tablespoons salt	½ level teaspoon pepper
½ pint/3 dl. white wine vinegar and water, in equal parts	

Wash the cucumber and slice thinly without removing the skin. Put the slices into a bowl and mix with the salt. Leave until the juices have run from the cucumber. Squeeze well to remove moisture and pour this away.

Put the cucumber slices into a fresh bowl. Pour the dressing made from the vinegar, water, sugar and pepper over the cucumber. Mix well and leave to chill for at least 1 hour before serving. Drain from the marinade and serve.
Advance preparation: Prepare and marinate the cucumber slices up to 4–6 hours before serving. They can be prepared in the morning for the evening.

Celery, orange and walnut salad

This salad is also delicious using crisp apples instead of the oranges. Quarter, core and dice the apples – leaving on the apple peel if it is a good red colour.

Serves 4

1 medium head celery	2 tablespoons roughly chopped
2 oranges	walnuts
4–5 tablespoons French dressing (page 127)	

Scrub the celery and remove 'strings' from the larger stalks. Then slice the celery thinly. Cut away outer rind and white pith from the oranges and then cut into segments and remove without the skin. Cut the orange into chunks and add to the celery. Add the French dressing and toss well. Fold in the roughly chopped walnuts just before serving.
Advance preparation: The celery, oranges or apples can be prepared and tossed in the dressing several hours before serving. Keep in a covered container and turn the ingredients in the dressing occasionally. Add the walnuts just before serving. Walnuts are inclined to darken in a dressing if left for a long period of time.

Red cabbage salad

Red cabbage makes a delicious colourful salad. Serve with cold roast game.

Serves 4

8 oz./¼ kg. red cabbage	2–3 carrots
4–6 tablespoons French dressing	1–2 crisp apples
	chopped parsley

Discard any coarse outer leaves, quarter the cabbage and shred finely. Place in a salad bowl with the French dressing. Peel and grate the carrots and peel, core and dice the apple. Fold the carrot and apple into the salad, toss well to mix and serve sprinkled with chopped parsley.
Advance preparation: Prepare the ingredients and toss in the dressing several hours in advance. Keep in a covered container and turn in the dressing occasionally. Sprinkle with parsley before serving.

Florida salad

This colourful salad of fresh fruits in a French dressing is very good served with cold chicken, gammon or pork.

Serves 4

1 orange	4 oz./100 g. black grapes
1 grapefruit	2–3 tablespoons French
2–3 sticks celery	dressing (page 127)
1 banana	crisp lettuce leaves

Using a sharp knife, cut round the outer rind of the orange and grapefruit to remove the outer peel and white pith, leaving only the flesh of the fruit. Cut into each segment of fruit and remove in one piece. Discard any pips and place the segments in a bowl. Scrub the celery and remove strings in larger stalks. Shred the celery finely. Peel and slice the banana, and halve and deseed the grapes. Add these with the celery to the fruit in the bowl. Toss the salad ingredients together with sufficient dressing to coat the ingredients and flavour the salad.

Line a salad bowl with lettuce, pile the salad in the centre and serve.
Advance preparation: Prepare the orange and grapefruit segments, the celery and grapes. Place together in a covered bowl with the dressing. Chill for several hours. When ready to serve, add the banana and arrange in the salad bowl with the lettuce. Lettuce can be washed and kept crisp in a polythene bag in the refrigerator.

Marinated sweet pepper salad

Where possible use a mixture of red and green sweet peppers or use only green peppers. This salad looks very pretty served as an hors d'oeuvre with sliced salami. Otherwise serve as one of a choice of salads.

Serves 4

2 red peppers	¼ pint/1½ dl. French dressing
2 green peppers	chopped parsley or chives

Use either a mixture of both red and green peppers or all green peppers. Place the peppers under a hot grill and cook them until the skins crinkle and split. Turn occasionally so they grill on all sides – this takes about 10 minutes. Alternatively, spear the peppers on a fork and hold over the gas flame until the skins char and split. While hot, peel or scrape away the skins under cold water. Split the peppers open lengthwise. Remove seeds and core and shred peppers lengthways, put in a shallow serving dish. Pour over the prepared dressing and leave to marinate for several hours or over night. Toss or turn the peppers occasionally. Sprinkle with parsley or chives and serve.
Advance preparation: This salad can be prepared well in advance. Toss or turn the peppers in the dressing occasionally.

Potato salad

To get the maximum flavour, blend the ingredients for this salad while the potatoes are still warm. Make in advance and serve with cold meats, chicken, salmon or salmon trout.

Serves 4

1½ lb./¾ kg. new potatoes	3 tablespoons mayonnaise
1 small clove garlic	2–3 tablespoons single cream
4 spring onions	crisp lettuce leaves
2 tablespoons chopped parsley	*to garnish:*
salt and freshly milled pepper	chopped mint or chives

Scrape the potatoes and cook in boiling, salted water until just tender, about 10–15 minutes. Drain, cool for a moment then cut the potatoes into large dice.

Rub the inside of a mixing bowl with the cut clove of garlic and put in the potatoes. Add the trimmed and chopped spring onions, chopped parsley and a seasoning of salt and pepper. Blend the mayonnaise and cream – the addition of cream gives the dressing a more subtle flavour and a better consistency for coating the potatoes. Add the mayonnaise and blend the ingredients gently together.

When ready to serve, line a salad bowl with crisp, washed lettuce leaves. Pile the potato salad into the centre and sprinkle with chopped mint or chives.

Advance preparation: This salad is excellent made in advance. Prepare and blend the potatoes with the dressing. Arrange in the salad bowl of lettuce when ready to serve. Lettuce can be washed and kept crisp in a polythene bag in the refrigerator.

Home freezing of vegetables

Many kinds of vegetables freeze very well. Remember, however, that no salad vegetables or any vegetables that are required to remain crisp should be frozen.

Vegetables for freezing should be very fresh and of first class quality. They should be prepared and frozen as soon after picking as possible. Vegetables are blanched before freezing to inactivate enzyme action. This is a chemical change that takes place in all living matter. It is responsible for the flavour, colour and quality of the vegetable. Unless this is inactivated to a certain degree, off flavours will develop and the colour in vegetables is not retained well.

Blanching of vegetables

A large amount of water should be allowed for blanching. Allow about 2 quarts (2¼ litres) of water for every 1 lb. (½ kg.) vegetables. The same water may be used several times, so long as it is for the same vegetable.

1. Bring the water to the boil.
2. Add the vegetables in a basket – use a blanching wire basket with a small mesh. Using a basket means you can control the time of blanching exactly. Placing the vegetables in the water and removing them at the correct time.
3. Notice how long the water takes to reboil after the vegetables are added – it should be within a minute. Blanch according to the chart taking the time from the moment the water reboils.

4. Remove immediately and plunge in iced water to cool. (Make blocks of ice in cake tins in the freezer prior to blanching, in readiness.) Cool in the iced water for the same length of time as the vegetables were blanched.
5. Drain, but do not dry on cloths. Vegetables freeze better with a little coating of water.

Packing and freezing

1. Pack vegetables in quantities suitable for using afterwards. Use polythene freezer bags or waxed cartons.
2. Exclude the air. This particularly applies to those in polythene freezer bags. Then tie tightly and seal.
3. Place in the freezer near the base or side, close to the refrigerant. Allow air to circulate round the packs so that they freeze quickly. Do not pack too closely together.
4. Twenty-four hours later, move the packs to the main storage part of freezer until required.

FREEZING VEGETABLES CHART

Store up to 12 months, but use all vegetables before the next harvest. Vegetables can be cooked straight from the freezer. Cooking times will be slightly less than for fresh, to allow for the partial cooking time that has taken place during blanching and should be timed from the moment the water reboils.

Vegetable	Preparation	Freezing	Cooking
Beans (broad)	Select young tender beans. Pod and grade beans in even sizes. Blanch for 3 minutes.	Pack in polythene bags.	Add frozen to boiling, salted water. Simmer for 8–10 minutes.
Beans (French)	Select fresh beans that snap. Wash then top and tail. Leave whole if small, others cut in half. Blanch for 2–3 minutes.	Pack in polythene bags.	Add frozen to boiling, salted water. Cook for 8–10 minutes if whole or sliced for 5–6 minutes.
Beans (runner)	Select fresh young beans that are not too large. Wash, string and cut off ends. Slice thinly. Blanch 2 minutes.	Pack in polythene bags.	Add frozen to boiling, salted water. Cook for 8 minutes.
Broccoli and calabrese	Trim any leaves and stalks. Cut in even lengths for packing. Select fresh young heads. Soak in salt water. Divide into sprigs. Blanch 3–4 minutes.	Pack in waxed cartons.	Add frozen to boiling, salted water and cook for 8 minutes.
Carrots	Freeze only young, new carrots. Trim top and base. Blanch whole and rub off skin. Leave whole or dice. Scald 4 minutes.	Pack in polythene bags.	Add frozen to boiling, salted water. Cook for 8–10 minutes.
Cauliflower	Choose firm white cauliflowers. Break the head into even sized sprigs. Soak in salted water and drain. Blanch 3 minutes.	Pack in waxed cartons.	Add frozen to boiling, salted water. Cook for 8 minutes.
Peas	Select tender young peas and pod. Blanch 1 minute.	Pack in polythene bags.	Add frozen to boiling, salted water. Cook for 8–10 minutes.
Onions	Select small button onions. Cut a slice off the top and base of each one. Cover with boiling water and allow to stand 5 minutes. Drain and strip off skins. Blanch 3–5 minutes.	Freeze in a single layer on trays. Cover with polythene to prevent odour spreading. Tip onions into polythene freezer bags when hard.	Add frozen to casseroles or stews. Cook in boiling, salted water for 8–10 minutes, serve in white sauce.

Desserts for summer entertaining

During the spring and summer months, there is ample opportunity to use a wide variety of fresh fruits. Freeze fresh summer fruits to serve during the winter months. Many of the recipes given here can be made using frozen fruit, particularly those which are packed dry without sugar added.

A mixture of fruits can be cooked as a compote or served fresh, marinated in wine and liqueurs. Try sliced pineapple with Kirsch or peaches in brandy. Serve fresh strawberries with Petit Suisse sprinkled liberally with sugar, or raspberries on their own. Cream desserts, mousses or soufflés provide more elaborate desserts. They should be served cold, but not chilled. Remove from the refrigerator at least 1 hour before serving.

Most of these desserts can be made in advance, avoiding any last minute work or anxiety. They make an ideal choice for party menus.

Fruits rafraichis

This method of preparing a salad of fresh fruits can be used for any variety of fruits depending on the season. As a basis, oranges, apples and pears are always used. In summer, strawberries, raspberries and apricots could be included. In autumn, plums, peaches and melon and in winter, bananas, fresh pineapple and grapes. A combination of white wine and Kirsch or champagne and cognac are used to marinate the fruits. Choose a pretty glass serving dish which will show off the colours of the fruit. Prepare each fruit in turn and place in the serving dish, arrange them in layers so that the colours contrast attractively.

Serves 6

2 oranges	1 lb./½ kg. strawberries or
4 oz./100 g. castor sugar	raspberries
2–3 apples	1 wine glass white wine or
8 oz./225 g. black grapes	champagne
8 oz./225 g. cherries	2 tablespoons Kirsch or cognac
2–3 ripe pears	

Using a sharp knife, cut a slice from the top and base of each orange. Then cut round each orange and remove the outer peel and white pith, leaving only the orange flesh. Cut into each orange segment to loosen and remove it, so that it comes away without any skin. Place in the serving dish and sprinkle with a little of the sugar. Peel, quarter and core the apples. Cut across into thin slices and add to the oranges with more sugar. Halve, deseed and arrange the grapes in the dish and halve and stone the cherries. Add the fruit to the bowl with some sugar. Peel, quarter and core the pears and slice across. Add in a layer with more sugar. Finally, hull the strawberries and cut in half. Arrange over the top of the fruit and add all the remaining sugar.

Pour over the white wine and add the Kirsch. Leave to stand for several hours. Press the fruits down so that they become covered with juice and will not discolour. Chill well before serving.

Advance preparation: This salad of fruits should be made several hours in advance of serving for the best flavour. Allow to stand for up to 12 hours.

Summer pudding

Any mixture of summer fruit such as black and red currants, raspberries, loganberries, strawberries, gooseberries and cherries may be used. For the best flavour and richest colour, use plenty of blackcurrants and raspberries.

Serves 4–6

8–10 thin slices day old bread	4–6 oz./100–175 g. castor sugar
2 lb./1 kg. mixed summer fruits	¼ pint/1½ dl. water

Rinse out a 1½-pint (1-litre) pudding basin with cold water. Trim the crusts from the bread. Cut a circle to fit the bottom of the basin and some wedge shaped pieces to fit around the sides. Press the bread firmly in to line the basin, leaving no gaps. Reserve some pieces of bread to cover the top.

Prepare the fruit according to kind and remove any stones from the cherries. Place the sugar and water in a pan and stir over low heat to dissolve. Add the tough skinned fruits first – gooseberries, black or red currants – and stew gently until tender. Then add the soft fruits and cook for a few more minutes. Strain off most of the juice and reserve.

Turn the fruit into the lined pudding basin. Cover the pudding top with a circle of bread. Stand the basin on a plate to catch any overflowing juices. Cover the top with a saucer or small plate and press down with a weight. Leave overnight. Boil up the reserved fruit juice until syrupy and well reduced, leave until cold.

Run a knife round the sides to loosen the pudding and turn out on to a serving dish. Spoon the sauce over the pudding and serve with cream.

Advance preparation: Make summer pudding and leave overnight. Do not unmould until ready to serve.

Danish fruit pudding

This fresh flavoured dessert can be made using a mixture of blackcurrants, redcurrants, raspberries or rhubarb. Allow 1 lb. (½ kg.) of fruit for every 1 pint (½ litre) of water, sweeten and thicken accordingly.

Serves 4

8 oz./225 g. redcurrants or	about 2 tablespoons cornflour
rhubarb	(see recipe)
8 oz./225 g. raspberries	6 oz./175 g. castor sugar
1 pint/6 dl. water	1 oz./25 g. flaked almonds

Wash or wipe and prepare the fruit according to kind. Place in a saucepan with the water, bring up to the boil and cook gently until the fruit is quite soft. Draw off the heat and rub the fruit and juices through a sieve to make a thin purée. Measure the purée back into the saucepan and for every ½ pint (3 dl.), blend 1 tablespoon cornflour with a little water to make a thin paste.

Add the sugar to the fruit purée and bring up to the boil. Add a little of the hot mixture to the cornflour blend, stir well and return the mixture to the saucepan. Stir over the heat until the mixture has thickened and is boiling. Allow to cool for a moment, then pour into a serving dish. Sprinkle the surface with a little castor sugar to prevent a skin forming and leave until quite cold.

Sprinkle with blanched flaked almonds and serve with cream.

Advance preparation: Make several hours in advance or the day before. Keep in the refrigerator but remove about 30 minutes before serving.

OPPOSITE **Savarin au rhum (page 177)**
Beat the savarin mixture until smooth with the hand.
Pour the mixture into the prepared savarin mould.
When cooked, the savarin should feel firm to the touch. Turn out of the mould and leave to stale overnight.
Place the savarin on a wire cake rack over a plate. Prick all over with a skewer and spoon over the hot syrup.
Prepare the fruit salad and spoon into the centre of the savarin.

Fresh pineapple slices with Kirsch

Pineapple is ideal to serve after a rich main course. The fresh sharp flavour goes perfectly with Kirsch. Reserve the leafy top for serving in the centre of the dish.

Serves 4–6

1 small fresh pineapple	2–3 tablespoons icing sugar
2 tablespoons Kirsch	

Cut away the leafy top from the pineapple, leaving a thin piece on the top. Reserve this for decoration. Stand the pineapple up and, using a sharp knife, cut away the outer rind. Cut the pineapple across into thin slices; depending on the size of the pineapple, it will make 8–10 slices. Using a sharp round cutter or a knife, cut out the hard centre core from each slice. Lay the slices in a serving dish, sprinkle the Kirsch over them and dust with the sieved icing sugar. Chill for a few hours, turning the slices occasionally and baste with the juices in the dish.

Arrange slices round the edge of a large flat dish with the leafy top in the centre.

Serve with cream.

Advance preparation: Make in advance of serving and leave fruit to marinate for several hours before serving.

Fresh peaches with raspberry syrup

This is a delicious way of serving fresh peaches. A dessert to serve in early August when both peaches and raspberries are plentiful.

Serves 6

6 ripe peaches	8 oz./225 g. raspberries
$\frac{1}{4}$ pint/1$\frac{1}{2}$ dl. water	2–3 tablespoons peach syrup
4 oz./100 g. castor sugar	(see recipe)

Place the peaches together in a basin. Cover with boiling water and allow to stand for 1 minute. Drain and then gently peel or rub away the skins. Cut each peach in half and remove the stone. If the peaches are a little difficult to separate into halves, place the knife blade in the cut and prise open gently.

Measure the water and sugar into a saucepan and stir over low heat to dissolve the sugar. Bring up to the boil, draw off the heat and add the peach halves. Replace over low heat, cover with a lid and simmer very gently for 5 minutes until the peaches are tender. Drain the peach halves into a serving dish and set aside.

Boil the peach syrup rapidly, uncovered, until reduced by about half. Draw off the heat and reserve. Using a wooden spoon, rub the raspberries through a sieve to make a purée, add a little of the peach syrup if liked towards the end to get all the raspberry flesh through. Discard the pips remaining in the sieve. Add extra peach syrup to make a fairly thin purée. Spoon liberally over the peach halves and serve.

Advance preparation: Prepare several hours in advance or the day before serving. Keep chilled but remove from the refrigerator about 30 minutes–1 hour before serving.

Strawberries with orange

A sensationally simple way of serving strawberries. The orange juice brings out the flavour of the fruit and forms a delicious syrup.

Serves 4

1 lb./$\frac{1}{2}$ kg. strawberries	2 oz./50 g. castor sugar
juice 1 orange	

Hull the strawberries and place in a serving dish. Squeeze the juice from the orange and pour over the strawberries. Sprinkle with the sugar and leave to stand for about 30 minutes. Turn the strawberries in the juices that form.

Serve well chilled with cream.

Advance preparation: Prepare several hours in advance and leave strawberries to marinate in the sugar and orange juice in the refrigerator. Turn fruit occasionally.

Pineapple and strawberry fruit salad

During summer months, small pineapples are plentiful and cheap to buy. Combine pineapple with strawberries to make a simple but effective fruit salad.

Serves 4–6

1 small pineapple	juice 1 lemon
4 oz./100 g. castor sugar	1 punnet strawberries

Slice away the leafy top and base. Then cut downwards round the pineapple, cutting away the outer skin. Remove any eyes and cut the pineapple into slices. Cut each slice in half and remove the core. Dice the pieces and place in a serving dish. Sprinkle with the sugar and add the strained lemon juice. Leave to stand for several hours, preferably in the refrigerator so that the mixture is chilled.

Hull and wash the strawberries and slice in half. Stir the pineapple to mix the juices and add the strawberries. Toss to mix before serving.

Advance preparation: Allow fruit plenty of time to marinate in the juices and develop flavour. Make several hours or a day in advance of serving.

Gooseberry and redcurrant compote

The addition of cornflour in this recipe may seem unusual and unnecessary, but it does give the compote a pleasant texture and an attractive glazed appearance.

Serves 4–6

1 lb./$\frac{1}{2}$ kg. green or dessert	6 oz./175 g. castor sugar
gooseberries	$\frac{1}{4}$ pint/1$\frac{1}{2}$ dl. water
8 oz./225 g. redcurrants	1 level tablespoon cornflour

Wash the fruit, then top and tail the gooseberries and place in a saucepan. Strip the redcurrants from the stalks, using the prongs of a fork, and add to the gooseberries, sugar and water. Bring slowly to the boil, stirring occasionally, to dissolve the sugar but taking care not to break up the fruit. Simmer for about 5 minutes or until the fruit is tender, but not soft and broken. Draw the pan off the heat. Blend the cornflour to a thin paste with sufficient cold water and stir into the fruit. Replace over a very gentle heat and bring back up to the boil, stirring very gently until the mixture is thickened and clear. Pour into a serving dish.

Serve warm or cold, with cream.

Advance preparation: Fruit compotes such as this, improve in flavour with standing. Make a day in advance of serving. Keep in a cool larder or chill until ready to serve.

Flambé bananas

A spectacular dessert and simple enough to prepare for a dinner party. The bananas are put to bake in the oven and require little attention. Bring the piping hot bananas and the hot rum to the table and flambé the dish before your guests.

Serves 6

6 firm ripe bananas	1 oz./25 g. butter
juice ½ lemon	3–4 tablespoons rum
3 oz./75 g. soft brown sugar	

Peel the bananas and cut in half lengthwise. Place cut side down in a well buttered, shallow baking dish. Sprinkle with the lemon juice and then the sugar. Top with dots of butter.

Place in the centre of a hot oven (400°F., 200°C., Gas Mark 6) and bake for 20 minutes or until the bananas are soft and glazed. Baste the bananas occasionally with the juices in the dish. Measure the rum into a saucepan and heat gently. Pour the *hot* rum over the *hot* bananas and flambé. The flames will burn for about 1 minute – shake the dish occasionally until the flames die, then cook for a further few minutes.

Serve at once with cream.

Advance preparation: Assemble ingredients but do not cook until ready to serve.

Gooseberry soufflé

This method of making a cold soufflé can be used with other fruits – blackcurrants or apricots are particularly delicious. About ½ pint (3 dl.) of sweetened fresh fruit purée would be required.

Serves 6

1 lb./½ kg. green gooseberries	4 large eggs
¼ pint/1½ dl. water	few drops green colouring
6 oz./175 g. castor sugar	¼ pint/1½ dl. double cream
½ oz./15 g. powdered gelatine	chopped walnuts

Prepare a 6–7-inch (15–18-cm.) soufflé dish, by tying a band of double thickness greaseproof paper around the outside of the dish. The paper should stand about 2 inches (5 cm.) above the rim of the dish.

Wash, top and tail the gooseberries. Place in a saucepan with the water and 4 oz. (100 g.) of the sugar. Bring to the boil slowly, stirring to dissolve the sugar. Cover with a lid and simmer gently for 10–15 minutes or until quite tender.

Meanwhile measure 3 tablespoons of cold water into a teacup and sprinkle in the gelatine. Set aside to soak for 5 minutes. When the gooseberries are tender, draw off the heat and add the soaked gelatine. Stir until the gelatine has dissolved in the hot mixture. Pass the juice and gooseberries through a nylon sieve to make a purée. Discard the skin and pips remaining in the sieve.

Separate the eggs, placing the yolks in one large basin and the whites in a second basin. Add the remaining sugar to the yolks and stir to blend. Add the hot fruit purée and whisk very thoroughly until the mixture is thick and light. Whisk in 2–3 drops green food colouring to give the mixture a pretty pale green colour. Set the mixture aside, until cool and beginning to thicken.

Lightly whip the cream and stiffly beat the egg whites. Using a metal spoon, fold the cream and egg whites gently but thoroughly into the gooseberry mixture. Pour into the prepared soufflé dish and leave in a cool place for several hours until set firm.

When ready to serve, loosen and peel away the paper. Coat the sides of the soufflé with finely chopped walnuts. Serve with cream.

Advance preparation: This soufflé can be made the day before serving. Leave the paper round the soufflé. Remove paper and decorate when ready to serve. Take out of the refrigerator at least 1 hour before serving.

Praline soufflé (page 138)

Tie a band of double thickness greaseproof paper round the dish, ensuring it stands at least 3 inches ($7\frac{1}{2}$ cm.) above the rim.

Melt the sugar in a pan over moderate heat and stir until it turns a caramel colour.

Fold the stiffly beaten egg whites and half the lightly beaten cream into the soufflé mixture.

When ready to serve, remove the paper collar from the edge of the soufflé.

Coat the sides of the soufflé with ground hazelnuts.

Decorate with whorls of cream and whole hazelnuts.

Fruit brûlée

A good recipe for a dinner party – there's a fair amount of work involved in preparing the fruit, but the whole dessert can be finished and put to chill hours before the guests arrive. Use fresh raspberries in place of grapes on another occasion.

Serves 8

1 lb./½ kg. green and black grapes, mixed	3 rounded tablespoons demerara sugar
1 pint/6 dl. double cream	

Peel, halve and deseed the grapes, then arrange over the base of a serving dish. Since the final dessert is put under a hot grill for a few minutes, choose a heatproof glass or china dish. Whisk the cream until thick, spoon over the grapes to cover and spread evenly. Set aside to chill thoroughly for several hours until the cream is firm.

Sprinkle the sugar over the top, then place under a preheated hot grill. Grill just long enough for the sugar to melt, turn the dish round so that the surface is caramelised all over. Replace at once in the refrigerator and chill again so that the sugar topping becomes quite crisp before serving.

Advance preparation: Prepare the fruit, cover with cream and chill well in advance. Sprinkle with sugar and caramelise about 1–2 hours before serving.

Orange jelly cream

Orange jelly cream is delicious served with summer fruits. The recipe can be moulded in a 1½-pint (1-litre) jelly mould. Turn out and surround with raspberries or strawberries or serve with fruit salad.

Serves 6

1 (6¼ oz./175 g.) can frozen orange juice concentrate	½ oz./15 g. powdered gelatine
1 pint/6 dl. water	4 oz./100 g. castor sugar
	¼ pint/1½ dl. double cream

Mix the orange juice concentrate with ¾ pint (4½ dl.) cold water and pour into a large mixing bowl. Measure the remaining ¼ pint (1½ dl.) water into a saucepan, sprinkle in the powdered gelatine and allow to soak for about 5 minutes. Add the sugar and stir over low heat until both the gelatine and sugar have dissolved but do not allow the mixture to boil. Draw off the heat and cool for a few minutes.

Slowly pour the gelatine mixture into the diluted orange juice. Whisk all the time to blend the mixture. Set aside until cold, stirring occasionally, until the mixture begins to thicken and shows signs of setting.

Lightly whip the cream and then pour a little of the orange mixture into the cream. Mix well then blend with the remainder of the orange mixture. Stir thoroughly to combine the ingredients. Pour into 6 individual glasses and chill for several hours until firm.

Advance preparation: Make several hours in advance or make the day before. Remove from the refrigerator about 30 minutes before serving.

Caramel oranges

Choose thin skinned seedless oranges where possible for this recipe. Allow the prepared oranges to chill for several hours, so that the flavour of the oranges blends with that of the syrup. A good recipe for a dinner party and one that can be prepared the evening before.

Serves 6

6 oranges	1–2 tablespoons Cointreau
8 oz./225 g. granulated sugar	*for the caramel topping:*
¼ pint/1½ dl. water	2 oz./50 g. granulated sugar
juice ½ lemon	

Either cut away the orange peel by working round the outside of the orange. Or, mark the peel of the oranges in quarters, put all the oranges together in a bowl and cover with boiling water. Leave to stand for 5 minutes, then drain and peel away the skins. Most of the white pith will come away with the peel, but any that remains can easily be scraped off with a knife. Slice the oranges thinly, remove any pips and place the slices in a serving dish.

Measure the granulated sugar into a large dry saucepan. Stir over the heat until the sugar melts and turns to a golden caramel brown. Draw off the heat and add the water. *Take care* since the mixture will boil up furiously with the addition of a cold liquid. Replace the pan over the heat and stir until the caramel has dissolved and a sweet syrup has formed. Add the lemon juice. Cool for a few minutes and then pour over the orange slices. Add the liqueur and put the oranges to chill for several hours or overnight.

Prepare the crunchy caramel topping for adding later. Place 2 oz. (50 g.) granulated sugar in a dry saucepan. Stir over the heat until the sugar turns to a caramel. Draw off the heat and pour into a lightly oiled cake tin or some other shallow container. Leave until quite cold and brittle.

When ready to serve, break or crush the caramel into small pieces and sprinkle over the top of the orange slices.

Advance preparation: Make the day before serving. These oranges keep very well. Leave in a cool larder or chill. Turn the oranges in the syrup occasionally.

Praline soufflé

Illustrated in colour on pages 136 and 137

Toast the hazelnuts in a hot oven for 5–10 minutes before using. While hot, tip all the nuts together into a tea cloth and rub hard to remove the papery brown coating. Toasting also gives them extra flavour, but allow the nuts to cool before using them in this recipe.

Serves 6

6 oz./175 g. granulated sugar	2 oz./50 g. castor sugar
5 tablespoons cold water	½ pint/3 dl. double cream
juice 1 lemon	*to decorate:*
½ oz./15 g. powdered gelatine	hazelnuts
5 eggs	

Select a round china soufflé dish approximately 6–7 inches (15–18 cm.) in diameter. Tie a band of double thickness grease-proof or waxed paper round the dish, making sure it stands at least 3 inches (7½ cm.) above the rim.

Measure the granulated sugar into a small heavy pan and stir over moderate heat until the sugar has melted and turned a golden caramel colour. Stir the mixture constantly so that the sugar melts evenly. Draw the pan off the heat immediately the caramel is dark enough – if it begins to burn and blacken, the taste will be too bitter. Meanwhile, measure 3 tablespoons of the water into a small teacup. Add the water all at once to the caramel – take care as the mixture will bubble furiously at this stage. Return the pan to the heat and stir until the caramel has dissolved and a syrup has formed. Set aside to cool until ready to use.

Measure the remaining water and strained lemon juice into a small saucepan. Sprinkle in the gelatine and set aside to soak for 5 minutes. Then stir over a low heat until the gelatine has dissolved. Do not allow to boil. When the mixture is clear, draw the pan off the heat. Crack 3 whole eggs and 2 egg yolks into a large mixing basin. Place the remaining egg whites into a separate basin. Add the castor sugar to the eggs and place the basin over a pan of hot water. Whisk until thick and light, then remove from the heat and gradually whisk in the caramel syrup. Whisk in the dissolved gelatine and set aside, stirring occasionally, until the mixture shows signs of setting. Fold in the stiffly beaten egg whites and half the lightly beaten cream. Reserve remaining cream for decoration. Pour the mixture into the prepared soufflé dish, there should be sufficient to come above the rim of the soufflé dish, as it is supported by the paper collar around the outside. Put in a cool place or in a refrigerator until firm.

When ready to serve, unpin and remove string around the paper collar. Loosen the inside top edge of the soufflé mixture with the tip of a knife blade. Then peel the paper carefully away from the edge of the soufflé. Using a hot damp cloth, clean away marks left by the mixture on the dish. Grind sufficient hazelnuts, either in a blender or through a mouli grater, to make 3–4 heaped tablespoons of ground nuts and use these to coat the sides. Pipe whirls of cream around the top edge and decorate with whole hazelnuts. If liked, the hazelnuts for decoration can be dipped in a little extra hot caramel.

Advance preparation: Can be made the day before serving. Leave the paper round the soufflé. Remove paper and decorate when ready to serve. Take out of the refrigerator at least 1 hour before serving.

Chocolate bavarois

Small ¼ pint (1½ dl.) metal pudding moulds are ideal for this recipe. Otherwise, use an attractively shaped large jelly mould. If chilled in the refrigerator, allow the unmoulded dessert to stand at room temperature for at least ½ hour before serving.

Serves 4–6

6 oz./175 g. plain chocolate	3 egg yolks
1 pint/6 dl. milk	1 oz./25 g. castor sugar
4 tablespoons cold water	1 tablespoon dark rum
½ oz./15 g. powdered gelatine	¼ pint/1½ dl. double cream

Break the chocolate into a saucepan and add ¼ pint (1½ dl.) of the milk. Stir over low heat until the chocolate has melted and the mixture is blended. Add the remaining milk and bring almost to the boil. Measure the cold water into a cup. Sprinkle in the gelatine and leave to soak for 5 minutes.

Meanwhile, in a basin, cream the egg yolks and sugar together, then gradually stir in the hot flavoured milk. Blend well and return the mixture to the milk saucepan. Add the soaked gelatine. Stir over low heat until the gelatine has dissolved and the mixture is as hot as the finger can bear. At this temperature, the egg yolks will be cooked. Draw the pan off the heat and add the rum. Pour into a large mixing basin and set aside to cool. Stir occasionally to prevent a skin forming. When cold and beginning to thicken, lightly whip the cream and fold into the mixture.

Pour the mixture into either 6 small individual moulds or into one 1½-pint (1-litre) mould. Leave in a cool place until set quite firm. To unmould, loosen the top edge of the mould, dip quickly into water (hot as the hand can bear) and turn out.

Serve with single cream.

Advance preparation: Make a day before serving. Remove from refrigerator and unmould about 1 hour before required.

Chartreuse of apples

A pretty, fresh flavoured jelly dessert that can be moulded in a pudding basin.

Serves 4

1 lb./½ kg. dessert apples
3 oz./75 g. castor sugar
½ pint/3 dl. water
juice 2 large, juicy oranges

juice 1 lemon
2 tablespoons cold water
1 tablespoon powdered gelatine

Peel, core and slice the apples. Add to a pan of boiling water, reboil and simmer for 1 minute and then drain. This blanching helps to maintain the light colour of the apples. Measure the sugar and the ½ pint (3 dl.) of water into a saucepan and stir over low heat to dissolve the sugar. Add the apple slices. Bring just to a simmer, then cover and poach gently for about 5 minutes or until the apples are tender but still whole.

Drain the apples from the poaching syrup and add the juice from the oranges and lemon. Measure the 2 tablespoons of water into a small basin, sprinkle over the gelatine and allow to soak for 5 minutes. Add the cake of soaked gelatine to the syrup and stir over low heat to dissolve the gelatine. Draw off the heat and pour into a basin. Leave until cold.

When the mixture begins to thicken and shows signs of setting, pour at once over the apple slices in a mould. Chill until set firm.

Unmould and serve with cream.

Advance preparation: Make up to 1 day before serving. Unmould when ready to serve.

Raspberry mousse

Raspberries make a mousse that has a vivid colour and a fresh flavour. The addition of fresh cream cheese in this recipe may sound unusual but it gives the recipe a richness and a texture that is extremely good.

Serves 6

1 lb./½ kg. fresh raspberries
4 tablespoons water
½ oz./15 g. powdered gelatine
2–4 oz./50–100 g. cream cheese

2 oz./50 g. castor sugar
¼ pint/1½ dl. double cream
2 egg whites

Press the raspberries through a sieve to make a purée. Measure the water into a small saucepan and sprinkle in the gelatine. Allow to soak for 5 minutes, then stir over a very low heat until the gelatine has dissolved and the mixture is clear. Draw off the heat.

Place the cream cheese and the castor sugar in a basin and beat with a wooden spoon until the mixture is soft and light. Stir in the raspberry purée and blend well. Slowly pour in the dissolved gelatine, whisking the mixture all the time to combine the ingredients well. Allow the mixture to stand until it begins to thicken and show signs of setting.

Lightly whip the cream and stiffly beat the egg whites. Fold in first the cream and then the egg whites, blend gently but thoroughly. Pour into a serving dish and chill until firm.

Decorate with a few extra raspberries before serving, if liked.

Advance preparation: This mousse should be prepared in advance and is even better made the day before. Remove from the refrigerator and decorate about 1 hour before serving.

Coffee and chocolate mousse

To make the coffee required in this recipe, stir 2 teaspoons of instant coffee into ¼ pint (1½ dl.) of boiling water. The combined flavour of coffee and chocolate taste very good.

Serves 6

6 oz./175 g. plain chocolate	½ oz./15 g. powdered gelatine
¼ pint/1½ dl. strong black coffee	3 large eggs
½ pint/3 dl. milk	1 oz./25 g. castor sugar
3 tablespoons cold water	

Break the chocolate into a saucepan and add the coffee. Stir over low heat until the chocolate has melted and the mixture is blended. Add the milk to the mixture and bring almost to the boil.

Measure the cold water into a cup and sprinkle in the gelatine. Leave to soak for 5 minutes. Separate the eggs, placing the yolks together in one basin and the whites in a second larger basin. Add the sugar to the yolks and cream the mixture thoroughly using a wooden spoon. Gradually stir in the hot, flavoured milk. Blend well and then return the mixture to the milk saucepan. Add the soaked gelatine and replace over low heat. Stir only until the gelatine has dissolved, do not allow to boil and then draw off the heat. Strain into a large bowl, rubbing through any soft pieces of chocolate that may still remain in the milk. Set aside to cool, stirring occasionally, until the mixture is cold and beginning to thicken.

Whisk the egg whites until stiff and, using a metal spoon, fold gently but thoroughly into the mixture. Pour into a serving dish and chill for several hours until set firm before serving.
Advance preparation: Make well in advance or a day before serving – the flavour improves. Remove from refrigerator about 1 hour before serving.

Summer trifle

A special recipe with a delicious flavour. A little Kirsch added to the fruit mixture makes it quite outstanding. An ideal dessert for a summer dinner party.

Serves 6

1 lb./½ kg. raspberries	2 oz./50 g. castor sugar
4 oz./100 g. redcurrants	2 level teaspoons cornflour
4 oz./100 g. castor sugar	1 pint/6 dl. single cream
4 individual trifle sponge cakes	few drops vanilla essence
for the custard:	*for decoration:*
6 egg yolks	few toasted, flaked almonds

Place the raspberries in a saucepan. Strip the redcurrants from the stems, wash well and add to the raspberries along with the sugar. Place over a low heat and cook gently, shaking the pan occasionally, until the juices run and the sugar has dissolved. Simmer for 5 minutes, then draw off the heat and allow to cool. Break the sponge cakes into the base of a glass serving dish and pour over the fruit and juices.

Crack the egg yolks into a basin. Add the sugar and cornflour. Whisk thoroughly to blend the ingredients. Heat the cream in a saucepan until very hot, then draw off the heat and stir into the egg mixture, a little at a time. Blend well and then strain the custard back into the saucepan. Stir over low heat constantly until the custard thickens and coats the back of a spoon – do not allow the custard to boil. Draw off the heat, add the vanilla essence and allow to cool for a few moments, then pour over the fruit. Cool, then chill until set firm.

Sprinkle with toasted, flaked almonds before serving.
Advance preparation: Make up this trifle several hours or a day before serving. Keep in a cold larder or refrigerator – if the latter, remove 1 hour before serving. Sprinkle with almonds only when ready to serve.

Pineapple cheesecake

This is an American style cheesecake which is not baked. The ingredients in this recipe are set with the addition of gelatine. It has a light texture and a pleasant flavour which contrasts well with the pineapple. This cheesecake makes an attractive dinner party dessert.

Serves 6

3 tablespoons cold water	12 oz./350 g. cottage cheese
½ oz./15 g. powdered gelatine	¼ pint/1½ dl. double cream
2 eggs	*for the crumb base:*
4 oz./100 g. castor sugar	8 digestive biscuits
1 (14½ oz./425 g.) can	1 oz./25 g. castor sugar
pineapple rings	2 oz./50 g. butter
finely grated rind and juice	
½ lemon	

Measure the water into a small basin and sprinkle in the gelatine. Set aside to soak for about 5 minutes. Separate the eggs, cracking the yolks into one basin and the whites into a second larger basin. Add the sugar to the yolks and, using a wooden spoon, beat thoroughly until creamy and light. Drain the juice from the pineapple, reserve the pineapple rings and make the juice up to ¼ pint (1½ dl.) with water – only 1–2 tablespoons water will be required. Pour the syrup into a saucepan and bring up to the boil. Draw off the heat and gradually stir into the egg yolk mixture. Blend well and then return the mixture to the saucepan. Add the cake of soaked gelatine and stir over low heat just long enough to dissolve the gelatine. Draw off the heat, add the finely grated lemon rind and set aside to cool.

Sieve the cottage cheese into a basin and stir in the lemon juice. Finely chop 3 rings of the reserved pineapple. When the custard has cooled and is beginning to thicken, stir it into the cottage cheese and pineapple pieces. Lightly whip the cream and stiffly beat the egg whites. Fold in first the cream and then the egg whites. Blend evenly and smoothly and then pour the mixture into an 8-inch (20-cm.) round cake tin, lined with a circle of greaseproof paper.

To prepare the biscuit base, crush the biscuits with a rolling pin and add the sugar. Melt the butter in a saucepan, add the crumb mixture all at once and stir with a fork until the crumbs are well coated with butter. Spread this evenly over the top of the cheese mixture – when the dessert is turned out this will in fact become the base. Set the cheesecake aside for several hours until quite firm. Then turn out on to a plate, remove the paper, and decorate with the remaining pineapple rings, cut into neat pieces.
Advance preparation: This cheesecake can be made the day before serving. Remove from the refrigerator 1 hour before serving.

Gooseberry fool

Gooseberries, blackberries, apricots and raspberries all make delicious fruit fools – these fruits have a good colour and flavour. With the exception of raspberries, the fruits are cooked gently first then puréed, raspberries can be pressed through a sieve raw.

Serves 6

1 lb./½ kg. green gooseberries	1 egg white
2 tablespoons water	½ pint/3 dl. double cream
4 oz./100 g. castor sugar	

Wash the gooseberries, no need to top and tail. Place in a saucepan with the water. Bring up to the boil, cover and simmer very gently for 10 minutes until tender and quite soft. Draw off the heat, add the sugar and stir to dissolve it in the heat of the pan. Then rub the fruit and juices through a nylon sieve to make a purée. Discard the skin and pips that remain in the sieve and put the purée to cool.

Add the unbeaten egg white to the cream and whisk both together until thick and light. Fold in the gooseberry purée. Spoon into a serving dish or individual glasses and chill for several hours until firm.

Serve with soft sponge fingers.

Note: To make a more economical recipe, use ¼ pint (1½ dl.) custard, that has been made and allowed to cool, and ¼ pint (1½ dl.) whipped double cream. In this case, omit the egg white.

Advance preparation: Make several hours or the day before serving. Serve chilled.

Lemon syllabub tart

Lemon syllabub tart looks pretty made in a 7-inch (18-cm.) white china, fluted flan dish. Stand the dish on a hot damp kitchen cloth for a few moments just before serving to loosen the biscuit crust on the base. This makes it easier to cut and serve.

Serves 4–6

8 digestive biscuits	4 tablespoons double cream
1 tablespoon castor sugar	rind and juice 1 large or 2 small
1½ oz./40 g. butter	lemons
for the filling:	*to decorate:*
1 small can condensed milk	4 oz./100 g. black grapes

Crush the biscuits with a rolling pin and add the sugar. Melt the butter in a saucepan over low heat. Draw off the heat and add the crushed biscuits and the sugar. Stir with a fork until the crumbs are quite buttery. Spoon the mixture into a 7-inch (18-cm.) china flan dish or pie plate. Using the back of a spoon, press the mixture over the base and around the sides of the dish. Chill until firm.

Mix together the condensed milk and cream. Stir in the strained lemon juice and finely grated rind. Stir gently and the mixture will thicken up in the bowl. Pour into the prepared crumb crust and spread evenly. Halve and deseed the black grapes and arrange around the rim of the tart.

Chill for several hours before serving.

Advance preparation: This dessert keeps well. Make a day in advance of serving. Serve chilled.

Lemon mousse

A lemon flavour is very refreshing. Choose large juicy lemons and rub them between the palms of the hands, the warmth helps the lemon juice to flow.

Serves 6

4 tablespoons water	juice and grated rind 2 large
½ oz./15 g. powdered gelatine	lemons
3 large eggs	¼ pint/1½ dl. double cream
4 oz./100 g. castor sugar	

Measure the water into a saucepan and sprinkle in the gelatine. Soak for 5 minutes then stir over low heat and allow the gelatine to dissolve. Draw the pan off the heat.

Separate the eggs, cracking the yolks into one large bowl and the whites into a second smaller bowl. Add the sugar, finely grated lemon rind and strained lemon juice to the egg yolks. Set the basin over a saucepan half filled with hot water and whisk the mixture until thick and light. Remove from the heat and whisk for a further few minutes to cool the mixture slightly.

Slowly pour the gelatine mixture into the egg mixture, whisking all the time until thoroughly incorporated. Set the mixture aside, whisking occasionally, until the mixture begins to thicken and show signs of setting. Stiffly beat the egg whites and lightly whip the cream. Using a metal spoon, fold both into the mixture, gently but thoroughly. Pour into a glass serving dish and chill until set firm.

Advance preparation: Flavour improves after several hours. Make a day before serving and remove from the refrigerator 1 hour before required.

Chocolate pots de crème with orange

Make these well in advance to get the best flavour and texture.

Serves 6

¾ pint/4½ dl. milk	4 egg yolks
finely grated rind 1 orange	1 oz./25 g. castor sugar
6 oz./175 g. plain chocolate	

Pour the milk into a saucepan and add the finely grated rind of the orange. Heat gently until just under boiling point, then draw off the heat and allow to infuse for 10–15 minutes so that the orange flavours the milk. Break the chocolate into a mixing basin and set over a saucepan half filled with hot water. Stir occasionally until the chocolate is softened and smooth. Remove the basin from the heat and beat in the egg yolks and sugar. Blend well and then gradually stir in the infused milk.

Strain the mixture into a jug and then pour into 6 individual ramekin or small soufflé dishes. Stand these in a baking or roasting tin containing ½ inch (1 cm.) cold water. Place in the centre of a very moderate oven (325°F., 170°C., Gas Mark 3) and bake for 45 minutes or until set firm. Remove from the heat, cool and then chill for several hours.

Serve plain or topped with a spoonful of lightly whipped cream.

Advance preparation: Make the day before serving. Remove from the refrigerator at least 1 hour before required.

Sherry soufflé

This attractive and easily made dessert is a suitable recipe for a dinner party. Prepare a day before serving so that the sponge lining is well soaked and the filling has a good flavour.

Serves 6

6 trifle sponge cakes	¼ pint/1½ dl. sweet sherry
2 tablespoons milk	4 eggs
2 tablespoons sweet sherry	3 oz./75 g. castor sugar
for the soufflé filling:	½ pint/3 dl. double cream
4 tablespoons cold water	grated plain chocolate
½ oz./15 g. powdered gelatine	

Split the sponge cakes in half and sprinkle the cut sides with the mixed milk and sherry. Arrange the cut sides inwards around the inside of a china soufflé dish or a glass serving dish, 2½–3-pint (1¼–1½-litre) size. Set aside while preparing the filling.

Measure the cold water into a small saucepan. Sprinkle in the gelatine and allow to soak for 5 minutes. Stir over a low heat until the gelatine has dissolved. Draw off the heat and add the sherry.

Separate the eggs, cracking the yolks into a large basin and the whites into a second basin. Add the sugar to the yolks and whisk together until light. Gradually whisk in the gelatine and sherry mixture. Allow the mixture to stand, whisking occasionally, until the mixture begins to thicken and shows signs of setting. This takes only a short time.

Lightly beat ¼ pint (1½ dl.) of the cream and stiffly beat the egg whites. Using a metal spoon, fold both into the mixture gently but thoroughly. Pour into the prepared serving dish, the mixture should come level with the top of the sponge cakes. Chill for several hours.

Lightly whip the remaining cream and spoon on top of the soufflé. Decorate with grated chocolate and keep in the refrigerator until ready to serve.

Advance preparation: Make 1 day before serving for best flavour. Remove from refrigerator 1 hour before serving.

Iced zabaglione

Sometimes a little diced fresh fruit (pears are particularly good) is placed in the base of each serving glass before pouring in the zabaglione mixture. Serve with sponge fingers.

Serves 6

4 egg yolks	2 oz./50 g. castor sugar
4 tablespoons Marsala wine or sweet sherry	¼ pint/1½ dl. double cream

Crack the egg yolks into a medium sized mixing basin. Add the sugar and the Marsala wine or sherry. Place the basin over a saucepan half filled with simmering water. Whisk the mixture continuously until thick and light – this takes about 5 minutes.

Remove the basin from the heat and whisk the mixture until cold. This can be greatly speeded up if the basin is set in a larger one filled with ice cubes and some cold water. When the mixture is well chilled, lightly whip the cream and fold in. Pour into 6 individual serving glasses and chill for several hours.

Advance preparation: Make 4–6 hours before serving to allow dessert to chill. Do not make the day before, the mixture is inclined to separate after about 12 hours. Serve chilled.

Strawberries with caramel cream

For this dessert, choose a glass serving dish to show off the layer of strawberries topped with the caramel coloured cream.

Serves 6

1 lb. fresh strawberries	4 tablespoons cold water
for the cream topping:	½ pint/3 dl. double cream
4 oz./100 g. granulated sugar	1–2 tablespoons brandy

Hull and wipe the strawberries. Reserve 6 for decoration and place the remainder in the base of a serving dish.

Measure the sugar into a dry saucepan. Place over moderate heat and stir until the sugar has melted and turns to a golden caramel brown. Draw the pan off the heat. Measure the water into a teacup and pour, all at once, into the hot caramel. Take care, as the caramel will boil furiously with the addition of a cold liquid. Replace the pan over the heat and stir until the caramel has dissolved and you have a thin caramel syrup. Pour into a basin and leave until cold.

Pour the cream into a mixing basin. Add the caramel and the brandy. Whisk the mixture until thick and light. Pour the caramel cream over the strawberries and chill for several hours.

Top with the 6 reserved strawberries and serve.

Advance preparation: Make several hours or the day before serving. Serve chilled.

Baked Alaska

This attractive party dish takes only minutes to put together. Have the sponge cake ready soaked and the ice cream in the freezer. Crack the egg whites in advance, ready to make the meringue and the oven preheated to the right temperature.

Serves 6

1 (8-inch/20-cm.) baked	*for the meringue:*
genoese sponge layer	4 egg whites
1 pint/6 dl. vanilla or chocolate	pinch salt
ice cream	8 oz./225 g. castor sugar
2–3 tablespoons sherry, Kirsch	
or brandy	

A genoese sponge layer can be baked in advance (page 171) and kept in the freezer with the ice cream, ready for use. At an early stage, pack the slightly softened ice cream into a round mould or soufflé dish, just a little smaller in diameter than the sponge and refreeze. Thaw the sponge before using, if necessary, but keep the ice cream frozen firm.

Preheat the oven (400°F., 200°C., Gas Mark 6) for at least 15 minutes before starting on the recipe. Sprinkle the sponge base with the sherry, Kirsch or brandy and place in an ovenproof serving dish. Remove the ice cream by holding a hot wet cloth round the mould for a moment and pushing a knife blade down the side to help release the ice cream; turn out on to the sponge.

Whisk the egg whites with a pinch of salt until stiff. Gradually beat in half the sugar and whisk until glossy. Fold in the remaining sugar. Spoon all the meringue on to the ice cream. Then quickly spread over the ice cream and sponge cake, taking care to completely cover the dessert. The meringue insulates the ice cream from the heat in the oven.

Place the dessert in the centre of the preheated oven and bake for 2–3 minutes or until the meringue is just beginning to brown. Serve at once.

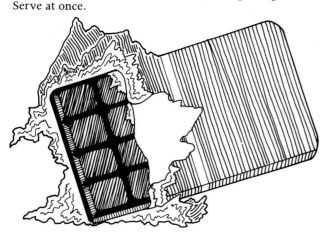

Ice cream pudding

This pudding gets its unusual name from the custard base, which when served cold does taste rather like vanilla ice cream.

Serves 4–6

2 oz./50 g. plain flour	2 egg yolks
½ oz./15 g. cornflour	1 pint/6 dl. milk
2 oz./50 g. butter	*for the meringue:*
2 oz./50 g. castor sugar	2 egg whites
few drops vanilla essence	4 oz./100 g. castor sugar

Sift the flour and cornflour on to a square of paper. Cream the butter and sugar until light and beat in the vanilla essence. Beat in the egg yolks and then stir in the sifted flour mixture.

Pour the milk into a saucepan and heat until almost boiling. Draw off the heat and gradually stir into the creamed mixture, whisking well all the time. Strain back into the saucepan and replace over the heat. Bring up to the boil, stirring constantly. Simmer for 1–2 minutes then draw off the heat and pour into a buttered 1½-pint (1-litre) shallow, fireproof baking dish. Set aside while preparing the meringue.

Whisk the egg whites until stiff. Whisk in half the sugar and beat until glossy. Using a metal spoon, fold in the remaining sugar. Spoon the meringue over the pudding and swirl evenly over the surface. Place in the centre of a very moderate oven (325°F., 170°C., Gas Mark 3) and bake for 20–30 minutes or until the meringue is lightly browned. Remove from the heat, allow to cool and then chill until ready to serve.

Serve with cream.

Advance preparation: Make several hours in advance and chill. Meringue tends to 'weep' and soften if left too long. It is not advisable to make this dessert the day before.

Chocolate refrigerator cake

This dessert consists of alternate layers of chocolate cream and sponge fingers. No baking is required but the cake must be allowed to stand for about 12 hours so that the cream sets firm and the sponge fingers soften.

Serves 6

2 oz./50 g. granulated sugar	4 oz./100 g. butter
3 tablespoons water	4 oz./100 g. icing sugar, sifted
2 tablespoons rum	4 egg yolks
about 15 sponge finger biscuits	*to decorate:*
for the chocolate cream:	few chopped walnuts
4 oz./100 g. plain chocolate	

Dissolve the sugar in the water over low heat. Bring to the boil and simmer for 5 minutes. Draw off the heat, add the rum and allow to cool until warm. Meanwhile, prepare the chocolate cream. Break the chocolate into pieces and place in a small basin set over a pan of hot water. Stir occasionally until the chocolate is melted and smooth. Cream the butter and sugar until light. Beat in the egg yolks one at a time, then beat in the melted chocolate.

To assemble the cake, divide the sponge fingers into three sets of five sponge fingers. Dip one sponge finger at a time in the warm, flavoured syrup. Arrange a neat row of five on a serving dish and spread with a layer of chocolate cream. Dip a second layer of sponge fingers and arrange on top. Spread with a layer of cream. Dip the remaining biscuits in the syrup and arrange on top of the cake. Sprinkle over any remaining syrup.

Spread the rest of the chocolate cream over the top and around the sides of the cake. Sprinkle with a few chopped nuts and chill for several hours or overnight. Cut into slices with a sharp knife, each slice should have a pretty striped appearance.

Advance preparation: This dessert improves with standing. Make a day in advance for best flavour.

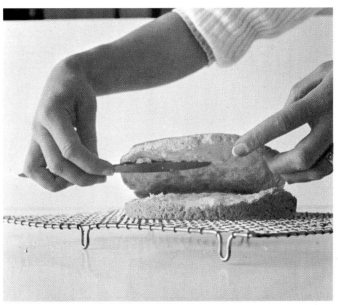

Strawberry shortcake (page 180)
Sift the flour and salt into a basin and rub in the butter.
Divide the mixture into two equal parts. Fit one circle of
shortcake into the tin, brush with melted butter, then place the
second circle of mixture on top.
When cooked, remove from the tin and separate the two layers
with a knife.
Fill the shortcake with some of the sweetened cream and
strawberries. Decorate the top with whorls of cream and
reserved strawberries.

Gingersnap dessert cake

This cake should be cut into six slices and it is important to cut it correctly. Using a sharp knife, cut at an angle as you would cut French bread. This way the biscuits will appear as thin strips through each slice and look most unusual and pretty. No extra cream is required for serving, the dessert is rich enough alone. Sometimes chopped crystallised ginger is sprinkled on top with the biscuit crumbs.

Serves 6

1 (8 oz./225 g.) packet   ½ pint/3 dl. double cream
  gingersnaps or gingernuts

Unwrap the biscuits and set aside any broken ones. Whip the cream until thick then, using not more than half the cream, spread the biscuits on one side lavishly with the cream. Arrange one on top of the other to make one long roll. Sometimes it is easier to build the biscuits up in stacks of three or four and then place them together. Lay the roll along the centre of a serving plate. Spoon over the remaining cream and, with the tip of a knife blade, spread over the top and sides to cover the biscuits completely. Rough up the surface a little to make it look pretty. Crush the remaining broken biscuits and sprinkle over the surface. Set aside to chill in the refrigerator for at least 6 hours, to allow the biscuits to soften. This is very important for serving, otherwise the dessert will not slice properly. Slice when ready to serve.

Advance preparation: Make 6 hours in advance or the day before. Biscuits must be given time to soften. Once firm cover with foil to prevent cream from drying out too much. Serve chilled.

Home made ice creams, water ices and sauces

Home made ice creams are very easy to prepare and make the most refreshing dinner party desserts. Use only the best ingredients and the results are always good. The finest cream ices, those with the best texture and flavour, are the ones made using a custard base of eggs and cream. These are the most expensive to prepare and take the most time. Other excellent ice creams and ones which are quicker to prepare, are those which combine a fruit purée with cream – a kind of frozen fruit fool. Strawberries, blackcurrants and gooseberries are among the fruit used to make this kind of mixture. Water ices are made using a sugar syrup to which flavouring is added and usually egg white which gives the mixture an aerated texture and the familiar light colour.

In order to obtain a creamy smooth consistency, it is necessary to stir the ice cream mixture while it is freezing. This helps distribute and break up small water crystals as they form during freezing. Any mixture simply poured into the container and left to freeze without stirring will be coarse in texture because of the large ice crystals that have formed. In most cases, all that is necessary is to stir the edges of the mixture as they freeze into the centre with a fork. Do this two or three times during the freezing and then towards the end give the mixture a good stir. In other cases, it is advisable to turn the mixture out when half frozen into a chilled bowl and whisk it thoroughly. This is usually necessary with water ices.

Ice cream can be frozen in large refrigerator trays or in shallow oblong polythene freezer containers. The advantage of the latter being that once the ice cream is ready, the container can be covered with the lid and the ice cream stored in the box ready for use.

Never serve ice cream very hard – straight from the freezer. Remove the container of ice cream and place in the refrigerator for 30 minutes to 1 hour before serving. Water ices, on the other hand, should be served very cold and straight from the freezer.

Lemon ice cream

An orange ice cream can be made by substituting the grated rind of 1 orange for the lemon and using 1 tablespoon orange juice and 1 tablespoon lemon juice.

Serves 6

¾ pint/4½ dl. single cream	4 oz./100 g. castor sugar
finely grated rind 1 large lemon	2 tablespoons lemon juice
4 egg yolks	¼ pint/1½ dl. double cream

Pour the single cream into a saucepan and add the finely grated lemon rind. Bring almost to the boil over moderate heat. Meanwhile, place the egg yolks and sugar into a bowl and beat well with a wooden spoon until thick and light.

Pour the hot cream into the egg and sugar mixture, stirring well to blend. Place the basin over a saucepan half filled with simmering water and stir until the custard has thickened. Remove from the heat, strain and leave to cool. Stir occasionally to prevent a skin forming.

When cold, stir in the lemon juice. Lightly whip the cream and fold into the mixture. Pour into a polythene freezer container or a large refrigerator ice tray. Freeze for several hours. Turn sides of mixture to the centre as they begin to freeze. Freeze until quite firm.

Cover and store in the container.

Green gooseberry ice cream

Fresh fruit can be used to make delicately flavoured ice creams. This recipe is quite suitable to serve for a dinner party dessert.

Serves 6

1½ lb./700 g. green gooseberries	½ pint/3 dl. double cream
1 tablespoon cold water	green food colouring (optional)
6 oz./175 g. castor sugar	

Wash the gooseberries and place in a saucepan – there's no need to top and tail them. Add the water and sugar. Cover with a lid and simmer very gently for about 15 minutes or until the fruit is quite soft.

Rub the fruit and juice through a sieve into a mixing basin, to make a thick purée. Discard all the pips and skin remaining in the sieve. Allow the purée to cool.

Lightly whip the cream and fold into the fruit purée. Add a few drops of green food colouring if liked, gooseberries tend to lose their colour on cooking. Pour the mixture into a large polythene freezer container or into a large refrigerator ice tray. Freeze for several hours. Turn sides to middle when beginning to freeze. Freeze for several hours until firm.

Cover and store in the container.

Orange water ice

This water ice recipe gets its delicious flavour from the use of frozen orange juice concentrate. It is an easy recipe to make.

Serves 4–6

4 oz./100 g. castor sugar	1 egg white
½ pint/3 dl. water	
1 (6¼ fl. oz./175 g.) can	
frozen orange juice	

Measure the sugar and water into a saucepan and stir over low heat until the sugar has dissolved. Bring up to the boil and simmer for 5 minutes. Draw the pan off the heat and add the concentrated orange juice. Stir to blend well and allow to cool.

Stir the unbeaten egg white into the mixture and pour the syrup into a polythene freezer container. Freeze until icy round the edges. Quickly spoon out into a chilled bowl and whisk until smooth and light in colour. Return to the container, cover and freeze until firm.

Advance preparation: Prepare a water ice several days before serving so that the flavour has a chance to develop.

Grapefruit water ice

Serves 6

1 pint/6 dl. water	juice 1 lemon
10 oz./275 g. castor sugar	2 egg whites
finely pared rind and juice	
2 grapefruit	

Measure the water and sugar into a medium sized saucepan. Add the finally pared rind of the grapefruits. Place over low heat and stir until the sugar has dissolved. Bring the mixture up to the boil and cook fairly rapidly for 5 minutes. Draw the pan off the heat, add the strained juice from both the grapefruits and the lemon. Set the syrup aside until quite cold.

Strain the syrup and stir in the unbeaten egg whites. Mix well and pour either into 2 large refrigerator ice trays or 1 large polythene freezer container. Freeze for several hours.

When partially frozen, spoon the mixture quickly into a chilled bowl and whisk until creamy and white in colour. Return to the container and freeze until quite firm.

Vanilla ice cream

Ice cream made using a custard base results in a rich, smooth texture. Where possible, use vanilla sugar to get a true flavour.

Serves 6

½ pint/3 dl. single cream	4 oz./100 g. vanilla sugar
4 egg yolks	½ pint/3 dl. double cream

Pour the single cream into a saucepan and bring almost to the boil. Meanwhile, place the egg yolks and vanilla sugar in a mixing basin and beat well with a wooden spoon until thick and light. Pour the hot cream into the egg and sugar mixture, stirring well to blend.

At this stage, the custard has to be cooked until the mixture thickens and it is advisable to do this over indirect heat. Either place the mixing basin over a saucepan half filled with simmering water and stir until the custard has thickened. An alternative, and quicker method, is to return the custard mixture to the saucepan. Place the pan in a second larger pan of simmering water and stir until the custard has thickened.

Remove from the heat. Strain and leave the custard to cool, stirring occasionally to prevent a skin forming. Lightly whip the double cream, fold into the cold mixture.

Pour into a large polythene freezer box or into a larger refrigerator ice tray. Freeze for several hours. Turn the sides of the mixture into the centre as they begin to freeze. Freeze until quite firm. Cover and store in the container.

Pommes bonne femme (page 162)
Peel and core the apples and wrap each in a strip of buttered, greaseproof paper.
Place the apples in a baking dish and fill the centre of each apple with mixed currants and sugar. Put a knob of butter on the top of the filling.
When cooked, lift the apples from the dish. Pour the juices in a saucepan and add the jam. Place over heat and bring to the boil. Remove the paper from each apple and replace back into the baking dish. Sift the tops with icing sugar and glaze under a hot grill.
Spoon over the hot apricot glaze and serve.

Melon ice cream

This unusual ice cream is served in an attractive container made from the melon shells. Select a fully ripe melon with a good green shell and scrub it clean.

Serves 6

1 honeydew melon	½ pint/3 dl. double cream
6 oz./175 g. castor sugar	few drops green food colouring
juice 2 lemons	

With a small, sharp pointed kitchen knife, cut into the melon at alternate angles – rather like cutting a grapefruit. Make sure that the knife tip goes into the centre each time and work round the melon from end to end. Pull the halves apart and discard the seeds. Using a dessertspoon, scoop out the flesh and rub through a sieve to make about ½ pint (3 dl.) purée. Keep the melon shells for serving.

Pour the melon purée into a saucepan, add the sugar and stir over low heat until the sugar has dissolved. Draw the pan off the heat, add the strained lemon juice and set aside to cool. Lightly whip the cream and then fold in the melon purée. Pour the mixture into two large refrigerator ice trays and place in the freezer compartment of the refrigerator or the home freezer. When the ice cream is practically frozen round the edges, scoop out quickly into a chilled mixing basin. Whisk, using a rotary beater, until smooth and creamy. Add a few drops of green colouring, if liked. Pour the ice cream quickly back into a large polythene freezer box. Cover with the lid and place in the freezer. Freeze for several hours until firm.

To serve, trim a slice from the base of each melon shell, not enough to make a hole but sufficient to hold them steady. When ready to serve, scoop the ice cream out using an ice cream scoop. Dip the scoop in cold water each time and mould the ice cream in the melon shells. Return to the freezer until ready to serve.

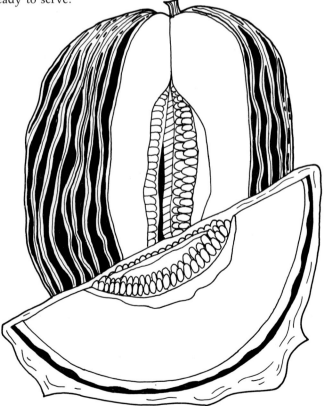

Sauces for ice cream

These are easy and quick to make if you prepare a sugar syrup for mixing the sauces. Dissolve 1 lb. (450 g.) granulated sugar in ½ pint (3 dl.) water, stirring over low heat. Bring up to the boil and simmer for 2 minutes only. Strain through muslin into a jug and allow to cool. Pour into a bottle, cover and store.

Chocolate sauce

Serves 4

5 tablespoons sugar syrup	4 oz./100 g. plain chocolate

Measure the sugar syrup into a basin. Add the chocolate, broken in pieces. Stand the basin in a shallow pan of hot water and stir over gentle heat, until the chocolate is quite melted and the sauce smooth and glossy. Add an extra tablespoon of syrup if the sauce seems too thick. Remove from the heat and cool until tepid before spooning over ice cream.

Melba sauce

Serves 4

4 tablespoons sugar syrup	juice 1 small lemon
4 heaped tablespoons raspberry jam	

Measure the sugar syrup into a saucepan. Add the raspberry jam and stir over the heat until almost boiling. Draw off the heat and pass through a fine strainer. Add the juice of the lemon and return the sauce to the pan. Boil for 1–2 minutes or until the mixture hangs in syrupy drops from the spoon. Cool before using.

Apricot sauce

Serves 4

4 tablespoons sugar syrup	juice ½ orange
4 heaped tablespoons apricot jam	

Measure the sugar syrup into a saucepan. Add the apricot jam and stir over the heat until almost boiling. Draw off the heat and pass through a fine strainer. Return the sauce to the pan and add the orange juice. Reboil and simmer for 1–2 minutes or until the mixture hangs in syrupy drops from the spoon.
Cool before using.

Ginger sauce

Serves 4

¼ pint/1½ dl. sugar syrup	¼ teaspoon finely grated lemon rind
1–2 tablespoons finely chopped crystallised ginger	

Measure the sugar syrup, ginger and lemon rind into a saucepan. Bring up to the boil and simmer together for 5 minutes. Draw off the heat and allow to cool. Cover and chill before serving.

Ideas for decorating desserts

Illustrated in colour on page 157

Chocolate

Plain chocolate is more suitable than milk chocolate, the darker colour being more effective as a colour contrast. To get more striking shapes and texture, chocolate should be melted and then used. Break the chocolate into a small mixing basin and place this over a pan of hot water – take care to select a basin that fits the pan neatly.

Heat the water in the pan until almost boiling and draw off the heat, before putting in the basin. Chocolate should never be melted over direct heat, nor should any water, even in the form of steam from the pan, be allowed to come in contact with it. Chocolate has unusual properties and its texture and shiny appearance can easily be spoiled. When melted, spread the chocolate on to a flat surface.

For chocolate curls, spread the chocolate thinly on marble or Formica and allow to cool, but not set firm. Then choose a fairly large, steel kitchen knife with a plain edge. Holding the knife tipped backwards at an angle, shave the chocolate into curls. As long as the knife is held at a sloping angle, the chocolate will curl into long cigarette shapes. Pick out the best shapes and place separately; broken shavings can be kept in a box. Store covered in a cool place, preferably the refrigerator.

To use: Chocolate curls look really attractive placed on top of chocolate gâteaux that are plainly iced with chocolate icing. Try also on the top of chocolate cup cakes and they look pretty sprinkled over the tops of creamy desserts or over ice cream.

Coconut

Desiccated coconut, being plain white, lends itself ideally to added colour for decoration. Spoon the required amount into a jar, unless specially required, do not colour more than 2 tablespoons at a time. Add a few drops of any edible food colouring – best to use are red, green or yellow. Cover with a lid, cap or piece of kitchen foil and shake vigorously to colour all the coconut evenly. Tip the coconut out on to a square of foil and leave in a warm place to dry before storing in the jar.

Toasted coconut is also effective; spread coconut over a square of kitchen foil in the base of a grill pan and toast under a high heat, shaking until evenly browned.

To use: Sprinkle over whipped cream toppings, particularly round edges of trifles or moulded milk puddings.

Nuts

Jars of nuts are invaluable for dessert decorations. Walnuts and almonds are the most useful.

Walnuts may be used whole or chopped. Coarsely chop walnuts, using scissors, and snip them into pieces. For finely chopped walnuts, chop them in the same manner as parsley. Never mince walnuts; the pressure squeezes out the nut oils and the fine pieces stick together, use a mouli grater.

Almonds may be purchased in their skins, blanched or chopped, or as almond nibs or flakes – finely sliced. To blanch almonds, that is to remove the outer skin on whole almonds, plunge the almonds into boiling water for 1 minute. Drain and quickly pop the almonds out of their skins. While they are still warm, it is a good idea to chop or slice them, if needed. When cold and hardened, they tend to break up. Toasted almonds have a delicious flavour and look prettier than the untoasted ones. Spread almonds out on a baking tray or grill pan under high heat. Either way shake the almonds occasionally to get even colouring and do not leave them – they burn very quickly.

To use: Chopped walnuts are attractive sprinkled over any custard based desserts, and over instant whips or ice cream. Flaked toasted almonds are delicious over creamed rice desserts, canned pears, especially pleasant with apricots, old-fashioned chocolate pudding, blancmange or apple snow.

Nut brittle

Gives a crunchy texture to custard and all creamy desserts. Particularly attractive served over the top of butterscotch instant whip pudding. Also attractive sprinkled over chocolate blancmange, fruit and milk jellies.

Delicious over flavoured ice cream with fruit or plain sauces, plain flavoured dessert, custard bases or baked custards.

Sugar rims

Sugar rims look attractive around chilled desserts or iced drinks. They also look pretty round the edge of glasses of apple snow, instant whip, particularly chocolate, or fruit compote served icy cold. Lemon or orange summer drinks look particularly pleasing served with this pretty rim, also fruit cups, punches and cider cups. Frost the rim of a glass serving dish with fruit salad in. Also pretty for glasses with coloured jellies set in them.

Try frosting the glasses for milk shakes, particularly for raspberry and other coloured ones. Fruit fools look much more attractive if served in a glass with a pretty sugar rim. Iced coffee looks delectable with the frosted rim, so does lemon tea and iced chocolate with cream floating on the top.

The rim of the glass or dish is first dipped into a saucer of lightly mixed egg white and then in castor sugar.

Glacé fruits

Glacé cherries and angelica are most suitable for decoration – other glacé fruit can be a little expensive. Glacé cherries can come in green and gold colours as well. Before using any glacé fruits, always wash off the sticky preserving syrup with warm water. Cherries may be cut in halves, quarters or they can be finely chopped.

Angelica may also be chopped, but is best cut into angelica leaves. To make these, first cut angelica into even strips about $\frac{1}{4}$–$\frac{1}{2}$ inch ($\frac{1}{2}$–1 cm.) wide. Then cut across at an angle to make diamond shapes. Arrange leaves and cherries together to make pretty designs.

To use: Glacé cherry halves can be placed in the centre of prepared grapefruit halves or in melon wedges. Chopped glacé fruits look pretty stirred into canned fruit, particularly pears or peaches. Decorate meringue toppings on lemon pie or queen of puddings with angelica and cherries. Arrange pretty designs in the base of jelly desserts, so when turned out they appear on the top.

Brandy snaps (page 174)

Melt the butter, sugar and golden syrup in a saucepan.
Stir in the flour mixture and lemon rind and juice. Spoon
teaspoons of the mixture on to oiled or lined trays.
When almost baked, quickly wrap each brandy snap round the
greased handle of a wooden spoon.
When crisp, slip the brandy snap off the spoon handle and
repeat the process with the next one.
If liked, pipe with whipped cream.

Home freezing of fruits

Fresh fruits frozen during the summer months can be used for a variety of desserts out of season. Quantities of fruits can also be stored for jam making later in the year. Choose fruit that is in prime condition and good quality. Where possible, freeze quickly after picking.

In all cases, fruit should be prepared according to kind. Hulls, stalks and stones removed. Fruit can be frozen in a dry pack and unsweetened – this is ideal for fruit to be used in recipes for jam making. To get the best colour and flavour, it is advisable to freeze fruit with sugar, either dry or in the form of a cold sugar syrup. Use this method for fruits to be served as a dessert from the freezer.

Dry pack: Fruits such as rhubarb, gooseberries, black and red-currants and raspberries can be frozen – prepared and packed with no sugar added. These fruits are very useful for using in dessert recipes, pies and for jam making.

Sugar pack: Sugar sprinkled over the fruit draws out the fruit juices and forms a sugar glaze. When frozen, this glaze protects the fruit. The fruit can either be sprinkled with sugar in a basin and left to stand at room temperature until the sugar goes into solution. Or the fruit can be packed in layers with the sugar in ridged wax containers. Allow to stand at room temperature until the juices run. Use approximately 4–6 oz. (100–175 g.) sugar for every 1 lb. ($\frac{1}{2}$ kg.) fruit.

Syrup pack: The use of a sugar syrup is particularly suitable for those fruits which discolour, such as apricots or peaches. Prepare a sugar syrup well in advance and allow to get cold. Where possible, chill before using. The strength of syrup used is determined by the tartness of the fruit. A medium syrup for stone fruits can be made by dissolving 1 lb. (450 g.) sugar in 2 pints (1 litre) water to make $2\frac{1}{2}$ pints ($1\frac{1}{4}$ litres) syrup. A heavy syrup for soft fruit can be made by dissolving 2 lb. (1 kg.) sugar in 2 pints (1 litre) water to make 3 pints ($1\frac{1}{2}$ litres) syrup.

Measure the sugar and water into a saucepan and bring up to the boil, stirring until the sugar has dissolved. Strain into a bowl, cover and leave to cool. Prepare sufficient syrup to allow 1 pint (6 dl.) syrup for every 2 lb. (1 kg.) fruit.

Packing and freezing

1. Dry packs of unsweetened fruit can be frozen in polythene freezer bags. Freeze in quantities suitable for using in recipes. Large amounts of fruit for jam making should also be placed in the freezer bags. Shape the contents of the bag into a neat flat shape for quicker freezing and neater stacking. Exclude air and freeze.

2. Fruit to be frozen in sugar or sugar syrup should be packed in ridged or wax containers. Add cold syrup sufficient to cover the fruit, leave at least $\frac{1}{2}$ inch (1 cm.) headspace at the top to allow for expansion during freezing. To keep fruit submerged, place a piece of crumpled waxed paper or foil between the fruit and the lid. The pressure keeps the fruit below the surface of the syrup.

3. Place packs in the freezer near the base or sides, close to the refrigerant. Allow air to circulate the packs so that they freeze quickly. Do not place too closely together.

4. Twenty-four hours later, remove the pack to the main storage part of the freezer until required.

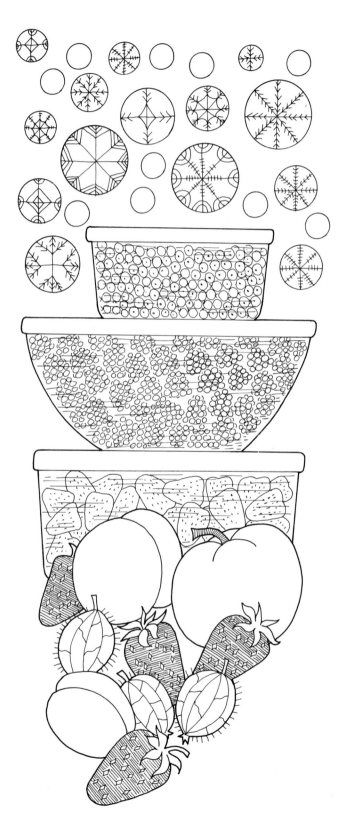

Fruit can be stored up to 12 months. Make use of fruit especially during the winter season and finish stocks before the new season starts again.

Fruits frozen in sugar or syrup should be thawed slowly in the unopened containers. For a 1-lb. (½-kg.) pack, allow 6–8 hours in the refrigerator or 2–4 hours at room temperature. Turn the container while thawing to keep the syrup circulating throughout the fruit. Dry packs of fruit for use in recipes or jam making should be used, wherever possible, while still frozen.

Fruit	Preparation	Freezing	Serving
Apples	Freeze only good cooking apples. Peel, core and slice. Scald for 3 minutes in boiling water to prevent discolouration.	Dry pack, unsweetened in polythene bags.	Use in fruit compotes, pies, crumbles.
Apricots	Wash, halve and stone.	Pack in ridged containers, cover with medium syrup.	Use in fruit salads, mousses and desserts.
Blackberries	Pick over and remove stalks.	Dry pack, unsweetened in polythene bags.	Use in pies, compotes and fruit mousses or for jam making.
Currants (red and black)	Remove from stems, using the prongs of a fork.	Dry pack, unsweetened in polythene. Pack in containers, cover with heavy syrup.	For use in jams and puddings. Thaw and serve chilled.
Gooseberries	Top and tail and freeze green gooseberries for cooking. Use dessert gooseberries for serving straight from freezer.	Dry pack, unsweetened in polythene. Sugar or syrup pack dessert gooseberries.	Use in jam, puddings, pies and mousses. Thaw and serve chilled.
Loganberries	Pick over carefully. Do not wash.	Dry pack, unsweetened in polythene bags. Pack in ridged containers with sugar or heavy syrup.	For jams, mousses, compotes or fruit salad. Thaw and serve chilled.
Peaches	Peel, stone and halve. Keep submerged in water while preparing, to prevent discolouration.	Pack in ridged containers with medium syrup.	Thaw and serve chilled. Use in fruit salads, mousses or trifles.
Plums	Freeze dark variety only. Wipe, halve and stone.	Pack in containers, cover with medium syrup.	Thaw and serve chilled. Use in fruit salads or trifles.
Raspberries	Select perfect fruit and remove hulls. Do not wash.	Dry pack, unsweetened in polythene.	Use in pies, mousses, fruit compotes, other desserts or jam making.
Rhubarb	Trim and cut stalks into 1-inch (2½-cm.) lengths.	Dry pack in polythene bags.	Use in compotes, pies, puddings or for jam.
Strawberries	Remove caylex. Leave whole or slice.	Sugar pack or cover with heavy syrup.	Thaw and serve chilled or use in trifles.
Strawberry purée	Hull and blend or purée 1 lb. (½ kg.) strawberries with 6 oz. (175 g.) castor sugar and the juice of 1 lemon.	Pour into ridged containers, cover and freeze.	Thaw and serve as a sauce with ice cream and puddings.

Winter puddings for the family

During the colder weather in winter months, desserts can afford to be more substantial and filling. This is the time of year to serve some of the more popular traditional recipes and others such as light, steamed or baked puddings. A variety of recipes in this section offers an interesting choice and much use is made of apples, being at their best in autumn and winter.

Ideas for decorating desserts
The explanatory captions to these decorations appear on page 151.

Old fashioned bread pudding

This traditional fruity, spicy pudding is still as popular as it ever was. For a darker pudding, use soft brown sugar and treacle in place of the golden syrup and castor sugar in the recipe.

Serves 6

12 oz./350 g. white bread, including crusts	1 level teaspoon mixed spice
4 oz./100 g. shredded suet	2 teaspoons golden syrup
2 oz./50 g. castor sugar	1 egg
6 oz./175 g. mixed seedless raisins, sultanas and currants	1 oz./25 g. granulated or demerara sugar
1 oz./25 g. candied peel, chopped	

Cut up the bread, or if using sliced bread place just as it is in a mixing basin. Cover with cold water and leave overnight to soak.

Empty the bread into a colander and squeeze by hand or using a potato masher, press out as much of the water as possible. Place the bread in a mixing basin and beat out any lumps with a fork. Add the suet, sugar, dried fruit, peel and mixed spice. Stir in the golden syrup and egg and mix thoroughly.

Turn the mixture into a buttered, shallow baking or small roasting tin. Spread evenly and sprinkle the top with granulated or demerara sugar. Place in the centre of a moderately hot oven (375°F., 190°C., Gas Mark 5) and bake for 1 hour. Turn out the pudding and cool slightly.

Serve warm or cold, cut in generous slices.

Advance preparation: Once baked, this pudding keeps for 1–2 days. Cut in slices and store in a lidded tin.

Apple brown Betty

The brown sugar, lemon and cinnamon give the apples in this recipe a delicious flavour.

Serves 4–6

4 oz./100 g. butter	grated rind and juice 1 lemon
4 oz./100 g. fresh white breadcrumbs	1½ lb./¾ kg. cooking apples
4 oz./100 g. soft brown sugar	3 tablespoons water
½ level teaspoon cinnamon	

Melt the butter in a saucepan over low heat. Draw off the heat and stir in the crumbs. In a small mixing basin, combine together the brown sugar, cinnamon and grated lemon rind. Peel, quarter, core and slice the apples.

Butter a 2-pint (1-litre) baking dish very thoroughly and then sprinkle a third of the buttered crumbs over the base of the dish. Cover this with a layer of the apple slices and then sprinkle over half the sugar mixture. Cover with another third of the crumbs and then the rest of the apple and sugar mixture. Spoon the water and lemon juice over. Finally, top with the remaining crumbs. Cover with a piece of buttered foil or greaseproof paper. Place in the centre of a moderately hot oven (350°F., 180°C., Gas Mark 4) and bake for 30 minutes. Remove the foil or greaseproof paper and bake for a further 30 minutes or until the apples are tender and the top is golden brown and crisp.

Serve hot or cold with thick cream.

Advance preparation: Assemble the pudding several hours in advance. Put to bake when required.

Baked lemon pudding

This pudding bakes with its own delicious lemon sauce underneath a topping of cake. Serve hot. It is a great favourite with children.

Serves 4

4 oz./100 g. self-raising flour	*for the sauce:*
pinch salt	4 oz./100 g. castor sugar
4 oz./100 g. butter	2 level tablespoons cornflour
4 oz./100 g. castor sugar	juice 1 lemon
2 eggs	*to decorate:*
finely grated rind 1 lemon	icing sugar
1–2 tablespoons milk	

Sift together the flour and salt and set aside. Cream together the butter and sugar until light and creamy, then gradually beat in the lightly beaten eggs and grated lemon rind. Add a little of the sifted flour along with the last few additions of egg, then fold in the remaining flour and enough milk to mix to a medium soft consistency. Spoon into a buttered 2–2½-pint (1–1¼-litre) baking dish and spread evenly over the base of the dish. Set aside while preparing the sauce.

In a mixing basin, combine together the sugar and cornflour, then stir in the lemon juice, made up to ½ pint (3 dl.) with hot, not boiling, water. Blend well and pour over the pudding. Place immediately just above the centre of a moderately hot oven (375°F., 190°C., Gas Mark 5) and bake for 40 minutes. While baking, the cake mixture will rise to the top and the sauce will go underneath.

Sprinkle with icing sugar and serve the pudding hot with its own delicious lemon sauce.

Advance preparation: Assemble ingredients but make and cook this pudding when required.

Eve's pudding

Serve Eve's pudding hot with vanilla ice cream or with cream. The apples can be flavoured with a pinch of cinnamon or mixed spice instead of grated lemon zest.

Serves 4–6

1–1½ lb./½–¾ kg. cooking apples	pinch salt
1 tablespoon water	3 oz./75 g. butter or margarine
½ oz./15 g. butter	3 oz./75 g. castor sugar
2–3 oz./50–75 g. castor sugar	1 large egg
finely grated zest ½ lemon	3 drops vanilla essence
for the topping:	1–2 tablespoons milk
4 oz./100 g. self-raising flour	icing sugar

Peel, core and slice the apples thinly. Put them into a saucepan with the water and the butter. Cover and cook very gently until the apple slices are soft. Shake the pan occasionally to prevent them sticking. When tender, add the sugar and lemon zest and beat the mixture to a purée. Spread the apples over the base of a greased 2-pint (1-litre) baking or pie dish. Set aside to cool while preparing the cake topping.

Sift together the flour and salt. Beat the butter or margarine and sugar until light and creamy. Lightly mix the egg and vanilla essence and gradually beat into the creamed mixture, a

Pouding à la royale

A pretty pudding when turned out. Choose plain, jam filled Swiss roll, any cream filling would spoil the recipe.

Serves 4

1 jam filled Swiss roll	*for the apricot sauce:*
½ pint/3 dl. milk	2–3 heaped tablespoons
1 oz./25 g. butter	apricot jam
3 eggs	2 tablespoons water
3 oz./75 g. castor sugar	2 level tablespoons castor sugar
1 oz./25 g. flour	juice 1 lemon

Thinly slice the Swiss roll and use the slices to line a well buttered 1½-pint (1-litre) ovenproof pudding basin. To completely cover the surface is not essential, one row of slices around the sides looks very attractive. The custard filling fills in any spaces between the slices of Swiss roll. Set the basin aside while preparing the filling.

Heat the milk and butter in a saucepan until hot. Separate the eggs, crack the yolks into one basin and the whites into a second basin. Add the sugar to the yolks and cream thoroughly. Add the flour and mix well. Stir in a little of the hot milk, blend well and pour back into the milk saucepan. Bring up to the boil, whisking well all the time until thickened and boiling. Draw off the heat. Pour the mixture into a large basin. Fold in the whisked egg whites. Pour into the lined basin. Set in a large roasting tin and pour boiling water to the depth of 1 inch (2½ cm.) into the tin. Place in the centre of a moderate oven (350°F., 180°C., Gas Mark 4) and bake for 40 minutes. Remove from the heat and leave to cool.

Sieve the apricot jam into a saucepan. Add the water, sugar and lemon juice. Stir over low heat to dissolve the sugar, then bring to the boil and simmer for 5 minutes. Draw off the heat and allow to cool.

Unmould the pudding on to a serving plate. Pour the sauce over and around the sides and serve.

Plum crumble

Serves 4

1½ lb./¾ kg. plums	*for the shortbread crumble:*
3–4 oz./75–100 g. castor sugar	6 oz./175 g. plain flour
½ oz./15 g. butter	4 oz./100 g. butter
1 tablespoon water	2 oz./50 g. castor sugar
icing sugar	

Halve and stone the plums. Place the fruit in a saucepan and add the sugar, butter and water. Cover with a lid and simmer very gently for about 5–10 minutes, or until the fruit is just soft. Pour into a buttered 1½-pint (1-litre) pie or baking dish. Where possible, choose a shallow rather than a deep dish for a crumble.

OPPOSITE **Gâteau aux fruits Chantilly (page 179)**
Pour the cake mixture into the prepared cake tin.
Sprinkle the two layers with sugar syrup. Spoon sweetened cream over the base. Prepare the fruit.
Arrange half the fruit over the cream and top with the second sponge layer, smooth side upwards.
Coat the top surface of the cake with hot apricot glaze. Quickly arrange remaining fruit over the glaze, then brush the fruit liberally with more hot glaze.

Leave the fruit to stand, while preparing the crumble topping.

Sift the flour into a bowl. Add the butter, cut in pieces, and rub into the mixture. Add the sugar and continue to rub in until the mixture clings together in large crumbs. Sprinkle the crumb mixture evenly over the top of the fruit and press down lightly. Place in the centre of a moderate oven (350°F., 180°C., Gas Mark 4) and bake for 1 hour or until the crumble is firm and golden brown.

Dust with icing sugar and serve with cream.
Advance preparation: Assemble pudding several hours in advance. Bake when required.

Old fashioned chocolate pudding

Chocolate pudding is a great favourite with most children. Sprinkle a little castor sugar over the surface of the hot pudding – this helps to prevent a skin forming on the surface as the pudding cools.

Serves 4

1½ oz./40 g. cornflour	1 pint/6 dl. milk
1 oz./25 g. cocoa powder	few drops vanilla essence
3 oz./75 g. castor sugar	

Measure the cornflour, cocoa powder and castor sugar into a basin. Mix to a smooth paste with a little of the milk taken from the pint. Take care at this point to make sure that the cornflour mixture is blended.

Pour the remaining milk into a saucepan and heat until almost boiling. When hot, stir the milk into the cornflour blend. Mix well and then pour the whole contents back into the saucepan. Place over moderate heat and stir constantly until the mixture is boiling and has thickened. Cook for 1–2 minutes then draw off the heat. Add a few drops of vanilla essence and pour into a serving dish. Serve warm or cold with cream.
Advance preparation: Assemble ingredients. The recipe is quick to make, prepare and cook about 2–3 hours before serving. Do not chill.

Baked apple compote

Choose a dish in which you can bake and serve the apples. These are particularly delicious if a little double cream is poured over the hot fruit when taken from the oven.

Serves 6

2 lb./1 kg. dessert or sharp	finely grated rind and juice
flavoured apples	1 lemon
1 oz./25 g. butter	4 oz./100 g. demerara sugar

Peel, quarter and core the apples and then slice them thickly. Using a little of the butter, well grease a shallow, fireproof baking dish. Arrange the apple slices over the base of the dish, packed close together and preferably in one layer. Sprinkle with the finely grated lemon rind and pour over the lemon juice. Sprinkle with the demerara sugar and dot with the butter, cut in small pieces. Cover with buttered paper or foil and place in the centre of a moderate oven (350°F., 180°C., Gas Mark 4) and bake for 35–40 minutes or until the apples are tender.

Serve hot, straight from the dish. Apples cooked this way are in a delicious sweet syrup with a refreshing lemon flavour made from the fruit juice, sugar and butter.

Danish apple cake

This is an excellent recipe to prepare in autumn when there are plenty of apples available. Where possible, make up the dessert in a glass serving dish, in order to show off the attractive layers.

Serves 4

2 lb./1 kg. cooking apples	*for the crumb mixture:*
3 tablespoons water	4 oz./100 g. butter
2 oz./50 g. castor sugar	4 oz./100 g. dry white
finely grated rind ½ lemon	breadcrumbs
¼ pint/1½ dl. double cream	2 oz./50 g. castor sugar
2 tablespoons redcurrant jelly	

Peel, core and slice the apples. Place them in a saucepan with the water. Cover with a lid and cook very gently for about 30 minutes. Stir occasionally and when the apples are very soft, draw the pan off the heat. Sweeten to taste with sugar and add the finely grated lemon rind. Set aside to cool.

Melt the butter in a frying pan. Add the mixed breadcrumbs and the sugar and fry very gently, stirring often, until they are brown and crisp. Leave to cool.

When both apples and crumbs are cold, spread a third of the crumbs in the base of a glass serving dish. Cover with half the apple purée. Repeat the layer of crumbs, top with remaining apple and then finally cover with remaining crumbs. Whip the cream until thick and spread over the top. Decorate with the redcurrant jelly. Chill until ready to serve.

Note: Traditionally, dry white breadcrumbs or rusk crumbs should be used.

Advance preparation: Assemble apple and crumb layers well in advance. Decorate when ready to serve.

Pommes bonne femme

Illustrated in colour on pages 148 and 149

The apples in this recipe are cooked in a delicious wine and sugar syrup, then glazed to a golden brown. Serve them hot with cream.

Serves 4

8 dessert apples, preferably	2 oz./50 g. butter
Cox's	4 tablespoons dry white wine
2 oz./50 g. castor sugar	1 heaped tablespoon apricot jam
1 tablespoon currants	icing sugar (see recipe)

Peel and core the apples, leaving them whole. Wrap each apple in a strip of buttered greaseproof paper about 2 inches (5 cm.) wide and place in a shallow baking dish or roasting tin. Buttered papers keep the apples white during baking; they should be only wrapped around the sides not over the top of each apple.

Mix together the currants and sugar and fill the centre of each apple. Using a knife, put a knob of butter on the top of the filling. Add the wine to the baking dish. Place in the centre of a hot oven (400°F., 200°C., Gas Mark 6) and bake for 45 minutes. When ready, the apples should feel quite tender when pierced with a thin skewer, but still firm.

Lift the cooked apples from the baking dish and pour the juices into a saucepan. Add the apricot jam – sieve first if there are any large pieces of fruit. Stir over low heat until ingredients are blended and bring up to the boil. Simmer for a moment, then draw off the heat. Meanwhile, carefully remove the paper from each apple and replace the apples in the baking dish. Sift the tops liberally with icing sugar and glaze quickly under a hot grill to caramelise the tops.

Spoon over the hot apricot glaze and serve at once.

Advance preparation: Assemble ingredients but put to bake when required.

Chaussons aux pommes

These are to be found in most French *boulangerie*. The moist apple filling combines perfectly with the crisp pastry. Chaussons aux pommes makes a marvellous picnic or packed lunch item.

Makes 8–10

1 lb./½ kg. cooking apples	1 tablespoon sultanas
½ oz./15 g. butter	8 oz./225 g. puff pastry
¼ teaspoon grated lemon rind	1 egg, beaten
2 oz./50 g. castor sugar	icing sugar

Peel, core and cut the apples up into pieces. Melt the butter in a saucepan, then add the apples and lemon rind. Cover with a lid and cook *very gently*, stirring occasionally, until the apples are soft – takes about 10 minutes. Draw off the heat, beat with a wooden spoon to purée the apples. Add the sugar and sultanas and leave until cold.

Roll out the puff pastry to a square about ¼ inch (½ cm.) thick. Using a 3-inch (7½-cm.) round fluted cutter, stamp out circles of the pastry. Take each circle of pastry and roll gently to elongate and make an oval shape. Dividing the apple mixture equally, spoon on to one half of each pastry shape. Brush the edges with beaten egg and fold the pastry over to make the 'chausson'. Press the edges well together to seal. Slash the top of each one with a knife – sometimes the slashes take the form of an elaborate pattern. Brush the pastries with beaten egg and leave to rest in a cool place for about 15–20 minutes before baking.

Arrange on one or more wetted baking trays. Place above centre in a hot oven (425°F., 220°C., Gas Mark 7) and bake for 10 minutes. Lower the heat to moderately hot (375°F., 190°C., Gas Mark 5) and bake for a further 20 minutes. Dust with icing sugar and serve warm or cold.

Advance preparation: Bake in advance. When cold, store in a lidded tin. Warm through in a moderate oven (350°F., 180°C., Gas Mark 4) for 10–15 minutes before serving.

Custard mixtures

Custards are milk puddings in which eggs are used as the thickening agent rather than starch. All mixtures such as these require steady, gentle cooking. Holes in the texture or a watery consistency can be caused by cooking the mixture too long, or by using too high a temperature. The protein in the white of egg becomes hardened and is unable to hold all the liquid. As a result, holes appear in the custard which give an uneven texture and a watery consistency. In spite of this, these desserts are among the easiest to make and many of the recipes are traditional childhood favourites.

Baked egg custard

This is one of the easiest puddings to prepare and one of the most neglected. Serve a baked custard cold with fruit compote – plums are especially nice.

Serves 4–6

4 large eggs	few drops vanilla essence
1 oz./25 g. castor sugar	scant 1 pint/scant 6 dl. milk

Crack the eggs into a large basin. Add the sugar and vanilla essence and whisk together to mix. Gradually whisk in the milk – use only a scant pint, otherwise the mixture will overflow the average sized 1½-pint (1-litre) baking dish. Strain the mixture into a jug. Butter a baking dish and place in a large roasting tin. Pour the custard mixture into the dish and fill the tin with cold water to the depth of about 1 inch (2½ cm.). Place in the centre of a slow oven (300°F., 150°C., Gas Mark 2) and bake for 1¼–1½ hours or until the custard is firm.

Serve hot or cold with cream or fruit.

Advance preparation: Baked custard keeps well, it can be made 1 day in advance if serving cold. Do not chill.

Bread and butter pudding

Bread and butter pudding should be served newly baked and hot from the oven. It tastes very good with cream or vanilla ice cream.

Serves 4

4 slices white bread, thinly sliced	2 oz./50 g. sultanas
butter	3 eggs
2 oz./50 g. castor sugar	¾ pint/½ litre milk

Spread the bread slices with the butter and trim away the crusts. Cut the bread into squares and place in a well buttered 1½-pint (1-litre) baking dish, in layers with the sugar and the sultanas. Whisk the eggs and milk together and strain over the ingredients in the pie dish. Let the pudding stand for 15–20 minutes to allow the bread to swell.

Place in the centre of a moderately hot oven (375°F., 190°C., Gas Mark 5) and bake for 45 minutes or until the pudding is risen and golden brown.

Advance preparation: Assemble ingredients and put to cook when required.

Caramel custard

Caramel custard can be moulded in a 1½-pint (1-litre) pie dish which gives an oval shaped custard or a small 6-inch (15-cm.) deep cake tin for a round pudding. Bake a caramel custard the day before serving.

Serves 6

6 large eggs	*for the caramel:*
3 oz./175 g. castor sugar	3 level tablespoons granulated
few drops vanilla essence	or castor sugar
1 pint/6 dl. milk	1 tablespoon water

First prepare the caramel for lining the dish. Measure the sugar into a dry saucepan. Place over moderate heat and stir all the time until the sugar has melted and turned to a golden caramel. Draw off the heat and add the water. Take care, the mixture will boil furiously with the addition of a cold liquid. Return the pan to the heat and stir until the caramel and water have formed a thick syrup. Pour this into an ungreased 1½-pint (1-litre) pie dish. Holding the dish in a cloth, tip in all directions so that the caramel runs over the base and around the sides of the dish to coat it. Set aside while preparing the custard.

Crack the eggs into a mixing basin. Add the sugar and vanilla essence. Whisk to break up the eggs and then whisk in the milk. Strain the custard into a jug and pour into the dish. Place the dish in a large roasting tin and fill this with cold water to the depth of about 1 inch (2½ cm.) around the sides of the pie dish. Place in the centre of a moderate oven (325°F., 170°C., Gas Mark 3) and bake for 1½ hours or until the custard has set. Remove from the heat and allow to cool. Leave until quite cold before serving.

Loosen round the top edge with a knife. Place a serving dish over the top and quickly reverse. Lift away the baking dish. Serve with cream.

Advance preparation: Baked custard keeps well and can be made 1–2 days in advance of serving. Unmould only when ready to serve. Do not chill.

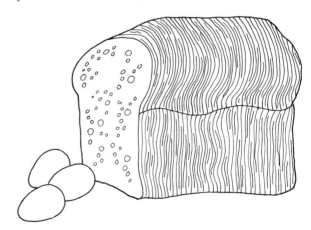

Fruit sponge pudding

Use left over stewed fruit for this simple pudding. Apples taste delicious, otherwise use plums, blackberries, raspberries or rhubarb – all of which look pretty and taste good.

Serves 4

½ pint/3 dl. stewed fruit	1 oz./25 g. castor sugar
2 trifle sponge cakes	½ pint/3 dl. milk
2 eggs	

Lightly butter a 1–1½-pint (½–1-litre) baking or pie dish and arrange the stewed fruit over the base. Slice the sponge cakes in half and place over the fruit, cut side downwards.

Crack the eggs into a basin and add the sugar. Whisk to mix then add the milk. Strain the mixture over the sponge cakes and fruit. Place the dish in a larger roasting or baking tin with cold water to the depth of ½ inch (1 cm.). Place in the centre of a moderate oven (325°F., 170°C., Gas Mark 3) and bake for 30–35 minutes or until the custard has set firm.

Serve warm or cold with cream.

Fruit pies

Home baked pies are a very special treat. Choose the pastry to suit the pie. Plain or sweet shortcrust for speed, and a flaky or puff pastry for a crisp, light crust. Home made pies can be baked all year round, using fresh fruit in season or using bottled, canned or frozen fruit for the filling. Serve pies hot with vanilla ice cream or cold with cream.

Fruit fillings for pies

Various fruits can be used for deep dish pies. The quantity of filling and pastry required for the various sized pie dishes are as follows:

4 oz. (100 g.) pastry	1 lb. (½ kg.) fruit	1-pint (¾-litre) pie dish serves 4
6 oz. (175 g.) pastry	1½ lb. (¾ kg.) fruit	1½-pint (1-litre) pie dish serves 4–6
8 oz. (225 g.) pastry	2 lb. (1 kg.) fruit	2-pint (1¼-litre) pie dish serves 6

Apple: Use tart cooking apples. Peel, core and slice the apples and place in layers with 4–6 oz. (100–175 g.) castor sugar. Add 2 good pieces of pared lemon rind for flavour and 1–2 tablespoons water. Equal quantities of apples and stoned, halved plums are very good.

Rhubarb: Wash and cut sticks of rhubarb into 1-inch (2½-cm.) lengths. Sweeten with 4–6 oz. (100–175 g.) brown sugar and flavour with grated orange rind. Add orange juice. Garden rhubarb is also excellent mixed with fresh raspberries or strawberries and should be sweetened with castor sugar.

Gooseberries: Use the hard green gooseberries. Top and tail the berries and place in layers with 4–6 oz. (100–175 g.) castor sugar. Add 1–2 tablespoons water.

Apricots: Use firm, ripe dessert apricots, halve and remove stones. Add 4–6 oz. (100–175 g.) castor sugar or brown sugar to sweeten. Squeeze over lemon juice instead of water.

Eight tips for perfect pies

1. Make the pastry in advance and chill for at least 30 minutes before rolling out to cover the pie. A relaxed cool pastry will shrink less in the oven heat.
2. When filling the pie, start and finish with a layer of fruit as sugar should never lie next to the pastry. Sugar makes a pastry top soft and sticky underneath.
3. The fruit filling should rise into a mound above the pie dish rim to hold up the crust. Where a soft bottled or canned fruit is used, use a pie funnel to help hold up the pastry.
4. Only use a small amount of water with the fruit for the pie fillings. Fruit juices will supply the extra juice. Where bottled or canned fruit is used, drain away the juices and add only 2–3 tablespoons to the pie dish.
5. When trimming the edges of a pie covered with pastry, hold the knife at a slant so that the pastry is a little wider at the top than at the edge of the pie dish. This allows for shrinkage during baking.
6. Use a baking sheet under pie plates and pie dishes to help spread the heat and cook the bottom pastry evenly.
7. Bake pies in a hot oven to set the pastry. The richer the pastry the hotter the oven is the general rule. Once the pastry has browned and is set, then lower the heat for the filling to cook.
8. Pies can be glazed with milk, with egg and milk which gives a golden crust, or only egg which browns best of all. Dessert pies are often enhanced if a little lightly mixed egg white is brushed over the baked pastry top. Dredge with castor sugar and return to the oven. Allow the sugar topping to bake crisp.

Dutch apple pie

This is the method for a shallow plate pie – a pie which is lined and covered with pastry. Spices, particularly cinnamon, go well with apples. To make a spicy pastry for this pie, add 1 level teaspoon ground cinnamon to the flour when mixing.

Serves 4–6

12 oz./350 g. sweet shortcrust pastry (page 11)	2 oz./50 g. soft brown sugar
castor or icing sugar	½ level teaspoon ground cinnamon
for the filling:	½ oz./15 g. butter
1½ lb./¾ kg. cooking apples	*to glaze:*
2 oz./50 g. sultanas	egg and milk

Divide the pastry into 2 portions, making one slightly larger than the other. Set the larger piece aside for the top of the pie. Roll the smaller of the two out to a circle large enough to line a 9-inch (23-cm.) shallow pie plate. Well butter the plate and line with the pastry.

Peel, quarter, core and slice the apples. Mix together the sultanas, soft brown sugar and cinnamon in a basin. Arrange layers of apple slices, and mixed sultanas and spiced sugar in the lined pie dish. Add a few dots of butter between the layers and finish off with a neatly arranged layer of apples. Damp the edges of the pastry rim.

Roll out the remaining pastry to make the pie top. Cut slits in the pastry and cover the pie. Seal the edges and trim off the surplus pastry from around the sides. Brush the pie with egg and milk to glaze. Place above centre in a hot oven (400°F., 200°C., Gas Mark 6) and bake for 20 minutes. Lower the heat to moderate (350°F., 180°C., Gas Mark 4) and bake for 45–50 minutes or until the pastry is golden and the apples are tender.

Serve warm, sprinkled with castor or icing sugar.
Advance preparation: Assemble pie. Put to bake when required.

Raspberry and redcurrant pie

The method here is for a deep dish pie – that is fruit baked in a pie dish with a pastry top. Deep pie dishes are never lined with pastry. The method is the same for any fruits, only the length of baking time may vary.

Serves 4

1 lb./½ kg. raspberries	6 oz./175 g. flaky pastry
8 oz./225 g. redcurrants	*to glaze:*
4 oz./100 g. castor sugar	egg and milk
2 tablespoons water	

Hull the raspberries. Rinse the redcurrants and, using a fork, strip the berries from the stem. Place half the fruit in a 1½-pint (1-litre) pie dish. Sprinkle with the sugar and add remaining fruit. Spoon over the water.

On a floured working surface, roll the pastry out to a shape about 1 inch (2½ cm.) larger than the pie dish all round. Place the pie dish on the pastry and using it as a guide, cut a top for the pie. Reserve the pastry strips for the pie rim.

Grease the rim of the pie dish and place the pastry strips on it. Trim them so that they fit neatly and there is no overlap. Damp the pastry border and cover the pie with the pastry lid. Press gently round the edge to seal them together. Trim round the edge with a sharp knife.

Flake or knock up the pastry edge, using a blade of a knife held horizontal with the pie. This seals the edges. Then flute the edges attractively with the back of the knife. Brush the pie with a little mixed egg and milk. Make a neat hole in the centre to allow the steam to escape. Decorate the pie with any pastry trimmings.

Place the pie on a baking tray and put on the shelf above centre in a hot oven (400°F., 200°C., Gas Mark 6) and bake for 20 minutes. Lower heat to moderate (350°F., 180°C., Gas Mark 4) and bake for a further 15–20 minutes – for soft fruits. For hard or stoned fruits allow 30 minutes.

Advance preparation: Assemble pie. Put to bake when required.

Steamed puddings

Steamed sponge and suet puddings are winter fare. Use foil pudding basins if there are no china or ovenproof glass ones to spare in the kitchen. Once the mixture is put to cook, they require little more attention. Check the pan occasionally and top up with boiling water, when necessary.

Notes on steaming puddings

1. Puddings need room to rise. Cover the top with double thickness greaseproof paper and fold in a pleat across the centre to allow for expansion. Tie the paper tightly with string, then cover with an extra layer of kitchen foil. It is a good idea to make a string handle over the basin so that it is easier to lift out the hot pudding.
2. If you have no steamer, you can cook the pudding in a deep saucepan, standing the pudding basin on an upturned saucer. Allow the boiling water to come one third up the sides of the basin.
3. Keep the water boiling briskly and steadily all the time. Add more water as required and make sure it is boiling.
4. To turn the pudding out cleanly, run a knife round the top edge. Put a warmed serving dish over the top, then quickly turn the basin over and lift it off.
5. Steamed puddings can be made in advance. They should be left in the basin after steaming and reheated over simmering water when required. Allow 20–30 minutes for the pudding to heat through.

Steamed chocolate sponge

A light, chocolate sponge mixture which can also be served with a vanilla or coffee flavoured custard.

Serves 4–6

3 oz./75 g. self-raising flour	icing sugar
1 oz./25 g. cocoa powder	*for the chocolate sauce:*
pinch salt	2 oz./50 g. plain chocolate
3 oz./75 g. butter or margarine	¼ pint/1½ dl. hot black coffee
3 oz./75 g. castor sugar	1 teacupful milk
1 large egg	2 rounded teaspoons cornflour
3–4 drops vanilla essence	sugar to taste
1–2 tablespoons milk	

Sift the flour, cocoa powder and salt on to a square of paper and set aside. Cream the butter and sugar until light. Lightly mix the egg and vanilla essence and gradually beat into the creamed mixture. Using a metal spoon, fold in the sifted dry ingredients. Add sufficient milk to make a medium soft consistency.

Well grease a 1½-pint (1-litre) pudding basin and spoon in the mixture. Cover with double thickness, greased greaseproof paper and tie securely. Steam briskly for 1½–2 hours.

Towards the end of the cooking time, prepare the sauce. Place the chocolate, broken in pieces, in a saucepan with the hot coffee. Stir until the chocolate has melted. Blend the milk with the cornflour and stir into the saucepan. Bring up to the boil, stirring all the time, until thickened; add sugar to taste.

Turn out the pudding, dust the top with icing sugar and serve hot with the chocolate sauce.

Steamed jam pudding

The addition of fresh breadcrumbs to a suet pudding mixture always gives a lighter texture to the finished result. If the breadcrumbs are omitted use 8 oz. (225 g.) flour.

Serves 6

6 oz./175 g. self-raising flour	milk
1 level teaspoon baking powder	1 tablespoon red jam
pinch salt	*for the jam sauce:*
3 oz./75 g. fresh white	2–3 tablespoons red jam
breadcrumbs	2 level teaspoons cornflour
4 oz./100 g. shredded beef suet	$\frac{1}{4}$ pint/1$\frac{1}{2}$ dl. water
4 oz./100 g. castor sugar	juice $\frac{1}{2}$ lemon
1 egg	

Sift the flour, baking powder and salt into a mixing basin. Add the breadcrumbs, suet and sugar and mix well. Lightly mix the egg and stir into the dry ingredients, along with sufficient milk to make a soft dropping consistency. Stir the ingredients thoroughly to mix.

Place the tablespoon of red jam in the base of a well buttered 1$\frac{1}{2}$–2-pint (1–1$\frac{1}{4}$-litre) pudding basin. Spoon in the pudding mixture, this should no more than two-thirds fill the basin. Cover with a double thickness of greased greaseproof paper, fold in a pleat to allow the pudding to rise. Tie tightly with string. Either put the pudding in a steamer over a saucepan half filled with simmering water, or place the basin on an upturned saucer in a saucepan and fill the pan with boiling water two-thirds up the sides of the basin. Either way, cover with a tightly fitting lid and steam for 2–2$\frac{1}{2}$ hours. Top up the pan with extra *boiling* water as required.

Towards the end of the cooking time, prepare the sauce. Measure the jam into a saucepan. Blend the cornflour with the water. Add to the pan along with the lemon juice. Stir over low heat to blend, then bring up to the boil. Simmer for 2–3 minutes until thick and syrupy.

Remove the pudding from the steamer, loosen the sides and turn out on to a hot serving dish. Serve with the jam sauce.
Advance preparation: If prepared in advance, draw the saucepan of water off the heat. Keep the pudding hot in the basin over the water. Turn out when ready to serve.

Guards pudding

This lovely old pudding could quickly become a firm favourite with the family. The mixture, flavoured and lightly coloured pink with the addition of raspberry jam, turns out a rich brown colour after steaming. Serve it hot with raspberry jam sauce.

Serves 6

6 oz./175 g. plain flour	milk to mix
$\frac{1}{2}$ level teaspoon bicarbonate of soda	*for the raspberry jam sauce:*
4 oz./100 g. butter or margarine	2 good tablespoons raspberry jam
4 oz./100 g. castor sugar	2 tablespoons castor sugar
2 eggs	2 tablespoons water
2 good tablespoons raspberry jam	juice 1 lemon

Sift together the flour and bicarbonate of soda. Cream the butter and sugar until light. Lightly mix the eggs and beat into the creamed mixture a little at a time. Beat in the raspberry jam and then fold in the flour, adding sufficient milk to make a medium soft consistency.

Turn the mixture into a well buttered 2-pint (1–1$\frac{1}{4}$-litre) pudding basin. Cover with double thickness greaseproof paper or foil and tie tightly. Steam briskly for 2 hours. Turn out and serve with raspberry jam sauce.

Sieve the raspberry jam for the sauce into a saucepan. Add the castor sugar, water and the lemon juice. Stir over the heat until the sugar has dissolved. Then bring up to the boil and simmer for 1–2 minutes. Cool for a moment before serving.

Marmalade pudding

Soft brown sugar and marmalade give this pudding a delicious flavour.

Serves 4

2 oz./50 g. self-raising flour	1–2 tablespoons milk
pinch salt	*for the marmalade sauce:*
1 level teaspoon baking powder	2 level teaspoons cornflour
2 oz./50 g. fresh white breadcrumbs	$\frac{1}{4}$ pint/1$\frac{1}{2}$ dl. water
2 oz./50 g. shredded beef suet	juice $\frac{1}{2}$ lemon
2 oz./50 g. soft brown sugar	2 heaped tablespoons marmalade
3 good tablespoons marmalade	sugar
1 egg	

Sift the flour, salt and baking powder into a bowl. Stir in the breadcrumbs, suet and sugar. Add 2 tablespoons marmalade and the lightly mixed egg. Stir the mixture thoroughly for about $\frac{1}{2}$ minute. Add milk as required to produce a medium dropping consistency.

Well grease a 1$\frac{1}{2}$-pint (1-litre) pudding basin and put in the remaining tablespoon of marmalade. Turn the pudding mixture into the basin and spread evenly. Cover with double thickness, greased greaseproof paper and tie securely. Steam briskly for 2 hours.

Meanwhile, prepare the marmalade sauce. Blend the cornflour and the water in a saucepan. Add the lemon juice and marmalade. Stir constantly over the heat until the mixture has thickened and is boiling. Taste and add a little sugar if necessary.

Turn out the pudding and serve hot with the marmalade sauce.

Lemon toffee pudding

The creamed butter and sugar form a toffee top to this pudding. When cooked, the lemon in the centre will be quite soft and can be eaten.

Serves 6

3 oz./75 g. butter	6 oz./175 g. shredded beef suet
3 oz./75 g. soft brown sugar	3 oz./75 g. castor sugar
for the pudding:	$\frac{1}{2}$–$\frac{3}{4}$ pint/3–4$\frac{1}{2}$ dl. milk
12 oz./350 g. self-raising flour	1 small lemon
1 level teaspoon salt	little soft brown sugar

Beat the butter and soft brown sugar until creamy. Spoon into the base of a well buttered 2-pint (1¼-litre) pudding basin. Set aside while preparing the pudding.

Sift the flour and salt into a mixing basin. Add the suet and the sugar. Stir in sufficient milk to make a medium soft consistency.

Put a large spoonful of the mixture into the pudding basin over the creamed sugar mixture. Peel and cut both ends off the lemon and dip the cut ends in soft brown sugar. Put it into the centre of the pudding and cover with the remaining mixture.

Cover the basin with double thickness, greased greaseproof paper and tie tightly. Steam briskly for 2 hours.

Turn out and serve with cream.

Tips on cooking and storing Christmas puddings

1. Christmas puddings need 6–8 hours total steaming to bring out the full flavour and to produce the rich, dark colour. The first steaming should last for at least 4 hours. Then cool, re-cover and store.

2. Before steaming, the pudding should be covered with a double thickness of greased, greaseproof paper and then with a pudding cloth. Keep old table napkins for this. Tie them over the basin with string, then pull out the opposite corners and tie across the top to make a handle.

3. After the first cooking, cool the pudding thoroughly, then re-cover with fresh paper (not greased) and store in a cool, dark place. Do not cover with airtight foil or any similar cover because moulds may develop.

4. If the pudding is to be kept from one year to the next, put on a fresh paper cover every 3 months. For a really super pudding, pour over a spoonful of whisky, rum or brandy two or three times during the year.

5. Before the final steaming, re-cover the pudding with greased paper and a pudding cloth. Then steam briskly for 2–3 hours to ensure that you get a really delicious, tender-textured pudding.

Christmas pudding 1

Mixing is an important part of the Christmas pudding and should be done very thoroughly. Let everybody in the house have a stir.

Serves 6 – makes 1 (1½-lb./700-g.) pudding

4 oz./100 g. self-raising flour	4 oz./100 g. sultanas
½ level teaspoon ground mixed spice	4 oz./100 g. seedless or stoned raisins, snipped
½ level teaspoon ground nutmeg	2 oz./50 g. chopped candied peel
pinch salt	
3 oz./75 g. fresh white breadcrumbs	2 eggs
3 oz./75 g. shredded beef suet	2 teaspoons treacle
4 oz./100 g. soft brown sugar	4 tablespoons milk, brown ale or stout
1 small apple or carrot	1–2 tablespoons brandy or rum

Sift the flour, mixed spice, nutmeg and salt into a large basin. Add the breadcrumbs, suet and sugar. Peel and grate the apple or carrot and add to the mixture with the dried fruit and candied peel. Lightly mix the eggs and treacle and stir into the mixture, adding the milk, ale or stout. Ale gives the best flavour. Mix well for 5–10 minutes.

Spoon the mixture into a well buttered 2-pint (1¼-litre) basin. The mixture should three quarters fill the basin. Cover with buttered papers and a pudding cloth and tie securely. Cover and steam gently for 4 hours. Allow the cooked pudding to cool. When cold, remove the cloth and papers and pour over 1–2 tablespoons brandy or rum. Re-cover with fresh ungreased papers and store in a cool place but not airtight.

On Christmas morning, re-cover with greased papers and steam briskly for 2 hours. This ensures a light texture and remember that the pudding will be darker after the second steaming. Turn out on to a hot plate and serve.

Christmas pudding 2

A mixture of flour and breadcrumbs gives lightness to rich steamed puddings, this recipe uses only breadcrumbs and makes a pudding with a very light texture.

Serves 8 – makes 1 (2-lb./900-g.) pudding

6 oz./175 g. fresh white breadcrumbs	4 oz./100 g. seedless raisins
6 oz./175 g. soft brown sugar	2 oz./50 g. chopped mixed peel
6 oz./175 g. shredded beef suet	pinch salt
8 oz./225 g. currants	$\frac{1}{2}$ level teaspoon mixed spice
8 oz./225 g. sultanas	3 eggs
	$\frac{1}{4}$–$\frac{1}{2}$ pint/1$\frac{1}{2}$–3 dl. Guinness

Measure all the dry ingredients into a large mixing basin. Add the lightly mixed eggs and the Guinness and mix to a medium soft consistency – quantity of Guinness required will depend on the freshness of the breadcrumbs. Dry breadcrumbs will absorb more than fresh. Allow the mixture to stand overnight. Check consistency, adding more Guinness if needed.

Spoon into a well buttered 2-pint (1$\frac{1}{4}$-litre) pudding basin. Cover with buttered, double thickness greaseproof paper – buttered side inwards, fold in a pleat to allow pudding to rise and tie securely. Steam gently for 5 hours. When the pudding is cool, remove damp papers and re-cover with fresh ungreased papers. Store in a cool place but not airtight.

To serve, re-cover with buttered papers and steam briskly for 2 hours.

Sauces for the Christmas pudding

Brandy butter: Cream together 3 oz. (75 g.) butter and 6 oz. (175 g.) sieved icing sugar until very light and creamy. Slowly beat in 1–2 tablespoons brandy.

Spoon into a serving dish and chill until ready to serve.

Sherry cream sauce: In a small saucepan over low heat, melt 1 oz. (25 g.) butter. Stir in 1 tablespoon flour and cook gently for 1 minute. Gradually stir in $\frac{1}{2}$ pint (3 dl.) single cream. Bring up to the boil, stirring all the time to get a smooth sauce. Draw off the heat and stir in 1 oz. (25 g.) castor sugar and 2 tablespoons sherry. Serve hot.

Rum sauce: In a small saucepan, cream together 2 oz. (50 g.) butter and 2 oz. (50 g.) castor sugar. Place over low heat to melt and bring up to the boil. Draw the pan off the heat immediately and stir in 3 tablespoons rum. Serve hot.

Rum butter: Cream 4 oz. (100 g.) butter and 4 oz. (100 g.) soft brown sugar until soft and light. Gradually beat in 4 tablespoons rum. Beat in $\frac{1}{4}$ teaspoon grated lemon rind, $\frac{1}{4}$ teaspoon ground cinnamon and $\frac{1}{4}$ teaspoon ground nutmeg. Press the mixture into a shallow pot and cover with a lid of kitchen foil. Chill until ready to serve. Cut into cubes and serve.

Custard sauce: Measure 2 tablespoons custard powder into small basin. Mix to a smooth paste with a little milk taken from $\frac{1}{2}$ pint (3 dl.). Place the remaining milk in a saucepan and bring almost to the boil. Stir into the custard blend, mix well and return the mixture to the saucepan. Bring up to the boil, stirring all the time. Add 2 oz. (50 g.) castor sugar to sweeten and draw off the heat. Serve hot.

Cakes for an occasion

Cake making is an art. It is a branch of cooking that demands care and attention and one that will result in much appreciation from the family or friends when entertaining. Cakes vary and can be served at tea time or for a coffee morning; there are also many of a more fragile nature, filled with fruit and cream, which make excellent desserts for entertaining. The average busy cook is more likely to bake a cake for a particular occasion and for this purpose the cake recipes given in this chapter have been carefully selected.

Cake making equipment

Baking requires tins and invariably one of a particular size and shape. Any cook who wishes to bake an interesting variety of cakes must be prepared to buy some good basic equipment. Buy good, well made tins that will wear for years. After using, clean them properly and dry them, preferably somewhere warm, before storing them away.

Deep round cake tins: These are the kind used for fruit cakes and for richer, plain cake mixtures. They can vary in diameter from 6–11 inches (15–28½ cm.) and from 3–4 inches (7½–10 cm.) deep. The two most useful tins to have are the 8 and 9-inch (20 and 23-cm.) sizes.

Because cakes baked in this type of tin usually require long slow cooking, it is important to line the tin to protect the cake. For the bottom, put the tin on a double thickness of greaseproof paper, mark round and then cut to give a circle of paper the size of the tin. For the sides, cut a double strip of greaseproof paper about 2 inches (5 cm.) higher than the depth of the tin and long enough to go round the sides and overlap about 1 inch (2½ cm.). Fold up a margin of about 1 inch (2½ cm.) deep all along the folded edge of the paper. Cut this folded margin at intervals with scissors, in a sloping direction. Well grease the tin and the papers. Place the strip of paper inside the tin, with the cut edge lying inwards and flat around the bottom. The lining should stand about 1 inch (2½ cm.) above the rim of the tin. Put the double round of greaseproof paper in the bottom to cover the whole surface.

Shallow sponge cake tins: Used for Victoria sandwich layers, for whisked sponges and genoese sponge layers. Also often used for meringue mixtures that are baked in layers for filling. The standard sizes are 6½, 7½, 8½ inches (16, 19, 21 cm.), all with straight sides of about 1 inch (2½ cm.) deep. Always have a pair of sponge cake tins. Most sandwich or sponge cake mixtures are baked in layers. Ideally, cut rounds of greaseproof paper to line the base in the same way as for the deep cake tins. On the other hand, it is more economical to cut squares of paper. Cut several at a time and keep them handy. Remember, as long as two thirds of the base of a round tin is covered, the cake will lift out easily.

Loaf tins: These are ideal for fruit breads, tea breads and for gingerbread or honey cake mixtures. Loaf tins come in 2 sizes – a small tin of approximately 7 × 3 × 2 inches (18 × 7½ × 5 cm.) and a larger tin of approximately 9 × 5 × 3 inches (23 × 13 × 7½ cm.). These tins are an ideal shape for afternoon tea breads and should not be confused with bread tins, which are deeper and different in shape. When lining loaf tins, remember that it is not necessary to line the 2 long sides. The baked cake or bread can easily be loosened along this edge with a palette knife. Cut a strip of greaseproof paper the width of the base of the tin and long enough to cover the base and the two opposite ends. Grease the tin, grease the paper and place it in the tin. If a slight overlap is allowed for, this sometimes assists in lifting out the baked bread or cake.

Shallow square or oblong tins: This type of tin is invaluable for baking the plainer, often spicy cakes such as gingerbread or honey cake, or cakes which are baked in one batch and then cut into squares for serving. The larger oblong tins are approximately 11 × 7 × 1 inch (28½ × 18 × 2½ cm.) and the smaller are 7½ inches (19 cm.) square. The same principle of lining tins applies to both these tins. Cover the base and the two opposite ends.

Swiss roll tins: These very shallow, oblong tins are designed specifically for baking Swiss rolls. They can also be used as baking trays and are used for the bar cookies or rich type of cake mixture that is baked as a whole and cut into pieces before serving. The smaller 11 × 7-inch (28½ × 18-cm.) tin is the traditional Swiss roll size and the larger 13 × 9-inch (33½ × 23-cm.) tin, although not strictly speaking a Swiss roll tin, is often used as such.

Clip sided pans: These have recently been introduced to this country from the Continent, where they are used a great deal. They are ideal for cheesecake or for cakes with baked fruit topping which cannot be turned out. The clip side of the tin can be opened and the baked cake remains standing on the movable base. The only British manufactured one is 8½ inches (21 cm.) in diameter, often sold with a set of three bases, one plain, one fluted and one tube. There are imported tins of 9–10 inches (23–26 cm.) in diameter, which are excellent for large cakes, particularly cheesecakes.

Before you start – be well organised

The temperature of ingredients is important when you mix a cake. Fat which is too cold will not cream easily. Cold eggs will quickly curdle when added to a creamed mixture. To get over this difficulty, bring the fat and eggs out of the refrigerator or cold larder some time in advance. While preparing other ingredients, fill the mixing bowl to be used with warm water and place the eggs in to warm them up. By the time everything else is ready, the eggs will be just the right temperature for cracking and whisking, and the bowl pleasantly warm for using.

Prepare the cake tins and set the oven to the right temperature, allowing it at least 15 minutes to heat up. Check that the shelves are at the correct height. Small cakes and sponge layers can be baked on the second or third shelf from the top, but large cakes need the centre of the oven for even baking.

Any additional ingredients, such as fruits, nuts, cherries or peel, should be prepared ready for use. Fruit should be cleaned, dried and picked over. Cherries or other glacé fruits need to be rinsed, dried and cut up; nuts are usually blanched and chopped.

Walnut layer cake

Freshen the walnuts by placing them in a moderate oven for a few minutes before using them. If preferred, this cake can be filled and covered with smooth American frosting (page 184).

Makes one 7½-inch (19-cm.) layer cake

8 oz./225 g. self-raising flour	buttercream (page 185)
pinch salt	*for the white icing:*
3 oz./75 g. walnuts, shelled	1 oz./25 g. castor sugar
4 oz./100 g. butter	2 tablespoons water
6 oz./175 g. castor sugar	8 oz./225 g. icing sugar
3 eggs	*to decorate:*
½ teaspoon vanilla essence	few walnut halves
1–2 tablespoons milk	

Sift together the flour and salt. Chop the walnuts very finely and add to the flour. Cream the butter and sugar very thoroughly until soft and light. Lightly mix the eggs and vanilla essence. Gradually beat the egg into the creamed mixture. Beat well after each addition of egg and add a little of the sieved flour, if necessary, with the last few additions of egg. Using a metal spoon, fold in the remaining flour, half at a time. Add sufficient milk to make a medium soft consistency.

Divide the mixture equally between 2 greased and lined 7½-inch (19-cm.) sponge flan tins and spread evenly. Place in the centre of a moderate oven (350°F., 180°C., Gas Mark 4) and bake for 25–30 minutes. Allow the cakes to cool, then sandwich with the buttercream, using half the recipe quantity.

Measure the sugar and water for the icing into a saucepan. Stir over low heat to dissolve the sugar and make a sugar syrup. Sieve the icing sugar into a basin. Bring the sugar syrup to the boil, draw off the heat and pour into the centre of the sieved icing sugar. Stir to blend, then beat thoroughly to mix. Pour the icing on top of the cake. Spread quickly and evenly over the top and sides of the cake. Press the walnut halves around the edges to decorate and leave untouched until the icing has set.

Iced genoese sponge

This genoese sponge mixture with the unusual feather icing makes an attractive cake for afternoon tea. The same recipe, split and filled with fresh fruit and cream could be served as a dessert.

Makes 8 portions

2 eggs	7 oz./200 g. icing sugar, sifted
3 oz./75 g. castor sugar	few drops food colouring
2½ oz./65 g. plain flour	*to decorate:*
1 oz./25 g. butter, melted	chopped walnuts or toasted
for the icing:	coconut
2 level tablespoons castor sugar	1 walnut half
2 tablespoons water	

Well butter an 8-inch (20-cm.) cake tin and sprinkle with a mixture of equal quantities flour and sugar – 1 tablespoon of each should be sufficient. Shake the mixture over the tin to coat evenly, then tap out the surplus.

Crack the eggs into a medium sized bowl and add the sugar. Place the bowl over a saucepan half filled with hot water and beat the mixture until thick and light – takes about 8–10 minutes. Remove the bowl from the heat and whisk for a further few moments until cool.

Sift the flour over the surface and, using a metal spoon, carefully fold the flour into the mixture. When the flour is half folded in, add the melted butter and blend ingredients gently until evenly mixed. Pour into the prepared tin and spread evenly. Place in the centre of a moderately hot oven (375°F., 190°C., Gas Mark 5) and bake for 18–20 minutes. Turn out on to a rack and allow to cool.

The glacé icing used to coat this sponge is mixed with a sugar syrup instead of water, which gives it more body. Dissolve the castor sugar in the water and bring up to the boil, then draw off the heat. Sieve the icing sugar into a basin and add sufficient of the sugar syrup to make a coating consistency. Take a teaspoon of the icing and add a few drops food colouring to make a good

deep colour. Adjust the consistency with a few drops of water or a little sieved icing sugar, if necessary. Put this into a small paper piping bag. Have ready a palette knife, scissors and a skewer.

Place the sponge to be iced on an upturned plate and spoon out the plain icing quickly on to the top of the cake. Using the palette knife, spread quickly all over the top and over to the edges of the cake. Snip the end of the piping bag with the scissors and pipe parallel lines about 1 inch (2½ cm.) apart across the cake in the contrasting colour. While the icing is still wet, draw the point of the skewer through the icing several times, tapering to a point. Spread the sides of the cake with the finely chopped walnuts or toasted coconut. Decorate the top at the tapered point of the icing with a walnut half.

Allow the icing to set before serving.

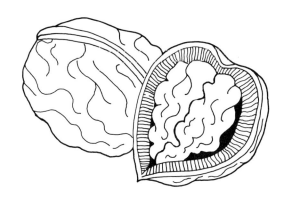

Almond cake

This is a pretty cake to look at when baked in a fluted ring mould. It tastes just as good baked in an 8-inch (20-cm.) round, deep cake tin. The ground almonds keep the mixture moist and the cake will store well for up to 2 weeks.

Makes 8–12 slices

5 oz./150 g. self-raising flour	4 large eggs
pinch salt	few drops almond essence
3 oz./75 g. ground almonds	*to decorate:*
8 oz./225 g. butter	icing sugar
8 oz./225 g. castor sugar	

Sieve the flour and salt on to a plate. Add the ground almonds and set aside. Cream the butter and sugar together until very pale and light. Lightly mix the eggs and almond essence. Gradually beat the egg into the creamed mixture, a little at a time. Beat each addition in well before adding the next. Add a little of the sieved flour mixture along with the last few additions of egg, if necessary. Using a metal spoon, fold in the remaining flour mixture and blend evenly.

Spoon the mixture into a well buttered 3½-pint (1½-litre) gugelhupf tin or fluted ring mould. Place in the centre of a preheated, moderate oven (350°F., 180°C., Gas Mark 4) and bake for 1–1¼ hours. Allow the cake to cool in the tin for 5 minutes, then turn out and leave until cold.

Dust lavishly with icing sugar before serving.

Swiss roll

Accurate measurements are important in a Swiss roll recipe. So that the mixture is pliable, there should be a higher weight of sugar than flour. When lining a Swiss roll tin, cut the grease-proof wide enough to cover the base of the tin and long enough to extend up the two short ends of the tin.

Makes 6 slices

2 oz./50 g. plain flour	1–2 tablespoons jam
2 large eggs	*to decorate:*
2½ oz./65 g. castor sugar	castor sugar

Fill a mixing bowl with *hot* water and allow to stand for about 5 minutes. Sift the flour on to a square of greaseproof paper twice to ensure lightness. Empty out and dry the mixing bowl. Crack the eggs into the warm bowl and add the sugar. Whisk the mixture until it is light and leaves a trail – when a little mixture is allowed to fall from the whisk back into the bowl, it rests on the surface of the mixture for a moment before it disappears.

Sift the flour over the surface and then, using the edge of a metal spoon, fold gently but thoroughly into the mixture. Spread the mixture evenly in a greased and lined 8 × 12-inch (20 × 31-cm.) shallow Swiss roll tin. Place at once above centre in a hot oven (425°F., 220°C., Gas Mark 7) and bake for 7 minutes. When cooked, the sponge should feel springy to the touch.

Turn the sponge out on to a lightly sugared cloth. Carefully strip away the lining paper. Allow to cool for 3–4 minutes then, using a sharp knife, trim off the crisp edges from the long sides. If these are left on, the sponge tends to crack when rolling up. Spread warm jam over the surface of the warm sponge and roll up. This is easily done by starting at the end farthest away from you, tuck the end of the warm Swiss roll in fairly closely to start and then draw the roll towards you, using the cloth underneath to help.

Leave to cool then dust generously with castor sugar. Once cold, trim away a thin slice from each end to present a neat appearance before serving.

Fresh strawberry cake

This is a good example of a Victoria sandwich layer being used to make a cake that is attractive and not necessarily the traditional finish. The filling of strawberries makes a pleasant moist cake that is delicious for tea and excellent for a picnic.

Cuts into 6–8 pieces

4 oz./100 g. self-raising flour	*for the filling:*
pinch salt	1 lb./½ kg. fresh strawberries
4 oz./100 g. butter	2 oz./50 g. castor sugar
4 oz./100 g. castor sugar	*to decorate:*
2 eggs	icing sugar
few drops vanilla essence	

Sift the flour and salt on to a plate and set aside. Cream together the butter and sugar until very light and creamy. The initial creaming in a mixture of this kind is very important and the creaming process should take about 10 minutes. Lightly mix the eggs and vanilla essence. Gradually beat the egg into the creamed mixture, a little at a time. Beat each addition in well before adding the next. If necessary, add a little of the flour along with the last few additions of egg. Using a metal spoon, fold the sifted flour into the mixture, half at a time.

Spoon the mixture into one greased and lined 8½-inch (21-cm.) sponge layer tin and spread evenly. Place in the centre of a pre-heated moderate oven (325°F., 170°C., Gas Mark 3) and bake for 45 minutes. Allow the baked cake to cool in the tin for 5 minutes, then turn out and leave until cold.

Wash and dry the strawberries and remove the husks. Place together in a basin and mash with a fork. Add the sugar. Slice the sponge cake in half and spoon the mashed strawberries over the base. Top with the remaining half and dust with icing sugar.

Gingerbread cake

This cake keeps well if stored in a covered tin or wrapped in foil.

Makes one 9-inch (23-cm.) cake

1 lb./450 g. plain flour	4 oz./100 g. (or 2 good
pinch salt	tablespoons) golden syrup
2 level teaspoons mixed spice	4 oz./100 g. (or 2 good
3 level teaspoons ground ginger	tablespoons) treacle
8 oz./225 g. castor sugar	8 oz./225 g. butter
6 oz./175 g. sultanas	1 egg
2 oz./50 g. crystallised ginger	1 level teaspoon bicarbonate of
4 oz./100 g. walnuts, chopped	soda
4 oz./100 g. cooking dates,	⅓ pint/2–2½ dl. milk
chopped coarsely	

Sift the flour, salt, mixed spice and ginger into a mixing basin. Add the castor sugar, sultanas, chopped ginger, nuts, dates and mix well.

Measure the syrup, treacle and butter into a small pan. Warm gently over a low heat until the syrup is soft and butter melted, but do not boil. Pour the heated mixture into the centre of the dry ingredients and add the egg. Stir the bicarbonate of soda into the milk and add at once to the mixture. Mix thoroughly and pour into a buttered and lined 9-inch (23-cm.) deep, round cake tin. Place in the centre of a moderate oven (325°F., 170°C., Gas Mark 3) and bake for 2 hours. Then lower to slow (300°F., 150°C., Gas Mark 2) and bake for a further 30 minutes. Allow to cool in the tin.

Chocolate layer cake

A chocolate layer cake is always popular. This recipe has a delicious flavour and makes a pleasantly moist cake.

Makes two 8¼-inch (21-cm.) layers

5 oz./150 g. self-raising flour	*for the frosting:*
1 oz./25 g. cocoa powder	3 oz./75 g. icing sugar
6 oz./175 g. butter	1 oz./25 g. cocoa powder
6 oz./175 g. soft brown sugar	1½ oz./40 g. butter
1 teaspoon vanilla essence	2 good tablespoons water
4 oz./125 g. plain chocolate	2 oz./50 g. castor sugar
3 tablespoons boiling water	¼ teaspoon vanilla essence
4 large eggs	

Sift the flour and cocoa powder on to a plate. Cream the butter, sugar and vanilla essence until soft. Break the chocolate into a small basin and add the 3 tablespoons of boiling water. Stir until the chocolate is melted and mixture blended. Beat the melted chocolate into the creamed butter and sugar. Separate the eggs, beating the yolks into the creamed mixture, one at a time, and placing the whites together in a basin. Gently fold in the sieved flour and then the stiffly beaten egg whites.

Spoon the mixture into 2 greased and lined shallow 8½-inch (21-cm.) sponge cake tins and spread evenly. Place in the centre of a moderate oven (350°F., 180°C., Gas Mark 4) and bake for 25–30 minutes, then turn out and allow to cool.

Sift the icing sugar and cocoa powder into a mixing basin. Measure the butter, water, sugar and vanilla essence into a saucepan. Place over low heat and, stirring gently over the heat, bring just up to the boil. Draw off the heat at once and pour into the centre of the sifted ingredients. Beat with a wooden spoon until the icing is smooth. At this stage, the frosting is fairly thin, but set aside, stirring occasionally, until the mixture has cooled and has become fairly thick. Use a little of the frosting to sandwich the cake layers, then pour the remainder on top of the cake and spread evenly over the surface, using a knife.

Jap cakes

Jap cakes are rather fragile in texture. They should be eaten with a fork since the buttercream filling makes them rather difficult to handle.

Makes 6 jap cakes

2 egg whites	few drops almond essence
4 oz./100 g. castor sugar	buttercream (page 185)
1 oz./25 g. ground almonds	*to decorate:*
1 oz./25 g. stale cake crumbs	1 oz./25 g. plain chocolate

Whisk the egg whites until stiff. Gradually whisk in 3 oz. (75 g.) of the castor sugar and beat to a stiff, glossy meringue. Mix together the remaining sugar, ground almonds and the cake crumbs. Using a metal spoon, gently fold these into the mixture with the almond essence.

Lightly grease 2 baking trays with cooking fat. Dust generously with flour and then tap the trays to get rid of the surplus flour. Using a 2-inch (5-cm.) plain round cutter, mark 6 circles on each tray – impress the cutter on to the surface leaving the mark of the ring. These are guide lines when piping the mixture.

Spoon the mixture into a large nylon piping bag, fitted with a ½-inch (1-cm.) plain nozzle. Pipe coils of the mixture, starting from the centre of each marked circle and working out to the edge. Keep within the marked circles. Place in the centre of a slow oven (300°F., 150°C., Gas Mark 2) and bake for about 20 minutes or until the jap cakes are crisp and dry. Tap the tray sharply to see if the cakes are loose. Remove from the tray and allow to cool.

Trim the circles of meringue with the same cutter used to mark the tin. Keep any trimmings for jap crumbs. Sandwich the circles of jap cake with buttercream, making the top a flat side. Spread the sides of each pair with buttercream and roll in the crushed jap crumbs. Melt the plain chocolate and, using a paper piping bag, pipe a button of melted chocolate in the centre of each. Keep the jap cakes in a cool place and allow several hours before serving.

Almond petits fours

Almond, ratafia or vanilla essence can be used to flavour these macaroon type biscuits. A little colouring can also be added to the mixture to give a variation.

Makes 2–3 dozen

5 oz./150 g. ground almonds	*to decorate:*
6 oz./175 g. castor sugar	glacé cherries
1½–2 egg whites	granulated sugar
few drops flavouring essence	

Measure the ground almonds, sugar and 1 egg white into a mixing basin. Beat with a wooden spoon to make a smooth, thick paste. Beat in the flavouring and add more egg white, but only sufficient to give a fairly thick paste, just soft enough to pipe. The amount of egg white required will depend on the size of eggs used.

Place the basin over a saucepan, half filled with hot water. Beat well until the mixture feels warm to the little finger. Remove from the heat. Spoon the mixture into a nylon piping bag, fitted with a rosette tube.

Pipe rosettes and other shapes on to sheets of plain greaseproof paper set on baking trays. Decorate with pieces of glacé cherry and sprinkle with granulated sugar. Place in the centre of a moderate oven (350°F., 180°C., Gas Mark 4) and bake for 15 minutes. Leave to cool on the paper before removing. Store in a tightly lidded tin.

American brownies

Brownies are squares of moist chocolate cake. They can be made with or without the walnuts added to the mixture. Use the unsweetened squares of American bitter chocolate if possible.

Makes 12 squares

4 oz./100 g. self-raising flour	2 eggs
pinch salt	½ teaspoon vanilla essence
2 oz./50 g. white cooking fat	2 oz./50 g. walnuts, coarsely
6 oz./175 g. castor sugar	chopped
1 tablespoon water	
2 oz./50 g. (2 squares)	
unsweetened chocolate	

Sift the flour and salt on to a plate and set aside. Measure the fat, sugar and water into a large saucepan. Place over moderate heat and bring just up to the boil, stirring to blend the ingredients. Draw off the heat and add the chocolate. Stir and beat well so that the chocolate melts. Allow to cool slightly.

Add the eggs, one at a time, and beat each one into the mixture thoroughly until the mixture is smooth and shiny. Stir in the vanilla essence and then add all the flour. Blend gently at first and then beat thoroughly to get a smooth mixture. Finally, stir in the walnuts.

Pour the mixture into a greased and lined 7 × 11-inch (18 × 28½-cm.) oblong baking tin. Place in the centre of a preheated, moderate oven (325°F., 170°C., Gas Mark 3) and bake for 20–30 minutes.

Cut in squares when cold and store in a tightly lidded tin.

Brandy snaps

Illustrated in colour on pages 152 and 153

Serve brandy snaps filled with cream for a dessert or without filling for an afternoon tea. Non-stick silicone paper used for lining the tins prevents them from sticking. Use the same sheet of paper for each batch.

Makes 2½ dozen

2 oz./50 g. plain flour	2 oz./50 g. butter
½ level teaspoon ground ginger	little grated lemon rind
2 oz./50 g. soft brown sugar	1 teaspoon lemon juice
1 heaped tablespoon (2 oz./50 g.) golden syrup	

Sift the flour and ground ginger on to a square of greaseproof paper. Put the sugar, golden syrup and butter in a saucepan. Stir over low heat to melt the butter and blend ingredients. Draw the pan off the heat and stir in the flour. Blend well and mix in the lemon rind and juice.

Line a baking tray with a sheet of silicone paper or oil the tray. Spoon on small teaspoonfuls of the mixture. Place on not more than six brandy snaps on one tray and keep well apart as the mixture spreads. Place in the centre of a moderately hot oven (375°F., 190°C., Gas Mark 5) and bake for 8–10 minutes.

Remove them from the heat and as soon as the mixture begins to firm up slightly, lift the snaps from the tray with a palette knife and wrap quickly around the greased handle of one or more wooden spoons. Continue with the next batch of brandy snaps. When crisp, slip the snaps off the spoon handles ready for the next ones.

Serve filled or unfilled. Whipped cream for filling should be piped into the centre of each one with the aid of a piping bag and rosette tube.

Advance preparation: Brandy snaps can be prepared several days in advance of serving and stored in an airtight tin. Do not fill with cream more than 1–2 hours before serving. The cream tends to soften the crisp attractive texture of the brandy snaps.

Petits fours glacé

This unusual recipe produces a light sponge cake with a very close texture. The texture is important because for petits fours glacé the sponge is cut into small shapes which must not crumble or break.

Makes 3 dozen

6 oz./175 g. plain flour	8 oz./225 g. butter
2 oz./50 g. cornflour	apricot glaze (page 183)
5 eggs	fondant icing (page 184)
pinch salt	cake decorations
9 oz./250 g. castor sugar	

Sift the flour and cornflour on to a square of paper and set aside. Crack the eggs into a large warmed basin, add the salt and sugar and whisk until the mixture is thick and light. This may take about 10 minutes. Once the mixture is thick, place the butter in a large saucepan and set over the heat to melt. Bring the butter up to the boil and immediately add the sifted flour mixture all at once. Draw the pan off the heat and whisk to blend the flour and butter. Add this to the beaten egg yolk mixture and, using a spatula or metal spoon, fold the ingredients thoroughly together to blend.

Pour into a buttered and lined shallow baking tin about 13 × 10 inches (33½ × 26 cm.) or a medium sized roasting tin. Spread the mixture evenly, particularly to the corners. Place in the centre of a hot oven (400°F., 200°C., Gas Mark 6) and bake for 25 minutes. When well risen and springy to the touch, remove the cake from the heat and turn over on to a flat board or clean working surface. Lift away the tin and replace on top of the cake with the base down and a light weight on top. This helps close the texture of the cake. Leave the cake until quite cold, then remove the tin and the paper lining.

Using a sharp knife, trim the sides of the cake evenly, then with pretty shaped cutters, stamp out pieces of cake as economically as possible. If no cutters are available, pretty shapes can also be cut using a knife. First cut the cake into strips, then cut across at an angle to make triangles or diamonds or straight across to make squares or oblongs.

Each cake must now be dipped into hot apricot glaze before icing. The hot glaze sets quickly on the cake, making a smooth surface and sealing in any crumbs that might otherwise spoil the smooth coating of fondant. Heat the apricot glaze in a saucepan and bring up to the boil. Draw off the heat and while the glaze is hot, spear each cake on to a fork and dip into the glaze to coat the top and sides. Place on a wire cooling tray and leave until the apricot glaze has cooled and is set firm.

Place the prepared fondant in a mixing basin and set over a saucepan half filled with hot water. Warm gently until the icing has softened and has a fairly thin coating consistency. Add a few drops of water if the fondant is very thick and a few drops of colouring if required. Keeping the mixture warm all the time you are working, spoon the icing over the cakes. Put a plate below the cooling tray so that any excess icing that runs off is not wasted. Coat all the cakes and then use any excess icing to pipe a decoration. Decorate the cakes with crystallised violets, rose leaves, angelica or glacé cherries. Leave until set firm before lifting off the tray.

Put the cakes in individual paper cases and serve.

Macaroon tarts

Crisp pastry shells with a little jam and a macaroon filling. These are always popular and keep well for several days. Store in an airtight tin so that the macaroon filling remains crisp.

Makes 12 tarts

4 oz./100 g. sweet shortcrust pastry (page 11)	2 egg whites
for the filling:	4 oz./100 g. castor sugar
1 tablespoon raspberry jam	4 oz./100 g. ground almonds
	few drops almond essence

On a lightly floured working surface, roll the pastry out thinly. Using a 2½-inch (6-cm.) plain round cutter, stamp out 12 circles and use these to line 12 tartlet tins. Place a little jam in the base of each tartlet.

Whisk the egg whites until thick. Add the sugar, a little at a time, and beat the meringue until stiff. Fold in the ground almonds and a few drops of almond essence. Dividing the mixture equally, spoon a rounded dessertspoonful of the mixture into each tartlet. Place in the centre of a moderate oven (350°F., 180°C., Gas Mark 4) and bake for 25 minutes.

Cool then store.

Chocolate truffle cakes

These cakes make use of the trimmings left over from a genoese sponge cake, particularly when making small petits fours. Otherwise trifle sponge cake crumbs could be used.

Makes 12 cakes

4 oz./100 g. stale sponge cake
  crumbs
4 oz./100 g. castor sugar
4 oz./100 g. ground almonds
2 tablespoons hot apricot jam
chopped walnuts or chocolate
  vermicelli

for the chocolate icing:
2 oz./50 g. plain chocolate
3 tablespoons water
4 oz./100 g. icing sugar, sieved
few drops vanilla essence

Rub the cake pieces through a coarse sieve to make crumbs. Add the sugar and ground almonds and enough hot apricot jam to bind the ingredients together. Divide the mixture into 12 equal portions, each about the size of a walnut. Shape each one into a round ball. Leave until quite cold and firm.

Cut or break up the chocolate for the icing into small pieces. Measure the water into a saucepan, set over the heat and bring up to the boil. Draw off the heat and add the chocolate. Stir until the chocolate has melted and the mixture is smooth. Add the icing sugar and a little vanilla essence and beat with a spoon to make a smooth icing. Dip the cakes one at a time in the warm icing. Lift out with a fork, drain for a moment and then roll in chopped walnuts or vermicelli. Place in paper cases and leave until set firm.

Honey cake

The best honey cake is made using a melted fat method, similar to a gingerbread. This recipe makes a moist, well flavoured cake which keeps well.

Cuts into 24 squares

7 oz./200 g. self-raising flour
pinch salt
5 oz./150 g. butter
4 oz./100 g. soft brown sugar
6 oz./175 g. clear honey

1 tablespoon water
2 eggs
to decorate:
flaked almonds

Sift the flour and salt on to a square of paper and set aside. Place the butter, soft brown sugar, honey and water into a saucepan. (To measure the honey, first weigh out the brown sugar and spread flat on the scale pan to form a bed of sugar. Add the necessary extra weights and then pour the honey into the scale pan. The sugar prevents it from sticking and they can both be tipped into the saucepan together.) Place the saucepan of ingredients over low heat and stir occasionally until the butter has melted and the ingredients are blended. Draw off the heat and allow to cool until the hand can be comfortably held against the sides of the pan.

Beat in the eggs, one at a time. Add the sifted flour all at once and beat very thoroughly to make a smooth mixture. Pour into a greased and lined oblong tin of approximately 11 × 7 inches ($28\frac{1}{2}$ × 18 cm.) or use a small roasting tin. Spread the mixture evenly and sprinkle with the flaked almonds. Place in the centre of a moderate oven (350°F., 180°C., Gas Mark 4) and bake for 30–35 minutes or until risen and firm to the touch. Remove the cake from the tin and leave until cold.

Cut into squares and store in an airtight tin.

Florentines

Florentines make an attractive addition to a buffet supper party or a picnic. They also make a pleasant gift. If you are at all nervous about florentines sticking to the baking tray, line each tray with a sheet of silicone paper first.

Makes 12 florentines

2 oz./50 g. castor sugar	2 oz./50 g. mixed preserved
2 oz./50 g. flaked almonds	fruits, finely chopped*
1 level tablespoon plain flour	2 oz./50 g. plain chocolate
1½ oz./40 g. butter	*glacé cherries, angelica and
1–2 tablespoons single cream	candied peel

Measure the sugar, almonds, flour, butter, cream and mixed fruits into a small saucepan. Stir over gentle heat until evenly blended, but *do not overheat*. Put about 6 teaspoons of the mixture on to each of two well greased baking trays. Flatten each heap out a little to help them bake in round shapes. Bake the florentines in batches. Place just above centre in a moderate oven (350°F., 180°C., Gas Mark 4) and bake for 10 minutes or until just set and golden brown. Allow to cool for 1–2 minutes then lift each one off the tray carefully with a knife. Leave until cold and crisp.

Beak the chocolate into a small basin. Place over a pan half filled with hot water. Stir until the chocolate is melted and smooth. Using a pastry brush or knife, coat the base of each florentine with the melted chocolate. Leave upside down until the chocolate has set.

Doughnuts without yeast

Soft sugary doughnuts are easy to make using this method. Make them in advance for a coffee morning and warm through before serving.

Makes 15–16 doughnuts

8 oz./225 g. plain flour	about 4 tablespoons milk
½ level teaspoon salt	oil for frying
1 level teaspoon baking powder	*for the cinnamon sugar:*
1½ oz./40 g. butter	½–1 level teaspoon cinnamon
2 oz./50 g. castor sugar	2 oz./50 g. castor sugar
1 egg	

Sift together the flour, salt and baking powder. Add the butter, cut in pieces, and rub into the mixture. Add the castor sugar, mix well and hollow out the centre. Mix the egg and milk and add to the ingredients all at once. Using a fork, mix to a rough dough in the basin, then turn out on to a lightly floured working surface and knead lightly to a dough.

Pat or roll out the dough to a thickness of about ¼ inch (½ cm.). Using a 2-inch (5-cm.) plain round cutter, stamp out as many rounds of the dough as possible – you should get about 15–16 circles. Using a smaller cutter, stamp out a small hole from the centre of each one.

Fry the doughnuts in hot deep oil until golden brown. Turn them to brown on both sides – takes about 5 minutes. Drain the hot doughnuts on crumpled greaseproof paper. Roll while still warm in the mixed sugar and cinnamon. Serve warm.

Almond slices

These keep well and can be prepared a day or two before serving. They are excellent for tea or for a coffee morning party.

Makes 16 slices

4 oz./100 g. rich shortcrust	2 small eggs
pastry (page 12)	few drops almond essence
1 tablespoon raspberry or	3 oz./75 g. ground almonds
strawberry jam	1 oz./25 g. plain flour
for the filling:	*to decorate:*
4 oz./100 g. butter	blanched flaked almonds
4 oz./100 g. castor sugar	

Roll the pastry out thinly to an oblong, approximately the size of a buttered, shallow 11 × 7 × 1-inch (28½ × 18 × 2½-cm.) Swiss roll tin. This rich pastry is difficult to handle but if a little on the small side the pastry can quite easily be pressed over the base of the tin to cover it completely. Spread the surface with a little jam and set aside while preparing the filling.

Cream together the butter and sugar. Gradually beat in the lightly mixed eggs and almond essence. Fold in the mixed ground almonds and flour and mix well. Spoon the mixture in to the pastry lined tin and spread evenly. Sprinkle with flaked almonds. Place in the centre of a moderate oven (350°C., 180°C., Gas Mark 4) and bake for 30–35 minutes. When baked, allow to cool in the tin. Loosen the sides, turn out and cut into 16 slices. Store in a tightly lidded tin.

French madeleines

For these pretty little cakes, you need the traditional shaped madeleine tins. Madeleines are excellent served with fresh fruit desserts and they keep for a week or more in a tightly lidded tin.

Makes 12 madeleines

2 oz./50 g. plain flour	few drops vanilla essence
2 eggs	2 oz./50 g. butter, melted
2 oz./50 g. castor sugar	

Sift the flour on to a square of paper and set aside. Crack the eggs into a basin and add the sugar and vanilla essence. Whisk until thick and light. Fold in the flour with a metal spoon, then lightly mix in the cooled, melted butter.

Have ready 12 buttered and floured madeleine tins. Add enough mixture to each tin to almost fill it evenly. Place above centre in a moderately hot oven (375°F., 190°C., Gas Mark 5) and bake for 10 minutes. Turn out on to a wire rack to cool.

Dessert cakes

Cakes served for dessert have one distinct advantage, they can be prepared in advance. Some cakes are soaked with flavourings, other crisp meringue types should be filled and allowed to stand so that the meringue softens slightly for easier serving. In most cases, these cakes need to be cut into neat portions for serving – take a confectioner's tip – a warm knife blade softens its way through a soft icing or cream and doesn't drag, spoiling the appearance. Choose a large, very sharp kitchen knife, preferably unserrated. Dip the knife blade into a jug of hot water to warm it for a moment. Shake away the drips and cut the slice of cake quickly and evenly. Clean and dip the knife again before cutting the next slice. Do this in the kitchen, before presenting the cake at the table.

Savarin au rhum

Illustrated in colour on page 133

A fruit filled savarin makes an attractive dinner party dessert. Although elaborate to prepare, most of the work can be done well in advance.

Serves 8

12 oz./350 g. plain flour	4 tablespoons rum
pinch salt	*for the glaze:*
¾ oz./20 g. fresh yeast or 3 level teaspoons dried	2 tablespoons sieved apricot jam
⅓ pint/2–2½ dl. milk	2 level tablespoons castor sugar
1 level teaspoon castor sugar	2 tablespoons water
4 large eggs	*for the fruit salad:*
4 oz./100 g. butter, melted	1 small honeydew melon
for the syrup:	8 oz./225 g. green grapes
12 oz./350 g. granulated sugar	2 oranges
1 pint/6 dl. water	2–3 bananas
juice 1 lemon	

Brush the inside of a 9–9½-inch (23–24-cm.) tube or ring mould with melted butter and sprinkle with flour.

Sieve the flour and salt into a large warm bowl and make a well in the centre. If using fresh yeast, blend the yeast with the warm milk and sugar. Add the beaten eggs, mix well and pour the liquid into the centre of the flour. Sprinkle with a little of the flour from the mixture, cover with a cloth and leave in a warm place to 'sponge'. This means until the yeast begins to bubble and starts to work – it usually takes about 15 minutes.

With dried yeast, the procedure is a little different. Sprinkle the yeast pellets over the hand hot mixed milk and sugar in a small basin. Set aside in a warm place for 10–15 minutes until the mixture has frothed up like beer, then add the beaten eggs and pour into the centre of the flour mixture.

Either way beat the batter by hand to a smooth mixture. Add the melted butter and beat in thoroughly.

Pour the mixture into the prepared mould, it should about halfway fill the mould. Set in a warm place to 'prove' until the mixture has risen and almost reaches the top of the tin – takes about 30 minutes. Place in the centre of a hot oven (400°F., 200°C., Gas Mark 6) and bake for 30 minutes or until golden brown and firm to the touch. When baked, allow to cool in the tin for 10 minutes, then turn out and leave to *stale overnight*. The reason for staling is mainly that the savarin will soak up more of the syrup. The baked savarin at this stage has little flavour and depends entirely on the syrup to give it a good flavour and a soft cakelike texture.

To prepare the syrup, measure the sugar and water into a saucepan and stir over low heat until the sugar has dissolved. Bring up to the boil and simmer for 10 minutes. Draw the pan off the heat and add the strained lemon juice and rum. Place the savarin on a wire cake rack over a shallow plate. Prick all over with a skewer. This helps the syrup to soak into the savarin more evenly. Spoon over the hot syrup. Excess syrup will collect in the plate below and should be spooned again over the savarin until all the syrup has been soaked into the cake. At this stage, the savarin will become soft and fragile, so lift very carefully on to a serving dish.

It is not necessary to glaze a savarin, but it does improve the appearance. Measure the jam, sugar and water for the glaze into a small saucepan. Stir over low heat to dissolve the sugar, then bring up to the boil and simmer until the glaze is thick and hangs in heavy drops from the spoon. Draw the pan off the heat and, using a clean pastry brush, brush the hot glaze over the whole surface of the savarin, or spoon over. Set aside while preparing the fruit salad.

Halve and deseed the melon, then quarter and remove the peel. Cut the melon flesh into thin slices. Halve and deseed the grapes, except for a few pairs which should be reserved for decoration. Peel the oranges and cut the segments into pieces. Peel and slice the bananas. If liked, toss the sliced banana in a little lemon juice to help preserve the white colour. Spoon the fruit into the centre of the savarin and decorate round the edge of the dish with the reserved grapes. Any extra fruit salad may be served separately.

Serve the savarin with cream.

Meringues Chantilly

Cream-filled meringues are a great favourite and not difficult to make. Use egg whites left over from another recipe for these.

Makes 8 filled meringues

2 egg whites	¼ pint/1½ dl. double cream
4 oz./115 g. castor sugar	

First prepare the baking trays, rub a little white cooking fat over the surface of 2 baking trays, then dust both lightly with flour and shake off the surplus.

Put the egg whites into a large clean bowl and, using a wire whisk, rotary beater or electric mixer, beat them slowly at first then faster as they begin to thicken. It is important to get the egg whites sufficiently stiff, so test them carefully as you beat. Lift the whisk out of the mixture and if the egg white adhering to the whisk stands up in a stiff unbending peak, then the whites are ready for an addition of the sugar.

Add two tablespoons of the measured sugar and beat this into the egg whites until the original stiff consistency is regained, then gradually sprinkle in remaining sugar, beating all the time until a thick light meringue is obtained.

Place a 1-inch (2½-cm.) plain or a star piping nozzle in a nylon or cotton piping bag. Fill the bag with the meringue mixture then twist the top to hold the mixture firmly inside. Keeping the bag upright, pipe out whorls of meringue on to the prepared baking trays, you should make about sixteen.

Put the meringues into a very cool oven, set at the lowest temperature (225°F., 110°C., Gas Mark ¼) and bake for 3–4 hours. They should slip off the tray very easily, but you can run a sharp knife under each if necessary. Cool them on a wire tray.

Whip the cream until it will hold its shape and pipe cream between pairs of meringues. Put the filled meringues in paper serving cases.

Mandlekuchen

This rich, elaborate gâteau could be served as a dessert for a dinner party. Other finely ground nuts, such as walnuts or hazelnuts, can be used in place of the ground almonds.

Serves 6–8

4 oz./100 g. ground almonds	8 oz./225 g. canned pineapple,
5 egg whites	seeded grapes or other fruits
10 oz./275 g. castor sugar	(see recipe)
1 teaspoon vinegar or lemon	*to decorate :*
juice	icing sugar
for the filling :	
½ pint/3 dl. double cream	

Lightly brush the insides of two 8½-inch (21-cm.) sponge cake tins with oil. Cut circles of greaseproof paper to fit the tins. Line the tins and brush with oil. Spread the ground almonds on a baking tray and toast in a moderate oven (350°F., 180°C., Gas Mark 4) for about 8 minutes. Remove from the heat.

Whisk the egg whites in a large basin until stiff. Beat in half the sugar, a little at a time, whisking well all the time until the meringue is glossy. Mix the almonds with the remaining sugar and, using a metal spoon, gently fold in the remaining sugar and almonds and the vinegar or lemon juice.

Divide the mixture equally between the 2 tins and spread the mixture evenly. Place in the centre of a moderately hot oven (375°F., 190°C., Gas Mark 5) and bake for 30–40 minutes. Allow the layers to cool in the tins. Loosen the sides with a knife, turn out the meringue layers and peel away the paper.

Sandwich the layers with lightly whipped double cream and drained canned pineapple slices or seeded, halved grapes. Alternatively, use fresh fruit such as raspberries or sliced strawberries. Dust the cake with icing sugar and allow to stand for about 1 hour before serving.

Meringue layer cake

Meringue layers always colour slightly during baking, this gives them an attractive appearance and enhances the flavour.

Serves 6–8

4 egg whites	¼ pint/1½ dl. soured cream
8 oz./225 g. castor sugar	¼ pint/1½ dl. double cream
few finely chopped walnuts	1 tablespoon brandy
for the filling :	
4 oz./100 g. plain chocolate	

Mark out three 8-inch (20-cm.) circles on separate sheets of greaseproof paper. Turn over so that the pencilled lines lie underneath and place on 3 separate baking trays. Fix at the corners with a smear of cooking fat so that the paper lies flat. Brush the circles lightly with oil and set aside.

Whisk the egg whites until stiff. Gradually beat in half the sugar, whisking all the time until the meringue is glossy. Using a metal spoon, gently fold in the remaining sugar. Dividing the meringue equally, spread over the marked circles, keeping within the pencilled outline. Select one meringue circle as the top and sprinkle with finely chopped walnuts.

Place the trays on separate shelves in a very cool oven (225°F., 110°C., Gas Mark ¼) and bake for 2½–3 hours or until dry. Change the meringue layers from shelf to shelf to get even baking. Towards the end of the baking time, turn the meringue layers on the paper upside down to allow the underneath to dry out. When the meringue layers are dry, the paper should peel off quite easily. Allow the layers to cool.

Place the chocolate in a basin over a saucepan, half filled with hot water. Stir as the chocolate melts. When smooth and melted, remove from the heat and stir in the soured cream. Lightly whip the double cream and fold into the chocolate mixture along with the brandy. Take care not to overmix.

Keeping the top layer aside, sandwich the other 2 layers with half the chocolate mixture. Spread with remaining chocolate mixture and cover with the top layer. Allow to stand for 2–3 hours so that the chocolate filling firms up and the meringue layers soften slightly.

Cut into serving portions with a sharp knife and serve with cream.

Coffee brandy gâteau

Serves 6

6 oz./175 g. plain flour	*for the syrup :*
½ level teaspoon salt	4 oz./100 g. granulated sugar
2 level teaspoons baking powder	¼ pint/1½ dl. strong coffee
5 oz./150 g. soft brown sugar	2 tablespoons brandy
2 eggs	*for the decoration :*
6 tablespoons corn oil	½ pint/3 dl. double cream
2 tablespoons coffee essence	grated plain chocolate
3–4 tablespoons milk	

Sift the flour, salt and baking powder into a large mixing basin, add the brown sugar and mix well. Crack the egg yolks into a small basin and whites into a second larger basin. Add the corn oil, coffee essence and milk to the yolks and mix with a fork. Pour into the centre of the dry ingredients and, using a wooden spoon, beat well to make a smooth batter. Whisk the egg whites until stiff and fold into the mixture. Pour into a greased and lined 8-inch (20-cm.) round, deep cake tin. Bake above centre in a moderate oven (350°F., 180°C., Gas Mark 4) for 40–45 minutes or until springy to the touch. Turn out and allow to cool.

Meanwhile, prepare the syrup. Measure the sugar and coffee into a small saucepan and stir over a low heat to dissolve the sugar. Then bring to the boil and cook quickly for 5 minutes – this concentrates the syrup. Draw the pan off the heat and stir in the brandy. When the cake is cold, stand it on a strip of kitchen foil and replace back in the original baking tin. The foil helps to remove the more fragile soaked cake at a later stage.

Prick holes over the top with a fine skewer – this helps the brandy syrup to soak in. Then pour over the hot syrup and leave overnight.

Next day, gently lift the cake base from the tin, using the folded kitchen foil support and place the gâteau on a pretty serving dish. Pour the chilled cream into a mixing basin and whisk until thick – there is no need to sweeten the cream, since the cake base is already very rich. Spoon all the whipped cream on to the top of the cake and then swirl over the top and around the sides. Decorate with grated plain chocolate and then put to chill until ready to serve.

Gâteau aux fruits Chantilly

Illustrated in colour on page 160

Vary the fruits used according to the season. In summer, this recipe can be made with strawberries, raspberries and cherries or fresh peaches and brushed with a redcurrant glaze.

Serves 6

6 oz./175 g. plain flour	2–3 bananas
3 large eggs	8 oz./225 g. black and green
6 oz./175 g. castor sugar	grapes, mixed
for the sugar syrup:	½ pint/3 dl. double cream
2 oz./50 g. castor sugar	1 oz./25 g. castor sugar
1 wine glass water	*for the apricot glaze:*
1 tablespoon Kirsch	4 tablespoons apricot jam
for the filling:	1 oz./25 g. castor sugar
½ small fresh pineapple	squeeze lemon juice
2 oranges	1 tablespoon water or Kirsch

Preheat the oven (375°F., 190°C., Gas Mark 5) and prepare the tin in advance. Use either one 8½–9-inch (21–23-cm.) 'moule à manque' or deep sponge layer tin. An attractive crust is baked on this type of light sponge cake by brushing out the tin well with melted butter – use unsalted to reduce the chances of sticking. Then sift equal parts – about one rounded tablespoon each – mixed flour and castor sugar into the tin. Shake evenly over the entire inside surface, then knock out the surplus. Set the prepared tin aside.

Sift the flour on to a square of paper and set aside in a warm place until required. As the egg and sugar mixture is beaten over warm water, it helps if the flour is slightly warm when added.

Crack the eggs into a large mixing basin and add the sugar. Although the mixture must be warmed while beating to get a better volume, it is important that it is not overheated. The best way is to heat the water to almost boiling point in a saucepan large enough to accommodate base of the mixing basin comfortably. Draw the pan off the heat and place the basin over the top. The base of the mixing basin should not touch the water. Using a hand or rotary beater, whisk the mixture until light in colour and thick. It should leave a trail over the surface when a little mixture is lifted. If using an electric hand beater, take great care not to overbeat the mixture. Lift the basin from saucepan and continue to whisk for a few moments to cool slightly.

Sprinkle or sift the flour over the surface of the mixture. Using a hand whisk or a metal spoon, gently fold in the flour. Turn the basin slowly round and round with left hand while gently folding in flour with an over and over movement with right hand. Take care to mix in the flour thoroughly. Pour the mixture into the prepared 'moule à manque' tin – it should be no more than three-quarters full. Place in the centre of a moderately hot oven (375°F., 190°C., Gas Mark 5) and bake for 35–40 minutes or until springy to the touch. Turn out, topside downwards, on to a cooling tray and allow to cool.

Split into two layers for filling. For this, use a very sharp knife. Keep the knife level with the centre of the cake to one side and cut slowly into the cake while turning it round. Put two layers apart, ready for filling. Remember that the wider top is, in fact, the base layer and the smaller half is the top layer.

Sprinkle the cake layers with a little sugar syrup before filling. For this, measure the sugar and water into a small saucepan and stir over low heat to dissolve. Bring to the boil and cook rapidly for 1 minute. Draw the pan off the heat, stir in the Kirsch and allow to cool.

Cut the outside of the pineapple, slicing downwards, remove any coarse pieces. Slice across and, using a round cutter or a knife, remove the centre core. Cut the rings into small segments. Slice both ends from each orange, then cut away outer peel, slicing downwards as if peeling an apple. Using a knife, cut into each segment, loosen and remove. Peel and slice the bananas – toss in lemon juice or juice from the pineapple to keep their white colour. Halve and deseed the grapes. Pour the cream into a mixing basin, half whip, add the sugar and whip again until thick.

Sprinkle the sugar syrup over the sponge layers, then spoon the sweetened cream over the base. Arrange half the fruit over the cream and top with the second sponge layer, smooth side upwards.

Once the cake is completed it is difficult to move and for this reason, it is best assembled where it will be served from. Before finishing the cake, prepare the apricot glaze. Sieve the apricot jam into a saucepan, add the sugar, lemon juice, water or Kirsch. Place over a low heat to dissolve the sugar and blend ingredients. Bring to the boil and cook rapidly until syrupy – take care the glaze does not scorch. Using a pastry brush, coat the top surface of the cake with hot glaze, then quickly arrange remaining fruit attractively over the glaze. Brush all the fruit generously with more hot glaze. Allow to cool before serving.

Advance preparation: The cake can be made in advance and stored in a tin. The glaze can also be made in advance and re-heated when needed. Assemble the cake on the day of serving.

Marrons mont blanc

Use bought or homemade meringue shells for these. Assemble them 2–3 hours before serving so that the meringue base has a chance to soften slightly.

Serves 6

6 meringue shells	1 (15½ oz./440 g.) can chestnut
¼ pint/1½ dl. double cream	purée
for the chestnut purée:	1 oz./25 g. butter, melted
2 oz./50 g. castor sugar	*to decorate:*
3 tablespoons water	icing sugar

Start by preparing the chestnut purée. Measure the sugar and water into a saucepan and stir over low heat to dissolve the sugar. Bring up to the boil and draw off the heat. Allow the syrup to cool slightly. Turn the chestnut purée into a basin and beat in the sugar syrup and the melted butter. Beat well to get a smooth mixture, then set aside for about 30 minutes or until the mixture is quite cold.

Place a meringue shell in the base of 6 individual paper serving cases. Lightly whip the cream and spoon a little into the centre of each meringue shell. Spoon the chestnut mixture into a large nylon piping bag, fitted with a small ¼-inch (½-cm.) plain nozzle. Pipe the chestnut purée in traditional wiggly lines (rather like a nest), piling it up on top of the cream. Chill for several hours.

Dust with icing sugar and serve.

Strawberry shortcake

Illustrated in colour on page 145

American shortcake should be made with a rich scone dough or, as the Americans call it, a 'biscuit' dough. In this recipe, melted butter brushed between the 2 layers of shortcake make it easier to separate the layers after baking. Once filled, the shortcake should be chilled for 1 hour – this makes it easier to cut.

Serves 6

8 oz./225 g. self-raising flour	½ oz./15 g. butter, melted
pinch salt	*for the filling:*
3 oz./75 g. butter	8–12 oz./250–350 g.
1 large egg	strawberries
3 tablespoons milk	1 oz./25 g. castor sugar
1½ oz./40 g. castor sugar	¼ pint/1½ dl. double cream

Sift the flour and salt into a basin. Add the butter, cut in pieces, and rub into the mixture until the fat is evenly blended and mixture is crumbly. Crack the egg into a basin, add the milk and sugar and mix thoroughly with a fork. Pour all at once into the centre of the dry ingredients. Mix to a rough dough in the basin. Turn out on to a floured working surface and, with floured fingers, knead very lightly to a smooth dough.

Divide the dough into 2 equal parts. Pat or roll out each piece to a circle slightly smaller than a shallow 7½-inch (19-cm.) sponge cake tin. (The choice of tin is important, the higher sides of a deep cake tin would prevent the top of the shortcake from browning evenly.) Butter the base and sides of the tin with a little of the melted butter. Place in one circle of dough and press lightly with the finger tips to make it fit perfectly. Brush the surface liberally with more melted butter. Place the second circle of dough on top and press lightly to make the dough fit to the edges of the tin.

Place the shortcake in the centre of a preheated, hot oven (425°F., 220°C., Gas Mark 7) and bake for 15 minutes. The shortcake should be risen and lightly browned. Cool for a few moments before removing from the tin then, using a knife, separate the two layers and cool them.

Hull the strawberries and slice any large ones in half. Add the sugar to the cream and whip until thick. Reserve a few of the nicest strawberries and a little of the cream for decoration. Fill the shortcake with the remaining strawberries and cream. Decorate with whorls of cream and the reserved strawberries.

Sachertorte

The chocolate cake layers for this mixture are best baked and left to stand for 24 hours before icing. The hazelnuts add a particularly good flavour, use a Mouli grater to grind them.

Cuts into 10–12 slices

4 oz./100 g. plain flour	7 oz./200 g. castor sugar
pinch salt	½ teaspoon vanilla essence
3 oz./75 g. ground hazelnuts	2–3 tablespoons sieved apricot
2½ oz./65 g. bitter cooking	jam
chocolate	*for the chocolate icing:*
4 oz./100 g. butter	1 oz./25 g. castor sugar
8 egg yolks	2 tablespoons water
7 egg whites	4 oz./100 g. plain chocolate

Butter and line two 8½-inch (21-cm.) sponge cake tins with buttered greaseproof paper. Sift the flour and salt on to a square of paper, add the hazelnuts and set aside. Place the chocolate and butter in a basin and set over a small saucepan, half filled with hot water. Stir occasionally until both are melted and blended, then remove from the heat.

Crack the egg yolks together into one large, warmed basin. Place the whites into a second basin. Add 3 oz. (75 g.) of the sugar and the vanilla to the yolks. Beat the egg yolks and sugar together until thick and light. Then stir in the melted butter and chocolate mixture. Beat the egg whites until stiff, whisk in the sugar and beat until glossy. Fold the egg whites into the chocolate mixture. Then carefully fold in the sieved flour and hazelnuts.

Divide the mixture equally between the prepared tins. Place in the centre of a moderately hot oven (375°F., 190°C., Gas Mark 5) and bake for 20–30 minutes. Turn out and allow the cake layers to cool.

Slice each cake in half horizontally and sandwich all the layers with apricot jam. Dissolve the sugar for the icing in the water over low heat. Bring up to the boil, then draw off the heat and allow to cool. Melt the chocolate for the icing in a small basin, set over a pan of hot water. When melted, stir in sufficient of the sugar syrup to make a smooth coating icing. Pour quickly on to the cake and spread over the top and sides. Leave until set firm.

Serve the sachertorte, cut in slices with whipped cream.

Cakes for Christmas

Cakes have always been baked for special occasions and Christmas is no exception. Most recipes for Christmas are fruity and spicy. Many can be made well in advance and will keep well, usually improving in flavour. Any fruit cake or bread should be allowed to become quite cold before storing. Although the richer fruit cakes keep for many weeks, the lighter fruit or glacé fruit cakes, that have achieved some popularity in recent years, should only be baked 2–3 weeks in advance. All cakes should be allowed to cool for 24 hours in the tins. Leave on the baking papers to help keep the crust soft and either wrap in foil or store in a tightly lidded tin.

Cinnamon iced gingerbread

To get the best flavour, wrap and store this gingerbread for a week or so before icing. A pretty recipe that is delicious to make for Christmas.

Makes 2 dozen squares

1 lb./450 g. self-raising flour	3 eggs
1 oz./25 g. ground ginger	1 level teaspoon bicarbonate
1 rounded teaspoon ground	of soda
cinnamon	*for the icing:*
8 oz./225 g. butter	8 oz./225 g. icing sugar
8 oz./225 g. soft brown sugar	¼ level teaspoon ground
4 oz./100 g. chopped mixed	cinnamon
candied peel	strained juice ½ small orange
4 oz./100 g. glacé cherries,	warm water (see recipe)
chopped	*to decorate:*
8 oz./225 g. currants	split blanched almonds
8 oz./225 g. sultanas	halved glacé cherries
8 oz./225 g. black treacle	angelica
¼ pint/1½ dl. hot milk	

Sift together the flour, ground ginger and cinnamon into a large mixing basin. Rub in the butter and add the sugar, candied peel, glacé cherries, currants and sultanas.

Measure the treacle into the hot milk and whisk in the eggs. Add the bicarbonate of soda and then stir into the dry ingredients. Mix well and pour the mixture into a greased and lined shallow baking or small roasting tin about 10 × 12 inches (26 × 31 cm.). Place in the centre of a moderate oven (325°F., 170°C., Gas Mark 3) and bake for 1½ hours, or until a warmed skewer pushed gently into the centre of the cake comes out clean. Leave until quite cold before icing.

Sift the icing sugar and cinnamon into a mixing basin, add the orange juice and then stir in a little warm water to mix to a thin paste. Pour this over the top of the gingerbread and spread evenly. When the icing has set, cut into small squares and decorate each one with a flower, using half a glacé cherry, three almonds for petals and a stalk and leaves of angelica.

Black bun

Black bun consists of a rich fruit mixture enclosed in a pastry case. The baked bun should be allowed to mature for at least 1 month before cutting. Traditionally served at Hogmanay in Scotland.

Makes 1 black bun

12 oz./350 g. plain flour	4 oz./100 g. castor sugar
½ level teaspoon baking powder	1 lb./450 g. raisins, stoned and
pinch salt	chopped
4 oz./100 g. butter	1 lb./450 g. cleaned currants
6 tablespoons water	3 oz./75 g. blanched almonds,
beaten egg	chopped
for the filling:	1 oz./25 g. chopped mixed
8 oz./225 g. plain flour	candied peel
¼ level teaspoon black pepper	¼ pint/1½ dl. milk
1 teaspoon ground cinnamon	1 tablespoon brandy
½ level teaspoon cream of tartar	
¼ level teaspoon bicarbonate of	
soda	

Sift the flour, baking powder and salt into a mixing basin. Rub in the butter and then mix with the water to make a stiff dough. Turn out on a floured working surface and knead lightly. Divide the dough into three equal portions. Roll out two of the pieces to a circle large enough to fit an 8-inch (20-cm.) deep, round cake tin. This makes the top and base of the black bun. Roll out the remaining dough to a strip about 2 inches (5 cm.) in depth and long enough to fit around the inside of the cake tin. Grease the tin and line the base with one circle of pastry and the sides with the strip. Press the edges well to seal together. Set aside while preparing the filling.

Sift the flour, spices, cream of tartar and bicarbonate of soda together into a basin. Add the sugar, raisins, currants, almonds and peel and mix well together. Stir in the milk and brandy and mix well. Pack the fruit mixture into the pastry lined cake tin and spread the top evenly. Turn in any edges of pastry around the sides, damp these and then cover with the pastry lid. Press down gently to seal and prick the top all over with a fork. Brush with a little beaten egg to glaze. Place in the centre of a moderately hot oven (350°F., 180°C., Gas Mark 4) and bake for 3 hours. Cover the pastry with a sheet of foil after 2 hours, if becoming too brown. Cool in the tin, then remove and keep for at least 1 month before cutting.

Christmas stollen

This rich, fruity bread should be made 2–4 weeks before Christmas. The texture is moist and rich and it should be served sliced and buttered.

Makes 1 stollen

1 lb./450 g. plain flour	8 oz./225 g. soft cream cheese
3 level teaspoons baking powder	4 oz./100 g. currants
½ level teaspoon salt	8 oz./225 g. seedless raisins
pinch cardamom	2 oz./50 g. blanched almonds,
pinch ground mace	chopped
8 oz./225 g. castor sugar	2 oz./50 g. ground hazelnuts
2 eggs	4 oz./100 g. chopped mixed
4 drops bitter almond oil	peel
1 teaspoon rum essence	*for the topping:*
4 drops oil of lemon	2 oz./50 g. butter, melted
4 oz./100 g. butter	2 oz./50 g. sieved icing sugar
2 oz./50 g. dripping or white	
cooking fat	

Sift the flour, baking powder, salt and spices on to a clean working surface. Add the sugar, mix well and make a hollow in the centre. Crack the eggs into the centre and add the essences. Stir and mix with just a little of the flour. Cut the butter into pieces over the top. Add the dripping or cooking fat, the cream cheese, currants, raisins, nuts and mixed peel. Draw the flour from the edges to blend ingredients and then knead with the hands, drawing all the ingredients together to make a smooth dough.

Shape the dough into a long loaf and place on a greased baking tray. Cover with greased foil. Place in the centre of a moderate oven (325°F., 170°C., Gas Mark 3) and bake for 1 hour. When baked, remove from the oven and, while hot, brush with the melted butter and dust generously with sifted icing sugar. Leave until cold before storing.

Bûche de Noël

This traditional French gâteau is served on Christmas eve. It makes a pretty and delicious centrepiece for a buffet supper party.

Serves 8

2 oz./50 g. plain flour
1 oz./25 g. ground almonds
3 large eggs
3 oz./75 g. castor sugar
for the filling and frosting:
crème au beurre (page 185)

2 oz./50 g. unsweetened
  chocolate
to decorate:
icing sugar

Sift the flour twice on to a square of greaseproof paper and add the ground almonds. Crack the eggs into a mixing basin, add the sugar and set the basin over a saucepan half filled with hot, but not boiling, water. Whisk until the mixture is pale and thick. Remove the basin from the heat and beat for a further few moments. Sprinkle the flour mixture over the contents of the bowl and, using a metal spoon, fold in gently but thoroughly.

Pour the mixture into a greased and lined shallow baking tin of approximately 13 × 9 inches (33½ × 23 cm.). Place above centre in a hot oven (425°F., 220°C., Gas Mark 7) and bake for 5–7 minutes or until the sponge is well risen and springy to the touch. Remove from the heat, loosen the sides and turn on to a clean cloth. Cover with a second cloth and leave until cold.

Flavour all but a small portion of the crème au beurre with the melted unsweetened chocolate. Spread the sponge with about half the cream and roll up by the long side. Cut off a slanting slice from one end and reserve. Cover the entire log with most of the remaining chocolate cream, and fix the cut slice in position at the side to make a jutting out branch. Coat this with chocolate cream. Smooth the flat ends of the log with a knife dipped in hot water.

Pipe circles of plain cream at either end of the log and draw these out with a pointed knife tip to make the wood markings life-like. With a fork dipped in hot water, make lines all over the surface of the log. Dust with a little sieved icing sugar for snow and chill for several hours.

Cut in slices to serve.

Plum bread

Plum breads are rich with fruit and often quite spicy. They are traditionally made for Christmas, often baked in October and kept for a month or more before serving. Like other rich fruit mixtures, the flavour improves and mellows on keeping. Serve thinly sliced and buttered.

Makes 2 large loaves

1½ lb./700 g. self-raising flour
1 level teaspoon salt
4 oz./100 g. butter
4 oz./100 g. lard
8 oz./225 g. soft brown sugar
2 eggs
2 tablespoons dark rum

½ pint/3 dl. milk
12 oz./350 g. currants
12 oz./350 g. sultanas
4 oz./100 g. chopped mixed
  peel
4 oz./100 g. glacé cherries

Sift the flour and salt on to a large square of greaseproof paper and set aside. Cream the butter, lard and sugar until soft and

light. Lightly mix the eggs and gradually beat into the creamed mixture, a little at a time. Using a metal spoon, fold in the flour along with the rum and milk and mix to a medium soft consistency. Fold in the currants, sultanas, chopped mixed peel and the glacé cherries, which have been rinsed and cut in half.

Dividing the mixture equally, spoon into 2 greased and lined 9 × 7 × 5-inch (23 × 18 × 13-cm.) large loaf tins. Spread the mixture evenly and hollow out the centre slightly. Place the loaves below centre in a moderate oven (325°F., 170°C., Gas Mark 3) and bake for 2 hours.

Cool, then wrap in kitchen foil and keep for up to 3 months.

Rich traditional Christmas cake

Preparing a Christmas or any rich fruit cake can be a lengthy process. This recipe is particularly useful in that the prepared cake can wait before baking, giving the cook a chance to choose a suitable time. Since the cake is baked at one temperature, it can be placed in the oven under the control of an automatic timer. This cake could also be used as the base of a single tier wedding cake or a christening cake.

Makes one 9-inch (23-cm.) round cake

1 lb./450 g. plain flour
½ level teaspoon salt
1 level teaspoon ground
  cinnamon
1 level teaspoon ground mixed
  spice
1 lb./450 g. sultanas, cleaned
12 oz./350 g. currants, cleaned
12 oz./350 g. raisins, stoned
  and chopped

8 oz./225 g. glacé cherries
2 oz./50 g. walnuts, chopped
12 oz./350 g. butter
12 oz./350 g. soft brown sugar
6 eggs
2 tablespoons black treacle
finely grated rind 1 lemon
4 tablespoons brandy or sherry

Grease a 9-inch (23-cm.) round deep cake tin and line with double thickness, greased greaseproof paper. Tie a band of double thickness brown paper round the outside of the tin for added protection.

Sift the flour, salt and spices on to a large square of greaseproof paper. Mix the cleaned sultanas, currants and the raisins in a large mixing basin. Rinse the cherries in warm water to remove the sugary coating, cut in half and pat dry. Add to the fruit along with the chopped walnuts. Add a quarter of the sifted flour to the fruit and mix well.

In a large mixing basin, cream the butter and sugar until light and fluffy. Lightly mix the eggs, treacle and lemon rind and add to the creamed mixture, a little at a time. Beat each addition in well before adding the next. Add a little of the sifted flour with the last few additions of egg. Using a metal spoon, fold in the remaining flour. Then fold in the fruit mixture and finally the brandy or sherry. Mix well and then spoon the mixture into the prepared tin. Spread the mixture evenly and then hollow out the centre slightly.

Place the cake on the shelf below centre in a preheated cool oven (300°F., 150°C., Gas Mark 2) and bake for 5–6 hours. Alternatively, the cake may be set in a cold oven with the automatic timer set for 6 hours. Cakes in a cold oven require about ½ hour more cooking time.

Allow the cake to cool in the tin. Do not remove the papers as they help to keep the cake moist. Simply wrap in foil and store in a cool dry place until required.

Glacé fruit Christmas cake

A fruit cake made using glacé fruits looks attractive and makes a very good alternative to the richer traditional Christmas cake.

Makes one 9-inch (23-cm.) cake

12 oz./350 g. plain flour	2 oz./50 g. angelica
pinch salt	12 oz./350 g. sultanas
6 oz./175 g. assorted glacé cherries	8 oz./225 g. butter
	8 oz./225 g. castor sugar
6 oz./175 g. glacé pineapple	4 eggs
2 oz./50 g. walnuts, shelled	finely grated rind 1 lemon
2 oz./50 g. candied peel	juice ½ lemon
2 oz./50 g. glacé or preserved ginger	3–4 tablespoons sherry or milk

Sift together the flour and salt. Set aside while preparing the fruit. Rinse the cherries to wash away the sugar syrup. Drain well and press dry in a cloth. Cut the cherries into quarters. Chop the glacé pineapple and walnuts. Remove any solid sugar from the peel and rinse the peel, ginger and angelica under hot water to remove all traces of sugar and press dry. Chop the peel, ginger and angelica into small pieces. Mix all the glacé fruits in a bowl and add the sultanas. Add a quarter of the sieved flour and mix well.

Cream together the butter and sugar until very pale and light – takes about 8–10 minutes. Lightly mix the eggs, grated lemon rind and strained juice, then gradually beat into the creamed mixture, a little at a time. Fold in the sifted flour mixture, then fold in the fruit and flour mixture. Blend the ingredients lightly but thoroughly, adding the sherry or milk to produce a medium soft consistency.

Spoon the mixture into a greased and lined 9-inch (23-cm.) deep round cake tin and spread evenly. Then, with the back of a tablespoon, make a wide but shallow dip in the centre of the cake. Place in the centre of a moderate oven (325°F., 170°C., Gas Mark 3) and bake for 1–1½ hours or until the surface of the cake has just set. Reduce the temperature to cool (300°F., 150°C., Gas Mark 2) and bake for a further 1–1½ hours. Finally reduce the temperature to 275°F., 140°C., Gas Mark 1 and bake for a final 1½ hours. The total baking time should be 4½–5 hours.

If the cake shows any tendency of becoming too brown on top, cover with a folded paper during the latter half of the baking. Allow the baked cake to cool in its baking papers. When quite cold, remove the papers and rewrap the cake in greaseproof or waxed paper and store in a tightly lidded tin until ready for icing.

Fillings and frostings

Most cakes, other than the very plain types, have a filling or a frosting on top to give extra flavour or to make the cake look pretty. The recipes listed here are some of the most popular. Different types of cakes require different types of frosting or icing. The use of each one here is clearly indicated.

Almond paste

This recipe makes a smooth almond paste that is particularly easy to handle. Use to cover rich Christmas cakes or other celebration cakes.

to cover top and sides of one 7–8-inch (18–20-cm.) cake:

1 egg	6 oz./175 g. icing sugar, sifted
6 oz./175 g. castor sugar	6 oz./175 g. ground almonds
½ teaspoon vanilla or almond essence	

to cover top and sides of one 9–10-inch (23–26-cm.) cake:

1 egg plus 1 egg yolk	8 oz./225 g. icing sugar, sifted
8 oz./225 g. castor sugar	8 oz./225 g. ground almonds
½ teaspoon vanilla or almond essence	

Place the egg and castor sugar into a mixing basin. Place over a saucepan half filled with hot water and whisk until the mixture is light in colour and feels warm. Whisk in the flavouring essence. Remove the basin from the heat and, using a wooden spoon, stir in the sifted icing sugar and ground almonds. Mix to a fairly stiff paste, then turn the mixture out on to a working surface lightly dusted with icing sugar and knead until smooth. Wrap the almond paste in polythene or kitchen foil and leave to mature for at least 1 hour before using.

Apricot glaze

Apricot glaze is invaluable for giving a professional shiny finish to flans and fruit decorated cakes. It is also essential to glaze cakes before icing to keep the gloss and before coating with marzipan, so that the marzipan sticks to the cake.

large quantity:

1 lb./450 g. apricot jam	¼ pint/1½ dl. water
8 oz./225 g. granulated sugar	

small quantity:

2 heaped tablespoons apricot jam	1 tablespoon water or lemon juice
1 heaped tablespoon granulated sugar	

Sieve the jam where necessary to remove any pieces of fruit. Measure the sugar and water into a saucepan. Stir over low heat until the sugar has dissolved. Add the apricot jam and stir over low heat until blended. Bring to the boil and cook steadily until the glaze hangs in heavy drops from the spoon.

Use while hot.

Fondant icing

The advantage of this particular icing is that it coats thinly and sets very quickly. When using fondant, great care should be taken not to overheat. This spoils the shine and the finished icing will look dull.

Makes 1 lb. (450 g.) fondant icing

$\frac{1}{4}$ pint/1$\frac{1}{2}$ dl. cold water
1 lb./450 g. granulated sugar

$\frac{1}{4}$ level teaspoon cream of tartar
1 tablespoon cold water

Measure the water into a heavy based saucepan and add the sugar. Use a strong saucepan when boiling mixtures to a high temperature. Stir over low heat until the sugar has dissolved then bring up to the boil. Brush down the insides of the pan with a clean pastry brush, dipped in cold water, to dissolve any remaining sugar crystals. Boil fairly rapidly to 240–242°F. (115–117°C.) on a sugar thermometer. Draw the pan off the heat, and allow the bubbles to subside.

Mix the cream of tartar with the cold water to a blend and add to the syrup, stirring once or twice. A chef's method at this stage is to pour the syrup on to a wetted marble slab for working, but an easier method for the home cook is to pour the mixture into a mixing basin, splashed with cold water. Leave to cool for about 20 minutes in the bowl. Then beat with a wooden spoon until the mixture turns white, then finally into a solid mass. Cover with a damp cloth and leave for 1 hour to mature. Then store in a covered container until required.

Place the fondant in a mixing basin, over the top of a saucepan half filled with hot water, and warm gently until softened and thin. Add a few drops of water if the icing is very thick. It is now ready to use.

American frosting

American frosting sets fairly quickly when it reaches the right stage in preparation. Have everything ready before starting on the recipe.

Makes sufficient for one 8-inch (20-cm.) cake

1 lb./450 g. granulated sugar
$\frac{1}{4}$ pint/1$\frac{1}{2}$ dl. cold water

2 egg whites

Measure the sugar and water into a saucepan. Place over low heat and stir until the sugar has dissolved. Wash down the sides of the pan with a clean pastry brush, dipped in cold water, to remove any sugar grains that might remain. Bring the sugar syrup up to the boil. Boil rapidly until 245°F. (118°C.) is shown on a sugar thermometer. Draw off the heat and allow to cool just long enough for the bubbles on the surface to subside.

Whisk the egg whites until stiff. Slowly pour the hot sugar syrup on to the egg whites, whisking all the time. Pour the syrup in a steady stream directly on to the area in the basin where being whisked. This incorporates the syrup immediately and in a few minutes the icing becomes thick and light.
For a smooth icing: continue whisking the mixture until the frosting coats the back of a spoon thickly. Quickly pour over the prepared cake. Fix any decoration when the icing has finished dripping but before it has set.

184

For a roughed up icing: continue whisking until the icing begins to crystallise. It clearly changes from a shiny soft mixture to a dull very light texture rather like cotton wool. Spread quickly over the prepared cake and rough up the surface. Fix on any decoration immediately.

Confectioners' custard

A smooth, rich custard that is often used along with fruits in open tarts. It is also used as a filling for eclairs, cream buns, mille feuille and other elaborate patisserie.

Makes ½ pint/3 dl.

½ pint/3 dl. milk	1 oz./25 g. plain flour
vanilla pod	pinch salt
3 egg yolks	1 oz./25 g. butter
2 oz./50 g. castor sugar	

Measure the milk into a saucepan, add the vanilla pod and warm through gently until hot and infused with vanilla. Cream together the egg yolks and sugar until light, then stir in the flour and salt and mix well.

Draw the milk off the heat, remove the vanilla pod and gradually stir the milk into the egg mixture. Blend well and pour back into the milk saucepan. Place over low heat and stir constantly until the mixture comes to the boil and thickens. Remove from the heat, beat in the butter. Stir very thoroughly and then turn into a basin. Allow the custard to cool, stirring fairly often to prevent a skin forming.

Use as required.

Crème au beurre

Crème au beurre is a rich buttercream that sets very firmly when chilled. It is widely used in Continental confectionery because it retains a firm attractive shape.

6 oz./175 g. castor sugar	4 egg yolks
½ pint/3 dl. water	8 oz./225 g. butter

Measure the sugar and water into a saucepan. Stir over low heat until the sugar has dissolved, then bring up to the boil. Cook rapidly until 240°F. (115°C.) is shown on a sugar thermometer or until a little dropped into a saucer of cold water forms a soft ball.

Put the egg yolks into a basin and whisk well. Slowly pour the hot sugar syrup on to the egg mixture, whisking well all the time. When all the syrup is added, the mixture should be quite thick. Beat in the butter (the butter should be at room temperature not cold from the refrigerator), small pieces at a time. Beat very thoroughly until the mixture is thick and light.

Use this mixture for filling or piping while still soft. If the mixture is chilled or kept any length of time after preparation and before using, allow it to stand until it has warmed up to room temperature, then beat well to get the light smooth texture.

Buttercream

Buttercream is suitable for either coating or filling a cake. If a softer, fluffier filling cream is needed, beat in a little golden syrup, using a dessertspoon of syrup for every 2 oz. (50 g.) of fat used.

4 oz./100 g. unsalted butter or margarine	flavouring and colouring to taste
6 oz./175 g. icing sugar, sieved	

Slice the butter or margarine and beat in a warmed bowl until softened. Add half the sifted sugar and beat until the mixture lightens in colour, then gradually beat in the remaining sugar. Colour and flavour as required, about ¼ teaspoon flavouring essence will be sufficient for this quantity.

Lemon buttercream: A fresher flavour is obtained by beating in 1 tablespoon of lemon curd. Colour pale yellow if liked.

Orange buttercream: Beat in 1 tablespoon of lemon curd and the finely grated zest of 1 orange. Add colouring if liked.

Chocolate buttercream: Break up 2 oz. (50 g.) plain chocolate and melt in a basin over a pan of hot water. Cool slightly before beating the melted chocolate into the buttercream. Add a few drops of vanilla or coffee essence.

Coffee buttercream: Beat in 2 teaspoons coffee essence, or a heaped teaspoon of instant coffee dissolved in a teaspoon of hot water.

Home preservation of fruits and vegetables

Most fruits and vegetables can be preserved in a form in which they can be used in recipes, or served during the time of year when the fresh varieties are out of season. The freezing of both and the bottling of fruits come under this category. On the other hand, they can be made into jams, pickles or chutneys – a form in which they can be served to enhance other foods.

Although preservation at home is no longer carried out on the scale it used to be, there is a great deal of satisfaction to be had from freezing your own home grown fruits and vegetables, bottling fruits and from making some of the more unusual jams, pickles and chutneys. All fruits and vegetables respond to some method of preservation, some better than others. It is as well to use each one in the right way, to get the best results.

Apples

Sound, ripe apples picked from the tree, especially late maturing varieties, are the ones to store. Among the best eating apples are the Cox's Orange Pippin, Laxton's Superb and Sturmer Pippin. Among the cooking varieties with the best flavour are Bramley Seedling, Lord Derby, Lane's Prince Albert and Newton Wonder. Pick these apples when fully ripe, that is when the stalks will part easily from the fruit.

To store apples whole, wrap each one separately in oiled paper, tissue or newspaper to prevent the spread of disease from one apple to another. Store in boxes, stacked in layers, in a dark not too dry atmosphere.

Apples are rich in pectin and may be used alone or mixed with other fruits to make jams or jellies. Blanched apple slices can be frozen alone or mixed with blackberries and placed in the freezer. Apples that are bruised or damaged should have those parts cut away and the apples can be used for chutney or for making a sweetened apple purée to bottle or freeze.

Herb jelly

Prepare this jelly using tart flavoured cooking apples and flavour it with the herb of your choice. Mint jelly goes well with lamb, parsley or thyme jelly with beef and sage jelly with pork.

Makes 6 lb./2 kg. 700 g.

4 lb./1 kg. 800 g. cooking apples	granulated or preserving sugar
2¾ pints/1⅓ litres water	(see recipe)
¼ pint/1½ dl. distilled malt	few drops green food colouring
vinegar	4–6 tablespoons chopped fresh
small bunch fresh mint, parsley,	mint, parsley, sage or thyme
sage or thyme	(use herb already chosen)

Wipe the apples then cut into quarters. There is no need to peel or core them. Place in a preserving pan and add the water and vinegar. Bring slowly to the boil and then simmer for about 1 hour. Stir occasionally and mash the apples well to reduce them to a pulp and extract all the pectin.
Draw the pan off the heat and ladle the juice and pulp into a scalded jelly bag or strong linen cloth. Allow to strain for several hours.

Measure the juice back into the preserving pan. Add the chosen bunch of herbs. Bring up to the boil and simmer for 5 minutes to flavour the jelly. Remove and discard the bunch of herbs. For each pint (½ litre) of juice, add 1 lb. (450 g.) sugar. Stir over low heat until the sugar has dissolved. Then bring up to a brisk boil. Cook rapidly to obtain a set or until a drop sets on a cold saucer and wrinkles when pushed with the finger. When ready, draw off the heat and skim. Add a few drops of green colouring and the chopped herb. Allow to stand for 5–10 minutes or until a skin forms on the surface, this ensures even distribution of the chopped herbs.

Stir gently and pour into clean jars. Cover and seal when hot. Label when cold.

Apple and lemon curd

Making lemon curd is a popular way of using up extra egg yolks. This recipe for apple curd is particularly good and makes an interesting change.

Makes 4½ lb./2 kg.

3 lb./1 kg. 400 g. cooking	grated rind and juice 4 lemons
apples	1 level teaspoon ground ginger
½ pint/3 dl. water	¼ level teaspoon ground nutmeg
2 lb./900 g. granulated sugar	8 egg yolks
2 oz./50 g. butter	

Peel, core and cut the apples into slices and then place in a saucepan with the water. Bring to the boil slowly and then cover with a lid. Reduce the heat and cook gently for about 10–15 minutes or until apples are reduced to a purée. Rub the apples through a sieve with a wooden spoon and return the purée to the pan. Add the sugar, butter, lemon rind, lemon juice and spices.

Place over a low heat and stir to dissolve the sugar. Bring the mixture gradually to the boil, stirring all the time. Draw the pan off the heat and stir in the egg yolks. Return the pan to the heat and cook gently until the mixture is hot and has thickened, but do not boil.

Pour into hot clean jars, cover and seal immediately. Store when cold.

Apricots

Fresh apricots have a delicate flavour and they must be used when just ripe.

Apricots can be bottled or frozen, or they can be made into preserves. The stones of fresh apricots have an attractive almond flavoured kernel inside, usually a few are included in apricot preserve. Apricots can be expensive to use in large quantities and it is worth noting that some of the best apricot jams and chutneys are made using dried apricots.

Apricot chutney

Serve apricot chutney with cold pork or veal. Use in sandwiches too; this chutney is very good with cheese.

Makes 4 lb./1 kg. 800 g.

8 oz./225 g. dried apricots	1 level teaspoon salt
4 oz./100 g. stoned raisins, chopped	3 teaspoons mixed pickling spice, tied in muslin bag
4 oz./100 g. sultanas	1 pint/6 dl. distilled malt vinegar
2 cloves garlic, peeled and chopped	1 lb./½ kg. apples, peeled, cored and chopped
juice and finely grated rind 1 lemon	1 lb./450 g. granulated sugar

Wash the apricots, cut into small pieces and soak overnight in cold water to cover. Drain and place the apricots in a large saucepan with the raisins, sultanas, garlic, grated lemon rind, salt, and bag of pickling spices. Add half the vinegar. Bring to the boil and cook gently for 30 minutes.

Add the apples, sugar and remaining vinegar. Stir over a low heat to dissolve the sugar, then cook gently for a further 30 minutes or until the chutney is quite thick. Stir frequently to prevent scorching. Draw the pan off the heat and remove the bag of pickling spices.

Pour into pots and cover with plastic lined screw caps or with a square of cotton material dipped in melted paraffin wax. Label and store for a few months before using.

Dried apricot jam

Apricots make one of the most popular jams. This recipe can be made any time of the year, but dried apricots tend to be more plentiful in the winter months.

Makes 12 lb./5 kg. 400 g.

2 lb./1 kg. dried apricots	7 lb./3 kg. 150 g. granulated sugar
3 good sized lemons	
5½ pints/3 litres 3 dl. water	

Wash the apricots, cut in half and put them in a large basin. Pare the rind from the lemons very thinly, using a potato peeler. Shred the peel finely and add to the apricots. Halve and squeeze the lemons and add the juice. Tie the lemon pips in a bag of muslin and add the bag to the apricots. Pour over the water and leave to soak for 24 hours.

Pour the soaked apricots, liquid and bag of lemon pips into a preserving pan. Bring up to the boil and cook rapidly for about 10 minutes or until the apricots are tender.

Remove the bag of lemon pips and add all the sugar. Stir over a low heat to dissolve the sugar, then bring up to the boil. Cook rapidly, stirring frequently, for about 20 minutes until setting point is reached. Draw off the heat, skim and allow to cool for 5–10 minutes.

Pour into clean, warm jars, then cover and seal while hot. Label when cold.

Beans

Broad, French and runner beans all freeze very well. French or runner beans can also be salted, although more often only runner beans are used. Runner beans are also one of several vegetables used for mustard pickle.

To salt runner beans

Fresh, young, newly picked beans are the only ones to salt. Ideally, beans picked from the garden are best. Limp or older beans only become tough using this process.

3 lb./1 kg. 400 g. fresh beans	1 lb./450 g. kitchen salt

As many beans can be salted as required, but use salt in the proportions given above. Do not wash the beans unless necessary. If they are washed, take care to dry them well. String the beans and then slice them thinly.

Select a large stone jar and put a layer of salt in the bottom. Put in alternate layers of beans and salt, pressing each layer down well. Finish with a layer of salt. As the beans shrink and the salt forms a brine with the moisture drawn from the beans, so more beans and salt can be added to the jar. Always finish with a layer of salt.

Cover the jar airtight for storing, otherwise the salt will draw moisture from the air. Use synthetic skin or cover with the lid of a jar and seal with melted paraffin wax.

To use the beans: Take out the quantity required and drain well. Place in a saucepan and cover with fresh cold water. Bring up to the boil and simmer for 5 minutes. Drain, re-cover with fresh cold water, bring up to the boil and cook until tender – about the same time as for fresh beans.

Mustard pickle

Illustrated in colour on page 117

This makes a fairly crisp pickle, the vegetables may be cooked for up to 10 minutes but take care not to overcook, otherwise they go soft and the pickle is spoilt.

Makes 5–6 lb./2 kg. 250 g.–2 kg. 700 g.

1 lb./½ kg. pickling onions	*for the mustard sauce:*
1 small cauliflower	3 oz./75 g. plain flour
1 lb./½ kg. marrow	4 oz./100 g. castor sugar
1 cucumber	2 oz./50 g. dry mustard
8 oz./225 g. runner beans	½ oz./15 g. turmeric powder
brine solution (see recipe)	2 pints/generous 1 litre malt vinegar

Clean, prepare and cut the vegetables into pieces of a suitable size for eating, leaving the onions whole and breaking the cauliflower into sprigs. Cover with a brine solution of 4 oz.

(100 g.) kitchen salt dissolved in $2\frac{1}{2}$ pints ($1\frac{1}{4}$ litres) water. Leave for 24 hours, then drain.

To prepare the sauce, measure the flour, sugar, mustard powder and turmeric into a saucepan. Add a little vinegar and blend to a paste, then stir in the rest of the vinegar. Stir over gentle heat until boiling and thickened. Add the drained vegetables and cook for 5 minutes. Pack the vegetables into clean hot jars, distributing the different varieties evenly. Pour over sufficient mustard sauce to cover.

Cover with plastic lined screw caps or with a square of cotton material dipped in melted paraffin wax. Label and store for a few months before using.

Beetroot

Fresh summer beetroot grown in the garden, will store very well covered in sand or ashes. Beetroot is also a popular vegetable for pickling. Only the small young beetroot can be frozen.

Pickled beetroot

As this is a root vegetable, the beetroot must be boiled and cooked before it is pickled. Pickle as many of the fresh young beetroot as you require. The spiced vinegar can be made up and kept ready for use. In fact, the best spiced vinegar is made by steeping the spices in the cold vinegar for a period of 2 months, after which the vinegar is strained and used. This pickle will keep about 6 months.

4 lb./1 kg. 800 g. fresh young beetroot	1 teaspoon cloves
	1 teaspoon mace
for the spiced vinegar:	1 teaspoon whole allspice
2 pints/generous 1 litre malt vinegar	6 peppercorns
$\frac{1}{2}$-inch/1-cm. piece stick cinnamon	

Wash the beetroots, taking care not to break the skins. Place in boiling, salted water and simmer gently for $1\frac{1}{2}$ hours or until tender. Drain and allow to cool. Then peel away the skins and slice into rounds about $\frac{1}{4}$ inch ($\frac{1}{2}$ cm.) thick.

Meanwhile, prepare the spiced vinegar. Place the vinegar and spices in a basin and cover with a plate. Place the basin over a saucepan of cold water and bring the water slowly to boiling point. Remove from the heat and leave to stand for 3 hours, then strain.

When the beetroot is cool, pack into bottles and cover with the cold, spiced vinegar. Cover with plastic tops or screw-top metal covers with a plastic coating on the inside.

Serve with cold meats and salads.

Note: For longer keeping, dice the beetroot while still warm, pack loosely in jars and cover with spiced vinegar that has been brought up to the boil.

Blackberries

Blackberries are available in the autumn. There are two types, the cultivated, larger blackberries which appear first in the shops and those wild berries (or brambles) picked from the hedgerow. The cultivated berries are larger and more juicy but the wild ones have the better flavour. Blackberries freeze very well and make excellent preserves. Jams and jellies are often combined with apples.

Blackberry and apple jelly

The distinct flavour of blackberries is a great favourite with children. Use this jelly as a filling for sponge cakes, scones and sandwiches.

Makes 5 lb./2 kg. 250 g.

4 lb./1 kg. 800 g. blackberries	granulated or preserving sugar
2 lb./1 kg. cooking apples	(see recipe)
2 pints/generous 1 litre water	

Pick over and rinse the blackberries. Wipe and cut up the apples, it is not necessary to peel or core them. Put all the fruit into a preserving pan and add the water. Bring up to the boil, then cover and simmer gently until the fruit is soft and pulpy.

Draw the pan off the heat and ladle the contents into a scalded jelly bag or strong linen cloth. Leave to strain for several hours. Do not squeeze the cloth or the resulting jelly will be cloudy.

Measure the juice back into the preserving pan. For every 1 pint (6 dl.) of juice, add 1 lb. (450 g.) of sugar. Stir over low heat to dissolve the sugar then bring back up to the boil. Boil steadily for a set, or until a drop sets on a cold saucer and wrinkles up when pushed with the finger – takes about 10–15 minutes. Draw the pan off the heat and skim.

Pour into clean, warm jars. Cover and seal while hot. Label when cold.

Blackcurrants

Blackcurrants have a rich colour and a rather sour flavour. They are rich in pectin and make excellent jam and jellies. Black-currants also freeze well. A quantity stored in the freezer can be used to make delicious puddings and desserts out of season.

Blackcurrant jam

This is one of the most economical jams to make. Blackcurrants are very high in pectin and can take $1\frac{1}{4}$ lb. (550 g.) of sugar per 1 lb. ($\frac{1}{2}$ kg.) of fruit, which gives an excellent yield.

Makes 9 lb./4 kg. 100 g.

3 lb./1 kg. 400 g. blackcurrants	$3\frac{3}{4}$ lb./1 kg. 700 g. granulated
$2\frac{1}{2}$ pints/$1\frac{1}{4}$ litres water	sugar or preserving sugar

Using the prongs of a fork, remove the berries from the stalks. Rinse in cold water and take care to remove any leaves. Drain the fruit well and place in a preserving pan. Add the water and simmer gently for 15–30 minutes or until skins are tender.

Add the sugar and stir over low heat until the sugar is dissolved. Bring up to a brisk boil and cook rapidly for a set, or until a drop sets on a cold saucer and wrinkles up when pushed with the finger – takes about 10 minutes. When ready, draw the pan off the heat and skim.

Pour into clean, warm jars. Cover and seal when hot. Label when cold.

Cabbage

Cabbage of one kind or another is in season all year round. Red cabbage, however, is seasonal in the autumn and is often pickled for use later in the year. Recipes for red cabbage cooked with apples or onion freeze very well.

Pickled red cabbage

Use pickled red cabbage within 2 months. After this time, the cabbage tends to soften.

Fills 4 (1 lb./½ kg.) jars

1 firm red cabbage, about 2 lb./1 kg.	1 small piece stick cinnamon
4 oz./100 g. coarse kitchen salt	6 cloves
for the spiced vinegar:	5 pieces mace
2 pints/generous 1 litre malt vinegar	2 bay leaves
	2 teaspoons whole allspice

Remove any discoloured outside leaves and cut the cabbage into quarters. Cut away any hard core and shred the cabbage finely. Place in a large bowl and sprinkle each layer with salt. Cover and leave to stand for 24 hours.

In the meantime, prepare the spiced vinegar. Place the vinegar and spices in a basin and cover with a plate. Place the basin over a saucepan of cold water and bring the water slowly to the boil. Remove the pan from the heat and leave the vinegar and spices to infuse for 2–3 hours. Then strain.

Drain the red cabbage and rinse off any salt. Pack loosely into 4 jars and pour over the cold spiced vinegar to come up to the neck of the jar.

Cover with snap-on plastic covers or screw tops with a plastic or waxed lining on the inside. Allow to mature for 1 week before using.

Cherries

The cherries most readily available are the dessert or eating type. For bottling or preserves, the sour Morello or May Duke cherries should be used. As a rule, cherries are best made into preserves or pickles. Cherries are not really suitable for freezing.

Pickled cherries

A delicious sweet sour pickle that is very good with cold meats. Use the acid type of cherry. Morello or May Duke are the best to use.

Makes 3–4 lb./1 kg. 400 g.–1 kg. 800 g.

3 lb./1 kg. 400 g. acid cherries	½ oz./15 g. stick cinnamon
1½ lb./700 g. granulated sugar	½ oz./15 g. whole cloves
1½ pints/scant 1 litre vinegar	½ oz./15 g. bruised root ginger

Rinse the cherries, remove the stalks and stones if liked, but the flavour is better if the stones are left in. Measure the sugar and vinegar into a saucepan. Tie the cinnamon, cloves and root ginger in a muslin bag and add to the pan. Stir over low heat until the sugar has dissolved, then bring up to the boil and simmer for 5 minutes. Add the cherries to the spiced vinegar, bring back to the boil and simmer for 3 minutes only. Draw the pan off the heat. Pour the cherries into a large bowl and leave overnight.

Drain the vinegar off the cherries. Bring the vinegar up to the boil, draw off the heat and pour back over the cherries. Leave overnight.

Strain the vinegar off the cherries and discard the spice bag. Bring the vinegar up to the boil. Add the cherries and boil for 1 minute, then draw off the heat. Strain the vinegar into a clean pan and continue to boil gently until the vinegar is reduced to a syrupy consistency. Meanwhile, pack the cherries into hot dry jars. Fill the jars with the boiling syrup to cover and seal the jars immediately.

Allow to mature for at least 6 weeks before using.

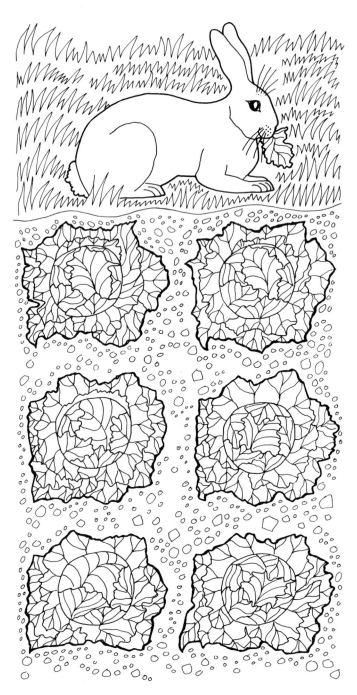

Cranberries

These bright red berries that appear in the shops around late autumn and Christmas have an acid sharp flavour. They make very good preserves and an unusually delicious relish. Cranberries freeze very well and 1-lb. ($\frac{1}{2}$-kg.) packs of cranberries bought in the shops can be stored in the freezer just as they are.

Cranberry and orange relish

This is an uncooked relish and a recipe which has a very good flavour. It keeps well for a week in the refrigerator or longer in the freezer. Use it to cheer up cold roast turkey, chicken or pork. Or serve with cold, cooked ham or bacon.

Makes $1\frac{1}{2}$ pints/9 dl.

1 lb./$\frac{1}{2}$ kg. fresh cranberries   1 lb./450 g. castor sugar
1 large orange

Pick over the cranberries and discard any soft berries or stalks. Rinse the berries under cold water and drain. Pare the rind from the orange very thinly, using a vegetable peeler. Cut away and discard the bitter white pith from around the orange, then coarsely cut up the orange flesh. Discard any pips.

Pass the cranberries, orange rind and the orange flesh through the fine blade on a mincer or a Mouli food mill. Place the minced ingredients in a deep bowl and add the sugar. Cover and leave for 1 day. The sugar will dissolve in the juices from the cranberries and orange. Stir well to blend.

Cover and store in the refrigerator. Use as required.

Cucumber

Cucumbers, which used to be a seasonal summer vegetable, are now available all year round. Some of the old fashioned sweet and sour pickles that were often made with summer cucumbers are still worth preparing.

Sweet spiced pickled cucumbers

A delicious pickle for those who like a sweet sour relish. Excellent with all cold meats. The cucumber can be cut into bite-sized pieces and served with little cubes of cheese and savoury biscuits on a cocktail tray.

6 large cucumbers (about 5 lb./   3 lb./1 kg. 400 g. granulated
  2 kg. 250 g.)   sugar
block salt (see recipe)   3 oz./75 g. mixed pickling spice
3 pints/1$\frac{1}{2}$ litres distilled malt   1-inch/2$\frac{1}{2}$-cm. stick cinnamon
  vinegar

Wash and trim the cucumbers and halve them lengthwise. Cut into 1-inch (2$\frac{1}{2}$-cm.) thick slices and then into chunky pieces. Put in an earthenware bowl and cover with a brine solution, allowing 2 oz. (50 g.) kitchen salt to every 1 pint (6 dl.) water. Cover and leave for 3 days.

Drain the cucumber and rinse well. Place in a saucepan and add 1 pint (3 dl.) of the vinegar. This should just cover the cucumber, add water if necessary. Bring up to the boil and then simmer gently for about 30–40 minutes or until the cucumber is tender and transparent looking. Drain and put the cucumber

in a large china or earthenware bowl; discard the liquid.

Add the remaining vinegar to the pan along with the sugar. Add the pickling spices and the cinnamon stick, tied in a muslin bag. Bring up to the boil and simmer for 5 minutes. Pour over the cucumber pieces and leave to stand for 24 hours. Next day, strain off the vinegar, boil it up again and pour over the cucumbers. Leave for 24 hours. Repeat this procedure once more and leave for 24 hours.

The cucumber is now ready. Strain off the vinegar and pack the cucumber pieces into warm, dry jars. Boil up the vinegar and simmer without a lid until reduced by about a third. Pour over the cucumber to fill the jars. Leave until cold, then cover and label.

Damsons

A small roundish, purple plum with yellow flesh. The damson is very sour and very good for preserves, both for jams and jellies. As a rule, damsons do not freeze well, better results are obtained when the fruit is bottled.

Damson jam

Do not attempt to stone damsons before making jam. The stones will float to the surface particularly after the sugar has been added and can easily be removed using a perforated spoon.

Makes 8 lb./3 kg. 600 g.

4 lb./1 kg. 800 g. damsons   5 lb./2 kg. 250 g. granulated or
1 pint/6 dl. water   preserving sugar

Wash the damsons and remove any stalks. Drain well and place the fruit in a preserving pan with the water. Bring up to the boil and simmer gently until the fruit is tender. Remove as many stones as possible during simmering.

Add the sugar and stir over low heat to dissolve it. Bring up to a brisk boil. Cook rapidly for a set, or until a drop sets on a cold saucer and wrinkles up when pushed with the finger – takes about 15–20 minutes. When ready, draw off the heat and skim well.

Pour into clean, warm jars. Cover and seal when hot. Label when cold.

Gooseberries

All jams, jellies and preserves should be made using the hard green gooseberries that come into season first. The dessert gooseberries which follow later are the eating variety. Both green and dessert gooseberries freeze very well and can be used later in the year for a number of puddings. Dessert gooseberries are the ones to choose for bottling.

Gooseberry chutney

Gooseberries make a particularly good chutney. Store for a few months before using, to allow the flavours to mellow and mature.

Makes 4 lb./1 kg. 800 g.

3 lb./1 kg. 400 g. green gooseberries	1 level tablespoon ground ginger
8 oz./225 g. onions	½ level teaspoon cayenne pepper
½ pint/3 dl. water	1 pint/6 dl. distilled malt vinegar
1½ lb./700 g. granulated sugar	
½ oz./15 g. salt	

Wash the gooseberries, then top and tail. Peel and slice the onions. Either pass both gooseberries and onions through the coarse blade of a mincer or chop both very finely.

Place the mixture in a large pan and add the water. Cook gently until mixture is quite soft and reduced to a pulp. Stir in the sugar, salt, ginger, cayenne pepper and vinegar. Bring to the boil, stirring to dissolve the sugar. Then simmer gently until all the ingredients are soft and the mixture is thick – should take about 1½–2 hours. Chutney should have a long, slow cooking time. It should be thick and smooth and no liquid should separate from the other ingredients when a spoon is drawn through the chutney across the base of the pan.

Ladle or pour the chutney into clean, dry jars. Cover with plastic lined screw caps or with a square of cotton material dipped in melted paraffin wax. Label and store when cold.

Gooseberry jelly

A small bunch of elderflowers tied in a muslin bag and added to the jelly after skimming and before bottling, gives the recipe a delicious muscat flavour. Stir in the jelly for a moment or two and then discard.

Makes 8 lb./3 kg. 600 g.

4 lb./1 kg. 800 g. green gooseberries	granulated or preserving sugar (see recipe)
cold water (see recipe)	

Rinse the gooseberries, there is no need to top and tail them. Place the fruit in a preserving pan and add the water, just enough to cover the fruit. Bring up to the boil and simmer for 20 minutes or until the fruit is tender and pulpy.

Draw the pan off the heat and ladle the contents of the pan into a scalded jelly bag or strong linen cloth. Leave to strain for several hours.

Measure the juice back into the preserving pan. For every 1 pint (6 dl.) of juice, add 1 lb. (450 g.) of sugar. Stir over low heat to dissolve the sugar, then bring up to a brisk boil. Boil steadily for a set, or until a drop sets on a cold saucer and wrinkles up when pushed with the finger – takes about 15 minutes. Draw the pan off the heat and skim.

Pour into clean, warm jars, cover and seal while hot. Label when cold.

Grapefruit

Grapefruit, like all citrus fruits, makes excellent marmalades. No other form of preservation is necessary since grapefruits are a year round fruit.

Grapefruit marmalade

Makes 8–10 lb./3 kg. 600 g.–4 kg. 500 g.

3 medium grapefruit	6 lb./2 kg. 700 g. granulated or preserving sugar
2 large lemons	
4½ pints/scant 2¾ litres water	

Scrub the fruit – the total weight should be about 3 lb. (1 kg. 400 g.). Cut the fruit in half and squeeze out the juice. Cut the peel in quarters and, using a sharp knife, first cut away all the flesh and tissue from the centre of each piece of fruit, then cut away as much of the white pith as possible. Coarsely cut up all this white pith and flesh and place with the pips in a large square, or even two squares, of muslin and tie loosely in a bag. Finely shred the peel of both the grapefruit and the lemons.

Place the shredded peel, the juice, the water and the bag of pips and pith, in a large saucepan. Bring to the boil, then lower the heat and simmer gently for about 2 hours or until the peel is quite tender. Squash the bag of pith occasionally, to encourage the extraction of all the pectin.

When the peel is tender, squeeze the bag of pips – best way to do this is to press the bag between 2 plates, then discard the bag. Add the sugar and stir over low heat until every grain has dissolved. Then bring up to the boil and this time boil rapidly until setting point is reached – takes 15 minutes. Draw off the heat, skim and then allow the marmalade to cool for about 10 minutes. Ladle or pour into clean dry jars. Cover and seal while hot. Label when cold.

Japonica

Japonica is the fruit of the ornamental japonica tree. The fruit should be used when beginning to turn yellow. It has a distinctive flavour and is used to make a delicious jelly.

Japonica jelly

Exactly the same method can be used to make quince jelly. Both are delicious served with roast game and roast pork.

Makes 6 lb./2 kg. 700 g.

4 lb./1 kg. 800 g. japonicas	granulated or preserving sugar (see recipe)
6 pints/3½ litres water	

Wash and cut up the japonicas. Place in a preserving pan and add the water. Bring up to the boil, then cover and simmer gently for about 1–1½ hours until the fruit is quite soft and pulpy. Squash the fruit with a potato masher while simmering, to encourage softening.

Draw the pan off the heat and ladle the contents into a scalded jelly bag or strong linen cloth. Leave to strain for several hours.

Measure the juice back into the preserving pan. For every 1 pint (6 dl.) of juice, add 1 lb. (450 g.) of sugar. Stir over low heat to dissolve the sugar, then bring up to a brisk boil. Boil steadily for a set, or until a drop sets on a cold saucer and wrinkles up when pushed with the finger – takes about 15 minutes. Draw the pan off the heat and skim.

Pour into clean, warm jars. Cover and seal when hot. Label when cold.

Lemon

The lemon is one of the most widely used fruits. In preserves, lemons are used for their flavour and also for their very acid juice, which helps other fruits to obtain a set.

Lemon marmalade

One of the easiest ways to remove lemon peel for marmalade is to mark the peel on each lemon in quarters and place the fruit together in a basin. Cover with boiling water and allow to stand for 5 minutes. Drain and the peel should come away from the fruit quite easily.

Makes 8 lb./3 kg. 600 g.

3 lb. lemons	granulated or preserving sugar
6 pints/3½ litres water	(see recipe)

Wash the lemons well and remove the peel in quarters. Using a sharp knife, cut the white pith away from the peel and shred coarsely. Shred the lemon peel finely. Cut up the lemon flesh coarsely and remove any pips. Place the pips and the coarsely shredded white pith in a square of muslin and tie in a loose bag.

Place the cut up lemons, the finely shredded lemon peel and the muslin bag of pith and pips into a preserving pan. Add the water. Bring up to the boil, cover and simmer gently for about 2 hours or until the lemon peel is quite tender. Remove the muslin bag and squeeze well by pressing between two plates to remove all the juices and liquid.

Measure the liquid and peel remaining in the preserving pan. For every 1 pint (6 dl.) of liquid, add 1 lb. (450 g.) sugar. Stir over low heat until the sugar has dissolved, then bring up to a brisk boil. Boil rapidly for a set, or until a drop sets on a cold saucer and wrinkles when pushed with the finger – takes about 15–20 minutes. Draw off the heat and skim.

Allow the marmalade to cool for about 15–20 minutes as this ensures even distribution of the peel. Pour into clean, warm jars. Cover and seal while hot. Label when cold.

Loganberries

Loganberries are a soft fruit with a dark red colour, similar, but slightly larger, than a raspberry. Loganberries are delicious eaten raw and they freeze very well. They are also used to make a delicious jam.

Loganberry jam

Loganberries or raspberries can be used to make jam. For a seedless preserve, pass the fruit through a nylon sieve after the sugar has dissolved but before bringing the jam up to the boil.

Makes 7 lb./3 kg. 150 g.

4 lb./1 kg. 800 g. logan-berries	4 lb./1 kg. 800 g. granulated or preserving sugar

Hull the fruit but do not wash. Place about a quarter of the fruit in a preserving pan. Using a wooden spoon, crush the fruit in the pan to form some juices. Add the remaining fruit and heat gently until the juices start to flow.

Add the sugar and stir over low heat until the sugar has dissolved. Bring up to a brisk boil and cook steadily for a set, or until a drop sets on a cold saucer and wrinkles up when pushed with the finger – takes about 8–10 minutes. When ready, draw off the heat and skim.

Pour into clean, warm jars. Cover and seal when hot. Label when cold.

Marrow

Although rather tasteless on its own, marrow is used a great deal with other fruits or vegetables to make a variety of chutneys and jams. Marrow is a watery vegetable and because of this does not freeze well.

Marrow and apple chutney

When marrow is prepared for preserves, there is a good deal of waste from the thick peel and the inner seeds, both of which are discarded. The quantity required in this recipe should be weighed after preparation.

Makes 3–4 lb./1 kg. 400 g.–1 kg. 800 g.

2 lb./1 kg. marrow	2 pints/generous 1 litre malt
2 level tablespoons salt	vinegar
1 lb./½ kg. cooking apples	½ oz./15 g. root ginger
8 oz./¼ kg. onions	2 teaspoons mixed pickling
8 oz./225 g. sultanas	spice
8 oz./225 g. soft brown sugar	

The marrow should be peeled and cut into cubes after removing the inner seeds. Place the marrow in layers in a basin and sprinkle the layers with the salt. Leave to stand overnight.

Drain the marrow from the juices that have formed. Rinse thoroughly and place in a preserving pan. Peel and chop the apples and onions. Add these to the marrow with the sultanas and sugar. Add the vinegar. Bruise the root ginger and tie in a muslin bag with the pickling spice. Add to the contents of the pan.

Bring the mixture slowly to the boil. Simmer gently for about 1½–2 hours, until the marrow is tender and the chutney is thick. When a wooden spoon is drawn across the base of the pan, there should be no free liquid. Draw off the heat and remove the bag of spices.

Ladle the chutney into clean warm jars. Cover with snap-on plastic covers or with a square of linen dipped in melted paraffin wax. Store for several months before using.

Medlar

This rather unattractive fruit is russet brown in colour and rather like a large rosehip. Once picked, medlars should be kept for 2–3 weeks until the fruit is really soft and mellow before using. Medlars are made into jam or jelly.

Medlar jelly

Medlars must be used when practically over-ripe. The set and taste are improved if lemon is added.

Makes 2 lb./1 kg.

4 lb./1 kg. 800 g. medlars
3 pints/1½ litres water
2 lemons

granulated or preserving sugar (see recipe)

Rinse the medlars, cut in half and place in the pan with the water and the lemons, cut in pieces. Bring up to the boil, cover and simmer gently until the medlars are soft and pulpy. Strain for several hours through a scalded jelly bag or strong linen cloth. Do not squeeze the bag or the resulting jelly will be cloudy and unappetising.

Measure the juice back into a saucepan. For every 1 pint (6 dl.) of juice, add 1 lb. (450 g.) sugar. Stir over low heat to dissolve the sugar, then bring up to a brisk boil. Boil steadily for a set or until a drop sets on a cold saucer and wrinkles when pushed with the finger – takes about 10 minutes.

When ready, draw off the heat and skim. Pour into clean, warm jars. Cover and seal when hot. Label when cold.

Nuts

Nuts sold in this country are all imported, that is with the exception of locally grown cob nuts. Almonds grown in this country are bitter, which although useful in small quantities for cooking are not suitable for eating. Our sweet chestnuts are too small in size to be of any practical use and walnut trees are scarce.

In September and October, fresh cob nuts are gathered along the Kent and East Sussex borders. These, perhaps, are the only ones worth storing. Cob nuts should be gathered when dry and the outer husks removed.

Spread the nuts out and leave in a warm place to dry very thoroughly. After this, they can be stored in boxes with layers of sand and kept in a cool place.

Some country gardens have walnut trees and the young walnuts can be gathered and pickled. Storing mature walnuts is a little uncertain. The nuts must be absolutely dry, otherwise they are subject to mould and the high oil content tends to make them go rancid.

Pickled walnuts

Walnuts used for pickling should be gathered in early summer while still green and before the shells have formed. Protect the hands when preparing these, walnut stain is very persistent.

Cover the walnuts with a brine made using 1 lb. (450 g.) kitchen salt to 1 gallon (4½ litres) water. Leave to soak for several days.

Drain the walnuts. Spread them out on newspaper and leave exposed to the air so that they will turn black. This takes about 1 day. When quite black, pack the walnuts into jars and cover with the following cold, spiced vinegar.

Place 2 pints (generous 1 litre) malt vinegar in a basin. Add 1 piece stick cinnamon, 6 cloves, 5 pieces mace, 2 bay leaves and 2 teaspoons whole allspice. Cover the basin with a lid, set in a larger saucepan of cold water. Bring the water slowly to the boil.

Remove the pan from the heat and leave the vinegar and spices to infuse for 2–3 hours. Strain and when quite cold the vinegar is ready to fill the jars.

Cover the jars of walnuts with snap-on plastic covers or screw tops with ceresin or waxed linings. Mature for 1 month before using.

Onions

Once taken in from the garden, onions should be spread out and allowed to dry. Hung up in bunches in a dry, dark place, they will store well and can be used as required. Smaller pickling onions are often pickled and served with cold meats. Button onions, which are used a good deal in cookery – particularly casseroles, tend to be seasonal and these can be frozen for using whole in recipes.

Pickled onions

Select small, even-sized onions and use a stainless steel knife for peeling to prevent them from turning black.

Makes 4 lb./1 kg. 800 g.

4 lb./1 kg. 800 g. small onions
coarse kitchen salt (see recipe)
for the spiced vinegar:
2 pints/generous 1 litre malt vinegar

1 small piece stick cinnamon
6 cloves
5 pieces mace
2 bay leaves
1 dessertspoon whole allspice

Using a stainless steel knife, trim away either end of each onion. Peel and then place the onion in a fresh brine, made using 8 oz. (225 g.) kitchen salt to 2 quarts (2¼ litres) cold water. Leave the onions to soak for 24–48 hours, making sure that they remain below the surface of the brine.

Meanwhile, prepare the spiced vinegar. Place the vinegar and spices in a basin and cover with a plate. Place the basin in a large saucepan of cold water and bring the water slowly to the boil. Remove the pan from the heat and leave the vinegar and spices to infuse for 2–3 hours, then strain. This spiced vinegar can be prepared in advance.

Drain the onions from the brine, rinse in cold water and drain very thoroughly. Pack the onions tightly into one or several jars, leaving the neck of the jar free. If any water settles in the bottom of the jars during packing, this should be poured away before adding the spiced vinegar. Cover the onions with the cold spiced vinegar, which should come at least ½ inch (1 cm.) above the onions to allow for evaporation.

Cover the jars with snap-on plastic covers or use screw tops with a ceresin or waxed lining on the inside. Keep for 3–4 months before using.

Oranges

Sweet oranges are available all year round, the bitter Seville oranges during the months of January and February only. Sweet or Seville oranges can be used with other citrus fruits to make marmalade. Sweet oranges can also be preserved as a sweet pickle, which is very good served with meat or poultry.

Sweet orange and lemon marmalade

This marmalade recipe can be made any time during the year. A useful recipe to make in autumn when stocks may be running low.

Makes 6 lb./2 kg. 700 g.

4 sweet oranges	about 4 lb./1 kg. 800 g.
4 lemons	granulated or preserving
4 pints/2¼ litres water	sugar

Scrub all the fruit and pick out the discs at the stalk end. Halve the fruit and squeeze out the juice. Quarter the peels and, using a sharp knife, cut away the excess white pith and bits of flesh. Tie the pips and chopped white pith loosely in a muslin bag. Shred the orange and lemon peel finely.

Place the shredded peel, the muslin bag of pith and pips and the juice in a preserving pan. Add the water. Bring up to the boil, cover and simmer gently for 1½–2 hours or until the peel is quite tender.

Draw the pan off the heat and remove the muslin bag. Squeeze the bag between two plates to remove all the juice. Measure the volume of peel and liquid remaining in the pan and for every 1 pint (6 dl.), add 1 lb. (450 g.) sugar. Replace over low heat and stir until the sugar has dissolved. Bring to a brisk boil and cook rapidly for a set, or until a drop sets on a cold saucer and wrinkles up when pushed with the finger – takes about 15–20 minutes. Draw off the heat and skim.

Allow the marmalade to cool for 15–30 minutes to ensure even distribution of the peel. Pour into clean, warm jars. Cover and seal when hot. Label when cold.

Seville orange marmalade

This recipe, where the cooked oranges are chopped or minced, is an easy one to make. Use a large preserving pan and boil fast for a quick set and a good flavour.

Makes 10 lb./4 kg. 500 g.

3 lb./1 kg. 400 g. Seville oranges	6 lb./2 kg. 700 g. granulated or preserving sugar
4 pints/2¼ litres water	2 lemons

Scrub the oranges and remove the small disc at the stalk end. Place in a large saucepan and cover with 3 pints (1½ litres) of the water. Cover with a lid and simmer gently for about 1 hour until the oranges are soft. Test by piercing with a knife.

Lift out the softened oranges, reserving the water they were cooked in. Cut each orange in half and scoop out the flesh and pips from the centre of each into a saucepan. Add the remaining pint of water to the flesh and pips, bring to the boil and simmer for 10 minutes.

Finely chop or mince the soft orange peel and put in a large preserving pan with the reserved cooking water. Add the sugar, the juice from the lemons and the strained water from the flesh and pips. Stir over low heat until the sugar has dissolved, then bring up to the boil. Boil briskly for a set – takes about 15–20 minutes.

Draw the pan off the heat and skim. Allow the marmalade to stand for about 20 minutes. This ensures even distribution of the peel. Ladle or pour into clean, warm jars. Cover and seal while hot.

Pickled orange wedges

This unusual sweet pickle is attractive and colourful. It goes particularly well with cold meat and poultry.

Makes 3 1-lb. (½-kg.) jars

4 medium oranges	12 whole cloves
½ level teaspoon bicarbonate of soda	1 (3-inch/7½-cm.) piece stick cinnamon
1 pint/6 dl. malt vinegar	½ oz./15 g. bruised root ginger
½ oz./15 g. whole allspice	1 lb./450 g. granulated sugar

Wash and cut each orange into 8–12 segments (leaving the skin on). Cover with water and add the bicarbonate of soda. Bring to the boil and simmer for 30 minutes. Tie the spices in a piece of muslin and simmer in a covered saucepan with the vinegar for 20 minutes.

When the orange peel is soft, drain off the water. Remove the spice bag from the vinegar. Add the sugar to the vinegar and stir over low heat to dissolve the sugar. Bring the vinegar to the boil and add the orange segments. Cover with a lid and simmer for a further 20 minutes.

Remove the orange segments with a draining spoon and put into hot dry jars. Boil the vinegar and sugar to reduce to a thick syrup. Fill the jars to the top with the syrup.

Cover with snap-on plastic covers or with a square of linen dipped in melted paraffin wax. Label when cold.

Seville orange and ginger marmalade

The addition of ginger gives this marmalade recipe a particularly good flavour.

Makes 6–8 lb./2 kg. 700 g.–3 kg. 600 g.

2 lb./1 kg. Seville oranges	4 lb./1 kg. 800 g. granulated or preserving sugar
1 lemon	
1 oz./25 g. root ginger	2 oz./50 g. crystallised ginger
4 pints/2¼ litres water	

Scrub the oranges well and pick off the small disc at the stalk end. Cut the fruit in half, squeeze out the juice and pips. Quarter the orange peel and cut away the excess white pith and flesh. Set the orange peels aside and coarsely shred the white pith. Tie the white pith, bits of flesh, pips and the bruised root ginger in a large square of muslin. The bag should be loose so that the water will circulate through and extract all the pectin.

Shred the orange peels finely and place in a preserving pan. Add the juices, the bag of pith and pips and the water. Bring to the boil, cover and simmer gently for 1½–2 hours or until the peel is quite tender.

Remove the bag of pith and pips and squeeze gently between two plates to extract all the liquid. Add the sugar and stir over low heat until the sugar has dissolved. Bring to a brisk boil and cook rapidly for a set, or until a drop sets on a cold saucer and wrinkles up when pushed with the finger – takes about 15–20 minutes. When ready, draw off the heat and skim.

Wash the sugar coating off the crystallised ginger and chop the ginger finely. Add to the marmalade and allow the marmalade to cool for about 15–30 minutes. This ensures that the peel is evenly distributed. Pour into clean warm jars. Cover and seal while hot. Label when cold.

Peaches

Peaches are imported from several countries. As a rule, being very low in pectin and with a delicate flavour, they do not make good jams or jellies. They do, however, respond to preservation in a pickle or with spirits such as brandy. Peaches discolour quickly and do not usually freeze well but are very good bottled. They are often combined with other fruit to make a bottled fruit salad.

Peaches in brandy

This is a recipe to prepare when peaches are cheap and plentiful. Prepare as many as the chosen jar or jars will hold, using the proportions of sugar and water for the syrup given here and the slightly less expensive grape brandy.

12–16 peaches	few cloves and piece stick
2 lb./900 g. castor sugar	cinnamon
1 pint/6 dl. water	1 bottle brandy (see recipe)

Using a perforated spoon, dip the peaches one at a time into a saucepan of boiling water. Allow to simmer for about 2 minutes then drain and immediately plunge into a bowl of cold water. Peel away the skins. Pack the peaches into one large or several smaller jars, choosing jars that have either a screw top or air-tight cover.

Measure the sugar and water into a saucepan and stir over low heat to dissolve the sugar. Bring up to the boil and simmer for 5 minutes. Draw off the heat and pour the syrup over the peaches, filling the jars not more than half full. Add a few cloves and a small piece of stick cinnamon to each jar and leave until quite cold. Top each jar up with the brandy to cover the peaches. Cover the jars with the tops and store for a month before using. Turn the jars gently occasionally to mix the liquid.

After a time, the peaches may darken in colour but this does not in any way impair the flavour. After a month the jar may be opened and the peaches used as required. Re-cover the jars each time. Serve as a dessert with cream or ice cream.

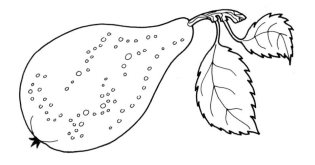

Pears

There are two types of pears – the hard cooking pear and the dessert pear. All pears should be picked off the tree before they are ripe. They should be allowed to ripen slowly in a warm kitchen temperature. Pears have a delicate flavour and are low in pectin content. Because of this, they do not make good jams or jellies but are excellent mixed with vegetables to make chutney, or with spice, sugar and vinegar to make a sweet pickle.

Pears do not freeze well but are excellent bottled. Use wind-fall pears for chutneys and dessert pears for bottling.

Sweet pickled pears

Sweet pickled fruits are good with cold meats. Spiced pears or peaches are particularly good with ham, gammon or pork. Use distilled malt vinegar and castor sugar to obtain a light colour in this sweet pickle.

Makes 4 lb./1 kg. 800 g.

4 lb./1 kg. 800 g. firm dessert pears	2 teaspoons whole cloves
2 lb./900 g. castor sugar	2 teaspoons whole allspice
1 pint/6 dl. distilled malt vinegar	3 (2-inch/5-cm.) pieces stick cinnamon
	1 piece root ginger

Peel, quarter and core the pears and place in a bowl of acidulated cold water as they are prepared.

Measure the sugar and vinegar into a large saucepan and add the crushed spices, stick cinnamon and bruised root ginger loosely tied in a muslin bag. Stir over low heat until the sugar has dissolved.

Bring up to the boil and add the pears. Simmer gently until the fruit is tender. Drain the fruit from the vinegar and remove the bag of spices. Replace the pan of vinegar over the heat and boil quickly until reduced to a thin, honeylike syrup. Meanwhile, pack the pears neatly into clean warm jars.

Draw the boiling syrup off the heat and fill each jar of pears with enough syrup to cover the fruit. Cover with snap-on plastic tops or with a circle of greaseproof paper and then a square of cotton dipped in melted paraffin wax.

Label and store for several months before using.

Plums

Of all varieties of plums, the Victoria plum is the most versatile. This is not only a good eating plum but is the best for bottling and preserves. Plums make excellent jams, often combined with apple. As a rule, plums do not freeze well but are excellent for bottling. Plums can also be made into chutney and a very good spicy sauce for meats.

Plum jam

Greengages, Victoria, red or purple plums all make delicious, fresh-tasting preserves.

Makes 7 lb./3 kg. 150 g.

4 lb./1 kg. 800 g. plums	4 lb./1 kg. 800 g. granulated
¾ pint/½ litre water	or preserving sugar

Choose slightly under-ripe fruit. Pick over and remove any stalks and damaged fruit. Slit the fruit through to the stone all round, following the line. Twist the two halves in opposite directions to separate them. Remove the stones.

If the stones are difficult to remove, cook the plums whole and remove as many of the stones as possible with a perforated spoon, as they rise to the surface. Place the fruit and water in a preserving pan and simmer gently for 10–20 minutes or until the fruit is tender.

Meanwhile, crack about a dozen of the stones and remove the kernels. Blanch these by dipping into boiling water for 1 minute, then drain. Reserve the kernels for adding to the jam.

Add the sugar and stir over low heat until the sugar is dissolved. Bring up to a brisk boil and cook rapidly for a set – about 15–20 minutes. Test after about 15 minutes and, when ready, draw off the heat. Add the kernels. Skim and pour into warm, dry jars. Cover and seal.

Plum chutney

Use ripe dark red or purple plums to make this chutney and for a pleasant fruity flavour use cider vinegar instead of malt.

Makes 4 lb./1 kg. 800 g.

2½ lb./1 kg. 200 g. plums	1 lb./450 g. brown sugar
1 lb./½ kg. onions	2 teaspoons cloves
2 lb./1 kg. cooking apples	2 teaspoons allspice
½ oz./15 g. salt	2 teaspoons black peppercorns
⅓ pint/2¼ dl. malt vinegar	small piece of bruised root
for the spiced vinegar:	ginger
½ pint/3 dl. malt vinegar	

Wipe, halve and stone the plums. Peel the onions and chop them finely. Peel and core the apples, chop into tiny dice. Put all these into a pan with the salt and the malt vinegar. Cover and simmer until soft.

Meanwhile prepare the spiced vinegar. Bring the vinegar, sugar and spices to the boil and simmer for 5 minutes. Draw off the heat and leave to infuse for 30 minutes. Strain the spiced vinegar over the softened fruit and continue simmering, stirring occasionally, until the mixture is soft and pulpy – takes about 2 hours.

Pour into hot dry jars. Cover with plastic snap-on covers or squares of linen dipped in melted paraffin wax. Label when cold and store for 2 months before using.

Raspberries

Raspberries are a soft, juicy fruit with a delicious flavour. They are one of the most popular summer fruits and freeze well. They can also be made into jams or jellies, often combined with redcurrants, since the two flavours combine particularly well.

Fresh raspberry jam

This is an uncooked preserve and will keep for 6–8 months in the freezer. It should be stored in small containers that seal airtight and used quickly once opened. Serve as a spread on hot toast or fresh scones. It can also be stirred to make a thick Melba sauce for ice cream.

Makes 4 lb./1 kg. 800 g.

1¼ pints/¾ litre crushed raspberries	2 tablespoons lemon juice
	½ bottle liquid pectin
2 lb./900 g. castor sugar	

Mix the crushed fruit, sugar and lemon juice. Allow to stand, stirring occasionally, until all the sugar has dissolved. This takes about 1 hour. Add the liquid pectin and stir for 2 minutes. Ladle into containers, leaving about ½ inch (1 cm.) at the neck. Allow to stand for 24 hours, or until set. Cover and place in the freezer.

Redcurrants

These bright red, very acid berries are similar to blackcurrants. Redcurrants freeze very well and, being high in pectin, make excellent jelly. The numerous seeds in redcurrants means that they are more often made into jelly than jam. Redcurrant juice is often added to other jam or jelly recipes to encourage the mixture to set.

Spiced redcurrant jelly

Serve this piquant flavoured jelly with roast lamb or pork and with cold meats.

Makes 5 lb./2 kg. 250 g.

3 lb./1 kg. 400 g. redcurrants	granulated or preserving sugar
1½ pints/scant 1 litre water	(see recipe)
3 cloves	distilled malt vinegar
½-inch/1-cm. stick cinnamon	(see recipe)

Wash the fruit and remove any leaves, but there is no need to strip the berries from the stem. Place the fruit in a preserving pan with the water. Add the cloves and cinnamon tied in a muslin bag. Bring to the boil and simmer gently for about 30 minutes or until the fruit is tender. Mash the fruit well and draw off the heat. Ladle the fruit and juice into a scalded jelly bag and leave to strain for about 30 minutes.

Measure the juice back into the preserving pan and for every 1 pint (6 dl.), add 1¼ lb. (550 g.) sugar and 2 tablespoons vinegar. Stir over low heat until the sugar has dissolved, then bring to the boil and simmer rapidly for a set – takes about 10 minutes. Draw off the heat, skim and pour into clean, warm jars. Cover and seal while hot.

Rhubarb

The first rhubarb available in the season is the tender, pink forced rhubarb. This has a pretty colour and very fresh flavour, and is excellent for freezing. The garden rhubarb which follows has a greenish pink stalk and a more acid flavour. Garden rhubarb is the kind to use for chutney or for jam.

Rhubarb and blackcurrant jam

Garden rhubarb can be picked right up until June. It is often used with soft fruits to make a more economical jam. In this recipe, rhubarb is combined with blackcurrants. The same recipe can be made with raspberries, using only $\frac{1}{4}$ pint ($1\frac{1}{2}$ dl.) water.

Makes 6 lb./2 kg. 700 g.

1 lb./$\frac{1}{2}$ kg. trimmed rhubarb	$3\frac{1}{2}$ lb./1 kg. 600 g. granulated
2 lb./1 kg. blackcurrants	or preserving sugar
$\frac{3}{4}$ pint/$\frac{1}{2}$ litre water	

Wash the trimmed rhubarb and cut the stalks into 1-inch ($2\frac{1}{2}$-cm.) lengths. Strip the blackcurrants from the stems, using the prongs of a fork. Rinse the berries. Place the fruit together in a large preserving pan and add the water. Bring up to the boil and simmer gently for about 30–40 minutes, to soften the fruit and draw out the juices.

Add the sugar and stir over low heat until dissolved. Bring back to a brisk boil. Cook rapidly for a set, or until a drop sets on a cold saucer and wrinkles up when pushed with the finger – takes about 10–15 minutes. Draw the pan off the heat and skim.

Pour into clean, warm jars, cover and seal when hot. Label when cold.

Strawberries

Strawberries are plentiful in summer and make delicious preserves. Strawberries are low in pectin and need lemon juice or fruit pectin added to get a set. They are often combined with other acid fruits such as redcurrants or gooseberries. Strawberries are very popular frozen, in spite of the fact that they tend to become soft. Strawberry purée is excellent for the freezer. Strawberries lose their colour when bottled and this method of preservation is not recommended.

Whole strawberry jam

The most popular strawberry jam is that in which the berries remain whole. In a recipe such as this, sufficient liquid pectin in the form of gooseberry or redcurrant juice or commercial liquid pectin should be added to get a set. Use small strawberries to get the best effect.

Makes 5 lb./2 kg. 250 g.

$2\frac{1}{2}$ lb./1 kg. 200 g. small	juice 1 lemon
strawberries	$\frac{1}{2}$ bottle commercial liquid
3 lb./1 kg. 400 g. granulated	pectin
or preserving sugar	

Hull the strawberries and place in a preserving pan. Cover with the sugar and leave to stand for 1–2 hours to draw out the fruit juices. Add the lemon juice and stir over low heat until the sugar has dissolved – take care not to crush the fruit. Bring up to the boil and boil briskly for 4 minutes. Draw the pan off the heat and stir in the liquid pectin.

Allow to cool for 30 minutes so that the berries are evenly distributed. Pour into clean, warm jars. Cover and seal.

Tomatoes

Usually surplus tomatoes are used to make chutneys or sauces and both ripe and unripe tomatoes can be used. Tomato purée used so much in cookery is not worth the time and trouble to prepare at home. Very large quantities of tomatoes are required to make the purée and it is not economical unless the tomatoes are very cheap. As a rule, whole tomatoes are too watery to freeze with much success. A purée can be frozen for use in recipes.

Tomato sauce

This sauce has a pleasant, mildly spicy flavour. Use the correct narrow necked bottles to hold the sauce. Corks and paraffin wax can be bought from a chemist shop.

Fills about 5 sauce bottles

6 lb./2 kg. 700 g. ripe tomatoes	$\frac{1}{2}$ level teaspoon ground ginger
8 oz./225 g. granulated sugar	$\frac{1}{2}$ level teaspoon mixed spice
2 level tablespoons salt	$\frac{1}{2}$ level teaspoon ground mace
$\frac{1}{2}$ pint/3 dl. vinegar	pinch cayenne pepper

Wash tomatoes, quarter and put in a large saucepan. Cook gently without a lid until the tomatoes are soft. Place a large sieve, preferably nylon or hair, over a mixing bowl and, using a wooden spoon, rub the tomato pulp through the sieve, leaving the seeds and skins behind.

Return the sieved tomato pulp to the saucepan and add the sugar, salt, vinegar, spices and pepper. Cook gently, stirring until the sugar has dissolved, then simmer uncovered until the pulp is thick and will coat the back of a spoon. When the sauce is the correct consistency, pour into a warm jug and fill approximately 5 warmed bottles to within 1 inch ($2\frac{1}{2}$ cm.) of the top. Cork lightly and tie with fine white string.

Place the filled bottles in a large pan, lined on the base with a layer of corrugated cardboard to make a double bottom. Fill with enough hot water to reach the necks of the bottles. Bring to the boil and simmer for 15 minutes. Remove from the hot water and allow to cool.

Press corks in firmly and dip tops in melted paraffin wax to seal. Label and store.

Bottling fruit

In spite of modern forms of preservation by freezing, many fruits – particularly apricots, cherries, peaches, pears and plums – retain a better flavour and colour when preserved by bottling than they do in the freezer. Small quantities of bottled fruits can be very useful and are worth making.

The process of fruit bottling depends on efficient sterilization for success. The object is to kill the yeasts and moulds present and then by sealing airtight, to prevent others from contaminating the contents of the jar. This is achieved by heat; the time required for fruits varies with the size of the jar and with the pack, which can be either whole fruit, sliced fruit or a purée. Fruit high in acid requires a shorter time than those low in acid.

Jars and seals

Use scrupulously clean jars, with either a screw top and a metal cap with a rubber ring such as the Kilner type, or those with a rubber ring and a clip top. The new, rather modern looking, Swiss Buclach preserving jars are of this type and they come in clear glass or green glass. The advantage of the green glass is that it helps preserve the colour of the fruit in the jar during storage. Preserving jars usually come in 1 lb. ($\frac{1}{2}$ kg.), 2 lb. (1 kg.), and 4 lb. (1 kg. 800 g.) sizes; the 1 lb. ($\frac{1}{2}$ kg.) and 2 lb. (1 kg.) are the most useful. Make sure the jars are perfect with no chips and that the rubber rings are new.

Preparing the sugar syrup

Most fruits retain a better colour and flavour when bottled in a sugar syrup. The strength of syrup used depends on the type of fruit to be bottled. Some fruits require a medium syrup and others heavy syrup – see chart. For a medium syrup, dissolve 4 oz. (100 g.) castor sugar or granulated sugar in every 1 pint (6 dl.) of water. For a heavy syrup, increase the sugar used to 8 oz. (225 g.). Dissolve the sugar in the water over low heat, bring up to the boil and simmer for 2 minutes. Draw off the heat and the syrup is ready for use.

The amount of syrup required for a number of bottles will depend on how tightly packed the fruit is in the jar. Prepare about 3 pints ($1\frac{1}{2}$ litres) syrup for every 6 (1 lb./$\frac{1}{2}$ kg.) jars of fruit. A little extra syrup can be made up very quickly, if necessary.

Method of sterilization

Although there are several methods of sterilizing the jars of fruit, the one that is most practical is the quick oven method. This method is ideal for a small quantity of bottled fruit and the timing is given in the following chart. Using this method, bottle not more than 6 (1 lb./$\frac{1}{2}$ kg.) jars of fruit at any one time.

Preheat the oven for 15 minutes at 300°F., 150°C., Gas Mark 2. Prepare the fruit – see chart. Pack the fruit into the jars up to the shoulders.

Add the boiling sugar syrup, pouring gently over the fruit and fill to within 1 inch ($2\frac{1}{2}$ cm.) of the tops. Place the jars on a baking tray lined with newspaper and arrange the jars so that they are at least 2 inches (5 cm.) apart. This allows the heat to circulate. Cover with the rubber rings and top or the metal caps. Do not seal airtight at this stage.

Place the tray in the centre of the oven and process for the time recommended on the chart. When the time is complete, remove the tray of jars from the oven and immediately place on screw tops and tighten up or press down the clips to close the jars and to seal them airtight. Cover with a cloth and leave until quite cold.

Preparation of fruit	Type of syrup	Time in oven at 300°F., 150°C., Gas Mark 2 for not more than 6 lb. (2 kg. 700 g.)
Apricots: Cut in half round the line on the fruit. Twist halves in opposite directions. Remove kernel stones, crack a few kernels – these may be added to the fruit. Pack fruit quickly to prevent discolouration.	Heavy	65 minutes
Blackberries: Pick over and discard any hard or under-ripe fruit. Remove hulls and examine carefully for maggots.	Medium	55 minutes
Blackcurrants: Blackcurrants bottle better than redcurrants. Strip berries from stems with a fork. Use only ripe currants.	Heavy	55 minutes
Cherries: Bottle at the firm ripe stage. Acid varieties of cherries give best results. Remove stalks but leave stones in for best flavour.	Medium	55 minutes
Damsons: Leave fruit whole. Remove stalks and wipe off any bloom from the skin which makes the syrup cloudy. Rinse in cold water.	Medium	55 minutes
Gooseberries: Choose acid green gooseberries. Pick over and top and tail, slicing off a small piece to allow syrup to penetrate.	Medium	55 minutes
Loganberries: Pick over fruit carefully, handling gently. Remove hulls and examine carefully for maggots.	Heavy	45 minutes
Peaches: Dip in boiling water for 1 minute, then plunge in cold water and peel off skins. Halve and remove the stone. Pack quickly to prevent discolouration.	Heavy	55 minutes
Pears: Use dessert pears only. Peel, halve and then scoop out cores with a teaspoon. Put fruit in water with lemon juice added as prepared, to prevent discolouration. Drain and pack quickly.	Heavy	65 minutes
Plums: Bottle Victoria plums when just turning pink, yellow plums when firm and purple plums when bright red. Halve and remove stones as for apricots. Wipe bloom off dark varieties.	Heavy	65 minutes
Rhubarb: Bottle tender stalks of early rhubarb. Trim and cut into even lengths of 1–2 inches (2½–5 cm.). Pour boiling syrup over fruit and leave overnight. Strain and reheat syrup for pouring over packed fruit.	Heavy	45 minutes
Raspberries: Handle fruit with care, to prevent damage. Do not wash. Remove hulls and examine carefully for maggots.	Medium	45 minutes

To test for a seal

Before testing for a seal, leave the jars preferably overnight. Unscrew metal rings or remove the clips, according to the type of jar used. Carefully lift each jar in turn, by the lid only. If the seal is secure, the vacuum inside the jar will hold it closed.

Storing

Place the jars in a cool, dark cupboard. Rub round the tops of metal caps with a little vaseline to prevent rusting during storage.

Cooking for a crowd

Whatever the occasion, the first and most important essential is to plan the menu. Choose foods that are suitable for the occasion and ones that fit in with the time you can allow for preparation. Be guided by the hints, recipe suggestions, ideas and quantities given in this chapter.

Food storage is important and notes on storing food in your refrigerator and freezer are given in this chapter.

Advance preparation

Make out a detailed shopping list. Recheck the shopping list carefully, nothing is more infuriating to a busy cook than to run out of an ingredient just when it is needed most. List the foods under two types, the dry groceries that can be ordered and bought days in advance and the perishable foods that can only be purchased when required for cooking. Check dry groceries in the store cupboard and order any that are running low.

The shopping for perishable foods can be completed 1–2 days before the food is required, provided there is adequate refrigerator space. Consult the detailed list of storage times for food in the refrigerator. Make sure you have plenty of refrigerator bags, covers for bowls, wax paper and foil for wrapping. Food carefully wrapped and protected will keep in the refrigerator in perfect condition for a limited time.

Plan and prepare some of the work in advance. Many parts of a recipe can be made up ahead, ingredients can be measured, sauces prepared and pastry made. Even parts of a recipe, like breadcrumbs to make and cheese to grate, can be done the day before. Most recipes have a stage up to which they can be prepared in advance. Others can be kept hot without spoiling. Spread the load of work by having one or more cold courses in a menu, that can be completely prepared the day before.

Cooking equipment

Large pans, but even more important, large adequately sized serving dishes are required for party foods. If you enjoy entertaining friends at home, it is wise to build up a collection of good sized serving dishes.

Large saucepans or aluminium preserving pans are ideal for top of the stove cooking. Very useful indeed are really large roasting tins – although not too large to fit your oven. These can be used for oven frying chicken joints or sausages, or as containers for large sized servings of lasagne or macaroni. Also useful for heating through rolls or baking lots of potatoes. Make sure you have plenty of mixing basins and several baking trays – these are particularly useful for baking several pizza, numerous layers of meringues for a buffet gâteau, or batch baking of cookies or scones for a coffee morning.

Quantities in recipes

One or two specially selected recipes in this chapter serve larger than average numbers of up to 12 portions. It is, however, easier to prepare and handle quantities of 6–8 servings. For 12–16 servings, simply double the ingredients. In this case, prepare the recipe twice simultaneously rather than attempt to cook double the ingredients in one pan. Cooking times can vary considerably when quantities are increased to large numbers. A single mistake or a wrong measure can ruin a whole batch of food.

Food storage and your refrigerator

The low temperature in a refrigerator will store all foods for a limited time. Food stored in the refrigerator must be protected properly since the action of refrigeration actually draws moisture. Flavours of different foods in the refrigerator will not be absorbed from each other if they are stored in containers, or kept wrapped or covered. For this reason, always have rolls of kitchen foil, waxed paper (greaseproof paper is no use because it is absorbent and allows evaporation to take place), and rolls of the new plastic film wrapping. The latter is very useful for placing over the surface of cakes, cheese or fresh fruit. The fine film clings to the surface over which it is placed. Plenty of plastic containers or tubs with airtight lids and polythene bags are useful too.

Different parts of the refrigerator are best for different foods.
1. Raw foods such as meat, bacon, poultry and fish should be kept directly under the frozen food compartment, in the coldest part of the refrigerator.

2. Vegetables and salad ingredients should be placed at the bottom of the refrigerator or in the vegetable crisper if there is one.

3. Cooked meats and any made up dishes can go on the middle shelf.

4. Butter and eggs usually have special compartments.

5. Frozen foods should go into the freezer compartment of the refrigerator, unless for immediate consumption. Accurate storage of frozen foods depends on the temperature of the freezer compartment. In other words, the lower the temperature, the longer the food will keep. If your frozen food compartment has one star, it means the temperature of the compartment operates at under 21°F. (−6°C.) and keeps frozen food for 1 week. With 2 stars, the frozen food compartment operates at below 10°F. (−12°C.) the frozen food will keep for a month. Three stars and a temperature of not higher than 0°F. (−18°C.) means that food will keep for up to three months.

DAIRY FOODS

Milk	Wipe bottles clean and put in space provided.	3–4 days
Buttermilk	Keep in container.	7–10 days
Cream	Dairy cream will keep longer in an unopened container; once opened cover with an extra piece of foil as cream will absorb other flavours quickly.	4–6 days
Sour cream	Same applies as above. Very useful for salad dressings and sauces in summer.	1 week
Yoghurt	Keep a few different varieties. Fruit flavoured ones are particularly good.	1 week

Meat	Remove meat from butcher's wrapping, unless in sealed vacuum pack. Raw meat should be left uncovered and placed in special meat containers. Otherwise lightly cover with waxed paper or foil and place in top half of the refrigerator. Bacteria attacks cut surfaces of meat, for this reason a large joint which has a single cut surface will keep in perfect condition for a longer period than minced beef which has many cut surfaces. Store as follows:	
	uncooked joints	3–5 days
	chops and steaks	3 days
	stewing steak	2–3 days
	minced beef	1 day
	offal, liver, kidneys (if latter are covered with suet leave on to protect them).	1 day
Cooked meat dishes	Cover and store in dish.	2 days
Beef or pork sausages	Give extra wrapping of foil.	2–3 days
Chicken	Remove chicken from butcher's wrappings. Remove giblets from inside bird. Lightly cover with foil.	2–3 days
	Chicken joints.	2 days
Frozen birds	Leave in original wrapping. Set in main part of cabinet for thawing. Once thawed, use quickly.	1 day
Cooked roast chicken	Remove stuffing from inside roast bird. Wrap in foil and store separately. Stuffing should be used up quickly.	2–3 days
Cooked poultry dishes	Keep covered in dish.	1 day
Sliced bacon	Keep vacuum seal packs intact. Watch date mark. Once opened, place bacon in covered container.	1 week
Bacon joints	Smoked or cured joints can be stored in the original wrapping if vacuum sealed. Otherwise wrap in foil and place on a low shelf. Bacon joints also keep in a cool larder.	1 week

Evaporated milk	One or two small cans in the refrigerator are useful for desserts. Chilled milk whips up much more quickly.	indefinitely
Hard cheeses	Keeps perfectly wrapped in foil or in a refrigerator box. When serving cheese, always remove from the refrigerator at least 1 hour before serving. Flavour is improved at room temperature.	2–4 weeks
Soft cheese	Some soft cheese such as Camembert or Brie are very perishable. Cream cheese wrapped in foil will keep well.	1–2 days 1 week
Blue cheese	Wrap blue, strong smelling cheese in foil.	2–4 days
Eggs (whole)	Store whole eggs small end down in the container provided. Otherwise far away from cold compartment. Remove eggs from refrigerator to warm up before using in recipes.	1–2 weeks
Egg (yolks)	If whole, cover egg yolks with water.	1–2 days
Egg (whites)	Keep in covered container. Mark number of whites on outside of container.	up to 1 week
Butter and fats	Leave in wrappings, these give sufficient protection. Remove butter for baking to soften slightly before using.	1 week
Suet drippings	Keeps almost indefinitely when stored in base of cabinet.	

FISH

	All fish are very perishable and should be eaten as soon as possible. Wipe or rinse and store unwrapped but covered with a sheet of waxed paper. Oily fish such as herring, salmon or trout keep fresh a shorter time than white fish.	1 day
Smoked fish	This will keep longer.	2–3 days
Cooked fish	Place in covered container.	2 days

FRUIT AND VEGETABLES

	Salad vegetables and citrus fruits benefit most from being stored in the refrigerator. Vitamin C deteriorates rapidly at room temperature and when exposed to the light. In this case, green vegetables such as spinach, cabbage and broccoli are better if washed, prepared and stored in polythene bags in the refrigerator. All salad vegetables should be washed and placed in the vegetable crisper, or in a polythene bag. Salad may even be prepared in advance and stored in a covered container, ready for use. Do not toss in dressing until ready to serve.	3–4 days
Cut lemons	Cover surface with foil or place in polythene bag and close the ends.	1 week
Soft fruits	Clean and keep in covered container.	2–3 days
Hard fruits	Lightly wrap or place in the crisper.	3–4 days
Avocado pears	Only ripe avocados, ready for eating, should be chilled. Unpeeled whole fruit keep without discolouration. Chill well before serving and open only when ready to serve.	1–2 days
Melon	Refrigerated to chill only. One hour is sufficient usually. Cover any cut surface with plastic film wrapping to stop odour spreading to other foods.	—
Bananas	*Do not refrigerate* – they will go black.	—

MISCELLANEOUS

Pastry	Puff or flaky pastry can be made in advance. Wrap in waxed paper, foil or put in a polythene bag. Allow to come to room temperature before using, for easy rolling out.	3–5 days
Salad dressing	During summer months make salad dressing up in quantity and store in a screw topped jar. Shake well before using.	2–3 weeks
Mayonnaise	Keep in covered container.	3–6 weeks
Mineral waters	Fruit juices and mineral waters take up valuable space in the refrigerator. If you plan on using them, tonic water, cans of tomato juice, fruit juice, beer, cider or lager can be chilled before serving.	—
Wine	White wine to be served with a meal is best chilled, about 1 hour before serving is usually sufficient.	—

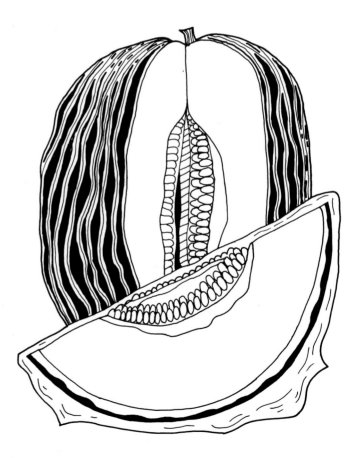

Food storage and your freezer

Keep in your freezer a selection of foods that can be used for everyday and party menus. Stock both home frozen and selected commercially frozen foods and plan on using them.

Check that the temperature in the freezer remains at below 0°F. (−18°C.) and food inside will keep in good condition. In every case, food has a recommended storage life in the freezer. Although bacteria is dormant and mould will not develop at this low temperature, there is a slow enzymic change in all foods. Items kept longer than the recommended storage time are not dangerous to eat, but will suffer from a noticeable deterioration in flavour and quality.

Soups and stocks	3 months	Soups thickened with potato freeze best. Spinach, sorrel, watercress and vichysoisse are good for parties. Stock should be well reduced to concentrate. Freeze in ice cube trays then turn into polythene bags for storing. Use in soups.
Sauces and gravy	1–2 months	Avoid egg based sauces. White sauce, brown and tomato sauce are useful for recipes.

FISH

Fish for freezing must be absolutely fresh and frozen within 24 hours of being caught.

Oily fish	2 months	Salmon or salmon steaks, cut 1-inch (2½-cm.) thick. Fresh trout – cleaned and gutted. Packs of commercially frozen trout and smoked salmon are very useful for recipes.
White fish	3 months	Steaks, fillets or small whole fish. Keep a selection of commercially frozen products.
Shellfish	1 month	Packs of prawns, prepared crab meat and potted prawns.
Smoked fish	2 months	Packs of smoked haddock or kipper fillets are useful.
Cooked fish dishes	2 months	Home made fish pie, fish cakes can be prepared for family meals. Potted salmon is good for a party.

MEAT

All meat for freezing must be of first class quality and correctly hung. If freezing a quantity of meat from a carcass, do not overload the freezer at one time. Freeze first those cuts which will deteriorate most quickly, cut up meat or minced meat, then chops and steaks and finally freeze the larger joints.

Beef	8 months	Pack steaks and chops in layers with waxed paper for easy separation.
Lamb	6 months	All cuts of lamb are excellent.
Pork	6 months	Score rind on pork joints while still frozen.
Veal	6 months	Veal escalopes for recipes. When convenient egg and breadcrumb before freezing.
Bacon	1 month	Not really advisable to keep bacon joints in the freezer. Bacon rashers freeze in vacuum sealed pack. Salt in bacon increases rancidity.
Sausages	1 month	Sausages with small amount of salt and seasoning will keep longer.
Minced meat and offal	2 months	Freeze in amounts suitable for use in recipes.
Cooked meat dishes	2 months	Underseason stews and casseroles as flavour intensifies during storage.

POULTRY AND GAME

Frozen oven-ready chickens available all year but seasonal game are worth freezing.

Chicken	6 months	Freeze poussin and spring chickens that are seasonal, also chicken portions for recipes.
Turkey	6 months	A small sized whole turkey for a special occasion. Sliced turkey breasts, egg and breadcrumbed for frying, are useful. Freeze stuffings for turkey or chicken separately.
Duck	4–6 months	Keep one or two oven-ready frozen birds in stock.
Goose	4–6 months	Buy a frozen oven-ready gosling for Christmas.
Hare	6 months	Freeze hare joints or, better still, cooked hare casserole.
Feathered game	6 months	All game must be hung first. Pluck, draw and truss ready for cooking.
Stuffings	1 month	Freeze quantities of mixed stuffing or dry mix without liquid added.
Cooked poultry and game dishes	2 months	Casseroles of hare, pheasant and chicken are excellent. Stir in cream or egg yolks, used to enrich poultry recipes, after thawing.

VEGETABLES

Vegetables must be blanched first. Always make a point of using up vegetables before the next season starts.

Green vegetables	12 months	Brussels sprouts, peas and beans are most popular. Red cabbage freezes well.
Root vegetables	12 months	Freeze new carrots, small quantities of new potatoes, tiny onions for casseroles.

Prepared vegetable dishes	6 months	Duchesse potatoes, croquette potatoes, ratatouille.
Herbs	12 months	Chopped fresh parsley and mint are both excellent to use in recipes.

FRUIT

Seasonal fruits are excellent to freeze and make especially good desserts in winter months. Use all fruit up before the next season starts.

Fruits	10–12 months	Freeze packs of individual fruits for compotes, puréed strawberries for sauce. All fruits frozen in syrup or dry sugar keep best.

PASTRY, BREAD AND CAKES

Pastry	3 months	Freeze puff or flaky pastry in quantities suitable for using.
Baked pastry	6 months	Baked unfilled pastry cases and tartlet cases.
Bread	2 months	Home baked brown or white soft rolls and malt loaves, also shop bought bread. Fresh yeast can be frozen for use in recipes.
Baked goods	2 months	Croissants, Danish pastries for a special occasion are best frozen after baking. Pizza also freezes well.
Cakes and scones	6 months	Freeze sponge layers for filling. Sponge flans or cake iced with butter cream, avoid glacé icing which goes thin on thawing. Scones and drop scones freeze well.
Sandwiches	2 months	White or brown sandwiches rolled or specially cut for a party. Avoid egg, cucumber, tomato or lettuce fillings.
Breadcrumbs	2 months	Freeze in quantities suitable for using in recipes. Use for stuffings, puddings, bread sauce and for coating foods.

DAIRY FOODS

Cream	3 months	Freeze double cream but not single cream. Transfer cream from a shop container to one large enough to allow $\frac{1}{2}$ inch (1 cm.) at the top for expansion during freezing.
Butter	6 months	Unsalted butter keeps best. Freeze flavoured butters made in advance for steaks and grills.

Cheese	4 months	Hard cheese freezes best. Use up left over pieces for grated cheese and store in freezer.
Ice cream	3 months	If home made and in a small container, allow to stand in refrigerator for 30 minutes before serving for best flavour.

MISCELLANEOUS

Ice cubes		Very useful for drinks. To keep cubes separate, remove from ice tray and arrange without touching each other on a flat tray. Place in freezer for damp sides to freeze dry. Then tip into polythene bag for freezing.
Pancakes	2 months	Prepare pancakes, using an enriched batter with melted butter or oil added.

206

Buffet supper party

When dining space is limited, a buffet is the obvious solution. This can readily be adapted to a variety of occasions and to the number of guests. If it is possible, arrange a separate room for seating, or for guests to move into with their food. A recreation room or, if the weather is fine, a patio or terrace can be most attractive. The position of the buffet table itself depends on the entertaining area. If the dining table is used, it may be left in the centre of the room, or in a smaller room pushed against the wall to provide more space. Use a small sideboard or table for the dessert. Coffee is best served from a trolley at a later stage.

Guests should be able to move round the table and food should be within easy reach. Make sure each dish has its own serving utensil in or beside it. If possible leave space near each dish so that guests can put their plate down and serve themselves. Keep food hot in chafing dishes, on a candle warmer or on a hot tray and do not forget to warm the plates for these foods. Give careful consideration to the serving dishes – colourful casseroles, wicker baskets for bread and attractive boards for the cheese. A pretty centre piece is most important. Build one with fresh fruit or flowers and use tall elegant candles to produce soft, diffused lighting.

Foods that can be eaten without a knife are preferable. Plan an imaginative menu and include both hot and cold dishes and salads, allowing slightly more food per head than you would at a formal dinner party. Most guests can be relied upon to try one or two of the more interesting dishes, particularly if the buffet is left there during the evening. Chilled Spanish summer soup, hot sorrel soup, chicken liver pâté or kipper mousse could be a choice for a starter. For the main course, cold roast turkey or rare roast beef, salmon or crab quiche, sugar baked gammon with spiced peaches or boeuf en croûte are all delicious cold with salads. Hot beef goulash, chicken paella, boeuf bourguignonne or kedgeree could be an alternative hot course. For dessert, items that can be served individually are ideal such as strawberries with orange, meringues Chantilly or a gâteau that cuts into portions, Lindy's cheesecake or coffee brandy gâteau would be excellent. Alternatively, choose soft fruit desserts that serve easily, such as summer trifle, gooseberry soufflé or lemon mousse.

Kedgeree

Kedgeree makes a delicious hot dish for a crowd. The fish can be cooked in advance and the liquor reserved ready for cooking the rice. If all the ingredients are assembled ready, it does not take long to put this recipe together.

Serves 8

2 medium smoked haddock, about 1½ lb./700 g.	1 onion, finely chopped
few parsley stalks	1 lb./½ kg. long grain rice
1 bay leaf	2 pints/generous 1 litre boiling
2 lemons	fish liquor (see recipe)
few peppercorns	2 hard-boiled eggs, chopped
salt and freshly milled pepper	1–2 tablespoons chopped
4 oz./100 g. butter	parsley

Rinse and cut up the haddock but do not remove the skin or bone. Place in a large pan with about 3 pints (1½ litres) cold water, the parsley stalks, bay leaf, 1 lemon, cut in slices, and a few peppercorns. Bring to the boil, then simmer very gently until the fish is tender. Strain off the liquor, measure and keep back 2 pints (generous 1 litre) for cooking the rice. Check the seasoning in the fish stock. Discard skin and bone from the fish and break the flesh into flakes.

Melt 3 oz. (75 g.) of the butter in a saucepan. Add the onion and rice and fry gently for about 5 minutes to soften the onions. Stir in the boiling fish liquor and, stirring gently, bring up to the boil. Cover with a lid and simmer very gently for 30–40 minutes or until the rice is tender and liquor absorbed. Fold in the reserved flaked fish, the chopped hard-boiled eggs, chopped parsley and remaining butter, in small pieces. Heat through, then check the seasoning with salt and pepper and add lemon juice from the remaining lemon to taste.

Pile into a hot serving dish and serve.

Paella

Paella is a popular Spanish dish consisting of chicken, shellfish and rice as the main ingredients, with onion, tomato, peppers and garlic added for flavour.

Serves 6

1 (3–3½ lb./1½–1¾ kg.) chicken	12 oz./350 g. long grain rice
salt and freshly milled pepper	1½ pints/9 dl. chicken stock
1 cooked lobster, about 1½ lb./ ¾ kg.	pinch saffron or tumeric
	1 (15 oz./425 g.) can tomatoes
4 tablespoons olive oil	2 green peppers
1 large onion	2 bay leaves
2 cloves garlic	

Joint the chicken into eight small pieces (page 102). Season the pieces and set aside.

Place the chicken carcass and giblets into a large pan and cover generously with about 2 pints (generous 1 litre) cold, salted water for stock. Split the lobster open and crack the claws. Remove flesh and add the crushed lobster shell to the stock for flavour. Reserve the lobster flesh for adding to the recipe later. Bring the stock to the boil, cover and simmer for about 1 hour. Strain the stock and measure out 1½ pints (9 dl.) for the recipe. Check seasoning and flavour of the stock.

Heat the oil in a large pan, add the chicken pieces and fry to brown on all sides. Peel and finely chop the onion and add to the pan. Fry gently for about 5 minutes until the onion is tender but not brown. Peel and finely chop the garlic and add to the pan with the rice. Stir to blend ingredients.

Stir in the *hot*, well seasoned, chicken stock and add a good pinch of saffron or tumeric to colour the rice. Bring up to the boil, lower the heat, cover with a lid and simmer for 10–15 minutes.

Drain the tomatoes from the can and chop coarsely. Peel, deseed and shred the green peppers. Add the tomatoes, green peppers and bay leaves to the paella. Stir with a fork, replace the lid and cook gently until the rice is tender and the liquid absorbed, about a further 20 minutes. Meanwhile dice the lobster flesh.

When the paella is ready, stir in the lobster meat, heat through for a moment and serve.

Kipper mousse

This is a recipe for a supper party. The mixture is very tasty and should be served in the same way as a pâté, with hot toast. Any left over makes a delicious filling for brown bread sandwiches.

Serves 6–8

1 lb./½ kg. kipper fillets	1 oz./25 g. flour
juice 2 lemons	4 oz./100 g. unsalted butter
½ pint/3 dl. milk	freshly milled pepper
1 bay leaf	¼ pint/1½ dl. double cream
1 oz./25 g. butter	

Separate the kipper fillets and pull away the skins from each one. Approximately two large packets (each serving four) frozen kipper fillets should yield about the amount required in the recipe. Arrange the kipper fillets flat in a shallow dish and pour over the squeezed lemon juice. Leave to marinate for several hours or overnight. Turn the fillets occasionally in the juice.

Meanwhile prepare a white sauce mixture used for binding the ingredients. Heat the milk in a saucepan with the bay leaf. When hot, draw away from the heat and leave to infuse for a while. Melt the butter in a saucepan and stir in the flour. Cook for a few moments until the mixture lightens in colour, then gradually stir in the hot milk. Bring up to the boil, beating well all the time to get a smooth mixture. Simmer gently for 1–2 minutes, then draw off the heat. Add no seasoning, pour the sauce into a shallow plate and cover with a square of buttered paper. Leave until quite cold.

Flake the kipper flesh into a basin, add the butter and pound or beat the two together. A smooth purée of these two ingredients is required and the easiest way to achieve this is to pass the mixture through a Mouli food mill. Otherwise rub or press through a coarse sieve, but this is rather hard work. Add the cold sauce to the butter and kipper blend and beat very well to a smooth mixture. Check flavour and add plenty of freshly milled pepper and salt only if required. Lightly whip the cream and fold into the mixture.

Spoon into a round, white soufflé or pâté dish. Chill for several hours before serving. This mixture keeps well in the refrigerator.

Advance preparation: This mousse can be made 2–3 days in advance.

Lindy's cheesecake

A delicious, very rich and creamy cheesecake. A recipe to make for a party. Any left over can be frozen.

Serves 20

for the pastry:	12 oz./350 g. castor sugar
4 oz./100 g. plain flour	3 level tablespoons plain flour
2 oz./50 g. butter	finely grated rind 1 orange
1 oz./25 g. icing sugar, sifted	¼ teaspoon vanilla essence
1 egg yolk	5 whole eggs
1 tablespoon water	2 egg yolks
for the filling:	¼ pint/1½ dl. double cream
2½ lb./1 kg. 200 g. Philadelphia cream cheese	

Sift the flour into a basin. Add the butter, cut in pieces, and rub into the flour. Add the icing sugar and make a well in the centre. Add the egg yolk and water and, using a fork, mix to a rough dough. Turn out on to a floured working surface and knead lightly. Shape into a ball, place inside a polythene bag and chill for 1 hour.

Roll the pastry out to a circle and use to line the base of a 9-inch (23-cm.) spring clip pan. Trim the edges neatly and prick the pastry with a fork. Place in the centre of a hot oven (400°F., 200°C., Gas Mark 6) and bake for 10–15 minutes or until golden brown. Allow to cool for a few minutes. Butter the sides of the pan and then fit to the base with the pastry inside.

Mix together the cream cheese and sugar. Beat in the flour, orange rind and vanilla essence. Using a wooden spoon, beat in the whole eggs and egg yolks, one at a time. Then stir in the double cream. Pour the mixture into the prepared tin and place in the centre of the hot oven (400°F., 200°C., Gas Mark 6) for 12 minutes, then lower the oven heat to 225°F., 110°C., Gas Mark ¼ and bake for 2 hours. Switch off the oven heat and leave the cheesecake in the oven until cold. Then remove from the tin, keeping the cheesecake on the metal base.

Allow to stand for 24 hours in a cool place before serving.
Advance preparation: Make the day before serving.

Wine and cheese party

A wine and cheese party offers an excellent way to entertain a number of friends informally and without too much expense. There are many varieties of cheese and types of wine to choose from. The requirements for a party depends on the number of guests and how hungry they are likely to be. If it is to be in place of a dinner party, then more must be provided than if guests have eaten beforehand. For a small informal get-together, have two or three types of cheese on a board so that people can help themselves. A basket of fresh bread, some crispbread and pats of butter will provide sufficient food. A supply of knives and plates completes the table. For a larger party, increase the number of varieties of cheese rather than just the quantities. If you start with Cheddar, Caerphilly and Wensleydale, try adding Cheshire, Leicester and Stilton. It is also advisable to cut some of the cheese into portions. Generally speaking, a light bodied red wine blends well with all cheese and choose a medium dry white wine. Although the fashion is for wine, there is no reason why there should not be a supply of beer and cider for guests who may prefer them.

The actual quantities of cheese and wine will vary, but as a rough average allow a quarter of a pound (100 g.) of cheese and half a bottle of wine per person. Arrange cheeses, keeping types separate, on the table with crusty French bread, rye or brown bread, pumpernickel and crispbread. Provide butter, fresh celery and dishes of nuts. Cut radish roses, black or green grapes, fresh apples, sliced cucumber or tomato can be used to garnish the cheeses attractively.

Serve fresh salad but not tossed in oil and vinegar dressing (vinegar ruins the taste of wine). Additional hot food could include hot toasted cheese, Swiss cheese tart, quiche Lorraine or other quiches such as salmon or asparagus, hot sausage rolls or a hot cheese fondue. For a dessert, serve fresh strawberries when in season, or perhaps a grapefruit or orange water ice.

Neuchâtel cheese fondue

The Swiss regard fondue as a meal. They would probably have a salad first, then follow it with fondue and a white wine to drink. Equal quantities of both kinds of Swiss cheese and a sharp white wine make the best fondue.

Serves 6

12 oz./350 g. Emmental cheese	2 tablespoons Kirsch
12 oz./350 g. Gruyère cheese	2 level teaspoons cornflour
1–2 cloves garlic	freshly milled pepper
½ pint/3 dl. dry white wine	pinch nutmeg

Grate the cheeses. Rub the fondue pan with a cut clove of garlic. Pour in the wine and place over the heat. When the wine is hot, add the cheese. Stir the mixture continuously – the Swiss use a wooden fork – until a smooth mixture has formed. Blend the Kirsch and cornflour, add to the cheese mixture, stirring well all the time. Stir until blended and just simmering. Season to taste with pepper and nutmeg. Remove the pan from the heat and place on a spirit burner. Lower the flame and allow the fondue to bubble gently. Stir occasionally so that the fondue does not stick on the base of the pan.

Dip squares of French bread into the hot fondue, using long forks.

Quiche Lorraine

Use the large quiche or French tart tins with a loose base. A tin 8 inches (20 cm.) in diameter makes a good sized quiche that will cut into several portions.

Serves 6–8

4–6 oz./100–175 g. quiche pastry (page 13)	½ oz./15 g. butter
for the filling:	2 oz./50 g. Gruyère cheese
4 oz./100 g. green or unsmoked bacon	3 eggs
	½ pint/3 dl. single cream
	salt and freshly milled pepper

On a lightly floured working surface, roll the pastry out to a circle and use to line an 8-inch (20-cm.) quiche or tart tin with a loose base. Trim the pastry edges. Place the lined tin on a flat baking tray so that it is easier to carry when the filling is added. Set aside while preparing the filling.

Trim away the rind and cut the bacon into strips. Blanch in boiling water for 2 minutes, then drain. Add to the hot butter, melted in a frying pan, and sauté gently until golden. Sprinkle the bacon over the pastry case and cover with the finely grated cheese.

Whisk the eggs and cream in a bowl and season with salt and pepper. Strain the mixture into the pastry case to cover the bacon and cheese. Place in the centre of a moderately hot oven (375°F., 190°C., Gas Mark 5) and bake for 40–45 minutes.

Advance preparation: One or more quiche Lorraine baked in advance should be arranged on baking trays when needing to be reheated. Cover completely with foil and heat through in the oven (350°F., 180°C., Gas Mark 4) for 10–15 minutes before serving.

Party picnic

The ideal picnic is a carefully planned cold meal. One which is cooked at home, packed thoughtfully and carried to the appointed site. Whether it is a picnic for a day trip or something as exciting as a visit to Glyndebourne or a race meeting, lavishness is the essential feature. Include a choice of cold foods, crisp fresh salads, wine, fresh fruits and cheese. This pre-planned picnic gives the hostess a chance to organise carefully. Choose foods that travel well:

Potted salmon or smoked cod's roe pâté carried in a pâté dish; raised pork pie, bacon and egg pie or Swiss cheese tart; chicken wrapped in foil or Jambon bourguignonne in its basin ready to unmould. All these go well with salads, crusty bread and butter. Newly baked chausson aux pommes or French madeleines to go with fresh strawberries; American brownies, almond petits fours or florentines could be served with fresh summer fruits.

Polythene containers with lids that seal are excellent, particularly for salads. Use insulated boxes or bags to keep foods cool or hot, as required. Remember these essentials for a grand picnic – cutlery, plates, tablecloth, napkins, glasses, a vacuum jug full of ice and rugs or cushions to sit on.

Swiss cheese tart

Cheese tart is very good served with a salad. Gruyère cheese gives the best flavour; if Cheddar cheese is used, increase the amount to 5–6 oz. (150–175 g.).

Serves 4

4 oz./100 g. shortcrust pastry	1 rounded teaspoon plain flour
for the filling:	salt and freshly milled pepper
4 oz./100 g. Gruyère cheese, grated	2 eggs
	¼ pint/1½ dl. milk

Roll out the pastry on a lightly floured working surface to a circle large enough to line an 8-inch (20-cm.) quiche or tart tin, or a flan ring set on a baking tray. Line the tin with the pastry, trim the edges and set aside while preparing the filling.

Mix the grated cheese with the flour and season with salt and pepper. Lightly mix the eggs and milk, add to the cheese and blend ingredients thoroughly. Pour into the lined pastry case. Check that the cheese is evenly distributed over the pie.

Place above centre in a moderately hot oven (375°F., 190°C., Gas Mark 5) and bake for 35–40 minutes. The pie should be well risen and golden brown. Serve warm with salad.

Drinks or sherry party

Informal and fun, a drinks party can be fairly easy to organise. As it is a stand up affair, the hostess can accommodate more guests than usual. A good many suitable items can be found at the delicatessen counter in any supermarket or food hall. Serve thinly sliced smoked chicken with lemon squeezed over, or thin slices of salami or garlic sausage. Serve fresh radishes with salt for dipping. Fresh celery with the hollow stem in each stalk filled with cream cheese and Roquefort cheese or smoked cod's roe pâté. Jumbo sized prunes that do not need soaking can have the stones removed and the space filled with cream cheese. If some form of canapé is essential, then spread small salty biscuits with smoked cod's roe pâté blended with lemon juice and seasoned with pepper, or with cream cheese and caviar. Try pumpernickel bread spread with Boursin cheese or topped with sweet marinated raw herrings. Serve flavoured dips surrounded by cheese or savoury biscuits. Allow some small hot savouries such as gougère, cut in slices, hot quiche or pizza, cut in small wedges that are easy to handle. Allow about 6–8 savouries per head depending on their size.

In addition to the sherry and spirits of your choice, make sure you have a selection of soft drinks and offer red or white wine for those guests who may prefer it. A glass of Vin chaud is a pleasant drink at a winter party.

Pizza

Pizza keeps well in the home freezer and can, therefore, be made ahead for a party. It is delicious hot, it reheats very well and is, oddly enough, very popular with children.

Cuts into 18 pieces

1 lb./450 g. plain flour	1 lb./450 g. sliced fresh or
2 level teaspoons salt	drained canned tomatoes
½ oz./15 g. fresh (or 2 teaspoons	freshly milled pepper
dried) yeast	1 teaspoon dried basil or thyme
¼ pint/3 dl. water	*for the topping:*
½ level teaspoon castor sugar	anchovy fillets
(optional)	streaky bacon rashers
1 tablespoon oil	black olives
for the filling:	fried onions or mushrooms
1 lb./450 g. strong Cheddar	sliced salami
cheese, grated	

Mix the flour and salt into a mixing basin. Blend the fresh yeast with the warm water and add to the dry ingredients with the oil. If using dried yeast, dissolve the sugar in the warm water and sprinkle in the dried yeast. Leave to stand in a warm place for about 10 minutes until frothy, then add to the flour as above. Mix to a rough dough in the basin. Turn the dough out on to a clean working surface and knead for about 5 minutes or until the dough is firm and elastic. Shape into a ball, place in a basin and leave in a warm place until doubled in bulk.

Turn the risen dough out on to a floured working surface and press firmly with the knuckles to knock out the air. Divide the dough into four pieces. Shape each one into a ball and roll out each to an 8-inch (20-cm.) circle. Place each circle of dough on to a greased baking sheet. Brush the dough with olive oil and cover with a layer of grated cheese and sliced or canned tomatoes. Season with pepper and sprinkle with basil or thyme. Decorate each one with the topping of your choice. Use anchovy fillets or bacon rashers, black olives, fried onions or mushrooms and salami. Set the prepared pizza aside in a warm place for about 15–20 minutes before baking.

Bake the pizza in a preheated hot oven (425°F., 220°C., Gas Mark 7) for 15–20 minutes. Cut in wedges and serve warm.
To freeze: To store the pizza in the home freezer, bake for only 15 minutes. Cool, wrap in polythene or foil and seal. Store until required. Thaw at room temperature for about 2 hours. Reheat in a hot oven (400°F., 200°C., Gas Mark 6) for 10 minutes.

Vin chaud

This should not be kept hot too long, prepare it spontaneously. It takes only a few minutes. A bottle of wine will stretch to 10 glasses this way.

Serves 4

1 bottle red wine	1–2-inch (2½–5-cm.) stick
¼ pint/3 dl. water	cinnamon
6 oz./175 g. castor sugar	1 lemon

Put the wine, water and sugar into a saucepan. Add the piece of stick cinnamon and the thinly *pared* rind of the lemon. Bring slowly to a simmer, stirring to dissolve the sugar. Cover the pan with a lid and allow the mixture to infuse over the lowest heat for about 10 minutes. Then draw off the heat and remove the cinnamon, otherwise the flavour gets too strong.

Meanwhile, thinly slice the lemon and remove any pips. You should have a slice of lemon for every glass. If necessary, use a second lemon but pare away the rind before slicing. Pour the hot (but never boiling) wine into the glasses, placing a dessertspoon in the glass first and pouring the wine on to the back of the spoon. This lessens the shock which the glass would otherwise have to withstand. Serve at once.

Barbecue supper party

For a party of this kind, precise timing of foods cooked over a barbecue is essential, so practice on the family first. Have all the equipment – tongs, long forks, charcoal, lighter fluid, gloves and serving implements – set out before your guests arrive. Choose the accompanying foods – rice, vegetables, salads, seasoning, sauces, hot breads and desserts which can be prepared indoors and brought out at the appropriate time.

The number of guests invited will be limited by the size of the garden or eating area and the facilities for cooking. Comfort aids enjoyment to a meal, so provide guests with seats and tables in the garden. Although preferable to do the cooking outside, have the actual seating in a covered or patio area. Arrange the tables, garden or trestle, simply but attractively arranged with perhaps a potted plant or two for decoration. After dark, the area can be lit with paraffin lamps or candles set inside glass for protection against the wind.

Some points to note

A charcoal fire takes time to become hot enough to cook over. Don't be tempted to cook too soon. The fire is ready when the flames have died down and coals look ash grey in daylight and have a red glow after dark. Start the fire in advance, most fires take about 45 minutes to heat up sufficiently.

Once the fire is established, disturb it as little as possible. Keep a supply of hot briquettes round the edges of the fire and move these into the centre when it is necessary to build it up.

To maintain even cooking, control the heat by adjusting the distance between the food and the fire. Most grids can be raised or lowered. Alternatively, use tongs to move the foods away or towards the hot centre of the fire.

All poultry and meat, especially steaks, intended for barbecuing should be at room temperature. Remove any meat for grilling from the refrigerator at least 1 hour before cooking. Spear some fat trimmings or a piece of bacon fat and rub over the grill before cooking, to prevent the meat sticking.

Have a sprinkler bottle of water handy to extinguish any sudden spurts of flames from fat dripping into the fire. To limit this danger, before cooking cut off most of the outside fat from the steaks and chops and score the remaining fat with a sharp knife to keep the meat from curling.

Start a barbecue supper party with cold cucumber and mint soup, chicken liver pâté or an hors d'oeuvre of sliced salami, fresh radishes, egg mayonnaise and tomato salad. Cook steaks, sausages, kebabs or chicken joints over the charcoal fire and serve with hot baked potatoes, Spanish rice and salad. Serve a large Swiss apple tart, or fresh strawberry shortcake for dessert. Make lots of iced coffee if the weather is warm or serve hot coffee if the evening is cool.

Swiss apple tart

The ground hazelnuts, sprinkled over the pastry base, absorb the fruit juices and keep the crust dry. This same method can be used for fruit flans made using fresh apricots or plums. This is a delicious recipe for a party.

Serves 8

8 oz./225 g. rich shortcrust pastry (page 12)	2 level tablespoons cornflour
	2 tablespoons milk
3 oz./75 g. ground hazelnuts	2 eggs
for the filling:	$\frac{1}{4}$ pint/1$\frac{1}{2}$ dl. sour cream or
2 lb./1 kg. sharp flavoured dessert apples	fresh double cream
	pinch salt
4 oz./100 g. castor sugar	

On a lightly floured surface, roll out the pastry and use to line a 12-inch (30-cm.) round tart tin. Prick the base with a fork and sprinkle with the ground hazelnuts. Peel the apples, halve them and remove the cores. Slice fairly thickly and arrange in circles to completely cover the pie. Sprinkle the pie with half the sugar and then place in the centre of a hot oven (400°F., 200°C., Gas Mark 6) and bake for 15 minutes.

Meanwhile blend the cornflour and milk together in a bowl and add the remaining sugar, eggs, cream and salt. Mix lightly to blend well and set aside until required.

Pour this mixture over the partly baked tart. Replace in the oven and bake for a further 15 minutes or until the custard sets and the pie is golden brown. Remove from the baking tin and allow to cool before serving.

Coffee morning

A coffee morning is a delightful way of uniting friends and providing a good atmosphere in which to deal informally with local business or charity affairs. Hot, freshly brewed coffee should be served with a collection of home baked goodies. Food should be easy to handle – warm scones with butter, chocolate cake, honey cake or warm doughnuts. Croissant and Danish pastries can be freshly bought and cake layers can be baked in advance and kept ready in the home freezer. Arrange a tray of biscuits, including home-made melting moments, almond slices, shortbread or macaroons, all of which could be baked in advance and stored separately in airtight tins.

Making coffee for a crowd

Make coffee in quantities that are practical for serving guests. It is not a good idea to keep prepared coffee standing after it is made. For each 1 pint (6 dl.) of water you should allow 4 heaped dessertspoons (1$\frac{1}{2}$ oz./40 g.) ground coffee. Allowing two cups of coffee per person, for twelve people you will require 4 pints (2$\frac{1}{4}$ litres) of coffee and about 2 pints (generous 1 litre) of milk or 1 pint (6 dl.) single cream.

Make the coffee using either the jug or the saucepan method, whichever is the most convenient for the hostess.

The jug method: Choose an enamel, earthenware or china jug and fill in advance with boiling water to heat through. Pour away the water and measure the coffee (use medium ground coffee) into the hot jug. Pour over the required amount of boiling water. Stir well and cover with a lid or saucer. Leave to infuse for 4 minutes. Stir once, gently, so that the grounds sink and strain the coffee through a nylon sieve into the coffee cups or into a hot jug for serving.

The saucepan method: Bring the required amount of water to the boil in a saucepan. Stir in the measured amount of coffee and leave over low heat until the coffee almost comes to the boil and begins to rise in the pan. Draw off the heat, cover and leave to infuse for 3–4 minutes. Strain through muslin or a nylon sieve into a hot coffee pot and serve.

Melting moments

These crisp, sweet cookies look very pretty. If liked, the cookies can be baked in advance and filled when ready to serve. Either way, store them in an airtight tin to prevent them from becoming soft.

Makes 13–14 pairs

3 oz./75 g. plain flour	*for the buttercream:*
1 oz./25 g. cornflour	1 oz./25 g. butter
pinch salt	2 oz./50 g. icing sugar, sifted
3 oz./75 g. butter	few drops vanilla essence
1 oz./25 g. castor sugar	few drops pink colouring
few drops vanilla essence	(optional)

Sift together the flour, cornflour and salt on to a plate. Cream the butter, sugar and vanilla essence until very soft. Add half the sifted ingredients and blend well, then add the remainder and mix to a smooth, fairly stiff dough.

Drop the mixture in rounded teaspoons on to a buttered baking tray, not too close to allow for spreading. You should get about 26–28 cookies. There will be enough to cover more than one tray so it is best to bake them in batches. Place in the centre of a moderate oven (350°F., 180°C., Gas Mark 4) and bake for 15–20 minutes or until just beginning to brown. Remove carefully from the tray and allow to cool.

To make the buttercream filling, beat the butter until soft then gradually beat in the sieved icing sugar and a few drops of vanilla essence. Add a few drops of colouring, the filling should be of the palest pink or left plain. Sandwich similar sized cookies in pairs with the filling.

Hot cheese scones

It is very important when making scones to preheat the oven well before putting them to bake. If sour cream or buttermilk is used for mixing, reduce the cream of tartar in the recipe to 1 teaspoon.

Makes 12 scones

8 oz./225 g. flour	pinch cayenne pepper
pinch salt	1 oz./25 g. butter
1 level teaspoon bicarbonate	3 oz./75 g. hard cheese, grated
of soda	$\frac{1}{4}$ pint/1$\frac{1}{2}$ dl. milk
2 level teaspoons cream of tartar	

Sift together the flour, salt, bicarbonate of soda, cream of tartar and pinch cayenne pepper into a basin. Add the butter and rub into the dry ingredients. Add the grated cheese and mix thoroughly. At this stage the mixture can be set aside until ready to bake.

Stir the milk into the dry ingredients and, using a fork, mix to a rough dough in the basin. Turn out on to a lightly floured working surface and knead for a moment to make a smooth, soft dough. Pat or roll out the dough to a thickness of no less than $\frac{1}{2}$ inch (1 cm.). Using a 2-inch (5-cm.) round cutter, stamp out 12 scones – it will be necessary to use up the dough trimmings to make the last two or three. Where no cutter is available, the scones can be cut into squares or triangles with a floured knife blade.

Place the scones on a floured baking tray and then dust the scones with flour. Place at once above centre in a hot oven (425°F., 220°C., Gas Mark 7) and bake for 10 minutes or until well risen and brown.

Serve warm with butter.

Advance preparation: One or more quantities of the dry ingredients can be weighed and sieved out in bowls ready for mixing. Stir in the liquid and put scones to bake early on the day of serving.

Late supper party

After a theatre or concert outing with friends, a late supper party is very pleasant. On this occasion, there is much to be said for a cold meal, although with careful planning one hot course could be produced without too much trouble. Avoid a lengthy meal, as some guests may have to return home for a baby sitter, and a meal that is too heavy or too rich so late at night. The menu for a supper party should be a little different and original, otherwise there is a danger that they become too much like dinner parties.

Serve a hot consommé, oeufs en cocotte or oeufs en gelée to start. A main dish could be cold roast duck, a quiche of salmon or fresh lobster salad. A hot main dish such as scampi in curry and cream sauce or lobster pancakes could be an alternative. If the occasion is informal, serve fondue bourguignonne and a salad or a large Spanish omelette with hot toast. Instead of a dessert, serve fresh fruit and cheese.

Fondue bourguignonne

Use the correct fondue pan – usually made in copper to withstand the high heat of the hot oil – and place over its own alcohol burner. Have the beef cubes at room temperature and the sauces ready before serving.

Serves 6

1$\frac{1}{2}$–2 lb./$\frac{3}{4}$–1 kg. fillet beef	salad oil for frying

Allow about 4 oz. (100 g.) of meat per person (a little more if the meat is untrimmed). Trim the meat and cut into bite-sized pieces. Keep in a cool place, if placed in the refrigerator allow the meat to come up to room temperature before using. Prepare all the sauces and set out in separate serving bowls. Each guest should have a fondue fork and a fondue plate. Put on each plate a serving of meat cubes and a selection of the sauces.

Pour the salad oil into the beef fondue cooker, fill the pan not more than half full. Place over the burner and allow to heat until hot enough for frying.

Each guest spears a beef cube with a fondue fork and holds it in the hot oil until cooked to required taste – only a few moments. The meat should then be *transferred to a dinner fork*, dipped in the chosen sauce on the plate and eaten.

Tomato sauce

2 tablespoons mayonnaise	1 teaspoon Worcestershire
2 tablespoons tomato ketchup	sauce
2 tablespoons cream	juice $\frac{1}{2}$ lemon

Measure the mayonnaise, ketchup and cream into a mixing basin. Stir in Worcestershire sauce and lemon juice to taste.

Mayonnaise with garlic and herbs

4 tablespoons mayonnaise	salt
$\frac{1}{2}$ small clove garlic	large pinch dried mixed herbs

Measure the mayonnaise into a mixing basin. Remove the papery outer skin of garlic and, using the blade of a knife, crush garlic with salt. Add the garlic and herbs to the mayonnaise and allow to stand to improve flavour.

Horseradish sauce

$\frac{1}{4}$ pint/1$\frac{1}{2}$ dl. double cream	salt and pepper
1 tablespoon lemon juice	dash Worcestershire sauce
4 tablespoons ready-made	
horseradish sauce	

Measure the cream and lemon juice into a mixing basin and stir until thick. Add the horseradish sauce, seasoning and Worcestershire sauce.

Curry sauce

4 tablespoons mayonnaise
2 level teaspoons curry powder

1 tablespoon sweet chutney –
   chop large pieces

Measure the mayonnaise into a basin, add the curry powder and chutney. Leave the sauce to stand to allow flavour to develop.

Sweet and sour sauce

5 tablespoons sweet chutney –
   chop large pieces

3 tablespoons redcurrant jelly
2 tablespoons vinegar

Combine the ingredients in a pan, heat until the jelly melts. Then allow to cool.

Mustard sauce

4 level tablespoons dry mustard
4 tablespoons boiling water
$\frac{1}{2}$ level teaspoon salt

2 teaspoons salad oil
1 tablespoon whole capers

Measure the mustard into a basin and gradually add the water, stirring well. Add the salt, oil and capers.

GUIDE TO FOOD QUANTITIES

	per serving	*for 12*	*for 25*	
Appetisers				
Soups	$\frac{1}{3}$ pint/2$\frac{1}{2}$ dl.	4 pints/2$\frac{1}{4}$ litres	8 pints/4$\frac{1}{2}$ litres	Serve soup hot or chilled.
Fish for cocktails	1 oz./25 g.	12 oz./350 g.	1$\frac{1}{2}$ lb./700 g.	For prawn, crab or tuna fish cocktails.
Pâté	2 oz./50 g.	1$\frac{1}{2}$ lb./700 g.	3 lb./1 kg. 400 g.	Allow 2 half slices of hot toast per person.
Meat and poultry				
Cold ham, tongue and salami	3 oz./75 g.	2$\frac{1}{4}$ lb./1 kg.	4$\frac{1}{2}$ lb./2 kg.	Sliced for salad. Make up total weight with a selection.
Chicken – roast	2–3 slices	3 (3 lb./1$\frac{1}{2}$ kg.) birds	6 (3 lb./1$\frac{1}{2}$ kg.) birds	Oven ready weight. Serve hot or cold with stuffing.
Chicken – cut up	3–4 oz./75–100 g.	2$\frac{1}{2}$–3 lb./1 kg. 200 g.– 1 kg. 400 g.	4$\frac{1}{2}$–6 lb./2 kg.– 2 kg. 700 g.	Weight without bone. Use in blanquette, casseroles etc.
Meat – roast with bone	5 oz./150 g.	3$\frac{3}{4}$ lb./1 kg. 700 g.	7$\frac{1}{4}$ lb./3 kg. 300 g.	Serve hot or cold with salads.
Meat – boneless, cut up	3–4 oz./75–100 g.	2$\frac{1}{2}$–3 lb./1 kg. 200 g.– 1 kg. 400 g.	4$\frac{1}{2}$–6 lb./2 kg.–2 kg. 700 g.	Meat for goulash or casseroles etc. or steak.
Turkey – roast	2–3 slices	8 lb./3 kg. 600 g.	16 lb./7 kg. 200 g.	Dressed weight. Serve hot or cold with stuffing.
Sausages	2	1$\frac{1}{2}$ lb./700 g.	3 lb./1 kg. 400 g.	For barbecue.
Pastry, sauces and pasta				
Bouchées	2	24	50	Allow 2 per person. 1 lb. (450 g.) puff pastry makes 50 bouchées.

	per serving	_for 12_	_for 25_	
Vol au vents	1	12	25	Allow 1 per person. 1 lb. (450 g.) puff pastry makes 25 vol au vents.
Gravy or sauce	3–4 tablespoons	1½ pints/1 litre	3 pints/1½ litres	
Rice or pasta	1½ oz./40 g.	1 lb. 2 oz./500 g.	2¼ lb./1 kg. 300 g.	For serving with blanquette, curries, bolognese etc.

Salads

	per serving	_for 12_	_for 25_	
Lettuce	2–3 leaves	2–3 heads	4–6 heads	Maximum quantity required for green salad, less for mixed salad.
Cucumber	2–3 slices	1–1½	2–3	Depends on size of cucumber, slice thinly.
Tomatoes	1–2	1½ lb./700 g.	2 lb./1 kg.	Peel skins away before using in salads.
White cabbage	2 oz./50 g.	1½ lb./¾ kg.	3 lb./1 kg. 400 g.	For using in coleslaw.
Potatoes	2 oz./50 g.	1½ lb./¾ kg.	3 lb./1 kg. 400 g.	For potato salad, combine with French dressing or mayonnaise.
Mayonnaise	2–3 tablespoons	generous ½ pint/3 dl.	1¼ pints/¾ litre	For serving alone. Less required as dressing for salads.
French dressing	2 tablespoons	generous ½ pint/3 dl.	1¼ pints/¾ litre	As above.

Desserts

	per serving	_for 12_	_for 25_	
Fruit salad	¼ pint/1½ dl.	3 pints/1½ litres	6 pints/3½ litres	Prepare in sugar syrup to keep colour of fruits.
Mousse or jelly	¼ pint/1½ dl.	3 pints/1½ litres	6 pints/3½ litres	Combine two or more recipes to total quantity.
Sorbet or ice cream	1 scoop	1 quart/generous 1 litre	2 quarts/2¼ litres	Allow more if the only dessert.
Cream	4 tablespoons	1½ pints/scant 1 litre	3 pints/1½ litres	To serve with desserts.
Cheese	1½ oz./40 g.	1 lb. 2 oz./500 g.	2¼ lb./1 kg. 300 g.	Serve with a selection of biscuits. Allow up to 4 oz. (100 g.) per person for a wine and cheese party.

Drinks

	per serving	_for 12_	_for 25_	
Coffee – instant	⅓ pint/2½ dl.	1½–2 oz./40–50 g.	3–4 oz./75–100 g.	Allow 2 coffee cups or 1 teacup per person.
Coffee – ground	⅓ pint/2½ dl.	4½–5 oz./120–150 g.	9–10 oz./250–275 g.	As above.
Cream for coffee	1 tablespoon per cup	1 pint/6 dl.	2 pints/generous 1 litre	Single or double.

Seasonal menus for entertaining

The choice of menu depends on many things — the occasion, the season of the year, the time required in terms of work and most important of all, the differing tastes and personal likes or dislikes of the hostess or her guests.

If the occasion is right, a perfect menu can be as simple as cheese, fresh bread, a salad and a bottle of wine. There are no hard and fast rules but the right menu does require thought and careful planning. Any menu should stimulate the palate with interesting flavours and different textures. Use herbs and wine to flavour dishes, serve young vegetables simply presented, provide crisp salads and use fruit in desserts. Avoid too many rich sauces and take care that within a menu there is no repetition of any foods that are too similar. Eye appeal is very important. Contrast the colour of the courses and of the parts of any one course, but avoid overgarnishing.

Lunch party menus

Generally speaking, a lunch party menu is less elaborate than a dinner party. Food should be light and interesting in flavour. Very often just two courses, perhaps a main dish and dessert followed by a varied selection of cheese and biscuits, are quite sufficient.

SPRING LUNCHES
Kebabs of pork with spiced orange sauce
Saffron rice

Vanilla ice cream

Spinach soup

Chicken Kiev
Mange tout peas
Watercress salad

Smoked cod's roe pâté

Swiss cheese tart
Lettuce and cucumber salad

Canneloni stuffed with chicken and spinach
Green salad

Chartreuse of apples

Fresh grapefruit

Omelette parmentier
Fresh tomato salad

AUTUMN LUNCHES
Barbecue chicken casserole
Creamed potatoes
French beans

Dutch apple pie

Swedish meatballs
New potatoes
Courgettes with parsley butter

Apple amber

Baked halibut with cider and tomatoes
Croquette potatoes
Leaf spinach

Butterscotch tart

SUMMER LUNCHES
Spatchcock of chicken
Peas with lettuce
New potatoes

Gooseberry fool

Jambon bouguignonne
French bread and butter
Salad

Cheese and fresh summer fruits

Scampi in curry and cream sauce
Boiled rice
Salad

Danish fruit pudding

Potted shrimps

Veal Parmesan
Sautéed potatoes
French beans

Spanish omelette
Green salad with 'fines herbes'

Green gooseberry ice cream

WINTER LUNCHES
Pork chops with piquante sauce
Creamed potatoes

Eve's pudding

Potage Parisienne

Lobster pancakes
Salad

Beef stew with herb dumplings
Brussels sprouts

Apple brown Betty

AUTUMN LUNCHES
Mixed grill
Hot baked potatoes with sour cream
Salad

Plum crumble

Baked stuffed marrow
Creamed potatoes

Marmalade pudding

WINTER LUNCHES
Steak with mustard sauce
Braised celery

Grapefruit water ice

Steak and kidney pudding
Glazed carrots

Baked apple compote with cream

Dinner party menus

Of all the forms of hospitality, a dinner party is, perhaps, the most rewarding for the hostess.

A well planned menu and an attractively decorated table contribute towards a pleasant atmosphere.

When choosing the menu, balance must be the primary consideration. Endeavour to vary the texture, the richness and, where possible, choose from foods in season which are plentiful and cheaper. A first course that can be served before guests sit down is a practical choice. Serve the main dish from a side table and allow the host to hand round vegetables for the guests to help themselves. Any salad in the menu is delicious served as a quite separate course. You might consider the Continental preference for serving a varied selection of cheeses before the dessert. The idea behind this is to offer an opportunity for finishing the wine from the previous courses. It clears the palate too. A separate wine can be served with the dessert if you wish.

To avoid confusion and possible embarrassment, seating arrangements should be worked out beforehand. Etiquette suggests that if there are guests of honour, that the woman sits on the right of her host and the man on the hostess's right. The hostess may exercise her discretion over seating other guests – she could place men and women alternately; but never husbands and wives side by side. The shape of the table should also be taken into consideration.

SPRING DINNER MENUS
Sorrel soup

Tarragon chicken
Mange-tout peas

Pineapple cheese cake

Grapefruit with prawns

Roast duckling with peaches
Fresh broccoli

Chocolate refrigerator cake

Potted salmon

Veal Cordon Bleu
French beans

Meringue Chantilly

SUMMER DINNER MENUS
Cucumber and mint soup

Salmon salad
New potatoes with chives

Strawberry shortcake

Spanish summer soup

Chicken with cream and asparagus sauce
New potatoes

Coffee and chocolate mousse

Beef galantine
New potatoes in butter
Garden peas

Strawberries with orange

SPRING DINNER MENUS
Pâté de campagne

Spring chicken with peas
Croquette potatoes with
almonds

Caramel custards

___

Avocado pear with cream
cheese

Paupiettes de veau
Courgettes with parsley butter

Fresh pineapple slices with
Kirsch

___

AUTUMN DINNER MENUS
Potage Parisien

Beef goulash
Buttered noodles

Dutch apple pie

___

Courgettes à la grecque

Kidneys with Bèarnaise sauce
Croquette potatoes

Lemon ice cream

___

Stuffed aubergines

Roast pheasant
Golden roast potatoes

Praline soufflé

___

Fresh melon

Chicken in paprika sauce
Boiled rice

Chocolate pots de crème with
orange

___

Salad of green peppers with
salami

Sole veronique
Baked tomatoes

Tarte aux pommes

___

SUMMER DINNER MENUS
Chicken liver pâté

Fricadelles
Boiled rice
French beans

Lemon mousse

___

Oeufs en gelée

Trout with tarragon
French beans

Summer trifle

___

WINTER DINNER MENUS
Smoked salmon

Filet de boeuf en croûte
Aubergine and tomato ragoût

Crêpes Grand Marnier

___

Chicken liver pâté

Roast leg of pork
Sweet and sour red cabbage

Coffee brandy cake

___

Eggs with tomato mayonnaise

Boeuf bourguignonne
Duchesse potatoes

Iced grapes

___

French onion soup

Roast chicken with
cranberry stuffing
Roast onions

Peaches in brandy

___

Arbroath smokies

Hot gammon with orange
sauce
Croquette potatoes

Meringue layer cake

___

Index